D1511702

Oklahoma Horizons Series

Oklahoma Bar Center

Oklahoma Horizons Series

AND JUSTICE FOR ALL:
THE LEGAL PROFESSION IN OKLAHOMA, 1821-1989

By
Orben J. Casey

Edited by Odie B. Faulk

**Published for the Oklahoma Heritage Association
by Western Heritage Books, Inc.**

Copyright © 1989
Oklahoma Heritage Association

All rights reserved. No part of this book may be re-
produced or utilized in any form or by any means,
electronic or mechanical, including photocopying and
recording, or by any information storage and retrieval
system, without permission from the publisher.

Manufactured in the United States of America for the
Oklahoma Heritage Association, Oklahoma City.

ISBN: 0-86546-076-0

PREFACE AND ACKNOWLEDGMENTS

This book is an attempt to survey the legal profession's role in the history of Oklahoma and outline the development of the Oklahoma Bar Association. I regret that space limitations and insufficient information prevented including references and anecdotes pertaining to many interesting and colorful lawyers important to the history of the state.

A work of this nature would have been impossible without the cooperation of numerous individuals and organizations. I especially thank the following Past Presidents of the Oklahoma Bar Association who took the time to visit with me relative to their experiences as lawyers and as officials of the Bar Association: W.E. Crowe, T. Austin Gavin, G. Ellis Gable, John M. Holliman, Robert W. Blackstock, LeRoy Blackstock, E.D. Hieronymus, Winfrey D. Houston, Thomas R. Brett, Jim F. Gassaway, Lee B. Thompson, Deryl L. Gotcher, C.D. Northcutt, William G. Paul, Wilson Wallace, William H. Bell, John M. Luttrell, and Leslie L. Conner, Jr.

Compilation of historical photographs was a task made easier by the cooperation of individuals across the state. The gracious assistance of the following is indeed appreciated: Martha M. Snow, Director of Communications of the Oklahoma Bar Association (abbreviated OBA under photographs); Dr. Bob L. Blackburn, Editor of the *Chronicles of Oklahoma*; Belva L. Henderson, Administrative Assistant for the University of Tulsa College of Law Library; Kay Zahrai, Photo Archivist for the Oklahoma Historical Society (abbreviated OHS under photographs), and

John R. Lovett, Photographic Archivist for the Western History Collections, University of Oklahoma.

Special thanks are also in order for Edward H. Palmer, Executive Director and Secretary-Treasurer of the Oklahoma Bar Foundation, as well as to Marvin C. Emerson, Executive Director of the Oklahoma Bar Association. The suggestions given by Dr. Kenny A. Franks, Director of Heritage Education for the Oklahoma Heritage Association, were greatly appreciated. The help and advice of Dr. Paul F. Lambert, Executive Director of the Oklahoma Heritage Association, were essential both to the compilation of photographs and publication of the book. The editor, Dr. Odie B. Faulk, was always helpful, especially during that climactic period when manuscript and photographs had to be assembled into one finished product.

In addition to those whose financial contributions made possible the publication of this book (listed on the "Special Acknowledgment" page), I am deeply indebted to Neil E. Bogan, elected President of the Oklahoma Bar Association for the year 1990. Not only did he suggest the book's title, but also his constant support and tireless fund-raising efforts assured publication without undue delay.

Finally, I affectionately dedicate this work to the person whose writing expertise, assistance, and everlasting patience were indispensable— Naomi Taylor Casey, my best friend and wife for almost half a century.

Orben J. Casey

SPECIAL ACKNOWLEDGMENT

Sincere appreciation and gratitude are extended to the following individuals and firms whose substantial financial contributions made the publication of this history of the legal profession a reality.

Jones, Givens, Gotcher, Bogan & Hilborne, P.C.

Fellers, Snider, Blankenship, Bailey & Tippens, P.C.

Kile, Rabon & Wolf

Fuller, Tubb & Pomeroy, P.C.

David K. Petty, P.C.

Luttrell, Pendarvis, Rawlinson & Poarch

Gable & Gotwals, P.C.

Phillips Petroleum Foundation, Inc.

Massad & Evans, Inc.

Hieronymus, Hodgden & Meyer, P.C.

Rhodes, Hieronymus, Jones, Tucker, Gable

Huffman, Arrington, Kihle, Gaberino & Dunn, P.C.

Kerr-McGee Corporation

Rogers & Bell (In memory of John Rogers and William H. Bell)

Marvin C. Emerson

Doerner, Stuart, Saunders, Daniel & Anderson

Richard L. McKnight

Stuart & Frieda, P.C.

Mock, Schwabe, Waldo, Elder, Reeves & Bryant, P.C.

PROFESSIONAL ASSOCIATIONS

Oklahoma Bar Foundation

Oklahoma Bar Association

Payne County Bar Association

CONTENTS

ILLUSTRATIONS

AND JUSTICE FOR ALL: THE LEGAL PROFESSION IN OKLAHOMA

1

A STATE IS BORN

President Theodore Roosevelt entered the cabinet room of the White House from his adjoining private office at 10:15 A.M. on November 16, 1907. He greeted the assembled Congressmen, newspaper correspondents, and interested citizens, then sat down at the head of a long conference table. While he signed his name the room was silent except for the scratching of his quill pen, which was made from the feather of an Oklahoma eagle. Then in his distinctive, raspy voice he announced, "Oklahoma is a state."

A few minutes later in Guthrie, the new state's capital of 12,000 people, city residents and visitors welcomed the telegraphed news of Oklahoma's Statehood with cheers, bell-ringing, and whistle-blowing. Shortly before noon an open, horse-drawn carriage occupied by Governor-elect Charles N. Haskell, Judge Frank Dale, chairman of the Statehood inaugural committee, and Leslie G. Niblack, a newspaper publisher, left Guthrie's Royal Hotel and rumbled along the brick-paved streets headed for the inaugural ceremonies to be held at the Carnegie Library.[1]

Two of the men seated in the carriage—Haskell and Dale—represented the two general types of lawyers influential in the past and future development of Oklahoma. Like most members of the profession of that time, neither possessed a formal legal education; both had "read law" in a lawyer's office. At the encouragement of United States Judge John R. Thomas, Haskell—a native of Ohio—had settled in Indian Territory a little more than six years earlier to engage in railroad construction. He was soon involved in Statehood activities that led to his election as Oklahoma's first governor.[2]

Unknown to the thousands who awaited Haskell's arrival at the Carnegie Library for the inaugural ceremonies, he already had taken the oath of office immediately after President Roosevelt signed Oklahoma's Statehood proclamation.[3] Less than ten minutes later he initiated the state's first legal action—an injunction to prevent the Kansas Natural Gas Company from completing the first pipeline intended to transport natural gas across the border from Oklahoma's Washington county into Kansas and points beyond.[4] Through this maneuver Haskell hoped to assure Oklahoma's industrial future by forcing manufacturing plants to locate within Oklahoma where natural gas, "the perfect fuel," was readily available. A month later the Legislature sanctioned the governor's action and thus established Oklahoma's leadership in the regulation of oil and gas among the energy-producing states; however, subsequent court cases defeated Governor Haskell's dream of a highly industrialized Oklahoma on the grounds that the "self-imposed Chinese Wall" was a hindrance to interstate commerce.[5]

In contrast to lawyer-entrepreneur Haskell, Frank Dale—the other man in the carriage headed for the inaugural ceremonies—could be described as a "lawyer's lawyer." Formerly an attorney in Kansas, he had participated in the "Run of 1889" that opened Oklahoma Territory to settlement, then had practiced law in Guthrie except for an interlude on the Supreme Court of Oklahoma Territory.[6] His Guthrie mansion, identified as one of the finest residences in the Territory, manifested the success of his law practice.[7] While chief justice of the Territorial Supreme Court, Dale had met head on the problem of lawlessness in the region by issuing one of the most drastic orders ever attributed to a Federal judge. "I have reached the conclusion that the only good outlaw is the dead one," he told United States Marshal Evett Nix. "I hope you will instruct your deputies to bring in dead outlaws in the future. That will simplify your problem a great deal and probably save some lives." He was pleased with the consequences of his order. Within six weeks nine members of the notorious Doolin Gang had been eliminated.[8]

The prominence of lawyers on Oklahoma's Statehood Day was indicative of the determinative role often played by the legal profession when significant political, economic, and social events occur. At the Statehood election on September 17, 1906, the voters entrusted lawyers with most of the

3

Charles N. Haskell, Oklahoma Governor, 1907-11.
(Courtesy Archives and Manuscripts Division, OHS.)

Governor-elect Charles N. Haskell, Judge Frank Dale,
and Leslie G. Niblack, newspaper publisher, on the way
to inaugural ceremonies at Guthrie's Carnegie Library.
(Courtesy The Daily Oklahoman.)

positions of leadership in the new state. In addition to the five members of the State Supreme Court from the legal profession, the electorate chose the governor, two United States senators, and four out of five members of the United States House of Representatives. The state's basic law—the constitution—had been written largely by 31 law-trained men among the 112 delegates to the constitutional convention. Subsequently the people approved it by a vote of 180,333 to 73,059.[9] A short time later the Oklahoma legislature chose lawyer Henry S. Johnston to be president pro tempore of the Senate and lawyer William H. "Alfalfa Bill" Murray to be speaker of the House of Representatives.

The selection of lawyers to guide Oklahoma in its initial stages assured a continuation of the contribution already made by the legal profession in the settlement, development, and formation of Oklahoma and Indian Territories into a state. On the national scene the decisions of two lawyer-presidents ultimately led to Oklahoma Statehood—Thomas Jefferson's decision to acquire the Louisiana Territory from France and Andrew Jackson's decision to insist on removal of the Indian people westward to a portion of the Territory. Jefferson had used his treaty-making power to initiate the purchase of Louisiana Territory and almost double the national domain of the United

States. All of present Oklahoma except the three Panhandle counties were included.

The laws that preceded lawyers to the newly acquired region were first administered through courts of Indiana Territory. Pursuant to a Congressional act of March 26, 1804, three judges appointed for four-year terms were to hold two sessions of court annually at a location convenient to settlers in the region.[10] Apparently no sessions of that court were ever held in what is now Oklahoma, which became a part of the Territory of Missouri in 1812 and part of the Territory of Arkansas seven years later.[11] Then in 1820 the General Assembly of the Territory of Arkansas created Miller County; it embraced parts of Arkansas and Texas as well as the present Oklahoma counties of McCurtain, Choctaw, and Pushmataha and the southern one-third of LeFlore and Latimer counties.

At that time the county seat for Miller County's 1000 residents was a trading station named "Miller Courthouse," located a few miles south of present Idabel, Oklahoma. The Court of Common Pleas for Miller County—the first court for white citizens within the present boundaries of Oklahoma—held its first session at the home of one Claiborne Wright on July 23, 1821. In accord with Territorial law, "three respectable house-holders" of the county sat as judges. Two terms of court

Judge Frank Dale is third from left, front row, in this photo of Bar Commision officials on the Oklahoma County Courthouse lawn in June 1912. Back row, L to R: Alvin Richards, law clerk to Justice Jesse J. Dunn of the Supreme Court; J.G. Ralls, Atoka; D.A. McDougal, Sapulpa; W.J. Horton, McAlester; J.W. Bolen, Ada; W.H.L. Campbell, clerk of the Supreme Court; Reuel Haskell, Jr., assistant clerk of the Supreme Court. Front row, L to R: C.H. Parker, Enid; E.F. Lester, Wilburton; Frank Dale, Guthrie; Ben F. Williams, Norman; C.A. Cook, Muskogee; Nestor Rummons, Hobart. (Courtesy Archives and Manuscript Division, OHS).

were held in 1821. Wright earned a total of $13 for the use of his residence during the July term of three days and a December term of four days. In October of that year the Arkansas General Assembly replaced the Territory's Courts of Common Pleas with a system of circuit courts.[12]

The General Assembly also established a court for the newly organized Lovely County at Nicksville, a logging settlement on Sallisaw Creek in what is now Sequoyah County, Oklahoma.[13] President Jefferson in 1803 had contemplated removal of the Indian people to lands acquired by the Louisiana Purchase to make more room for the onrush of white settlement in the Southeastern United States.[14] During the next quarter of a century removal of the eastern Indian tribes became established governmental policy. Removal treaties concluded in 1828 required Arkansas Territory to relinquish Miller and Lovely Counties, thereby

closing the first courts for white people within the present area of Oklahoma.[15]

After the early 1800s the American frontier moved steadily westward, while in the southwestern United States white settlers longed for the rich agricultural lands owned by the Five Civilized Tribes: the Cherokees, Choctaws, Creeks, Chickasaws, and Seminoles. Land occupied by the Cherokee Nation in Georgia proved doubly attractive after the discovery of gold in 1828. The Cherokees embarked on a valiant effort to retain their status as an independent nation. In two landmark court cases they battled Georgia legislation that subjected Cherokee lands to state law. They lost their first case, however, when the United States Supreme Court declined to accept jurisdiction on the grounds that the Cherokee Nation was not "a foreign state, in the sense of the constitution, and [could not] maintain an action in the courts of United States."[16]

In the second case the United States Supreme Court ruled a Georgia law unconstitutional; however, that state refused to comply with the court's decision.[17] President Andrew Jackson was unwilling to use executive authority to enforce the court's ruling. To him is attributed the comment, perhaps apocryphal, that "[Chief Justice] John Marshall has made his decision, now let him enforce it."[18] Jackson, a Tennesseean, like most frontiersmen of the day favored vigorous government policy to move the Indian tribes west of the Mississippi River. At times he engaged personally in negotiations that led to almost a hundred treaties intended to legalize removal.

The sordid tale of physical removal in the 1830s of the peaceful Five Civilized Tribes across hundreds of miles of rugged terrain, an operation graphically termed the "Trail of Tears," has been told many times. Thousands lost their lives in what remains one of the most tragic episodes in American history. Uprooted from their ancestral homes, the Five Tribes settled in what is now the state of Oklahoma and began rebuilding their laws and institutions.

2

BENCH AND BAR OF THE FIVE CIVILIZED TRIBES

Expressed in rough geographical terms of present Oklahoma, treaties with the Five Civilized Tribes (or Nations) divided the state into three sections. Generally the Cherokees acquired land in northern and northeastern Oklahoma except the Oklahoma Panhandle. South and east of the Cherokees in central Oklahoma was the Creek-Seminole domain. The Choctaws and Chickasaws were ceded all of southern Oklahoma, although Texas claimed the area west of the North Fork of the Red River. A number of smaller tribes, including the Senecas, Shawnees, and Quapaws, were located northeast of the Cherokees in present Ottawa County.[1]

The Commission of Indian Affairs in 1844 reported the population of the tribes then owning Indian Territory as:[2]

Cherokees	25,911
Quapaws	400
Chickasaws	4,111
Seminoles	3,136
Choctaws	12,410
Senecas	125
Creeks	24,594
Seneca-Shawnee band	211

The various governments of the Five Civilized Tribes reflected a combination of primitive Indian customs, and, except for the Seminoles, had written laws and constitutions patterned after those of federal and state governments. All land was held in common with title vested in the tribal governments. The Cherokees, Creeks, Choctaws, and Chickasaws provided for a bicameral legislature, a "Principal Chief," or "Governor," and a judicial system consisting of a Supreme Court and lower courts. Trial court procedure resembled that of state courts except for the small Seminole Nation where the National Council served as both legislature and judiciary, and litigating parties appeared before the Council without lawyers. The Council's decisions were final although criminal cases could be appealed to the Seminole Principal Chief.[3]

Each nation had a force of mounted police,

"Lighthorsemen," to carry out the orders of the chief magistrate and the decisions of the courts. Accepted punishment in capital cases was execution by hanging or firing squad. Originally, public whipping was a popular form of punishment for minor offenses in all five tribes; however, the Cherokee Nation abolished whipping posts in the 1870s after a national jail was built at Tahlequah.[4]

The routine practice of a Cherokee lawyer was perhaps no different from that of lawyers in nearby states, and his education and ability appear to have been generally the equal of practitioners in those states. Some had merely read law in a lawyer's office; the elite studied in the East, the favorite educational institutions being Princeton and Dartmouth. W.W. Hastings, later an Oklahoma congressman for 18 years, and Judge William P. Thompson who served on the Oklahoma Supreme Court Commission from 1923 to 1926, were both graduates of the Law Department of Vanderbilt University.[5]

The proficiency of members of the Bar appeared to be of no great concern to the Cherokee legislative body.[6] Cherokee law required no examination, and an aspiring lawyer needed only to purchase a $5 license to practice in the district and circuit courts. For an additional $5 fee he could practice before the Supreme Court. Any person could conduct his own law suit. Attorneys in good standing in other Indian nations could practice in a Cherokee court if properly recommended by a Cherokee attorney and approved by the presiding judge.

Judges and members of the executive council were expressly prohibited from practicing law.[7] In the 1870s the National Council also included the executive secretary in that category because of the actions of W.L.G. Miller, an adopted white citizen of the tribe. Miller, the trusted executive secretary to Chief Charles Thompson, was also a lawyer and had been inclined to seek impeachment of any judge whose decisions were unfavorable to him.[8]

An aggrieved party in the Cherokee Nation

Indian Territory, 1866-1889. (From Historical Atlas of Oklahoma, 3rd Edition, by John W. Morris, Charles R. Goins, and Edwin C. McReynolds, University of Oklahoma Press, 1986.)

Cherokee Capitol Building, Tahlequah. (Courtesy Archives and Mansucripts Division, OHS.)

could obtain damages and disbarment of any attorney by proper showing of deceit, malpractice, gross misconduct, willful neglect of his client's interests, or collusion.[9] However, the Supreme Court seemed reluctant to effect disbarment. In one instance, the Cherokee National Council specifically directed the court to cancel the license of two attorneys accused of violating their oaths. The court refused to do so on the grounds that statutory procedure had not been followed and that disbarment would involve "taking property without due process of law."[10]

Laws of the Choctaw Nation charged judges of the Supreme Court with the responsibility of examining an applicant to practice law as to his good character and whether he possessed "a competent share of law knowledge."[11] To practice in the Creek Nation, no legal training was required, but one had to be "of good moral character" and pay a fee of $10 to practice in a district court or $20 to practice in all courts.[12]

Until the year 1892 any individual who wished to practice law in the Chickasaw Nation was expected to demonstrate only "sufficient law knowledge" to a judge of the Supreme Court and pay a fee of $15.[13] The "sufficient law knowledge" pertained to Chickasaw law only. In October, 1892, however, the Chickasaw Legislature addressed itself to an unusual problem, explained in the introductory paragraph of "An Act Relating to the Issuing of License to Practice Law in the Chickasaw Nation," providing that:[14]

Whereas, many of the citizens of this Nation who do not wish to leave their homes when summoned to serve as jurymen at any of the terms of the Chickasaw Court, and in order to exempt themselves from such jury duties, they apply to the Supreme Court of this Nation and obtain a license as a lawyer merely to exempt them from such duty, when at the same time they do not intend to practice law before the courts, and at the same time again they are not qualified to practice and should not have such law license.

The Legislature made a license more difficult to obtain by requiring "three good practicing attorneys," appointed by a district judge, "to examine said applicant on all points of law, the treaties and constitution of the Chickasaw Nation, and all kinds of legal procedure had in the Chickasaw Courts, how to sue and defend suits and how to conduct criminal prosecution and defend the same as practiced by the courts of this nation...."[15]

The selection of judges in the Indian nations, done either by general election or more often through a vote of the legislative body, was generally based more on reputation for honesty and on political considerations than on knowledge of the law.[16] Nevertheless, in the Cherokee courts many of the judges were retired lawyers familiar with the "general elementary principles of law." There was little uniformity in Cherokee decisions, however, owing to some non-lawyer judges and the fact that the judge acted as both judge and jury in appealed civil cases. In addition, translation back and forth between English and

Tobucksy County Courthouse, Choctaw Nation. (Courtesy The Daily Oklahoman.)

Chickasaw Nation Capitol Building, Tishomingo. (Courtesy The Daily Oklahoman.)

Cherokee was a definite handicap. In the process of translation, judge and jury often lost important ideas in testimony and argument.[17]

The Cherokee Supreme Court could be subjected to criticism-as shown by an anonymous letter published in the *Vinita Indian Chieftain* in 1887. Joseph Abasalom Scales, Cherokee statesman, lawyer and judge, was a zealous defender of the court over which he presided for many years. He obtained the name of the letter writer—J.H. Akin, a Vinita attorney—and answered with scathing sarcasm in his letter printed on March 10, 1887:[18]

> I...was curious to know which of the attorneys before the supreme court was so wanting in decency as to write such an article. I inferred from the internal evidence that it was the product of some disappointed pettifogger who desired to attain notoriety by attempting to cast odium upon the court and its officers. But singularly protected by your utter insignificance your name did not occur to me, and I did not like to go skunk hunting in the dark.
>
> It is not my intention to defend the decisions of the court. They need none, and besides I am not responsible for them. I may however be allowed to say that the court has been able to discriminate between a constitutional requirement and a provision of the statute in relation to formal' defects, and it has also been able to judge whether some of the literary curiosities called 'bonds' were really such, and some times it has thought they were not. In this it is different with the fools who thought otherwise, but of course the court would think it beneath its dignity to enter into a newspaper controversy with every lying scribbler who might wish

to avail this method through spleen or malevolence, to ventilate his imaginary grievances.

Judge Scales closed his denunciation of Akin by writing, "You have been abundantly blessed with ignorance and self conceit and had not the good Lord benevolently made you an ass, you would have been a scoundrel."

J.B. Sharp, a white lawyer who practiced 14 years in the Chickasaw Nation and after Statehood served on the Oklahoma Supreme Court Commission and the Supreme Court of Oklahoma, observed that the legal knowledge of most Chickasaw judges did not surpass that of "the ordinary justice of the peace in a sparsely settled backwoods district."[19] Moreover, according to Sharp, "The laws of the Nation were never suited to the protection of great property interest such as began to accumulate during the latter part of the eighties."[20]

Nevertheless, a Chickasaw magistrate could be jealous of his sphere of authority. J.H. Franklin was presiding judge at the Panola County Court House in what now is Bryan County, Oklahoma, in the early 1880s when A.B. Pearson, a prominent Texas attorney, appeared in court in behalf of a client. Opposing counsel objected that Pearson was not licensed to practice in the Chickasaw Nation. Pearson countered, "I have a license to practice anywhere in the United States." Judge Franklin hastened to inform him that "the Chickasaw Nation and Panola County are not in the United States." Non-citizen lawyers were never permitted to practice in Chickasaw courts.[21]

The Creek Council in the 1870s provided for

Joseph A. Scales, Cherokee statesman, lawyer, jurist. (Courtesy McFarlin Library, University of Tulsa.)

log courthouses, but until then court had been held in any convenient place—the judge's home, a schoolhouse, or the town square. The judges were usually illiterate so no written proceedings were required in civil cases. The plaintiff merely explained the nature of his case to the judge and gave him the names of the defendant and any witnesses. The judge then instructed the Lighthorse police to notify the parties involved.[22] A Creek judge acted at his peril if he was dilatory in holding court. One statute warned that, "Any Judge who shall fail to hold court at the time prescribed by law, unless prevented by death, or other circumstances beyond his control, or who shall willfully violate any other provisions of the law, shall be guilty of a misdemeanor, and be liable to impeachment and expulsion from office."[23]

The Creeks allowed former Negro slaves to hold positions of responsibility. One of these was Jesse Franklin who testified before a congressional committee in 1878 that he had been a judge of the Creek Supreme Court for three years and earned $5 a day when court was in session.[24] Another freedman, Sugar George, worked as a blacksmith but in the first three months of 1875 earned $25 as prosecuting attorney for the Ar-

kansas District of the Creek Nation. He later served as a judge in the Muskogee District.[25]

Especially busy was Creek freedman David A. Lee. His printed letterhead identified himself as judge, lawyer, postmaster, notary public, and grocer. He held court in a one-room log cabin at the trading post of Lee—named after him—which was located three miles northwest of Boynton. Another black lawyer, also a schoolteacher, was A.G.W. Sango, who was hired as attorney for the Creek Nation in 1895.[26]

Joseph G. Ralls of Atoka, the peppery, outspoken pioneer member of the Indian Territory Bar Association and the Oklahoma State Bar Association, presented a paper on the Choctaw courts at a meeting of the Indian Territory Bar in 1903. He was a strong critic of Choctaw courts and lawyers as reflected in one paragraph of his paper:[27]

> There has never been any uniform practice; the judges and lawyers have never claimed to be possessed of any legal training; they despise to see a law book in a court room, and the library of the Choctaw lawyer consists of the Code and a few session laws, costing about three dollars. He charges his client from one dollar up, and many with the privilege of selling out to the other side. Too frequently these same lawyers are elected as judges, when they find themselves in a very embarrassing and restrained position, as they are unable to 'sell out' to both sides. The corruption is so appalling that many of the honorable Choctaws are anxious that the Federal courts be given exclusive jurisdiction of both civil and criminal cases as well as all probate matters.

The code referred to by Ralls was probably the "J.P. Code," the basic law book of the Choctaw Nation after it was published in 1869 under the title, *Constitution and Laws of the Choctaw Nation and Treaties of 1855, 1856, and 1866.*[28] Its Choctaw author, Joseph P. Folsom, spent 10 years in schools in the East and was graduated from Dartmouth College in 1854. Probably the best educated of any Choctaw lawyer until 1900, he was, as one writer noted, "profound in Latin and Greek and thinks the English nothing but a borrowed language." He used his legal training to great advantage in the political life of the Choctaw Nation.[29]

Another well-trained Choctaw lawyer was Alinton Telle, who attended Kemper Military Academy then received a degree from Southwestern

Alinton Telle, Choctaw lawyer. (Courtesy Archives and Manuscripts Division, OHS.)

Presbyterian University of Clarksville, Tennessee, in 1880. A year later he earned a law degree from Union University at Albany, New York. He was admitted to practice in New York but chose to return to the Choctaw Nation.[30] A Choctaw district judge, J.B. Connors, described Telle: "Alinton Telle was a genial, full-blood Choctaw who did not mind pleading guilty to laziness. One day among a crowd of friends, one of them accused him of being lazy and reminded him of the Scriptural admonition to work and earn his bread by the sweat of his face. He replied that he did not believe that God intended for a man to work all the time or He would not have given him so many wonderful and interesting things to think about."[31] Telle served as National Secretary for the Choctaw Nation and represented the Choctaws before the Dawes Commission. His penmanship was so outstanding that a committee of handwriting experts, when shown an official communication written by Telle to the Department of the Interior, "pronounced it the most perfect example of handwriting they had ever seen."[32]

Judge Connors marveled that Telle formed a partnership with George Pate, an intermarried Choctaw citizen of entirely different personality. Of Pate, Connors said, "He was the kind of man that the trouble makers considered best to let alone. He was about as nervous and active during his sleep an in the daytime. Once while handling a case in the district court near Wilburton and following the first day of trial, he worked on his evidence during most of the night. He would lie down, think awhile, get up and begin working on his papers, take another cat-nap and begin again. The next morning while enjoying a breakfast of broiled venison, he told his adversaries that he was ready for them as he had enjoyed a fine night's rest and was rearing to go."[33]

In 1891 Telle and Pate represented the defendants in a suit involving the "Number Six" coal mines, located near Lehigh for a monetary amount of $25,000. According to Joseph G. Ralls who narrated the case to the Indian Territory Bar Association at the 1903 convention, the Choctaw district judge was also attorney for the plaintiffs and failed to comply with proper procedure for issuing the summons. Telle and Pate made a special appearance to quash the summons and were amazed when the special judge appointed by the regular judge overruled their motion. They appealed to the Choctaw Supreme Court. Ralls described the actions of a lawyer confident he would win his case:[34]

> Mr. Pate was so certain he would win he decided if he did not win he would hang himself; but that court, like many other august bodies, was looking for ways to affirm, and did so. Mr. Pate was true to his word, and purchased a rope and swung himself off, but fortunately J.A. Hale, a member of our Association, chanced to pass by and cut the rope in time to save Mr. Pate's life, and today Mr. Hale preserves a piece of the rope as a souvenir.

Despite George Pate's eccentricities he was considered an able lawyer. When young Robert L. Williams, future governor and Federal judge, first came to Indian Territory in 1896, he worked as a law clerk for Pate. A short time later they formed a partnership with Pate located in Atoka and Williams in Durant.[35]

Unlike the other four tribes the small Seminole Nation had little need for a legal profession. The General or (National) Council prided itself on swift justice in its capacity as both legislature and judiciary. Trials were conducted in the simplest possible manner. The parties appeared before the Council, made their statements, produced witnesses, then awaited the Council's verdict. The parties were not represented by counsel. In a criminal case the Principal Chief always had the

Grant Foreman, lawyer-historian, in his Muskogee office. (Courtesy OHS.)

Stand Watie, Cherokee part-time lawyer and Confederate general. (Courtesy OHS.)

power to pardon the accused at any time before punishment was inflicted. The Chief had to act speedily, however, for any punishment was usually administered by Lighthorse police during the session of the council that tried the case.[36]

Throughout Indian Territory non-citizens were not subject to any law applicable to credit transactions among themselves or with the Indian people. Commercial organizations outside the Territory extended credit to its residents at their own risk, so the Territory became an attractive home for unscrupulous debtors.[37] Cherokee, Creek, and Seminole judicial processes could be utilized to collect debts between their own citizens; however, neither Choctaw or Chickasaw law permitted civil actions for debts.

One pioneer recalled that in the Cherokee Nation any individual who needed money could usually borrow from neighbors, and only those suspected of dishonesty had to furnish security. In fact, he said, "When notes and chattel mortgages were first introduced into the Cherokee country the real old full-bloods thought that they were made for the crooks."[38] The lack of a collection law seemed to present no great hindrance to Choctaw internal transactions for debts were seldom incurred.[39]

One historian of the Choctaws has pointed out that if a member of that tribe did incur a debt, it was always paid if and when the means became

available. A physician practicing in the Choctaw Nation told of lending $60 to a young Indian. When from time to time he inquired about payment, his only reply was a grunt. The physician had almost forgotten the debt when 20 years later a middle-aged Indian knocked on his door and said, "Here's your sixty dollars," and walked away.[40]

The Chickasaws had such strong objection to a collection law that the Legislature enacted "An Act prohibiting the collection of debts in the courts of this Nation":[41]

> Sec. 1. Be it enacted by the Legislature of the Chickasaw Nation, that as there never has been any law for the collection of debts from the Nation, or from individuals, it is hereby enacted that no courts of this Nation shall allow any case of indebtedness to be entered upon the records of said court, except bonds and fines and such other indebtedness as is provided for by the laws of this Nation.

Sharp commented to the lawyers attending the 1903 Indian Territory Bar convention, "What a haven of refuge for the dishonest debtor, subject to its jurisdiction, was the Chickasaw Nation."[42]

A debate arose in the Chickasaw Legislature after a young member, recently graduated from the University of Texas, introduced a bill to allow collections of debts through judicial process. In rebuttal, one man named Grayson advanced the

11

following argument that assured the bill's defeat: "Young man say this is progress. Under white man law you have a horse; I have a horse. You think my horse best; I think your horse best. We make trade. After trade you find my horse best. White man law don't give thing to correct my judgment when no lie is passed [meaning when there is no fraud]. Now I want borrow hundred dollars. You think me 'honorable.' I got no honor. I borrow hundred dollars. Don't pay. What business in law curing your judgment on hundred dollars, anymore than correct judgment on horse trade."[43]

Grant Foreman, long-time Muskogee lawyer and Oklahoma historian, noted that the court records of the Five Civilized Tribes "are not extensive nor very illuminating."[44] However, while doing historical research in the Library of Congress, Foreman discovered that John Howard Payne, the actor, playwright, and journalist who wrote the song, "Home, Sweet Home," had written a detailed narrative of the 10-day criminal trial of one Archilla Smith at Tahlequah in 1840. As a guest of Chief John Ross, Payne had visited the Cherokee Nation that year to write a history of the Cherokees. The next year the *New York Journal of Commerce*, published an account of the Smith trial drawn from Payne's notes and court transcripts.

Payne wrote that the trial was conducted in a hut 18 feet square with a dirt floor. It was furnished with rough board benches for all participants except that Judge Looney Price was permitted the luxury of a chair and the court clerk had both a chair and table.[45] One of the defense attorneys was Stand Watie, later a revered Cherokee leader who fought for the Confederacy in the Civil War and became the last Confederate general to surrender.[46] Watie, then 35 years old, conducted a part-time law practice usually confined to commercial transactions.[47]

The trial, which ended with the conviction and hanging of the defendant, included the ordinary elements of a criminal case today. Its simplified approach, however, was appropriate for a developing nation of 25,000 people not long removed from the unwritten law of the clan. The proceedings were in accord with Chief John Ross' suggestion made not long after the first Cherokee Constitution was adopted in 1827, "The mode for conducting suits in courts should be free from all

Old Eagletown Courthouse and whipping tree, Choctaw Nation. (Courtesy Western History Collections, University of Oklahoma Library.)

complicated formalities, and no other *form* should be required than, to let both parties know distinctly, what is alleged."[48]

John Howard Payne was impressed by the friendly atmosphere throughout the trial. The jury was free to interrupt to ask questions, and participants and spectators alike seemed completely at ease.[49] Defendant Smith smoked his pipe contentedly. Payne commented, "...His judge, and most of his jury, every now and then would get up and go across the log-court to him with 'Arley, lend me your pipe:' and received his pipe from his mouth (as is the Indian custom); and revel in the loan of a five minutes' smoke."[50]

More than 50 years later, in 1892, another journalist, George E. Foster, reported the custom of pipe-smoking in the Cherokee courts endured— and had indeed flourished, for now everyone had his own pipe. Foster told of his experience in *The Green Bag*, a publication for lawyers:[51]

As the case proceeded, and the evidence grew more complicated, the jury dropped into apparently deep meditation. Finally one drew out a long pipe, filled it with tobacco, and commenced to smoke. Another and another of the jurymen followed with a pipe. The interested audience outside the bars also lit their pipes, and at length the judge, five of the jurymen, and nearly the whole audience were smoking.

Informality prevailed with one exception; As Foster sat by an open window, the room "blue with the smoke of tobacco," he put on his cap to protect his head from the cool air. A court official politely asked him "not to wear his hat in the presence of the judge."[52]

In the Choctaw Nation, one of the first trials after removal took place in the Red River District on September 10 and 11, 1834. Judges George W. Harkins, Israel Folsom, and Silas L. Fisher presided at the trial of a Negro slave named "Bob" who was charged with murder of a Negro woman. Sixteen of the 24-man jury found "Bob" guilty and sentenced him to die. However, because neither the slave nor his white owner was a Choctaw citizen, Indian Agent F.W. Armstrong directed military authorities to hold "Bob" until Armstrong could submit the problem to Washington for a ruling. The eventual outcome is unrecorded, but Armstrong's action at once forecast jurisdictional problems that the Indian nations would encounter until their courts were eventually abolished by the Curtis Act of 1898.[53]

3

JURISDICTIONAL PROBLEMS: THE GOINGSNAKE COURTHOUSE TRAGEDY

Where Indians went, whites were never far behind. Recognizing that fact, Congress in 1834 supplemented Indian tribal law with legislation that placed the non-Indians of present Oklahoma under the jurisdiction, for the most part, of the Territory of Arkansas. Provisions were made for the licensing of tradesmen, regulation of relations with Indian tribes, fines and removal of intruders, and prohibition of the liquor traffic. Crimes confined solely to Indians were left to the Indian courts, but United States law governed when non-Indians were involved. This important legislation was to remain basic law for the Indian country until after the Civil War.[1]

President Jackson felt the "Indian problem" had been resolved by their removal to the West and the legislation of 1834. In his message of December, 1835, he said, "The pledge of the United States has been given by Congress, that the country destined for the residence of this people, shall be forever secured and guaranteed to them'...A barrier has thus been raised, for their protection against the encroachment of our citizens, and guarding the Indians, as far as possible, from those evils which have brought them to their present condition."[2]

At first the Five Civilized Tribes functioned virtually as five independent republics with complete control over immigration and citizenship. However, the "silent immigration" that acquired lands for the United States west to the Pacific Ocean and south to the Rio Grande, also helped destroy President Jackson's "barrier" of protection for the Indian nations.

As had happened in their Eastern homelands, the Indian people themselves were partially responsible for white intrusion. Their rich agricultural lands were communal property, although crops belonged to the Indian citizen who cultivated the land. Resourceful Indian entrepreneurs utilized black slave labor to cultivate large tracts prior to the Civil War. After emancipation

The Five Civilized Tribes Union Agency, 1875-78, Muskogee, now the Five Civilized Tribes Museum. (Courtesy Five Civilized Tribes Museum.)

of their slaves, they procured black or white labor by use of government permits. Although outright lease of the land was forbidden, the Indian landlord attained essentially the same objective by an agreement whereby the agricultural laborer exchanged his services for a share of the crops. This proved a satisfactory arrangement for all parties, and agricultural "laborers" soon outnumbered other permit holders such as missionaries, teachers, and tradesmen.[3]

In addition to tribal courts and the federal courts that existed only outside Indian Territory, local practicalities encouraged formation of a third tribunal—the office of United States Indian agent. Originally the agent was, in the main, a diplomatic representative of the United States government; but later he became responsible for "general tribal well-being." After 1874, when all agencies for the Five Tribes were consolidated into a single "Union Agency" at Muskogee, the agent with increasing frequency conducted informal hearings. The disputes voluntarily submitted to him often involved large sums of money.[4]

The Indian agent could call on United States marshals at Fort Smith for assistance, and after 1878 he had access to a company of 35 to 40 Indian police, called "Lighthorsemen," who helped enforce tribal law, federal liquor statutes, and other laws affecting American citizens.[5] United States Indian Agent John Q. Tufts told the Commissioner of Indian Affairs in 1883, "In civil cases between white men and Indians and in cases of differences between the tribes, this agency is the court."[6]

The dual system of jurisprudence that tried Indians in tribal courts but required United States courts where a non-Indian was involved naturally led to confusion in jurisdiction. The United States Supreme Court in 1846 held that a white man was still subject to United States law despite his claim to Cherokee citizenship. The Cherokees received no comfort from a further statement by Chief Justice Roger B. Taney that Congress had the power to punish any offense committed in Indian Territory whether by white man or Indian.[7]

When the Federal District Court for Western Arkansas under Judge Daniel Ringo was established in Van Buren in 1853, the Five Civilized Tribes had more cause for alarm. Deputy marshals from the Van Buren Court, who earned fees based on the number of prisoners taken and the miles traveled, did not hesitate to enter Indian Territory to arrest Indians for violation of laws over which Indian courts claimed cognizance and to place them in the Van Buren jail.[8]

Indian violators of the law against introduction of liquor into Indian Territory furnished a fruitful source of revenue for arresting officials. Enraged Creeks rescued one prisoner from the marshals and threatened armed resistance to continued intrusions. Congress awakened to the problem, and in March, 1854, it enacted legislation to prevent United States law from extending to offenses committed by Indians in their own country and punishable under Indian law.[9] But Cherokee authorities still complained that their citizens accused of crimes against the United States often were held in the Van Buren jail for months—as much as a 100 miles from home, un-

Choctaw Lighthorsemen, 1893, Antlers, Indian Territory. (Courtesy Western History Collections, University of Oklahoma Library.)

15

familiar with court procedure, and without benefit of counsel.[10]

The Van Buren court in 1856 handed down its first death sentence. This was to accused murderer Thomas Beard, a white blacksmith living in the Cherokee Nation 14 miles from Fort Smith. One of Beard's defense attorneys was Benjamin T. DuVal, a lawyer whose long legal career identified him with many outstanding cases before the Federal District Court of Western Arkansas.[11] When the body of the man allegedly murdered by Beard was found, it was beyond identification. A man staying at Beard's home was missing, and because only circumstantial evidence pointed to Beard as the murderer, the defense persuaded Judge Daniel Ringo to advertise for Beard's missing house guest in a few Eastern newspapers and in newspapers within a several-hundred-mile-radius of Fort Smith. This highly publicized defense maneuver was unsuccessful, for the missing man never appeared. The case itself made legal history being what was reported to be the first Arkansas conviction for murder based on circumstantial evidence.[12]

Congress moved the Van Buren tribunal to Fort Smith on March 3, 1871. There Judge Henry J. Caldwell, an appointee of President U.S. Grant, convened court in May, 1871, to try John Childers, a mixed-blood Cherokee accused of murdering a peddler in the Cherokee Nation. A defense argument lasted two and a half days, but after a short deliberation the jury pronounced Childers guilty. Thus he became the first of 87 victims of the newly erected gallows inside the walls of the abandoned fort for which Fort Smith, Arkansas, is named.[13] A year later the Cherokee Nation's fight with Fort Smith officers in "The Goingsnake Courthouse Tragedy" intensified the problems of dual jurisdiction that confronted the Five Tribes after the Civil War.

In that war the tribes generally had participated on the side of the Confederacy. Consequently the United States government considered tribal agreements abrogated and required new treaties executed in 1866 to incorporate provisions for freeing slaves, granting railroad rights of way, and permitting plains Indians to live on the land in western Indian Territory. At the same time all Five Tribes agreed that the United States could establish courts within tribal domain.[14]

Zeke Proctor, Cherokee Indian, initiated the Goingsnake Courthouse tragedy. (Courtesy OHS.)

The Cherokees insisted on a clause, unique to their treaty, by which Cherokee courts retained "exclusive jurisdiction in all civil and criminal cases arising within their country in which members of the nation, by nativity or adoption, shall be the only parties, or where the cause of action shall arise in the Cherokee Nation, except as otherwise provided in this treaty."[15]

The latter clause was frequently referred to in jurisdictional squabbles which reached a peak in the early 1870s after an argument in which Zeke Proctor accidentally killed another Cherokee, Polly Kesterson, and wounded her husband, James, an adopted-white Cherokee citizen.[16] Kesterson filed a complaint against Proctor in Fort Smith in expectation that the Cherokee courts would free Proctor. Judge Black Hawk Sixkiller and other Cherokee officials, aware that United States deputy marshals planned to take Proctor, were well prepared on the morning of April 15, 1872, when a posse headed by Deputy Marshal James G. Owens approached the Whitmire School in the Goingsnake District, the site where the Proctor trial was in progress. Someone fired a shot into the courtroom. In the ensuing battle 10 men died, and several were wounded. One of the dead was a defense counsel, the elderly Moses Alberty, who had been sitting at the clerk's table reviewing evidence in the case.[17]

"The Goingsnake Courthouse Tragedy" re-

Robert L. Owen, Indian Agent, became Oklahoma's first United States Senator. (Courtesy OHS.)

ceived the attention of both houses of Congress and President Ulysses S. Grant. The government apparently relied on an investigation made by Enoch Hoag, Superintendent of Indian Affairs at Lawrence, Kansas, as well as that by John B. Jones, Indian Agent for the Cherokee Nation. Both Hoag and Jones supported the Cherokee allegation that their jurisdictional treaty rights had been violated.[18]

On the other hand, Fort Smith officials accused the Cherokee government of past failures to cooperate and even of hindering the proper exercise of United States authority in the Cherokee Nation. They pointed out that at the May and November terms of the previous year, Judge Caldwell's court had convicted four persons of resisting marshals operating in the Goingsnake

District and that already in the early part of 1872 one deputy marshal had been killed in that area.[19]

Deputy United States Marshal James W. Donnelly claimed that Zeke Proctor belonged to an organization of "Pin" Indians sworn to kill any Indian or Cherokee citizen who testified against another Indian or Cherokee citizen in the Federal courts. The Goingsnake affair reached an impasse with conflicting statements and accusations from both sides, and all charges were finally dismissed.[20]

To avoid jurisdictional problems in the future, Indian Agent Jones suggested the creation of a court in Indian Territory as contemplated by the treaties of 1866. That solution had the support of President Grant, who told the United States Senate in his report of the Goingsnake incident on May 7, 1872, that "a judicial district court within the Indian Territory...will afford the most immediate remedy for the existing troubles."[21]

However, the first session of the court proposed by President Grant did not occur for another 17 years. Meanwhile, white migration into Indian Territory proceeded apace, especially after the coming of railroads in 1871 and the expanded coal mining activity. And conditions were developing that caused Indian Agent and future United States Senator Robert L. Owen to describe Indian Territory in 1886 as, "a blackspot on the map of the United States. .., [an] asylum for absconding debtors, thieves, gamblers, outlaws, murderers; in fact the scum of the worst element found on the frontier."[22]

Probably no other available applicant was so well qualified to furnish judicial leadership in that chaotic frontier setting as Isaac C. Parker, who would become known as the "Hanging Judge" as he presided over the Federal District Court at Fort Smith.

4

THE COURT OF NO APPEAL

In late 1872 young William Story, a "carpet-bagger," appointee of President Grant, succeeded Henry J. Caldwell as judge of the federal court at Fort Smith. Story's 14-month term as judge was tainted with corruption. Apathetic toward law enforcement, his court was distrusted by bar and public alike. Trials and convictions were few—no action was taken to avenge more than 50 murders in addition to sundry other crimes said to have been committed during Judge Story's tenure. Many witnesses and jurors were unpaid although court costs of $400,000 for the 14 months were considered extravagant and wasteful. Judge Story resigned in June of 1874 in the face of impeachment proceedings.[1]

A physician in the Creek Nation town of Muskogee explained the apparent lawlessness in that vicinity to an amazed visitor in 1872: "The fact is there is no government actually, but lots of trials. If both parties were Indians—that is, have 'head rights' in the Nation—it's tried by Indians under their laws; if either's a white man, it's tried at Fort Smith, and that's just no trial. My protection and government is in these stone walls, a shot-gun and six shooter."[2]

On the Fort Smith legal scene is 1875 appeared 36-year-old Isaac Charles Parker of St. Joseph, Missouri. Parker had taught school while attending Barnesville Academy in Ohio and had moved to Missouri after being admitted to the Bar in 1859. At St. Joseph he served consecutively as city attorney, prosecuting attorney, and two years as judge of the Twelfth Judicial Circuit of Missouri. He had twice been elected to Congress from the Sixth Missouri District. In March of 1875 President Grant appointed him Chief Justice in the newly created Territory of Utah, but a short time later the president withdrew that appointment and made him judge of the Western District of Arkansas—a post Parker apparently preferred—at an annual salary of $3500.[3]

The man Professor John H. Wigmore of Northwestern University's law school described as "one of the greatest of American trial judges"

never actually held court within the confines of present Oklahoma, but his actions and decisions dealt almost exclusively with the people and conditions in that future state.[4] The Parker court was to be unique in the history of America jurisprudence. Over the western half of Arkansas it exercised a jurisdiction not unlike that of any other federal court, with the state of Arkansas providing court machinery for most civil and criminal litigation. But for more than 70,000 square miles—from the western boundary of Arkansas to the shadow of the Rocky Mountains—Judge Parker's court reigned supreme in criminal cases except those involving Indians only, and under certain circumstances the court even assumed jurisdiction over Indian cases.

For 14 years, until a congressional enactment of February 6, 1889, no appeal was possible from a conviction in that district court. Presidential clemency was the only hope for a convicted criminal. With such unlimited power the vigorous Judge Parker embarked on a program of law enforcement that was to have a potent civilizing influence on Indian Territory. He worked tirelessly to reduce the court's backlog of cases. The customary May and November court terms merged into one continuous term, convening no later than 8:30 and lasting until dark. The only holidays were Sunday, Christmas Day, and perhaps the Fourth of July.[5]

The distance from points in the Indian Territory to the Fort Smith court always created a problem in obtaining witnesses. One Indian Territory citizen, Ninnian Tannehill, said that he once appeared as a witness in a whiskey selling case, for which he was allowed 10 cents per mile for travel and $1.50 per day expenses for the two months he had to stay in Fort Smith. "It was a costly matter for most people," he said, "and for that reason many things were never reported in order to avoid the trip to Fort Smith."[6] Another pioneer, Peter B. Arthur, said, "It was the custom in those days when any one was found murdered to bury him in a grave near the place where the

Isaac Charles Parker, the "Hanging Judge," served as judge for the Western District of Arkansas from 1875 until his death in 1896. (Courtesy OHS.)

body was found. This was done to avoid the long weeks of attending trials at Fort Smith, Arkansas."[7] Indian Agent Robert L. Owen reported a case north of Muskogee where a husband had cut his wife's throat, but a local doctor refused to render medical aid because he had no desire to expend the time and money involved if he had to go to Fort Smith to testify.[8]

Judge Parker later recounted the problem he encountered, when he first convened court on May 10, 1875:[9]

> At the first term of court it was rather hard to get good, honest men to come out of that country [Indian Territory] and give testimony against these desperate characters. A reign of terror existed over there, and the peaceful, law-abiding citizens would rather put up with the annoyances they were subjected to than to come out and testify against the criminals and thus incur the enmity of these bad men and their friends and risk life by assassination at their hands.

Nevertheless, at that court session 15 of the 18 persons charged with murder were convicted, and Parker sentenced six of them, all of whom had committed murder in Indian Territory, to the gallows. On September 3, 1875, they were hanged before 5000 enthralled spectators in a staged event that brought worldwide attention to Judge Parker and his court. The next year he

sentenced nine more men to be hanged and convinced everyone he was a believer in the frontier law, "Take 'em out, give 'em a fair trial, and hang 'em." By then he had earned the sobriquet, "Hanging Judge," for which he is still remembered.[10]

The tremendous drive and dedication of Isaac C. Parker are reflected in the workload completed in his 21 years on the bench: 13,490 cases docketed, 9,454 convictions, 344 trials of capital offenses in which 165 men were convicted, and 79 hanged.[11] The library available for Judge Parker's guidance consisted of the *Arkansas Reports, American Decisions, American Reports*, the old *American and English Encyclopedia, Wharton's Criminal Law, Story on Equity*, and a few other text books.[12]

Assisting Parker in accumulating the court's gruesome statistics was a company of 200 deputy marshals of whom 65 died in line of duty. They roamed the hills and ravines of Indian Territory seeking lawbreakers of any race—white, red, black, or mixed. Especially they wanted "criminal intruders," people illegally in the Territory, whom Parker despised. The list of outlaws brought to the United States District Court of Western Arkansas is a roster of Indian Territory criminals with names still familiar to Oklahomans, people such as Cherokee Bill, Belle Starr, the Buck Gang, Blue Duck, and Henry Starr.[13]

In 1883 Congress reduced Judge Parker's territorial jurisdiction by transferring the region west of the Five Civilized Tribes and North of the South Canadian River to the United States District Court for Kansas, with Wichita and Fort Scott as court towns. The court for the Northern District of Texas, headquartered at Graham, took charge of the region south of the South Canadian River.[14] The Parker docket received little relief, however, for the retained area of jurisdiction was the most populous of the Five Civilized Tribes.

The unusual volume of cases in Judge Parker's court—it probably heard more criminal litigation than any court in the land—made law enforcement a major industry in the city of Fort Smith. For 14 years local lawyers were reluctant to challenge the great power exercised by Judge Parker. But after the 1883 legislation, lawyers from both Kansas and Texas became more familiar with Indian Territory affairs. Few Indian lawyers ever practiced in federal courts, but they did occasionally gather evidence for the white law firms and

Law enforcement officers who served in Indian Territory and in eastern Oklahoma after Statehood. (Courtesy Western History Collections, University of Oklahoma Library.)

Israel G. Vore, a non-Indian lawyer in Muskogee, drafted most of the Creek Nation's laws and executive papers during the 1870s. See Murray B. Stewart's article in 55 Okla.B.J. 2645-55, December 29, 1984. (Courtesy Brueau of American Ethnology.)

help prepare cases for trial. Until 1889 no terms of federal court were conducted in the Territory, so virtually no white lawyers resided there except a limited number of adopted, intermarried citizens.[15] Nevertheless, the advisability of holding sessions of the United States court within the Territory itself, for the convenience of participants and as a possible crime deterrent, was often discussed.

Gideon Morgan, a Cherokee Indian and later a member of the Oklahoma Legislature, told of an incident that indicated Judge Parker's reaction to holding a court term in Indian Territory. Morgan, after being tried and acquitted in Judge Parker's court for shooting a trespasser, wrote his cousin, Senator John T. Morgan of Alabama, to complain of the distance prisoners and witnesses had to travel from the Territory to Fort Smith, where they sometimes were forced to remain as long as a year without "healthy recreation" while awaiting trial.

Senator Morgan and Massachusetts Senator Henry L. Dawes, later head of the Dawes Commission, came to Fort Smith to investigate. Gideon Morgan reported the following conversation:[16]

Senator Morgan: The court will have to move and become a moving court.

Judge Parker: That's not respectable nonsense. You couldn't get a jury.

Senator Morgan: But it's time to educate those west of the river to be citizens. You hold one term one hundred miles west and let them become acquainted with customs and usage of the Court.

Judge Parker: I must be excused. If I crossed the river, I would be shot.

Senator Morgan: Do I understand you to say, Judge, that holding your position, that this government can't protect you one hundred miles. The Court is going.

No doubt Parker's popularity and influence in strategic political places helped prevent Senator Morgan from ever carrying out his own preference.

On February 6, 1889, Congress passed legislation obviously directed at the "Hanging Judge." The measure authorized the United States Supreme Court on writ of error to review death sentences pronounced by any United States trial court.[17] This law was strengthened two years later by an act permitting direct review by the Court of all capital or otherwise infamous criminal cases.[18]

Judge Parker's lengthy charges to the jury were often flavored with statements in support of the prosecution and resulted in many reversals. Even then some justices recorded strong dissenting opinions. And it seems that Parker, with his broad experience in criminal trials, may occasionally have been more perceptive and ahead of his time than the cloistered tribunal that overruled him.[19] Plain spoken individual that he was, Parker could not forever remain silent in the wake of continuing criticism of his decisions. He began openly to denounce the Supreme Court. He had been mentioned frequently as a possible appointee to that court; however, his unjudicial comments probably closed the door on such an appointment.[20]

The case of Crawford "Cherokee Bill" Goldsby—self styled "half Indian, half Negro and half white," perhaps the most vicious desperado ever to operate in Indian Territory, provoked Judge Parker's strongest censure of the Supreme Court. After Parker sentenced Goldsby to die for the murder of a prominent citizen of Lenapah, defense counsel J. Warren Reed took the case to the Supreme Court on writ of error. While the Supreme Court studied the matter, Goldsby, still in jail a month after the execution date set by Judge Parker, somehow obtained a pistol and killed one of his guards in an attempted escape. Judge Parker was in St. Louis, Missouri, at the time, and a *Globe Democrat* reporter secured an interview in which the angry judge bared his heart:[21]

You ask why...murders are largely on the increase? Why, I attribute the increase to these reversals. First, the convicted murderer has a long breathing spell before his case comes before the Supreme Court; then when it does come before that body, the conviction may be quashed; and wherever it is quashed it is always upon the flimsiest technicalities. The Supreme Court never touches the merits of the case. As far as I can see, the court must be opposed to capital punishment, and therefore, tries to reason away the effect of the law...At the present time there seems to be a criminal wave sweeping over the country, the like of which I have not seen before. It is due to the laxity of the courts.

Attorney Reed exhausted his repertoire of legal maneuvers: Continuance on the grounds of public prejudice, demurrer to Parker's jurisdiction, appeal to the Supreme Court, and appeal for presidential clemency. Goldsby was hanged on March 17, 1896.[22] A few months later the 58-year-old Judge Parker, thought to be in the best of health, was stricken with his first and last serious illness.[23] Already in 1889 Congress had reduced Parker's role as a major trial judge by creating a court at Muskogee in Indian Territory with jurisdiction over minor offenses.[24] Legislation in March of 1895 provided that, beginning in September of 1896, a new court system would have complete jurisdiction over Indian Territory.[25]

Judge Parker tried to conduct court business from his sick bed, but his health seemed to worsen as the September 1 deadline approached. His "court was his idol," wrote one biographer, and "with its destruction his mission ended." He died on November 17, 1896, two and a half months after the effective date of the expansion of the Indian Territory court's jurisdiction.[26]

Justice in Indian Territory now lay almost exclusively with a contingent of colorful members of the bench and bar who were to control its destiny for the next decade.

5

INDIAN TERRITORY'S FIRST UNITED STATES COURT

Government officials had long realized the need for a "white man's court" in Indian Territory. However, political realities discouraged lawmakers from depriving the border towns—Fort Smith, Arkansas, Graham, Texas, Wichita and Fort Scott, Kansas—of the financial benefits that accrued to them as court towns with jurisdiction over parts of the Indian country. Opponents had also argued for delay in creating a new court within the Territory because of the difficulty in assembling competent jurors. The influx of white people all but eliminated the latter objection, and in the meantime civil controversies multiplied while the area, notorious as an outlaw sanctuary, also flourished as a haven for debtors.

Understandably displeased with the situation were creditors in St. Louis, Kansas City, and border cities who sold goods and services regularly within the Territory but who could not enforce payment under either federal or Indian law. They joined with other interested persons to discuss their mutual problems at Baxter Springs, Kansas, in December of 1888 and at Fort Smith the following month. Subsequently, they petitioned Congress for a new court. No doubt the political pressure from creditors had much to do with the enactment of March 1, 1889, that established the "United States Court in Indian Territory."[1]

Congress at first favored Fort Gibson, long the military center of Indian Territory, as the seat for the court; however, the Cherokee Nation objected to locating the court within its boundaries. A prominent Creek Nation official, Pleasant Porter, recommended that Congress place the court in Muskogee—a Creek Nation village established in 1872 when tracks of the Missouri-Kansas-Texas Railroad reached there. For 15 years Muskogee had been headquarters for the Union Agency of the Five Civilized Tribes. When opponents objected because Muskogee lacked a courtroom and adequate hotel facilities, Clarence Turner, F.B. Severs, Pleasant Porter, and others won federal approval of a court in their city by promising to provide any facilities needed for its operation.[2]

The jurisdiction assigned to the new tribunal was limited. In deference to the border towns of Fort Smith, Arkansas, and Fort Scott, Kansas, Congress permitted their courts to retain Indian Territory jurisdiction as it then existed over all offenses punishable by death or imprisonment at hard labor. A federal court established at Paris, Texas, maintained full jurisdiction over the southern portion of the Choctaw and Chickasaw Nations along with certain Texas counties.[3]

The Muskogee court's jurisdiction over the remainder of Indian Territory included civil cases where the amount in controversy was $100 or more, certain misdemeanors, and all controversies arising out of mining leases or contracts for mining coal made by the Indians. The court was to have no jurisdiction over controversies between persons of Indian blood only. Two court terms annually were to be held in Muskogee. The court was to follow Arkansas laws and rules for pleading and practice, and jurors had to be at least 21 years old and understand the English language.[4]

The morning of April 1, 1889, began a great day for the approximately 500 residents of Muskogee, Indian Territory. Swelling the population were the curious, eager to be present at the opening of the long-awaited court, numerous prominent attorneys and statesmen from the border states, and aspiring lawyers moving to Muskogee to share in the litigation that was to come. But the most important individual to alight from the Missouri, Kansas and Texas Railway train that morning was James M. Shackelford, the new United States judge dressed in his high silk hat and Prince Albert coat.[5]

Shackelford's Civil War reputation had preceded him into the Territory. Born in Kentucky in 1827, he had practiced law there after his admission to the Bar in 1853. In July of 1863, two months after attaining the rank of brigadier general in the Union forces during the Civil War, he

Officials of the first United States Court in Indian Territory. Front, L to R: Major William Nelson, Clerk; James M. Shackelford, Judge. Back, L to R: Thomas B. Needles, United States Marshal; Zachary T. Walrond, District Attorney. (Courtesy Archives and Manuscripts Division, OHS.)

The first United States court building in Indian Territory. (Courtesy Archives and Manuscripts Division, OHS.)

commanded the troops who captured the romantically famous General John Hunt Morgan, otherwise known as "Morgan the Raider." After the war Shackelford practiced law at Evansville, Indiana, until March 26, 1889, when his friend, President Benjamin Harrison, appointed him to the Indian Territory post.[6]

To serve with Shackelford as District Attorney was Zachary T. Walrond, a specialist in criminal law from Kansas. Major William Nelson of Indiana was to be clerk of the court, and Thomas B. Needles of Illinois was the United States marshal.[7] Flags waved from the few buildings Muskogee boasted at the time, and a gala holiday air prevailed as the four officials were escorted up the stairs to a small hall used by the town's lodges over the *Muskogee Phoenix* newspaper office.[8]

At 10:30 the beaming Judge Shackelford called the crowd of citizens and visitors to order and asked Reverend J.Y. Bryce, pastor of the Methodist Episcopal Church South, to offer the invocation. The judge then directed Marshal Needles to convene court, and with his "Hear ye, Hear ye," the proceedings of the first United States Court for Indian Territory were under way. The first session was brief—District Attorney Walrond sub-

mitted to the judge the credentials of the court officials. They were properly approved, and court was adjourned until nine o'clock the next morning.

The business of Tuesday morning, April 2nd, consisted of defining the rules for admitting attorneys to practice before the court. Judge Shackelford announced that attorneys would be admitted after furnishing satisfactory proof of admission before any United States Circuit or District Courts, or before any Supreme Court of any state. Otherwise, applicants were to be examined by a committee of three attorneys appointed by the judge.[9] The records of the Court Clerk of Muskogee County show the names of the following attorneys admitted to practice before the United States Court on April 2, 1889. Beside each name was shown what was believed to be the attorney's home state or Territory: 1. Zachary T. Walrond, Kansas [admitted on his own motion] 2. D. Stewart Elliott, Kansas 3. Townsend N. Foster, Illinois 4. Napoleon B. Maxey, Illinois 5. Walter A. Ledbetter, Texas 6. S.E. Jackson, Indiana 7. Ridge Paschal, Indian Territory 8. Sampson O. Hinds, Kansas 9. E.C. Boudinot, Arkansas 10. Preston S. Lester, Tennessee 11. Joseph Ralls, Arkansas 12. Robert L. Owen, Indian Territory 13. J.H. Crichton, Kansas 14. W.D. Crawford, Arkansas 15. G.W. Pasco, Texas 16. S.S. Fears, Texas 17.

James H. Atkin, Indian Territory 18. D.M. Wisdom, Arkansas 19. W.C. Jackson, Arkansas.[10]

Of the first 19 admitted to practice before the court, three were members of the Cherokee Nation: Elias C. Boudinot, long-time practitioner in federal courts and considered one of the ablest attorneys in the Southwest; Ridge Paschal, whose father, a white man, had been a well known jurist; and Robert L. Owen, later a United States senator and youngest of the three Cherokees but already active in Indian Territory affairs.[11]

On April 4 Judge Shackelford admitted four more attorneys: James Brizzolara of Arkansas and Leroy Neal, W.N. Patterson, and Thomas George, all of Kansas. On Wednesday, April 3, Judge Shackelford, District Attorney Walrond, and 14 attorneys met to form the Muskogee Bar Association, the oldest Bar Association now functioning in Oklahoma. The first officers were Judge Shackelford, President; Z.T. Walrond, Vice President; R.L. Owen, Secretary; and N.B. Maxey, Treasurer.[12]

Several of the newly admitted lawyers lost little time in making their availability known to the public. Five days after the court was established, a front page advertisement in the April 6, 1889, issue of *Our Brother in Red*, a Muskogee Methodist publication, announced that S.E. Jackson and Benjamin Dye "will practice in any Territorial, State or United States Courts. Collection of uncertain accounts a specialty." Their office was "Opposite Cottage House, east side R.R. Track." W.D. Crawford's front page announcement said he would "practice in all the Courts of Arkansas." Judge Shackelford had announced that a special session of the court would begin on June 3, 1889, to conduct "all business lawfully within its cognizance." As that court term approached, other attorneys also advertised their services available to the creditors who had so long been denied assistance by the courts.[13]

Until then no officials in the Indian country had the authority to issue marriage licenses to white people so the marriage ceremony had often been a simple announcement to family and friends that a couple was henceforth to be considered man and wife. The Clerk of the Court now issued 1324 marriage licenses in the court's first 30 days, "permitting a lot of laggards to catch up with their vows."[14]

The local Methodist publication, with an eye on

Indian Territory's first United States court in session with Judge James M. Shackelford on the Bench, April 1, 1889. (Courtesy Archives and Manuscripts Division, OHS.)

the wealth of legal talent suddenly available, lightheartedly warned:

> He who courts and runs away,
> May live to court another day,
> But he who courts and will not wed,
> May find himself in court instead.[15]

In the meantime lawyers were busily preparing for the upcoming court term. After the April 22, 1889, settlement of the Unassigned Lands in what was to become Oklahoma Territory, the court's docket grew considerably due to controversies falling within its limited jurisdiction over that area. By May 25 a total of 182 cases had been filed with the Court Clerk with still more than a week left before the June 3 court date.[16]

Twenty-four attorneys were qualified to practice before the court when it convened to try its first case on Monday, June 3, 1889. Judge Shackelford, overwhelmed by more applications for admission, appointed an examining committee composed of Hinds, Owen, Ledbetter, and Wisdom and instructed them to begin at once. By two o'clock that afternoon the committee recommended admission of 26 more lawyers, and by the end of the week a total of 56 were listed on the court roll.[17]

The court prepared to try its first case—that of *United States v. Wilson McDonald, H. Sandler, J.T.*

McDonald, and W.A. Husted, accused of intimidating and assaulting settlers in the "Oklahoma" country. A jury was impaneled, and Pleasant Porter, the Creek leader, in recognition of his help in bringing the court to Muskogee, was accorded the honor of being the first juror summoned to serve. Although the lawyers, officers, jurors, witnesses, and visitors must have looked forward with some excitement to the opportunity to view the first actual case in the new court, their anticipation went unfulfilled—the required witnesses were absent so the court adjourned until afternoon. Another problem delayed the trial again that afternoon. Prosecuting Attorney Walrond pointed out that an important point had been overlooked when the jury was chosen. The defendants were entitled to a jury of their peers, and only United States citizens were competent to try their fellow citizens. Unfortunately, all but three of the 36 selected jurors were Indian citizens. The error was immediately corrected by calling a jury of United States citizens, but as the local newspaper commented, "The Government will have a lot of incompetent jurors on hand to pay."[18]

The trial was still in process when court adjourned at 6:00 P.M. The next morning, Congressman Silas Hare of Sherman, Texas, representing Husted, challenged the court's jurisdiction over the "Oklahoma" country. Judge Shackelford reserved his decision on the challenge, which he later overruled, and went on with the trial. The jury deliberated all night and returned to the jury box Wednesday morning with a verdict of guilty against A. Husted only.[19]

As the court proceeded with the trial docket, a pressing question arose stemming from one of the main reasons the new tribunal had been established—the collection of debts. Should the Statute of Limitations apply to debts incurred before March 1, 1889, the date the court was created by Congress? Most of the lawyers present had a vested interest in the question, and Judge Shackelford, "pleasant and courteous in the extreme" as one newspaper noted, was liberal in allowing everyone to be heard.[20] Long suffering creditors could breathe more easily after the judge ruled that debtors residing within Indian Territory had lived beyond the jurisdiction of any competent court; therefore the Statute of Limitations had not begun to run. Enterprising lawyers made the

most of the judge's ruling, in some cases collecting debts incurred as far back as the Civil War.[21]

Later the Creek Council tried to nullify the effect of Shackelford's decision where Creek Nation debtors were involved by enacting an "exemption law." However, Judge Shackelford ruled that the Creek law was ineffective.[22]

During the first week of the term, the Bar filed numerous motions to quash summons and to dismiss attachments and other motions on the question of jurisdiction. Many attorneys were obviously unfamiliar with the Arkansas pleadings and practice followed by the court. Among the court's rulings were: answer and demurrer could not be filed at the same time, the Indian Nations were to be regarded as counties for the purpose of verifying instruments, and costs must be paid before the marshal could make returns on processes. Execution had been ordered in some cases, and a total of 50 default judgments was taken.[23]

Also during that first week, just as the court's business was progressing well, decisions being rendered, and cases resolved, Judge Shackelford announced that unless more funds for expenses could be found the session could not last more than two weeks. As he predicted, funds appropriated for the entire fiscal year were exhausted by June 22. Because no more cases could be tried, the court discharged the jury, and non-resident attorneys returned to their home bases to await the November, 1889, session.[24]

While the first court term drew to a close, Muskogee civic leaders Clarence W. Turner and Pleasant Porter completed plans for construction of the new Federal Court building. A day for another celebration was June 24, 1889, when the corner stone for the elegant three-story structure was laid at the southwest corner of Second and Court streets by members of the Grand Lodge of Masons. An estimated 2000 people enjoyed a giant barbecue. The building was ready for occupancy when the November term began. The courtroom and offices for court officials were furnished in fine taste, and as a newspaper proudly reported, "Lighted by gas throughout."[25]

As could be expected, immediate jurisdictional conflicts arose between the Muskogee and Fort Smith courts. Larceny cases were especially troublesome. Judge Parker issued an order for the Muskogee court to show cause for detention of prisoners for larceny, and within six months after

25

opening of the Muskogee court he had ruled on six habeas corpus cases. In decisions that definitely made the Muskogee court subordinate in criminal matters, Parker decided that the new court had no power to impanel a grand jury, that no person could be tried on a charge of larceny without first being indicted by a grand jury, and that the court had no jurisdiction over charges of assault with intent to kill.[26]

One of the habeas corpus cases required a distinction between aggravated assault, an offense punishable by the Muskogee court, and assault with intent to kill, relegated to the Fort Smith court. The question arose when a cowboy recklessly fired at the feet of a blacksmith in Purcell. The cowboy was subsequently charged with aggravated assault and sentenced to jail in Muskogee for six months. He was released by Judge Parker on a writ of habeas corpus, but the matter was appealed to the United States Supreme Court. When it finally appeared on the Supreme Court docket three years later, the court learned that the cowboy had since died in the Paris jail, where he had been confined for a homicide committed in the Chickasaw country, so the case was dismissed.[27]

One of the misdemeanors under the jurisdiction of the new court was "disturbing religious worship," or, in colloquial terms, "pestirin' a meetin'." Public worship in the rural areas was ordinarily held under brush arbors, and for years the local rowdies enjoyed riding their horses furiously around these assemblies while firing their guns. Besides a fine, the penalty was now imprisonment in the Muskogee jail, and with the help of deputy marshals and possemen Judge Shackelford soon put an end to that type of recreation.[28]

But if the offenders happened to fire their guns into the midst of the worshippers, another jurisdictional question presented itself. Judge Parker himself explained the problem in a September 20, 1892, letter replying to an inquiry about shots fired into a church. "If there were people in the church at the time it was fired into," the judge wrote, "it would be an assault with intent to kill; but if there were no people in the church, it would be a trespass on property. If the first case exists, the court here has jurisdiction. If the latter, the court at Muskogee has jurisdiction."[29]

The rapidly growing Muskogee Bar numbered

L to R: veteran lawyers Samuel Morton Rutherford and Walter A. Ledbetter. The third man is unidentified. (Courtesy Archives and Manuscripts Division, OHS.)

almost 125 lawyers by November of 1889—six months after the Muskogee court first convened—and already had underway an important project, enlargement of the court's jurisdiction. Prospects for Muskogee lawyers received a boost in September when the House Committee on Indian Affairs and Territories visited their community. At a reception held at the Katy Hotel, Pleasant Parker presided and Judge Shackelford delivered the welcoming address. The committee, described as "six fine looking gentlemen" by the local press, were on a tour of investigation that involved organizing Oklahoma Territory and establishing boundary lines between Oklahoma and Indian Territories.[30]

Bar members helped entertain the committee and had opportunities to discuss the subject of the new court's jurisdiction. At the House committee's suggestion, the Muskogee Bar, at its semiannual meeting on October 12, 1889, appointed a committee of 10 to make recommendations, each in his own area of expertise, to be included in a bill for submission to the next Congress.[31]

At one meeting devoted to the study of appropriate boundary lines between the two territories, John M. Allen, a prominent Mississippi congressman, mentioned the distance between Ardmore in the Chickasaw Nation and the Muskogee court and exclaimed, "The United States Court of the Indian Territory should hold one or two terms at Ardmore each year."[32] Present at the time of the Congressman's remark was 26-year-old Walter A. Ledbetter, later to be known as "Father of Oklahoma's Judicial System," who was then to become a leader in the movement to permit the court to sit at points other then Muskogee. Already one of the most active members of the Muskogee Bar,

Ledbetter had begun a career of more than four decades of service to the legal fraternity in both Indian and Oklahoma Territories.

On his 21st birthday he had been admitted to practice in Gainesville, Texas, and maintained his home there in 1889 while he tested the opportunities in the newly organized Muskogee court. He had the good fortune to be among the members of the Muskogee Bar who accompanied the visiting Congressmen on a hunting trip near Muskogee. During this enjoyable outing the hunting party bagged a large number of game birds and animals, including two timber wolves. Congressman Allen later remembered the Indian Territory experience with pleasure in a humorous speech on the floor of the House of Representatives.

During the hunting trip Congressman Allen invited Ledbetter's opinion of the Muskogee court, and Ledbetter agreed with Allen that court terms should be held in the more remote locations of the Territory. Ledbetter especially recommended Ardmore, a town he was familiar with, for over half of its population was made up of former residents of his home town of Gainesville, Texas. The Congressmen suggested Ledbetter should visit Ardmore and report to them on several relevant points such as the preponderance of its population, whether Indian or white, the community's agricultural and trade advantages, and !its railroad facilities.[33]

Ledbetter visited both McAlester and Ardmore and suggested that the citizenry should petition Congress to establish terms of court in their respective towns. Ardmore, then a city of several hundred people, showed the most interest and invited him to explain the proposition at a public meeting. The town's Indian population disapproved, but Ledbetter assembled a complete report favoring the court term and forwarded it to the committee.

He returned to Muskogee and a few weeks later received a long letter from Ardmore leaders asking him to go to Washington at once to promote the court matter before Congress. Most importantly they had deposited $1000 to his credit at a local bank for that purpose. For months he devoted most of his time in behalf of the Ardmore court, and finally in April of 1890 he returned to Ardmore confident that his objective had been accomplished. A short time later a wire from a member of Congress informed him of the bill's passage.

While on his way to Ledbetter's office with the wire, the excited telegraph operator spread the good news to everyone he met, and the crowd of citizens who accompanied him quickly lifted the young lawyer onto their shoulders for a happy ride about town. His popularity in the new court town dictated that his future as a lawyer lay in Ardmore. A few years later the Chickasaw legislature, incensed with Ledbetter's outspoken views in favor of Statehood and other legislation contrary to the legislature's interests, tried to expel him from the Chickasaw Nation. That effort was unsuccessful, and Ledbetter continued as one of Ardmore's most active citizens until he moved to Oklahoma City nearly 20 years later.[34]

The Act of May 2, 1890, which Ardmore greeted with such enthusiasm, divided the United States Court in the Indian Territory into three divisions: the first division covered the Creek and Cherokee country and the tribes of the Quapaw Agency located in the northeastern part of present Oklahoma; Muskogee was the court town for that division and continued as headquarters for the three divisions. South McAlester was the court town for the second division and covered the Choctaw country. Ardmore became the court town for the third division, the Seminole and Chickasaw country. Judge Shackelford was to hold at least two court terms annually at each location.

The Act was also Oklahoma Territory's "Organic Act" and created new courts for Oklahoma Territory, thus confining the Indian Territory court's jurisdiction to the area east of Oklahoma Territory. However, the Indian Territory tribunal now exercised jurisdiction over controversies between Indians of different tribes and over civil cases not exclusively delegated to tribal courts. Creditors were pleased to learn they could now secure execution against improvements to real estate even if the improvements were owned by adopted white citizens of an Indian tribe.[35]

The Indian Territory court's criminal jurisdiction was enlarged slightly; however, the courts for the Western District of Arkansas and the Eastern District of Texas maintained jurisdiction as in the past. Nonetheless, according to United States Attorney Walrond, "The people were now given an

Dew M. Wisdom, head of the Union Agency, with his wife and daughters at Muskogee, c. 1900. (Courtesy Archives and Manuscripts Division, OHS.)

object lesson in real civilization." Minor offenses for which there had been no redress for decades unless settled by *lex talionis*—the law of retaliation—now found their way into the court. Juries learned that "insulting words did not justify blows"and that the public welfare could be served by punishing such offenses as wife beating, malicious mischief, and cruelty to animals. By the end of the court's first year under the new legislation, it had a thousand cases on the criminal docket.[36]

A significant change permitted appointment of not more than three commissioners "learned in the law" for each division. Several Muskogee lawyers accepted appointments as commissioners—Joseph G. Ralls, for example, accepted the post at Atoka where he remained for a life-long legal career.

The commissioners served in a capacity similar to that of Arkansas justices of the peace, acting as committing magistrates in criminal matters and having civil jurisdiction over controversies involving $100 or less. Dew M. Wisdom, a respected lawyer placed in charge of the Union Agency at the specific request of tribal authorities, reported to the Secretary of the Interior that fees paid by the government to the nine commissioners totaled $40,000 to $50,000 annually. "Many of these officers receive more than the Federal judges received,"Wisdom said, "and the amount paid them is not in accordance with the services rendered or the qualifications required to fill the office."[37] Walrond confirmed that "The commissioners and

marshals reaped a harvest."[38] Judge Shackelford's salary was $3500 per year.[39]

Indian Agent Wisdom regretted that the Indian Territory court, "invested with such dignified and important civil jurisdiction," should be burdened with cases of "trivial character"appropriate for police judges and justices of the peace and which could be handled just as well by commissioners.[40]

Judge Shackelford must at times have shared Agent Wisdom's opinion, as for example in the trial of the young defendant accused of firing a charge of "bird shot" into a cow that trespassed onto his father's crop. The defense lawyer requested the judge to instruct the jury, "That they could not convict the accused unless they believed from the evidence that when he fired the shot, he was actuated by malice toward the cow." Shackelford refused to accept that doctrine, but the attorney would not give up. In desperation he finally informed the court, "But, Your Honor, there is a maxim in the law which should control the court in the disposition of this case, *'De minimis non curat lex'*!" "Yes, yes, gentlemen of the jury," agreed Judge Shackelford, "the law regards not mere trifles, and in law this case is too little to be noticed and should never have been brought to court." Counsel had indeed recited a maxim that freed his client. "Gentlemen of the jury," Shackelford concluded, "In this case I instruct you to bring in a verdict of not guilty."[41]

The new court town of South McAlester, described by United States Attorney Walrond as a "wilderness" at the time, soon became an active center for the legal profession due to railway and mining litigation involving large sums of money. As new lawyers began to arrive there, J.B. Connors, District Judge for Tobucksy County of the Choctaw Nation, said, "It seemed as if some law school had sent us its graduating class."[42] McAlester merchant Fritz Sittel enjoyed an increase in sales that necessitated building a large one-story frame structure with an attached "shed-room." To alleviate the shortage of facilities for the lawyers and doctors who now came to McAlester, Sittel rented his "shed-room" where "They all huddled together under this roof, except when either lawyer or doctor had a client or patient; at such times the others politely absented themselves until the conference or treatment was over."[43]

The practice of law was not an easy profession for newcomers to the Territory who were required to wrestle with problems of Arkansas law, federal law, and the jurisdiction of tribal courts plus the jurisdiction of the courts of the Western District of Arkansas, Eastern District of Kansas, and the Texas District of Paris.[44] And Judge Shackelford, as pioneer judge for the court, had few precedents to fortify his decisions. His military experience and discipline no doubt contributed to the success of a court in a country so long without a local means of settling controversies and punishing crime. C.L. Herbert, a practitioner in the Shackelford court, said, "When he came anything but law and order prevailed, but when he left the bench you could hear a pin drop upon the floor of his courtroom. His court had a limited jurisdiction, but he exercised the criminal part of it to the extreme limit, though judiciously and effectively."[45] In the years 1891 and 1892 the court heard the cases of 2700 persons charged with crime and found 2200 guilty.[46]

The Department of Justice had not expected the great increase in legal business before the court after the Act of May 2, 1890. Therefore, expenses budgeted for witness and jury costs were often exhausted before the docket was completed, which led to summary adjournment of court.[47]

Always aware of his limited budget, Judge Shackelford adopted the policy of being on the bench each morning at nine o'clock sharp to hear motions and demurrers in civil cases. He ex-pected every attorney to attend to these matters promptly so that, when the jury was called, all pleadings would have been already settled.[48] Also in an effort to eliminate expenses of trial, at the "motion hour" he allowed the accused in criminal cases to throw themselves on the mercy of the court. At such times, Judge Shackelford, who was said to be "a good reader of character," might relax his stern military manner and assess a lighter punishment.[49]

William B. Johnson, pillar of the legal community in Ardmore, once told how Judge Shackelford handled a unique situation. Johnson had moved from Gainesville, Texas, in 1890 to practice in the new Ardmore court—the Chickasaws called it the "sandy land" court to distinguish it from the "black lands" court at Paris, Texas.[50] One of Johnson's first clients was a young father who with his family had gone to church one Sunday morning and returned to find that a herd of goats had invaded their one-room home and "chewed up all their clothing and bed clothing, and …practically destroyed the furniture." The angry young man "got his shot-gun and killed 28 of the goats." At the first term of federal court ever held in Ardmore, Judge Shackelford tried the case in a Methodist church at the Corner of B Street and Broadway. Johnson's client pleaded guilty, but after listening to his account of what happened the judge fined him only one dollar and remitted costs. Johnson recalled, 'The young man was so excited that he ran to me and started to give me the dollar. I told him to keep the dollar and give it to the Judge, although I knew the Judge did not intend for him to pay the fine."[51]

6

"EMANCIPATION FROM AN ALIEN JUDICIARY": THE ACT OF MARCH 1, 1895

The Democratic administration of President Grover Cleveland in 1893 replaced Judge Shackelford with Charles Bingley Stuart of Gainesville, Texas, as judge of the United States Court in Indian Territory. Thus began a legal career of more than 43 years that earned Judge Stuart a reputation as one of the most admired lawyers ever to practice in Indian Territory, Oklahoma Territory, and the state of Oklahoma.

After graduation from Randolph-Macon College in Virginia, Stuart located in Marshall, Texas, studied law in the office of Major James Turner, and was admitted to the Texas Bar at the age of 21. Three years later, in 1883, while practicing in Waco, Texas, he sued Western Union in his own behalf because of that company's mishandling of a telegram calling him to his brother's deathbed. The telegram did not reach him until after his brother's death. His victory on appeal to the Supreme Court of Texas helped set a precedent for recovery of damages for mental suffering in the absence of physical injury and brought Stuart to the attention of the Texas legal community.

He moved to Gainesville, Texas, in 1884 and three years later formed a partnership with Joseph W. Bailey. In 1890 Bailey began a political career in the United States House of Representatives that eventually took him to the United States Senate. Stuart had been an active supporter of President Cleveland who, no doubt on the recommendation of Bailey, appointed Stuart to the judgeship—a political plum in Indian Territory.[1]

The trial and execution of Silon Lewis, a Choctaw Indian, during Judge Stuart's tenure demonstrated how three United States agencies—Department of Interior, Department of War, and Department of Justice—could become involved in internal tribal affairs. Political disputes had brought the Choctaw Nation to the verge of civil war in 1892, and a group of Choctaws accused of political assassinations surrendered to Indian Agent Leo E. Bennett. Nine of them were tried in the Choctaw court of Judge N.J. Holson and sentenced to be shot. Defense attorneys applied to Judge Stuart for a writ of habeas corpus which he denied on the grounds that the federal courts had no jurisdiction.[2]

Agent Bennett, on behalf of the Department of Interior, appealed to Choctaw Governor Wilson N. Jones to exercise his pardoning power, which the governor refused to do. But under pressure from the Department of War he granted a series of reprieves, and eventually only Silon Lewis, the admitted killer of Joe Haklotubbee, a highly respected full-blood Choctaw, received the death sentence. The trial was conducted before Judge Holson in a one-room log building near Wilburton.[3] Judge Stuart recommended that President Cleveland grant a stay of execution, but the president's telegraphed approval did not arrive until mid-morning on the day Lewis was to be executed later in the afternoon. To stop the execution, Deputy Marshal James Brazell rode three different horses in a frantic 40-mile dash from McAlester to the Choctaw Courthouse grounds east of Wilburton. When he arrived, he found Lewis bare-chested and seated on a coffin. Close by was Lewis' executioner, a rifle in hand, awaiting orders to fire at a spot marked above the condemned man's heart.

Deputy Marshal Brazell found Judge Holson in the courthouse nearby and handed him the notice of the president's stay of execution. The judge's failure to understand that document caused additional delay while the marshal located an interpreter, Choctaw Attorney Gilbert W. Dukes, who explained the stay of execution to the judge. Finally, according to Brazell, Judge Holson "stepped out and told the sheriff to turn him [Lewis] loose and that the white man had for the first time in history interfered with our government."[4]

Brazell's wild ride accomplished the last reprieve for the harried Lewis. The Choctaw Supreme Court reviewed the case and affirmed the

For more than 43 years, Charles B. Stuart, appointed second judge of the United States Court in Indian Territory in 1893, was an outstanding lawyer in the Oklahoma area. (Courtesy Harold C. Stuart.)

Gilbert W. Dukes, Choctaw attorney who interpreted the stay of execution that temporarily delayed the death of Silon Lewis. (Courtesy T.F. Dukes.)

murder conviction. Silon Lewis' execution took place on November 5, 1894, before some 300 spectators, one of whom was pioneer McAlester attorney Joe Hulsey, then only a boy. A Choctaw deputy sheriff used white powder to mark a target over Lewis' heart. Another deputy sheriff fired an accurate shot into the middle of the target, but according to one eyewitness Lewis lived for 15 minutes before an officer placed a red bandana handkerchief over his mouth and nose to smother him to death. The execution of Lewis reportedly was the last legal execution in the Choctaw Nation.[5]

A faction led by Jacob Jackson, a defeated candidate for governor, continued to charge that the Lewis trial and conviction were in violation of the law, especially because of the fact that Governor Jones and his supporters had influenced the venue of the trial.[6] The uproar caused by political disturbances and the widely publicized trial and execution of Silon Lewis probably hastened extinction of tribal governments.

Even the relatively remote Oklahoma and Indian Territories did not escape the devastating impact of the "Panic of 1893"—one of America's most severe depressions prior to that time. Approximately 8000 of the nation's business firms failed in six months, and overexpansion of the railroad industry in the 1880s ended with more than 150 railroads in receivership. One of these was Indian Territory's Choctaw Coal and Railway Co., which went into receivership in 1891. Accepting the well-paying post of receiver for that company was Major William Nelson, who had accompanied Judge Shackelford from Indiana to take the post of clerk of the Muskogee court.[7]

Wholesale creditors in the Territories, eager to preserve their rights, lost no time in attaching the inventory of defaulting merchants during the depression. Assignments for the benefit of creditors together with disputes over payment preferences were common. Advertisements of one law firm insisted that its assignments "would hold kerosene." But money was a scarce commodity in the Territories, and law practices suffered. In other locales lawyers could acquire business from title and lien litigation affecting real property, but that type of practice did not exist in Indian Territory where all land was held in common.[8]

Half of the lawyers' practice in federal court had formerly been devoted to criminal trials, but now liquor peddlers and cow thieves could easily exhaust their available funds in the preliminary examination alone. Having no funds for more attorney fees, the accused might choose to enter a guilty plea on the best terms the prosecution

A widely publicized photo of the Choctaw Nation's execution of Silon Lewis. (Courtesy Judge Ben P. Choate, Jr., Workman's Compensation Court.)

would accept without regard to the maxim, "Let the government prove its case."

The depressed times encouraged numerous settlers to take their chances in the race for the nearly 10,000 square miles of land in the Cherokee Outlet, which was opened for settlement on September 16, 1893. Even the Chicago World's Fair of 1893 helped deplete the Territories of their inhabitants. Some attorneys who had entered the Territories only a few years before with such hopeful aspirations now drifted west and northwest with others seeking better living conditions.[9]

Enlarged jurisdiction for the United States court and establishment of other court towns were to furnish some relief for lawyers preferring to remain in Indian Territory. The Muskogee Bar Association appointed a committee headed by two of its better-trained and more articulate members, William T. Hutchings and Napoleon Bonaparte Maxey, to head a committee to peti-

tion Congress for improvements in the Indian Territory court system. Hutchings, a graduate of Yale Law School, worked as a clerk for several years in the United States House of Representatives and spent a year in Fort Smith before settling in Muskogee in 1889.[10] Maxey attended the University of Chicago for two years, studied in a law office, and was admitted to the Illinois Bar in 1881. He came to Muskogee via Gainesville, Texas, and became the fourth man on the roster of attorneys admitted on the court's opening day, April 1, 1889.[11]

The Hutchings-Maxey committee argued that the Indian Territory court had little more than police court authority and was encumbered with a multitude of actions such as assault and battery, gambling, disturbing the peace, and the ever-present liquor cases—all to the detriment of more important criminal and civil matters. Because only one judge was assigned to the court, frequent trial delays as well as distances to the three

William T. Hutchings, Muskogee attorney instrumental in expanding the Indian Territory court system. (Courtesy Law Library, University of Tulsa.)

major court seats involved extraordinary expenses for travel and lodging of deputy marshals, defendants, and witnesses.[12] Even when found guilty, the accused might be fined only $15 to $20, far less than the cost of $100 to $500 to the federal government. Expenses in the Indian Territory courts were reported to comprise one-seventh of the federal government's total judicial expense.[13] Indian Agent Dew M. Wisdom thought expenses could be substantially reduced "by giving the commissioners power to finally dispose of misdemeanors subject to right of appeal, and perhaps also by increasing the number of commissioners."[14]

Also, inhabitants of Indian Territory continued their strong objections to assignment of capital offenses to Arkansas and Texas courts where defendants and witnesses had to travel long distances and appear before strangers unacquainted with the Territory's people and conditions.[15] The Hutchings-Maxey committee contended, that unlike the situation in earlier days, jurors in the Territory were now competent to try any type of criminal or civil case.[16]

On April 8, 1894, Senator Henry M. Teller headed a committee that visited Muskogee and returned to Washington with a report that resulted in the Act of March 1, 1895, by which Congress divided Indian Territory into three judicial

districts:[17] 1) Northern District: the Creek, Seminole and Cherokee Nations, including the Quapaws Indian Agency, the Miami townsite. Court towns: Vinita, Miami, Tahlequah, Muskogee. (2) Central District: the Choctaw Nation. Court towns: South McAlester, Atoka, Antlers, Cameron. (3) Southern District: the Chickasaw Nation. Court towns: Ardmore, Purcell, Pauls Valley, Ryan, and Chickasha. In addition to exclusive civil jurisdiction, the courts acquired complete criminal jurisdiction effective September 1, 1896, that spelled the end of Judge Parker's sovereignty in Indian Territory as well as that of the Kansas and Texas court.[18]

Each of the three judges was to receive an annual salary of $5000, an increase of $1500 over that previously paid the first Indian Territory judge.[19] Salaries of judges in Oklahoma Territory remained at $3000 until raised to $4000 not long before Statehood.[20] The salary differential between the two territories may have been due to the more complex nature of conditions in the Indian country.

With an apparent hope that Indian Territory matters would be resolved locally, Congress created a "Court of Appeals" composed of the three district judges, neither of whom was to sit when the appeal was from his own decision. This court was to convene semi-annually in South McAlester; appeals were to go to the Circuit Court of Appeals for the Eighth Judicial Circuit in St. Louis.

United States commissioners were now to be "duly enrolled attorneys," and the attractive income received by some commissioners under the fee system was now stabilized at $1500 annually with all fees paid to the court. Two new district attorneys were to be appointed by the president, each at a salary of $4000, and deputy marshals, appointed by district judges, were to receive $1200.[21]

Local courts could now serve nearly 400,000 people, and, at last, all citizens of Indian Territory could be tried in their own districts before a jury of their peers. Thus, September 1, 1896, marked the end of an era. Many Indian Territory towns held mass meetings that day to celebrate what they termed "emancipation from an alien judiciary."[22]

The United States Court for the Northern District of Indian Territory could claim the immediate distinction of being the leading court in the world in criminal business transacted. Criminal lawyers who had endured lean years in their practice before the Indian Territory court now enjoyed a measure of prosperity. Former United States Attorney Z.T. Walrond, then practicing in Muskogee, philosophized as to the reason: "Often the hot-tempered man, charged with the commission of a violent and felonious assault, is a man of industry and thrift, has accumulated property and is able to pay for his defense."[23]

In 1909 W.A. Ledbetter, during a ceremony in commemoration of the deceased judge of the United States Court for the Southern District, Hosea Townsend, described the functions of the United States courts in Indian Territory after the 1895 legislation:

"In a constitutional sense the court over which [Townsend] presided was one of limited jurisdiction of United States Circuit and District Courts, civil and criminal, including the powers of a court of bankruptcy, and all the powers now exercised by the district and county courts of the State of Oklahoma, including general common law, and equity jurisdiction, and probate jurisdiction; besides, by special act of Congress, his court was given jurisdiction to hear and determine applications for citizenship in the Indian tribes. The Court of Appeals for the Indian Territory, of which he was a member, exercised appellate jurisdiction over all controversies arising in the trial courts, embracing every subject of which the Criminal Court of Appeals and the Supreme Court of the State of Oklahoma, the United States Circuit Court of Appeals and the Supreme Court of the United States now have appellate jurisdiction.

It would be hard to imagine a situation that would produce more varied litigation, or a greater number of difficult questions, calling for determination, than that covering the ten years preceding Statehood. There was a constant struggle between the individual and the law; and the rights of personal liberty, so much prized by the pioneer, were in constant conflict with the plenary power of the Government exercised in the effort to prepare the country for Statehood. The territorial courts were required to apply, in almost every conceivable form, the elementary principles of government, and by their decisions to mark the boundary line between individual liberty and governmental restraint.[24]

To serve with Judge Charles B. Stuart of the

William M. Springer, Judge of the United States Court in Indian Territory and author of the Springer Amendment. (Courtesy McFarlin Library, University of Tulsa.)

Central district, President Cleveland named two former Congressmen to the judicial posts created by the Act of 1895: William M. Springer to the Northern District, and Constantine B. Kilgore to the Southern District. Springer, an Indiana University graduate, was a veteran of 10 consecutive terms in Congress from Illinois and was author of the "Springer Amendment" to the Indian Appropriation Act of 1889 which opened the "Unclaimed Lands" in Oklahoma Territory for settlement.[25]

Kilgore, from Wills Point, Texas, was a personal friend of President Cleveland and was said to have made an impressive appearance—more than six feet tall, and attired in Prince Albert coat, waistcoat, flowing tie, high wing collar, and yellow boots. Lawyers in the Territory called him the "kicking judge" because of an incident in the United States House of Representatives during the tenure of "Czar" Thomas B. Reed. Reed enforced a rule that any member could be counted as present for purposes of a quorum even though he refused to vote on a bill, and if at roll call the member decided to leave the House chambers he was likely to be stopped by the sergeant-at-arms standing in front of locked doors.[26] During one controversial roll call vote, the Republican speaker refused to let Democrat Kilgore leave the chambers. Kilgore headed for the exit and, in the presence of the sergeant-at arms, cooly kicked the door open and departed. His absence defeated the quorum and passage of the Republican measure "Czar" Reed advocated.[27]

Congested court dockets in Indian Territory led Congress less than two years after the Act of 1895 to authorize an additional judge who had the rank and power of the other three but functioned on the "floater system" (with no assigned district).[28] Congress in 1904 added four more judges, and the number remained at eight until Statehood.[29] President William McKinley selected as the "floater" judge 57-year-old John Robert Thomas, an Illinois Congressman from 1879 to 1889. For his service while chairman of the Com-

mittee on Naval Affairs, Thomas had been named "father of our modern navy" by some metropolitan newspapers. He chose to establish residence in Muskogee, still an unincorporated town without utilities but with a steadily growing population of nearly 3500. Judge Thomas was to serve the local legal community as judge and lawyer until 1914 when while visiting the McAlester penitentiary on legal business he and four others were murdered by escaping prisoners.[30]

A few months after his appointment, in the latter part of the year 1897, Judge Thomas' court in the case of *United States v. Cyrus R. Brown* became the first court to levy a death sentence in Indian Territory. Brown, a drifter, had murdered his benefactor, an elderly fisherman, while the latter

The account of the Seminole Indian burning published in the New York Herald on June 18, 1899. (Courtesy Archives and Manuscripts Division, OHS.)

slept. Alice M. Robertson, Oklahoma's first Congresswoman, described Judge Thomas' conduct during the Brown trial:[31]

Throughout the trial Judge Thomas saw that exact justice should be done the prisoner, that every right to which he was entitled should be extended to him. With many others I was in the court room when sentence was passed. An impressive silence held all those present as the prisoner was brought before the judge...

The Judge administered implacable justice, his voice quivering with horror of the crime and yet with ineffable pity for the criminal. No impassioned pulpit orator, thundering the terrors of everlasting punishment, had ever brought to me such a realization of sin, of justice and judgment, as the kindly faced judge who performed the, to him, abhorrent duty of sentencing a human being to death.

On December 30, 1897, only a few days after Judge Thomas decreed the death sentence for Cyrus Brown, two Indian men believed crazed with whiskey purchased from "line saloons" (across the border in Oklahoma Territory), assaulted and murdered Mrs. Julius Laird at her farm home near Maud in the Seminole Nation. An infuriated mob of white settlers singled out two young Seminole Indians, Lincoln McGeisey and Palmer Sampson, as the criminals, chained them to a tree, and burned them before some 300 spectators.

Later information verified that McGeisey could not have been present when the murder occurred, and it was doubtful that Sampson was there at the time. The "Indian burning" case was well publicized, and demands for prosecution of the mob leaders poured into offices of the Department of Justice. Congress appropriated $25,000 for a complete investigation. The Department of Justice appointed Horace Speed as special prosecutor for an agreed fee of $10,000. Speed, originally from Kentucky, was then 46 years old and had been in Oklahoma Territory since the "Run of '89." While serving as the first United States District Attorney for Oklahoma Territory, he had earned a reputation for his relentless prosecution of several hundred perjury cases dealing with the settlement of Oklahoma Territory.

While gathering evidence after his special appointment in the Indian case, Speed set up a tent

Horace Speed in his Tulsa office about 1920. (Courtesy Archives and Manuscripts Division, OHS.)

on a street corner in Tecumseh where he talked with more than 60 men already arrested and with any others willing to give information. Everywhere he was greeted with jeers and taunts, and one local organization was reported ready to pay a thousand dollars for his murder. Despite threats and intimidation, he stayed in Pottawatomie County until October 12, 1898, then made a public announcement that he had sufficient evidence to convict the mob's ringleaders.

During the December court term at Muskogee, he secured the indictment of United States Deputy Marshal Nelson M. Jones and 20 citizens of Oklahoma Territory. The first "Indian burning" cases were tried before Judge Thomas at the May, 1899, term of the Muskogee court. Nationwide interest brought reporters from as far away as Washington and New York, and they remained for the entire May term—the most important session in the history of any Indian Territory court. An interpreter translated the testimony of Seminole witnesses. The proceedings were reminiscent of the Fort Smith trials, for Judge Parker's nemesis, J. Warren Reed, was defense counsel for Deputy Marshal Jones at the first trial.

Horace Speed's meticulous preparation was evident throughout. The deputy marshal was found guilty of having encouraged the torture and murder of the Indians and was assessed the maximum sentence of 21 years at the Missouri State Penitentiary. At that term of court one defendant was found not guilty, and two others re-

36

ceived 10-years sentences. Eight more participants received jail sentences in the next court term. Judge Thomas eventually disposed of 30 "Indian burning" cases. The Federal government's insistence on punishment of the wrong-doers had not been popular with many white settlers in Oklahoma Territory, and Judge Thomas underwent tremendous pressure from relatives of the prisoners. His daughter, Carolyn Thomas Foreman, recalled, "I was a young girl at the time of the outrage, and we did not discuss such matters at home..., but I can remember father's indignation when members of the white prisoners' families came here to try to talk to him about helping their sons and brothers."[32]

7

WHITE LAWYERS IN INDIAN TERRITORY

The 13 court towns established in Indian Territory in the six years from 1889 to 1896 greeted the coming of the federal courts in much the same manner as a town of today would welcome a new industry. The courts not only brought permanent new residents but court sessions that could be social events almost on par with horse races, circuses and community fairs. Court officials and participants were joined by rural families, who, with proper timing of their occasional visits to town could keep abreast of the news and hear lawyers wax eloquent in courtroom arguments. At Ardmore it was not unusual for the court to set two to three hundred cases for trial in one court term. In the December, 1900 term Judge Hosea Townsend scheduled approximately 330 cases on his "Criminal Trial Docket," including larceny, adultery, assault with intent to kill, introducing liquor, embezzlement, fencing Indian lands, disturbing peace, gaming, seduction, robbing United States mail, illicit distillery, perjury, and obstructing process.[1]

To the visitors a wagon was like a mobile home today. One could sleep in or around it and cook meals on a nearby fire. Lawyer James Mathers opened a law office in Ardmore in 1896 and had a vivid memory of those days. "It was easy to tell when court was in session," he said, "by looking at the city on the courthouse grounds—a swarming mass of humanity, horses, mules, and for those with young children, a friendly cow to provide an adequate supply of warm, nourishing milk."[2]

Visitors provided their own lodging for reasons of necessity as well as economy, for sleeping accommodations in the new court towns left much to be desired. One Atoka pioneer remembered that when court was in session the local hotel sometimes would sleep three in a bed and still be unable to accommodate all the visitors in town.[3]

The judge's journey from court to court was much like that of the circuit-riding preacher except the judge had company. Where he went, lawyers also went—as did other officials and sometimes prisoners, litigants, and witnesses. To some of the legal fraternity of the Southern District, perhaps no court session was more welcome than the one at Purcell in Indian Territory near the South Canadian River. That river was the boundary between Indian Territory and Oklahoma Territory to the north where the sale of alcoholic liquor was legal. Just past the center of the river on the Oklahoma Territory side, enterprising saloon keepers constructed "Box Saloons," wooden buildings resting on posts anchored in the river bed. A path of 12-inch boards on posts spanned the 40 or 50 yards from the south shore to a saloon.

When the judge and his traveling cavalcade had concluded a hard day in court, they could find relaxation at a "Box Saloon" where that day's losing barrister then suffered a financial loss—the purchase of the first round of drinks at 10 cents each. As noted by lawyer Mathers, the trip out to the saloon on the 12-inch boards was easy, "but the return trip to the shore sometimes involved a rather difficult piece of navigation."[4]

Unlike the judge, a lawyer did not always have the companionship of others in his travels. Lawyer J. R. Charlton, later a long-time district judge in Bartlesville, recalled the ordeal of travel as he pursued his profession in frequent trips throughout the territory:[5]

In the late 90s while practicing law at Kansas and in the territory courts, and doing a general collecting business through the Territory, I made many trips with a span of ponies and a buggy, driving to Nowata, Vinita, Muskogee and Pawnee to Court. This was before there were any railroads in this part of the Territory.

Our roads were mere trails that could scarcely be driven over. We had no bridges and crossed the rivers and streams by ferry boats or drove across at the fords.

I would leave Caney early in the morning, drive to Pawhuska for dinner, on to Gray Horse and Ralson, crossed the Arkansas River on a ferry at Ralson, then to Pawnee by night to attend court the next day.

Charlton also remembered the first law suit

J.R. Charlton, pioneer Bartlesville attorney and judge. (Courtesy The Daily Oklahoman.)

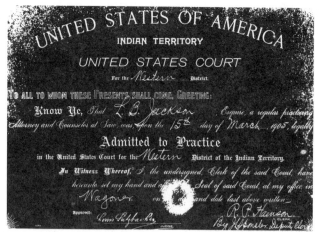

License to practice law in Indian Territory, 1905. (Courtesy William C. Jackson, grandson of L.B. Jackson.)

ever tried in Bartlesville, a replevin action before United States Commissioner Harry Jennings in about the year 1900. "That term of court was held in the open air on the banks of the Caney River at the edge of the peach grove about 100 yards west of the Johnstone and Keller store, in what is now the city park," said Judge Charlton. "We took nail kegs and boxes from the store and 2 x 12's from the lumber yard and made seats for the jury and attorneys. W. A. Chase and I tried the first case that was called, and after both sides had done their best the jury retired to the shade of the grove to deliberate upon the verdict."[6]

Applicants for admission to practice in the federal courts in Indian Territory continued to be examined by a committee appointed by the local judge in the manner decreed by Judge Shackelford in 1889. Such a committee examined Wellington Lee Merwine when he settled in Okmulgee, the capital of the Creek Nation, to fulfill a boyhood dream after graduating from a law school in the East. The fact that Merwine had to ride horseback from Okmulgee to Muskogee when he had a case in federal court apparently did not bother him, for, according to Merwine, "As there was then little to do for any one in the profession, save to defend the indicted cattle rustler or the gun-fighter, I found that I had much time for hunting and adventure, for both of which I had an intense liking."[7]

Muskogee in 1895 became an attractive stopping place for lawyers entering the Territory. Indeed, in the words of former United States Attorney Z. T. Walrond, it was a "dumping ground" for attorneys coming from all directions.[8]

The problem of preparing for examination by the Ardmore board of examiners was related by C. T. Huddleston many years later. In the mid-1890s he was a schoolteacher in a subscription school at Stonewall, Indian Territory. Like numerous other male schoolteachers, he decided to prepare for the legal profession:[9]

I got the catalogue of study required by the Cumberland Law School of Lebanon, Tennessee, and bought the books therein prescribed for study. I studied this course for four or five years, including Story on Equity Jurisprudence, Greenleaf on Evidence, and Parson on Contracts. When I left the school at four o'clock I went directly to my room and studied until something like 11 to 12:00 o'clock and the same thing on Saturdays and Sundays, usually.

Date Crawford, who is now a lawyer at Ada, Oklahoma, and I went to Ardmore, Oklahoma, to be examined for license to practice law. Our conveyance was a wagon going to Davis and we each paid $2.00 apiece to ride out there, and were to walk up the hills. We were two days on the trip. I remember very distinctly it appeared to be all up hill. We went to Ardmore and were examined, and on May 9, 1899, we got our license to practice law.

In that same year the Ada Bar was also expanded by the addition of John Crawford, afterward one of the city's leading attorneys. His Ada practice began in an office six feet by eight feet—adequate space for a table and chair, his only furniture. His two-volume library—the *Mansfield Digest of Arkansas* and *Arkansas Justice* rested on the table.[10]

The thriving court town of Atoka lured a young Texan, Isaac Lorenzo Cook, who arrived there with $500 in his pocket, bought a law library, opened an office and waited for clients. Weeks passed; no clients appeared, and Cook began to doubt the wisdom of his move. But as he walked down the street one morning, a man stopped and asked him if he was a lawyer. Cook's affirmative reply produced a $25 retainer fee and his law practice began. Before the day was over he had earned $75.[11]

Although the federal district court for the Durant area was in Atoka, the town of Durant had a United States commissioner court and was an attractive location for lawyers in the 1890s. For about four dollars a month two young attorneys, W. H. Ritchey and W. A. Durant—the latter one of the family for whom the town was named—shared a room with a dentist. The practice of law was separated from the practice of dentistry by a large cotton sheet that hung from the ceiling.[12] When Walter L. Boner arrived in Durant in 1898, he was fortunate enough to have his own private office adjoining one occupied by a doctor and another occupied by an undertaker. They frequently described their close professional co-operation: the doctor administered a fatal dose to his patient, the undertaker provided the funeral service, and Lawyer Boner then administered the estate.[13]

By 1895 the presence of a federal court had attracted more than 100 lawyers to Ardmore, almost one lawyer for every 30 local residents. Their customary professional attire was a Prince Albert coat with a polished shirt front and high collar.[14] Offices of the more prosperous attorneys boasted stenographers, good libraries, and elegant carpets. Prominent among the law firms was Johnson, Cruce and Cruce. Youngest of the Cruce brothers was Lee, only 15 years away from becoming the second governor of Oklahoma. The firm had just completed building what the *Daily Ardmoreite* called "the handsomest structure in the city": a two story building, 32 by 90 feet with a lower front made of plate glass and iron."[15]

The appointive office of United States commis-sioner, whose duties were similar to those of a justice of the peace, may have had unusual financial rewards at the time, but communities unaccustomed to law and order could make life difficult for the commissioner. That was the situation at Roff in the Chickasaw Nation where racial tension followed a fight between a white man and a black man. When the commissioner summoned the white man for a preliminary hearing, he was intoxicated and could not testify coherently. A mob administered the commissioner a whipping because he conducted a hearing while the white defendant was not in command of his faculties. According to one account this episode caused the federal court to be established at Ada instead of Roff, and at Statehood it made Ada the county seat of Pontotoc County.[16]

President Cleveland named 58-year-old William M. Springer to the judgeship of the Northern District pursuant to the Act of 1895. In turn Judge Springer appointed Elijah G. Tollette, Jr., of Tennessee to set up a commissioner's court in Tulsa.[17] Tulsa at the time was a village of only a few hundred people existing despite polluted well water, quagmire streets, and no sanitation. Nevertheless, formation of the commissioner's court attracted several ambitious lawyers to the community, including Edward Calkins, a disabled Union veteran of the Civil War. Although in later years he achieved the success lawyers dream of, Calkins was already 59 years old when he arrived in Tulsa in 1895. Reported to have been "brilliant but eccentric" and with meager financial resources, Calkins made judicious investments along Tulsa's present Main Street and in little more than a decade was considered a wealthy man. He was instrumental in organizing the Tulsa town government in 1898, was Tulsa's first mayor, and was the organizer and first president of the Tulsa Bar.[18]

Commissioner Tollette for some reason used his influence to move the main office of the commissioner from Tulsa to Claremore. He was a capable lawyer but encountered strong opposition in his conduct of the commissioner's office. Citizens under his jurisdiction were no doubt relieved when, according to one report, he "gave up in disgust."[19]

Tollette's successor was David W. Yancey, who came to Claremore from Missouri. Although the court of a United States commissioner was in legal effect like a justice of the peace court, the term at Tulsa presided over by individuals with legal ability like Tollette and David W. Yancey was of tremendous importance to the broad region it served. The commissioners heard litigants who traveled, in a time of no bridges and few roads, from Bartlesville, Claremore, Catoosa, Coweta, Okmulgee, Sapulpa, and later Bristow. Misdemeanors and preliminary examinations for felonies were tried in the court, as were all suits involving $100 or less. In some instances the limit was as high as a thousand dollars.[20]

It was not long before Yancey, like the commissioner at Roff, suffered the discomfort of frontier vengeance. He was a sociable young man, and on one particular evening he joined his friends in attending a public dance in the country some distance from Claremore. According to the account told by Yancey's friend, lawyer David Dickey, a band of outlaws operating in the vicinity of Claremore had been dissatisfied with Yancey's treatment of one of their members who had appeared in his court. At the dance they overpowered the commissioner and his friends and dragged him outside where they laid him flat on his back and forced him to drink whiskey from a jug. Friend Dickey's comment, "If you think this was not real revenge, try it sometime."[21]

Harry Campbell, a graduate of Northwestern University's law department, drove his mule team into Tulsa on April 28, 1895, carrying his worldly possessions that included only one law book. He soon tripled his library when he purchased Arkansas' *Mansfield Digest* and received a volume of Creek Nation statutes as a gift.[22] After Tulsa was incorporated in 1898, Campbell's knowledge of the town's ordinances won a case for Colonel Lynch, charged with allowing his cows to run loose on Main Street. Campbell produced the exact terminology of the ordinance that permitted an individual to let as many as six cows and five hogs run loose. Fortunately the colonel had only two hogs and three cows. Proving that court decisions are often forerunners of new law, the town fathers decided to repeal the ordinance and allow all hogs and cattle to roam at will on Main Street.[23]

President William McKinley in December of 1899 appointed his friend, Republican Joseph Albert Gill, as judge in the Northern District to succeed Democrat William M. Springer, who then moved back to Washington as resident counsel for

Harry Campbell, Northwestern University law graduate, settled in Tulsa in 1895. (Courtesy Law Library, University of Tulsa.)

the Cherokee and Creek Nations.[24] Gill had moved to Colby, Kansas, in 1887 from Illinois. Politics became a corollary of his profession as a lawyer and rewarded him with the Indian Territory judgeship which he held until Oklahoma's Statehood in 1907.[25] Judge Gill in 1929 described his experiences as an Indian Territory judge to a writer for the *Tulsa Daily World*, saying:

If you can imagine the opening of one of the United States courts, the bringing in of from 20 to 40 prisoners, the presentation of each case, the plea of the prisoner, the consideration of the plea and the sentence to jail or the penitentiary of from 20 to 35 men a day—beginning at 9 o'clock in the morning and continuing sometimes until after 10 o'clock at night—you will have some idea of the work of the court in the administration of justice in Indian Territory in the older days.

Upon the conclusion of a term of court the government would send in a special passenger coach barred like a jail, and it would be placed in charge of a marshal, who oversaw the loading on of from 50 to 100 prisoners to be taken to different penitentiaries throughout the United States.[26]

Judge Gill observed that, although many Indians and blacks were among the criminals, most of them were illiterate whites less than 25 years old. The predominance of white criminals he attributed to the lack of public schools for the white race in a land where Indians and blacks were entitled to an education free of charge.[27]

TWO INDIAN TERRITORY LAWYERS:
ROBERT L. WILLIAMS AND ALFALFA BILL MURRAY

Robert Lee Williams, future jurist and one of the ablest of Oklahoma governors, was among the young lawyers attracted by new opportunities in Indian Territory after the Congressional legislation of March 1, 1895. Williams held an A. B. degree from Southern University in Greensboro, Alabama, at the time he began to read law in the office of William S. Thorington in Montgomery, Alabama. He compressed the usual two-year course of study into six months, and in 1891 at age 23 passed a three-hour oral bar examination conducted by the state attorney general and two associates.[1]

Two years later Williams gave up what appeared to be a growing law practice in Troy, Alabama, to travel west with the intent of settling in the Cherokee Outlet on the designated opening date of September 16, 1893. At Guthrie he purchased a copy of the *Oklahoma Territorial Statutes* for 1893 and proceeded to Orlando, Oklahoma Territory, to await the opening of the Outlet. But there all the discomforts caused by heat and wind, along with the exorbitant prices charged aspiring homesteaders for food and lodging, dampened his pioneer spirit. He complained that the "eternal dust is getting on my nerves as well as in my eyes" and told acquaintances that back in Alabama he "could buy whiskey cheaper than he could buy water in Orlando."[2] He sold his one law book to W. N. Boles on an extended credit arrangement and returned to Troy.[3]

Back in Alabama he was caught up in the emotional atmosphere of a revival conducted by the great evangelist of that time, Sam Jones, and decided to return to Southern University to study for the ministry. At the end of the nine-month term, he received a Master of Arts degree and a license to preach. However, two years as a Methodist circuit rider in Texas convinced him that his calling remained with the law rather than the ministry, and he headed back to the future state of Oklahoma. But this time instead of the northwestern plains he decided to settle in the wooded regions of the Choctaw Nation that had terrain similar to his Alabama homeland.[4]

In August of 1896 Williams arrived in Atoka, a court town of a few hundred people, where he accepted employment as a $50-a-month law clerk for George A. Pate. Pate was an intermarried Choctaw citizen who had practiced law in Atoka for seven years. The Dawes Commission had recently announced the rules for enrollment of Choctaw and Chickasaw citizens, and Pate's office was contacted for help by hundreds of applicants. Williams soon convinced Pate of his legal ability, and within four months he was a partner in the new firm of Pate and Williams, Attorneys and Counsellors at Law.

A month later, in January of 1897, the new partnership expanded 32 miles southward into Durant, a flourishing community of some 1500 people.[5] As resident partner in those beginning years in Durant, Williams did his own clerical work—often until midnight. After a full day in his office or in court he frequently drove by horse and buggy 20 or 25 miles into the country on legal business, returning home around 11:00 or 12:00 o'clock.[6]

Williams was to practice law in Indian Territory less than a decade before his election to the first Supreme Court of Oklahoma. During that time he maintained his law practice on the premise that "a fair compromise was better than a risk of losing the case after a hard expensive fight." If he was certain that his client in a criminal case was guilty, he advised the client to plead guilty. Williams would then argue for leniency on the grounds that the government had been spared the expense of trial. If the client denied guilt, Williams applied his best efforts, but if the defense was weak he did not hesitate to cloud the issue by "prosecuting" or "convicting" the United States attorney.[7]

Williams was federal district judge for Eastern Oklahoma when he spoke at the State Bar Convention in 1933. D. A. Richardson, a judge of the

Robert L. Williams, Oklahoma governor and jurist. (Courtesy OHS.)

A scene in early Durant, where Robert L. Williams practiced law. (Courtesy The Daily Oklahoman.)

state Criminal Court of Appeals, asked him how he set his fee in a criminal case when he was practicing law. "Why Judge," Williams replied, "when I defended a man and he was convicted, I tore up all the mortgages and notes and gave them to his wife. I hadn't done him any good. And when I cleared him, I took everything he had." The audience interrupted with laughter, after which Judge Williams continued, "I said: 'Public justice required him to be punished.' [Laughter] You see that was my philosophy—my philosophy of right and wrong."[8]

After four years in Durant, Williams in 1901 formed a partnership with William E. Utterback, a 28-year-old University of Mississippi graduate and recently discharged captain in the Spanish-American War. In outward appearances at least, Williams and Utterback were a study in contrasts: Utterback was six feet tall, immaculate, with a winning personality and the bearing of a soldier; Williams was about five and a half feet tall, careless in appearance, and gruff in manner.

Williams, while always a controversial figure, went on to the Supreme Court of Oklahoma, to the governorship, to the bench of the Federal District Court of Eastern Oklahoma, then to the Circuit Court of Appeals. Utterback, president of the Oklahoma State Bar Association in 1932, proved to be a capable law partner, and their friendship

ended only with the death of Judge Williams in 1948.[9]

In 1898, a year after Robert L. Williams settled in Durant, another young lawyer—28-year-old William Henry Murray—arrived in Tishomingo to start his law practice. With little formal education, Murray had worked as a farmer, schoolteacher, reporter, and newspaper editor in Texas.[10] While in the newspaper business in Corsicana, he had considered attending a university to study law, but Congressman Roger Q. Mills had advised him the better approach was to work in the office of a good lawyer.[11]

He studied for several months with Judge John Rice before he applied to the district judge for examination in open court as required by Texas Law. The examination was one in name only, Murray later recalled, for a committee of three lawyers merely joked with him a few minutes and asked no serious law questions before reporting to the judge that they found him "eminently" qualified.[12]

He practiced briefly in Corsicana, then moved to Fort Worth where he survived as a bill collector while studying municipal law under Judge W. D. Harris.[13] In August of 1897 he visited his father in Marlow, Indian Territory, and returned to Fort Worth convinced that his future lay in Indian Territory. With borrowed funds he rode a train to

William H. "Alfalfa Bill" Murray, one of Oklahoma's most colorful characters. (Courtesy OHS.)

Ardmore.[14] Unimpressed by the prospects for a new attorney there, he proceeded north to Pauls Valley. There he encountered several lawyers coming out of the Pauls Valley courthouse, of whom one was W. B. Johnson, then the United States district attorney for the Southern District.

Murray visited with Johnson who informed him that Tishomingo, capitol of the Chickasaw Nation, would be an excellent place to practice law. Tribal money was plentiful there, Johnson said, white people were settling in the Chickasaw Nation, and it had "the greatest Criminal Commissioners district in the United States."[15]

Without a cent in his pocket Murray rode a mail hack into Tishomingo, then bluffed the driver into postponement of payment of the one dollar fare.[16] He was already assured of lodging because during the trip he had engaged in pleasant conversation with another passenger—the stepdaughter of the operator of a Tishomingo hotel.[17] During his first few days in his adopted home, Murray, according to plan, visited with the seven or eight lawyers practicing there and, in his words, "Each day regaling these fellows with bits of speech and Classical Literature, and discussions of Constitutional Law. It may be observed that I was using all the blandishments possible with these country lawyers, all of whom were young men just beginning the practice, and that

was largely true of ninety per cent of the lawyers in the Indian Country."[18]

Madison Lucas, a law partner of Stephen C. Treadwell, gave Murray his first opportunity to exhibit his skill as a trial lawyer. One "Horn," a farmer of large stature, filed suit against "Gray," a much smaller man, for threatening him with a fence rail. Gray retained Lucas for his defense, and Lucas paid Murray half of the $20 fee to conduct the jury trial. Murray sized Horn up as a "swift witness"—one who, when given the opportunity would talk more than he should. Horn produced as evidence a fence rail almost as large as his accused assailant. By exploiting Horn's garrulous manner, as well as the ridiculous size of the fence post, Murray easily won the case. A few days later he won another law suit and accepted an invitation to join the new firm of Treadwell, Murray and Lucas.[19]

Thereafter Murray's legal career in Tishomingo was assured. The knowledge of municipal law gained in Fort Worth gave him a virtual monopoly in that field after the Congressional legislation allowing incorporation of towns in Indian Territory.[20] In criminal cases requiring a jury trial, he could usually choose which side he preferred to represent.[21] He even felt safe in discarding the Prince Albert coat and derby hat—the conventional dress of a Texas professional man—and adopted the loose, comfortable attire popular in the Chickasaw Nation.[22]

His practice flourished even more after Douglas H. Johnston, governor of the Chickasaws, selected him as legal advisor. He was in an especially favorable position to plead the numerous citizenship cases for those seeking to have their names placed on the tribal roles.[23] In land title and citizenship cases one-fourth of the settlement was his customary fee. One land case brought him the extraordinary fee of $7500. Like other lawyers he sometimes had to engage in a barter arrangement: his defense of a band of cattle thieves rewarded him with a bronco appropriately named "Bullet."[24]

His defense of Lake Munday, a Chickasaw citizen, was, according to Murray, later published in an Arkansas law journal. Munday was a benevolent landlord, always protective of the tenants who rented his farms in what is now Marshall County. On a farm nearby lived "Wild Bill" Holland and his three grown sons. The Holland fam-

Murray, shown here with his wife and children, was only 36 years old when his financial situation permitted retirement to his farm near Tishomingo. (Courtesy Archives and Manuscripts Division, OHS.)

ily had become especially abusive of Munday's tenants, who for the most part were church-going families. On one occasion a tenant named Jones was on his way to church accompanied by his wife and children when the Hollands accosted them, calling Jones a "woolly-headed son-of-a-bitch."

Munday retained Murray to prosecute the Hollands on a charge of using profane language in the presence of females. Lawyer Buck Garrett defended the Hollands on the theory that the words used were not profane per se—that even friends often described each other in those terms.

Murray took full advantage of his right to discuss freely anything in the court record, when he arose and addressed the jury. "Gentlemen of the jury," he began, "it is all right for any friend who has another who don't object, to call him a 'son-of-a-bitch.' " Murray turned to the four Hollands seated in front of the jury, and pointed to each of them in succession as he continued, "It is all right for a son-of-a-bitch like that and that and that and that to call themselves and their families and one another a son-of-a-bitch, but when four sons-of-bitches like these," Murray again pointed to each of the Hollands, "call a Christian gentleman in the presence of his wife and daughter a son-of-bitch, I insist that the sons-of-bitches ought to have the limit of the law." The Hollands were convicted. Thereafter local lawyers chuckled when someone mentioned Bill Murray's "Son-of-a-Bitch case."[25]

By his marriage to the niece of Governor Johnston of the Chickasaw Nation, Murray gained Chickasaw citizenship and tribal allotments to his growing family placed large tracts of land under his control. He devoted one large tract to growing alfalfa, and his frequent lectures to farm organizations about that crop earned him the sobriquet of "Alfalfa Bill."[26] In less than a half dozen years after his entry into the Chickasaw Nation as a penniless lawyer, Murray's improved financial situation allowed him to retire to his farm at Twelve Mile Prairie. He then devoted most of his time to politics and the study of a constitution for the new state that was only a few years in the future.[27] When he attended the Sequoyah Statehood convention in Muskogee in August of 1905, his name was heard often during the deliberations owing to his familiarity with the basic legal instruments of nearly every state and many foreign countries. In 1906 he was elected president of Oklahoma's Constitutional Convention, and the following year he became the first Speaker of the Oklahoma House of Representatives. He was elected to the United States House of Representatives in 1912 and 1914 and to the governorship of Oklahoma in 1930.

9

CITIZENSHIP LAW AND THE DAWES COMMISSION

In the mid 1890s more than 350,000 white people lived in Indian Territory. They engaged in all types of business enterprise, in cities and towns where no municipal government existed. They were governed by the common law, Federal law, and by Arkansas statutes, but inasmuch as all land was owned in common by the Indian tribes, no laws covered the filing or recording of mortgages or other conveyances of property. Corporations could not be chartered, and no foreign corporations except railroads could legally do business in the Territory. These conditions, along with a never-ending influx of whites, foretold inevitable change in the structure of Indian government. Few doubted that Congress would soon abolish the Indian system of communal land tenure and distribute all land in severalty. Thus non-citizens could recognize the future value of Indian citizenship, and the practice of "citizenship law" developed.

For a $50 fee citizenship attorneys of the Cherokee Nation would complete a citizenship application form and submit it to tribal authorities. One report told of a lawyer who made a short promotional trip into the Southern states to tell citizens of the Five Civilized Tribes who had not moved west of the fortune to be gained from sharing in the ownership of fertile Indian Territory land. He contracted to file citizenship claims for 20 applicants and earned $1000 for his trouble. In Tahlequah the citizenship business attracted a new enterprise—a newspaper that published the Cherokee National Council's daily agenda along with the names of citizenship claims scheduled to be presented to the Council on a given day. The paper had a wide circulation among attorneys who regularly mailed copies to clients to show that their claims had been filed. The attorney earned his $50 fee in that manner, but the client who rejoiced and awaited notice of citizenship was usually disappointed, because comparatively few new citizens were ever enrolled.[1]

In 1893 Congress, with a view toward "the ultimate creation of a State or States of the Union" in the Indian Territory, established a commission to the Five Civilized Tribes known as the Dawes Commission.[2] Its duty was to negotiate with the Tribes and extinguish tribal title to their lands, which were then to be allotted in severalty to tribal citizens. However, the Commission encountered strong opposition from local citizens, and tribal officials refused even to meet with the Commission.[3] Consequently, Congress adopted a more forceful approach to division of Indian lands in an act of June 10, 1896; this declared that the United States government had a duty "to establish a government in the Indian Territory which will rectify the many inequalities and discriminations now existing in said Territory and afford needful protection to the lives and property of all citizens and residents thereof."[4]

The act authorized the Dawes Commission to determine Indian citizenship by accepting tribal citizenship rolls and giving consideration to the applications of persons not on the rolls. To evaluate citizenship claims, the commission became a quasi-judicial agency empowered to administer oaths, compel attendance of witnesses, and take all steps necessary to determine the rights of claimants to citizenship. These claimants included full-blood Indians, intermarried citizens, and former slaves and their descendants freed from their Indian owners after the Civil War. Congress brought the already overloaded United States courts into the program by making them the appellate courts for all decisions of tribal authorities and the Dawes Commission.[5] Heretofore citizenship attorneys had to seek out claimants, but now hordes of people from neighboring states journeyed to the various tribal enrolling sites to file citizenship applications.

The practice of citizenship lawyers flourished, but it was the elite of the Indian Territory Bar who enjoyed the most lucrative remuneration derived from representing the Five Tribes themselves. Each tribe sought to avoid the diminution of tribal shares which would occur by the enrollment of more citizens. Representing the Choctaw Nation was the firm of Stuart, Gordon and Bailey

The Dawes Commission meeting with an Indian delegation. (Courtesy OHS.)

of South McAlester, headed by former Judge C. B. Stuart. W. B. Johnson of Ardmore, soon to become District Attorney for the Southern District, joined with H. F. Paine to represent the Chickasaws.[6] The Choctaw Nation in 1898 placed former Judge James M. Shackelford on a retainer of $5000 for a year, and the Chickasaw Nation retained Mansfield, McMurray and Cornish of South McAlester under a similar arrangement. The Choctaws later engaged Stuart, Lewis and Gordon at a fee of $15 and expenses for each name they succeeded in removing from Choctaw rolls.[7] In 1901 Mansfield, McMurray and Cornish entered into a new contract with the Choctaw and Chickasaw Nations that established a fee of nine percent of the value of property saved for the two Nations.[8] The value of each share of tribal property at that time was deemed to be worth $4800.[9]

The tenacity of Choctaw-Chickasaws tribal leaders and their attorneys was rewarded in 1902 when Congress created a Choctaw-Chickasaw Citizenship Court consisting of three judges appointed by the president at a salary of $5000 annually. In previously unheard-of legislation, the new court had jurisdiction to set aside court judgments previously rendered under the Act of June 10, 1896, and retry the cases on the theory that local United States courts had admitted persons to citizenship without proper notice to the Choctaw and Chickasaw Nations, and had conducted trials *de novo* when they should have reviewed only the findings of the Dawes Commission.[10]

Largely due to the reopening of previously adjudicated cases, the Mansfield firm eventually calculated savings of approximately $16 million for the two Nations on which its fee would have been $1,440,000. While litigation was in process, the Secretary of the Interior proposed to reduce the contingent fee of nine percent, but the Mansfield firm refused to accept any modification of its contract. Congress assigned to the Citizenship Court the responsibility of setting the fee. One of that court's last acts before dissolution granted Mansfield, McMurray and Cornish a fee of $750,000.[11]

Public announcement of awarding the $750,000 fee and its payment in March, of 1905 caused another series of legal squabbles. Two tribal executives and the members of the Mansfield firm were indicted by a grand jury. Charges unsupported by the evidence accused the judges of the Citizenship Court of accepting bribes. But all such efforts to rescind payment of the $750,000 fee were unsuccessful. Historians familiar with the Choctaw-Chickasaw Citizenship court seem to agree that the Mansfield firm was clearly entitled to its fee.[12] Historian Angie Debo, often critical of the Bar's dealings with the Indian people, has said, "The fee, large as it was, was an excellent investment, for the amount recovered represented one-eighth of the Indians' possessions. The real blame rests with a federal policy that drove the tribes to such ruinous measures of defense."[13]

Appraisal, classification, and allotment of the land by the Dawes Commission was a slow process. Its work lasted some 12 years and was similar to the function of a giant probate court, determining the division of the assets of five great estates. Twenty million acres of tribal land were divided among 100,000 tribal citizens sifted from 300,000 claimants.[14] To perform its duties, the Commission hired hundreds of employees through political patronage.[15] It drew heavily on the local Bar for law clerks and stenographers to work in Commission headquarters at Muskogee. Many of its lawyers came from across the nation, and when the Commission's work was completed they chose to remain in the Territory. Thus the Indian Territory Bar grew in numbers and talent and assumed a more cosmopolitan quality.[16]

Notable among the Bar's new members was Grant Foreman, a law graduate of the University of Michigan who accepted employment with the Dawes Commission at Muskogee in 1899. Four years later he formed a law partnership with Judge John R. Thomas and married the judge's daughter,

Creek Indians awaiting enrollment at the Dawes Commission office in Muskogee in 1898. (Courtesy the Daily Oklahoman.)

A Dawes Commission dining tent. (Courtesy OHS.)

Carolyn, in 1905. Foreman retired from his law practice in 1920 to devote full time to the research and writing of Oklahoma and Indian history. Long before his death in 1953 he was recognized as one of Oklahoma's foremost historians.[17]

Another Dawes Commission employee who enjoyed a prosperous career in Oklahoma was Wirt Franklin. He interrupted law studies at George Washington University to accept a political appointment as a stenographer on the Commission's staff in Muskogee. The 19-year-old Franklin spent an unforgettable first night in Muskogee's Edmondson Hotel Annex where, unfamiliar with the hazards of electricity, he used a light bulb to warm his feet. Be-

fore long his mattress was on fire. He survived that ordeal, made peace with the hotel proprietor by promising to pay for the mattress out of his first month's salary, and reported for work the next morning to Law Clerk H. C. Ristine.[18]

Franklin himself achieved law clerk status two years later, and with his own wagon, stenographer, and interpreter he set about tracking down recalcitrant Choctaws and Chickasaws trying to avoid enrollment by the Dawes Commission. After almost four years with the Commission, Franklin resigned to study for the Bar examination. He was admitted to the Indian Territory Bar in 1906 and immediately formed a partnership in Ardmore with S. A. Apple. Their clientele was composed largely of Indians in dispute with the federal government. Of necessity the legal fees earned by the firm could usually be paid only in land, a circumstance that proved profitable for Franklin in view of later oil discoveries. After eight years of law practice in Ardmore, Franklin left his partnership with Apple to devote full time to the oil interests that soon made him wealthy. As president of the Wirt Franklin Petroleum Corporation and later president of the Independent Petroleum Association of America, he became a well-known spokesman for the nation's oil industry.[19]

The opening of a United States court at Muskogee in 1889 foretold the beginning of the end for

Law office of Judge John R. Thomas, right foreground, and Grant Foreman, at Judge Thomas' right. (Courtesy Archives and Manuscripts Division, OHS.)

the Indian court system. Agreements with the Five Civilized Tribes provided for the termination in 1906 of all tribal government as previously known. United States law was to be supreme in every detail, for tribal courts had been abolished by the Curtis Act of June 28, 1898.[20] Thus, as observed by lawyer-historian George H. Shirk, "There passed from the scene tribunals unique in American jurisprudence, courts set up under the sponsorship of independent sovereignty, yet functioning side by side with those of the white man."[21]

White immigrants in the eastern portion of Indian Territory after the Civil War had hastened the demise of tribal government. To the west, other erstwhile settlers had sought homesteads in the so-called "Unassigned Lands." The activities of a Cherokee lawyer, Colonel Elias Cornelius Boudinot, expedited the white settlement of the "Unassigned Lands" and eventually led to formation of the state of Oklahoma.

Wirt Franklin, Dawes Commission clerk who became a wealthy oil man. (Courtesy The Daily Oklahoman.)

Governor Dewey F. Bartlett, left, presents a miniature Oklahoma flag and Okie pin that orbited the moon with Astronaut Tom Stafford, to lawyer George Shirk, Oklahoma Historical Society president and former mayor of Oklahoma City. (Courtesy The Daily Oklahoman.)

ALLOTMENT DEED.   Creek Indian ROLL. No 3671

THE MUSKOGEE (CREEK) NATION,
INDIAN TERRITORY.

To all Whom These Presents Shall Come, Greeting:

WHEREAS, By the Act of Congress approved March 1, 1901 (31 Stats., 861), agreement ratified by the Creek Nation May 25, 1901, it was provided that all lands of the Muskogee (Creek) Tribe of Indians, in Indian Territory, except as therein provided, should be allotted among the citizens of said tribe by the United States Commission to the Five Civilized Tribes so as to give to each an equal share of the whole in value, as nearly as may be, and

WHEREAS, It was provided by said Act of Congress that each citizen shall select, or have selected for him, from his allotment forty acres of land as a homestead for which he shall have a separate deed, and

WHEREAS, The said Commission to the Five Civilized Tribes has certified that the land hereinafter described has been selected by or on behalf of _____

__ Alexander L. Posey _____, a citizen of said tribe, as an allotment, exclusive of a forty acre homestead, as aforesaid,

NOW, THEREFORE, I, the undersigned, the Principal Chief of the Muskogee (Creek) Nation, by virtue of the power and authority vested in me by the aforesaid Act of the Congress of the United States, have granted and conveyed and by these presents do grant and convey unto the said

Alexander L. Posey

all right, title and interest of the Muskogee (Creek) Nation and of all other citizens of said Nation in and to the following described land, viz:__ The West Half of the North East Quarter, and the South East Quarter of the North East Quarter of Section Seventeen (17), Township Ten (10) North, and Range Fifteen (15) East,

of the Indian Base and Meridian, in Indian Territory, containing__ One Hundred and Twenty (120) _____

acres, more or less, as the case may be, according to the United States survey thereof, subject, however, to all provisions of said Act of Congress relating to appraisement and valuation, and to the **provisions of the Act of Congress approved June 30, 1902 (Public No. 200).**

IN WITNESS WHEREOF, I, the Principal Chief of the Muskogee (Creek) Nation, have hereunto set my hand and caused the Great Seal of said Nation to be affixed this **3rd** day of **September**, A. D. 190**2**.

P. Porter
Principal Chief of the Muskogee (Creek) Nation.

Department of the Interior.

Approved

Acting Secretary.

Allotment Deed for land acquired by Alexander L. Posey, gifted Creek Indian writer. (Courtesy OHS.)

COLONEL ELIAS C. BOUDINOT, CHEROKEE LAWYER-BOOMER

The father of Cherokee lawyer Elias C. Boudinot had been one of the leaders who signed the Treaty of New Echota that required Cherokee removal to the West. The older Boudinot was killed in 1839 by tribesmen who considered the signing of that treaty an act of treason. After the death of his father, four-year-old Elias Boudinot was taken to New England where he received a good education. He studied civil engineering for a while, but at age 21 he settled in Fayetteville, Arkansas, to read law in the office of A. M. Wilson. At the outbreak of the Civil War he was commissioned a major in the Confederate army and later promoted to colonel. He was a delegate to the Confederate Congress in 1863 where he worked hard in behalf of the Southern Cherokees. When the war ended he served with the Cherokee treaty delegation at Fort Smith as one of its most resourceful members.[1]

Probably it was Colonel Boudinot with an eye toward the future who was responsible for Article 10 in the Cherokee Treaty of 1866 which permitted residents of the Cherokee Nation to sell farm products, live stock or "any merchandise or manufactured products" and pay any United States tax on only "the quantity sold outside the Indian Territory."[2]

Soon after the end of the war Boudinot resolved to build a tobacco factory in the Cherokee Nation and informed Internal Revenue authorities of his intent to do so. He continued with his plans despite Congressional legislation in July of 1868 which imposed taxes on liquor and tobacco products "produced anywhere within the exterior boundaries of the United States, whether the same shall be within a collection district or not."[3] In November of 1868, with the help of his uncle, Stand Watie, a Cherokee who attained the rank of brigadier general in the Confederate army, Colonel Boudinot erected a tobacco factory in Indian Territory just west of Maysville, Arkansas. They produced "Boudinot & Watie" plug tobacco, capitalizing on the commercial value of two famous Cherokee names. At a price unburdened by federal revenue tax, their tobacco as well as that sold by three other factories operating near the Arkansas border quickly pre-empted the market in nearby Arkansas, western Missouri, and northern Texas. Owners of factories in St. Louis, Louisville, and New York could not compete with untaxed tobacco and protested to federal authorities.[4]

The Commissioner of Internal Revenue maintained that the Act of July 20, 1868, superseded the 1866 treaty with the Cherokees and that the Boudinot-Watie factory owed revenue taxes. Litigation of the matter reached the United States Supreme Court where Boudinot himself appeared before the court, assisted by eminent attorneys Albert Pike, R. W. Johnson, and B. F. Butler. Justice Swayne delivered the court's opinion in the December, 1870, term, noting that, "considering the narrowness of the questions to be decided, a remarkable wealth of learning and ability have been expended in their discussion." By a four-to-two decision the justices affirmed that the Indian country should be considered a part of the United States and that an Act of Congress could at any time supersede an Indian Treaty.[5]

"The Supreme Court has decided the tobacco case against me; it is the Death Knell of the Nations," Boudinot wrote Watie.[6] Boudinot's tobacco case did indeed constitute a legal landmark in the subsequent erosion of the Indian Nations. The court's opinion underscored the tenuous nature of hundreds of Indian treaties made since 1778. All were now susceptible more than ever to legislative politics. A breakdown of protection against white encroachment was imminent. Only a short time after the Supreme Court's decision was publicized, W. R. Laughlin, a Workingman's Party gubernatorial candidate in Kansas cited the "Cherokee Tobacco Case" in defense of white settlement of Indian land.[7]

About that time an Indian appropriation bill

SOUTHERN CHEROKEE DELIGATION TO WASHINGTON D. C. 1866

John Rollin Ridge   Saladin Watie   Richard Fields   Elias C. Baudinot   William Penn Adair

Thirty-one-year-old Colonel Boudinot was a valuable member of the delegation involved in drafting a new treaty with the United States after the Civil War. (Courtesy OHS.)

was being prepared by the 41st Congress. A member of the conference committee was Kansas Congressman Sidney Clarke, a former Massachusetts newspaperman who had supported the opening of Indian Territory lands since he moved to Kansas in 1859. At Clarke's suggestion, the appropriation bill included a now-famous provision that the United States no longer would recognize Indian tribes as independent nations for treaty purpose. In this manner Congress strengthened the ruling in the Cherokee Tobacco Case so that the Five Civilized Tribes thereafter could be controlled by United States law. Congressional charter could authorize railroad construction through Indian Territory that had formerly been subjected to the treaty-making process. The coming of railroads together with white encroach-

ment eventually created a situation Indian leaders were powerless to resist. Congressman Clarke wrote, "I think it is safe to say that had it not been for the abrogation of the treaty system at that time, the settlement of Oklahoma would have been much longer delayed."[8] Clarke, who attained his license to practice after reading law in the office of Kansas Senator James H. Lane, later participated in the opening of Oklahoma's Unassigned Lands, and as a prominent citizen of Oklahoma City he was known as "the Statehood evangelist" in the drive for Statehood.[9]

During the 1870s Colonel Boudinot spent a great deal of time in Washington both as an employee and consultant in the House of Representatives. Dark and handsome, a talented orator and musician, he was a favorite of Washington so-

53

Sidney Clarke, Kansas congressman, later Oklahoma's "Statehood evangelist." (Courtesy Archives and Manuscripts Division, OHS.)

ciety. Benjamin T. DuVal of the Fort Smith Bar observed, "He was on familiar and easy terms with the learned justices of the Supreme Court, with stately senators, members of Congress, distinguished military men, and, indeed, with every class of society."[10] On one occasion while he was an adviser to the House Committee on Indian Affairs, that body was discussing a name for the territory to be carved out of Indian Territory. The colonel virtually assured the name of "Oklahoma" for the future state by reminding the committee that Reverend Allen Wright of the Choctaw Nation had suggested "Oklahoma" as an appropriate name during the treaty negotiations of 1866.[11]

Like his father, Colonel Boudinot seemed to realize the inevitability and benefits of Indian assimilation into the mainstream of the Unites States populace. This philosophy fit well with the policy of the railroad interests, and, although any business affiliation was not publicized, Boudinot may have been on retainer for the railroads. The *Chicago Times* in February of 1879 published an article attributed to Colonel Boudinot that insisted the United States held "absolute and unembarrassed title" to nearly 14 million acres of land purchased from the Five Civilized Tribes as a part of the Treaties of 1866. Boudinot referred to the vast area in western Indian Territory, including the Cheyenne-Arapaho, the Comanche-Kiowa,

and Apache reservations along with Greer County, then in dispute with Texas. The tract receiving the most attention was the Unassigned Lands—the "Oklahoma District"—containing almost 2 million acres that included the rich bottomland of several rivers and their tributaries near the center of present Oklahoma. In the newspaper article, supplemented by a form letter and map which Boudinot sent to a deluge of readers requesting more information, he argued that the government had abandoned its original intent to settle Indians or freedmen on the land and that it was now available for settlement as part of the public domain.[12]

By joining the "Boomers"—those who promoted the opening of the Indian country to non-Indians—Colonel Boudinot incurred the disapproval of many of his fellow tribesmen. His article, reprinted throughout the United States, suited the railroad companies but was contrary to the argument of government attorneys. They pointed out that the Creek and Seminole residual interests attached to any land not devoted to Indian use must first be extinguished before it could be opened for settlement. However erroneous, the Boudinot argument accomplished its purpose and became an important catalyst in 10 years of persistent agitation that eventually forced the opening of the land to homesteaders.

An almost immediate effect of Boudinot's writings in February of 1879 was the assembling of an "Oklahoma Colony" in Kansas by Charles L. Carpenter, swashbuckling adventurer. The federal government stationed soldiers at strategic border locations, a move that temporarily countered the enthusiasm for entry onto the Indian lands. Carpenter's successor, David L. Payne, proved to be a more tenacious advocate of the Boomer movement. From 1879 until his death in 1884 Payne, with the encouragement of his good friend, Colonel Boudinot, conducted several expeditions into the forbidden land. Ejected by United States soldiers, he nevertheless attained hero status as he argued Boudinot's "public domain" theory in the federal courts of Fort Smith, Wichita, and Topeka.[13]

The federal government relied on the Non-Intercourse Act of 1834 and an enactment of August 18, 1856, both of which were directed at such unauthorized entry. However, penalty for the first intrusion was merely ejection of the intruders accompanied by a warning; a second intrusion subjected the intruder to a thousand dollar fine. Because of its jurisdiction in Indian Territory, Judge Parker's federal court in Arkansas heard many cases dealing with intruders into the Territory. W. L. Couch, a Boomer leader, testified in 1885 before a Senate Committee that 365 judgments against the Boomer intruders had been obtained in the Fort Smith court and that 800 suits were still pending in the District Court at Wichita, Kansas.[14]

One of the important Boomer suits was that of the United States against David L. Payne tried at Fort Smith in 1881. Tribal representatives accused the Boomer leader of being a tool of the railroads and greedy businessmen, and they raised almost $5000 to assist United States District Attorney William H. H. Clayton in the prosecution. Representatives from all five Indian nations attended the trial. Judge Parker's decision announced on May 2, 1881 was that, contrary to Colonel Boudinot's argument, the Creek and Seminole ceded lands were still a part of Indian Territory. The judge levied the statutory $1000 fine against Payne, but the government's victory ended in a barren judgment, for Payne had no assets.[15]

Bills were frequently introduced in Congress to make intruders criminally liable, but all such measures failed to pass.[16] The activity of the Boomers continued until their Congressional victory in 1889 when the Springer Amendment opened the land to settlement. Like their non-Indian neighbors among the Five Civilized Tribes, the settlers of the Unassigned Lands were also to experience life in a country without local forums for the administration of justice. The evolution of government in the new land constitutes another chapter in the Bench and Bar's contribution to the history of Oklahoma.

11

PROVISIONAL GOVERNMENT IN OKLAHOMA TERRITORY

After years of battle with the direct pressure of individual homeseekers and the indirect pressure of railroads and other business interests, Congress acknowledged defeat. The Indian Appropriation Act of 1885 authorized the president to negotiate with the Creeks, Seminoles, and Cherokees for payment of their claims to the "Unassigned Lands" in Indian Territory in order to open these lands to settlement. In early 1889 the interests of the Creeks and Seminoles in the nearly 2 million acres of Unassigned Lands, known as the "Oklahoma District", were satisfied by payment of an additional $4,193,779.[1]

Indian leaders were on the scene in Washington in the winter of 1888-1889 to fight opening this area to settlement, but any hope of doing more than postponing it fast disappeared. Congressman William M. Springer, who a few years later was appointed a United States judge in Indian Territory, thought the Indian representatives were a lazy group enjoying vacations at the expense of their fellow tribesmen. To prove what an indolent lot they were, he arranged to have them appear before the House Committee on Territories. The first to be called before the Committee was Lucien B. Bell, a graduate of Cane College in Arkansas. The following exchange occurred:[2]

> Mr. Springer: "Mr. Bell, tell the Committee what you do for a living—what is your trade, calling or occupation?"
> Mr. Bell: "Various things. I practice law a little, farm some, run for office occasionally, now and then take a hand at poker and never miss a horse race if I can get to it. The rest of my time I spend in trying to fool God like you white folks do."

Bell's reply almost broke up the hearing. If Springer was somewhat taken aback, he recovered enough to author the "Springer Amendment" to the Indian Appropriations Bill of 1889 that opened the Unassigned Lands to settlement.[3]

Consequently, on the bright spring day of April 22, 1889, an estimated 50,000 homeseekers and speculators used various means of transportation to race into lands situated near the center of present Oklahoma and comprising the major parts of Kingfisher, Logan, Payne, Canadian, Oklahoma, and Cleveland counties. In that famous "Run" the "'89ers" populated the communities of Guthrie, Oklahoma City, Kingfisher, El Reno, Norman, and Stillwater, and within days the Oklahoma country claimed 27 villages and towns.[4]

A settler could eventually acquire a town lot or a 160-acre tract of farm land under the homestead laws by being the first to stake his claim and file the necessary papers in the United States Land Office at Guthrie or Kingfisher. The territory's first lawyers derived their principal income from filling out such forms for fees of 25 cents to two dollars per instrument.[5] Townsites consisted of 320 acres, but no adequate statutes prescribed how towns should be created or town lots transferred. The number of claimants far exceeded the quarter-sections and town lots available. Therefore land disputes occupied territorial and federal courts for years and sometimes went as far as the United States Supreme Court.

The opening of the Unassigned Lands was an opportunity for any aspiring young lawyer to begin his career in a new country. For the older lawyer it was an opportunity to begin anew. But the recently arrived lawyers encountered the novel experience of trying to practice law in a land without local judges or courts of general jurisdiction. In its haste to attach the Springer Amendment to the Indian Appropriation Act, Congress had not provided for local government or laws.

United States marshals and a few soldiers were stationed near the larger towns to preserve order. Congressional leaders relied primarily on the federal court at Wichita to exercise jurisdiction over offenses punishable by death or imprisonment at hard labor, while the court at Muskogee, organized only seven weeks before the "Run," had jurisdiction over most other offenses.[6]

Especially in the townsite communities, the

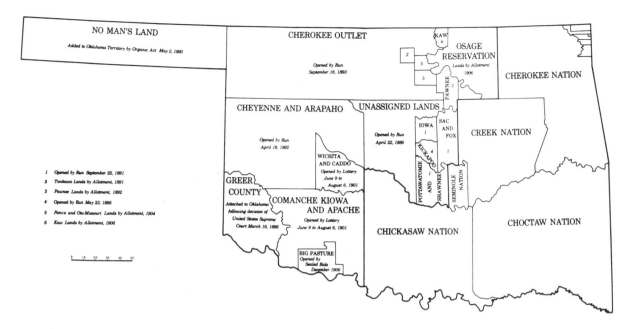

Within the map:

NO MAN'S LAND

Added to Oklahoma Territory by Organic Act May 2, 1890

CHEROKEE OUTLET

Opened by Run
September 16, 1893

KAW 6

OSAGE
RESERVATION

Lands by Allotment
1906

CHEROKEE NATION

CHEYENNE AND ARAPAHO

Opened by Run
April 19, 1892

UNASSIGNED LANDS

Opened by Run
April 22, 1889

PAWNEE 3

IOWA 1

SAC
AND
FOX 1

CREEK NATION

WICHITA
AND CADDO
Opened by Lottery
June 9 to
August 6, 1901

KICKAPOO

POTTAWATOMIE
AND
SHAWNEE

SEMINOLE
NATION

GREER
COUNTY
Attached to Oklahoma
following decision of
United States Supreme
Court March 16, 1896

COMANCHE KIOWA
AND APACHE
Opened by Lottery
June 9 to August 6, 1901

CHICKASAW NATION

CHOCTAW NATION

BIG PASTURE
Opened by
Sealed Bids
December 1906

1 Opened by Run September 22, 1891
2 Tonkawa Lands by Allotment, 1891
3 Pawnee Lands by Allotment, 1892
4 Opened by Run May 23, 1895
5 Ponca and Oto-Missouri Lands by Allotment, 1904
6 Kaw Lands by Allotment, 1906

0 10 20 30 40 50

Land Openings in Oklahoma Territory. (From Historical Atlas of Oklahoma, 3rd Edition, by John W. Morris, Charles R. Goins, and Edwin C. McReynolds, University of Oklahoma Press, 1986.)

Lucien B. Bell, Indian lawyer, who explained his interesting sidelines to a congressional committee. (Courtesy Archives and Manuscripts Division, OHS.)

proximity of individuals on lots of 25 or 50 feet with two or more claimants called for "provisional government" or government by "common consent" until Congress could provide for local government. Guthrie, Oklahoma City, and Kingfisher each held mass meetings a few days after the opening on April 22, 1889, and elected town officials to pass and enforce laws, levy taxes, and impose fines and jail sentences. Arbitration boards—Oklahoma's first "courts"—decided town lot disputes and issued certificates of title. Inasmuch as provisional municipal governments functioned without legal sanction, some dissatisfied individuals labeled them "kangaroo governments." In Oklahoma City a citizens committee elected on April 24 took testimony and made "on the spot" decisions as to ownership of town lots. To ward off the crowds who gathered around them, they operated inside a triangular fence which they carried from lot to lot.[7]

In July and August following the land run, 96 delegates assembled in Guthrie and prepared a memorial requesting Congress to convene in special session to organize a territorial government. From the lawyers' viewpoint, among the more pressing needs were provisions for wills, rules of descent, and probate of estates; procedures for conveying land, creating trusts, public and private corporations, and all types of liens; laws for the care and adoption of children, solemnization of marriages, assignments by insolvents, regulating rates of interest; and methods of raising revenue by taxation.[8] For nearly 13 months, however, the Territory was without law and order except that supplied by the provisional govern-

Open air law offices ready for clients after the "Run" of April 22, 1889. (Courtesy William J. Baker.)

A scene at Guthrie the day of the "Run." Note the Lauck & Lauck law office. (Courtesy Western History Collections, University of Oklahoma Library.)

ments, a few United States marshals, and a detachment of the United States Army.

In order to circumvent the 320-acre limitation on townsites, enterprising Guthrie settlers created side by side the towns of East Guthrie, South Guthrie, West Guthrie, Capitol Hill, and Dyer's Guthrie.[9] Their provisional governments established elaborate judicial systems which included municipal, appellate, and superior courts.[10] As many as 20 police officers preserved order. Frank P. Cease's police court averaged 50 cases daily involving lot-jumping, gambling, bootlegging, and complaints against "dives" and dance halls.[11]

During the first few days after the "Run," grocery stores, restaurants, and the offices of doctors and lawyers lined Guthrie's Harrison Avenue.[12] Among the 152 lawyers reported to be in Guthrie at the time were three future judges who arrived by train from Kansas: John H. Cotteral, the first United States District Judge for the Western District of Oklahoma and later appointed Circuit Judge by President Calvin Coolidge; Frank Dale, second Chief Justice of the Oklahoma Territory Supreme Court; and A. G. C. Bierer, a justice of

the Territorial Supreme Court long active in Oklahoma's legal affairs.[13]

The 25-year-old Cotteral had studied two years at Michigan University, then received legal training in his brother-in-law's office in Garden City, Kansas, where he specialized in land title cases.[14] Frank Dale, 50 years old at the time of the Run, had studied law and practiced at Wichita, Kansas, then served as Assistant County Attorney. In 1885 he was appointed registrar of the United States land office.[15] Bierer, 25 years old, grew up on a Kansas farm, studied in his father's law office, and received a law degree from Washington's Georgetown University in 1886. Bierer and Cotteral opened a partnership in Guthrie immediately after the "Run," but Bierer divided his time between Garden City and Guthrie until 1891 when he moved to Guthrie and soon afterward was appointed city attorney.[16]

A well-known '89er and Oklahoma lawyer of later years was Roy Hoffman, World War I general and first of a prominent Oklahoma banking family. Hoffman was a "flaxen-haired boy" not yet 21, therefore ineligible for a homestead when he

Arbitration boards, Oklahoma Territory's first "courts," promoted peaceful settlement of town lot disputes. (Courtesy OHS.)

John H. Cotteral, an "'89er" who became the first federal judge for the Western District of Oklahoma. He later was appointed to the Circuit Court of Appeals. (Western History Collections, University of Oklahoma Library.)

A.G.C. Bierer, '89er lawyer and judge long prominent in Territory and state legal circles. (Courtesy The Daily Oklahoman.)

arrived in Guthrie by train from Arkansas City on the day of the Run.[17] His only possessions were a typewriter, a blanket, and a sack of canned food. He had already begun the study of law at Fort Scott, Kansas, but decided to interrupt his studies to participate in the opening.[18] Hoffman staked his claim to a lot near the land office, but a man jumped from one of the trains and rushed up to where Hoffman stood. "Whose lot is this?" he asked. When Hoffman answered, "It's mine, sir," the man said, "Oh, hell, you're nothing but a kid, move on," and sent the youth on his way. Later Hoffman felt justice was served, for a survey placed the lot in the middle of a Guthrie street and no compensation was allowed the man who ejected him.[19]

The graphic phrase of the West, "land office business," described the activity at the little Guthrie land office that had been constructed from boards and shingles shipped into Guthrie just before the opening on April 22. The building's two small rooms and "store front" appearance little suggested the magnitude of its function—the transfer of title of much of the land in present northern Oklahoma from the United States government to private ownership.[20]

Already on the afternoon of the opening day,

hundreds of homestead claimants formed lines before the land office, and young Hoffman saw an opportunity to utilize his knowledge of shorthand and typing. He applied to Registrar John I. Dille and Receiver Cassius M. Barnes for the job of recording testimony which customarily had been taken in long hand in disputed land cases. Hoffman recalled"

I suggested and urged upon the Registrar and Receiver that it would take a tremendous force and also endless time to take the testimony in long hand and unravel the claims of the multitudinous contestants of Guthrie, and that the testimony be taken in shorthand…The lawyers objected, one objection being that no one could read the stenographer's notes except himself and that he might misinterpret; thus they urged that the testimony be written out at the time taken. I then urged permission to take the testimony on typewriter at the government price of 15 cents per hundred words. This method was finally adopted, and I was soon earning $15.00 to $20.00 per day.[21]

An important case recorded by Hoffman was the contest of Frank Gault for land that later became a part of downtown Oklahoma City. When the decision in favor of Gault was announced, his attorney, Frank Dale, told Hoffman, "Roy, I get

Lawyer Roy V. Hoffman, a "flaxen-haired boy" on the day of the "Run," used his stenographic ability in land dispute cases. Later he was a World War I general and prominent state banker. (Courtesy Western History Collections, University of Oklahoma Library.)

half of that land of Frank's as my fee, and I believe I should go down and look it over, it ought to be worth something, for Oklahoma [City] might make a town some day."[22] The success of Frank Dale and other land attorneys may have encouraged Hoffman to continue his law studies, for he became a lawyer four years later.[23]

Six weeks after the settlement of Oklahoma City, a newspaper reported that a "careful, conscientious count" showed 280 different business establishments which included 23 law firms with 42 members.[24] Dan Peery, an 89er pioneer, territorial legislator, and official of the Oklahoma Historical Society, has written, "There must have been more than a hundred lawyers in Oklahoma City a week after the opening. Most of these fellows claimed to be expert land office lawyers and could win your claim for you if you were contested, and if you wanted to file a contest against some other person, they would furnish the evidence and win the claim for you for a little additional consideration." Peery also noticed that there were "shyster" doctors as well as "shyster" lawyers, for no medical degree was required. "A horse doctor from Kansas could practice on human animals here in Oklahoma," so one employed a doctor at his own risk. However, Peery

softened his criticism of the medical and legal professions by adding, "There were good lawyers and skilled physicians who were a credit to their professions."[25]

An election for the important judicial post of police judge in Oklahoma City's provisional government pitted the scholarly A. C. Scott against O. H. "Posey" Violet, a lawyer who had journeyed eastward from California. Scott's academic credentials included degrees from the University of Kansas and the George Washington University Law School. He was described by Dan Peery, however, as "an honorable man and an educated, cultured gentleman" better fitted to be "the president of a female seminary" than police judge.[26]

Violet won the election by a vote of 687 to 586. Scott later was appointed United States Commissioner, and W. F. Harn, Horace Speed, and others kept him busy for the next 18 months binding over defendants accused of committing perjury in their land affidavits.[27] In 1889 Scott was appointed president of what is now Oklahoma State University where he served until 1908.[28]

Police Judge "Posey" Violet was quick to assess fines and jail terms against violators of town ordinances.[29] Dan Peery wrote, "He was not bothered with a conscience…His ear was deaf to the appeals of attorneys and his heart was flint to those who asked for mercy in his court."[30]

One account of the Oklahoma City police court proceedings told of the newly arrived lawyer whose client was to be tried before Judge Violet. The lawyer suspected his client's rights would be better protected elsewhere so he filed a motion for change of venue. Judge Violet informed him no court of similar jurisdiction existed and denied the motion. The determined advocate then filed a motion to appeal. Judge Violet also denied that motion and stressed that his decision was final. "Your honor," said the exasperated attorney, "I must bow in humble submission. I have been practicing law for 20 years but this is the first time I have ever represented a client before the supreme court of the universe."[31]

One of Oklahoma City's first lawyers was Seymour A. Steward, later Oklahoma County's probate (county) judge. Steward had studied for three years at Knox College in Illinois, then read law in a Kankakee, Illinois, office before admission to the Illinois bar. He was 26 years old when he arrived in Oklahoma City on the first train

Anton H. Classen, University of Michigan graduate, homesteaded a claim in Oklahoma Territory and achieved financial success in real estate. (Courtesy OHS.)

from the north on the day of the "Run," put up his tent, and hung a sign, "Attorney-at-Law and Notary Public." His office furniture consisted of two soap boxes—one was his desk the other his chair. Lumber yards and general merchandise stores were especially active, and Steward partially supported himself by submitting credit reports to the Wilbur Mercantile Co. of Chicago and to the predecessor company of Dun & Bradstreet. Prior to his early death at the age of 36, he had became a successful railroad attorney.[32]

One of the best prepared and eventually among the most affluent of early Oklahoma attorneys was Anton H. Classen. As a 25-year-old law student at the University of Michigan, Classen had been intrigued by Western land openings and had written his senior thesis on "How to Obtain Title to Government Lands." Two years later at the opening of the Unassigned Lands, he secured a homestead, then opened a law office in nearby Edmond where he, like so many other lawyers, engaged in the real estate business. He also edited the *Edmond Sun*. President McKinley appointed him Receiver for the Oklahoma City land office in 1897, and he later became successful in the real estate business.[33]

Representative of blacks who sought opportunity in the new land were lawyers like George N.

Perkins, S. H. Scott, and W. H. Harrison. Perkins, a Civil War veteran, migrated from Little Rock, Arkansas. While practicing law and serving as justice of the peace, he found time to edit the *Oklahoma Guide*, Oklahoma Territory's first black newspaper.[34] A black lawyer active in the fight for political control of Oklahoma City shortly after settlement was S. H. Scott. Albert McRill, longtime lawyer and former city manager of Oklahoma City described Scott as "a spellbinder of the first order."[35] W. H. Harrison, a black attorney admitted to the Bar by Territorial Judge B. F. Burwell about 1900, was remembered by Oklahoma City lawyer Albert S. Gilles as "the greatest natural orator I have ever heard."[36]

As a revenue measure Guthrie's provisional government passed an occupation tax ordinance that included a $20 assessment against practicing attorneys. Those who failed to pay were barred from practice in local courts. The ordinance was enforced apparently without difficulty.[37] However, a similar measure in Oklahoma City met opposition when, as Oklahoma City's first historian, who called himself "Bunky," put it, "the lawyers were asked to give up their gold." Judge Violet jailed a few members of the town Bar who refused to pay the tax. He released them after their lawyer friends made a hurried journey to the Muskogee court and obtained a restraining order.[38]

The absence of federal laws against gambling brought a swarm of gamblers to Oklahoma Territory to practice their profession. In Guthrie the city council took steps to fill city coffers by appropriate fines for gambling.[39] The power of the gambling fraternity in early Kingfisher tested the ability of that town's provisional government to enforce the law and brought into prominence Matthew J. Kane, destined in 1909 to be Chief Justice of the Oklahoma Supreme Court. Kane was a native New Yorker who had graduated from Georgetown University in 1887 and went west to Wichita, Kansas, to practice law.[40] The 24-year-old lawyer joined the firm of Carlisle & Carlisle in Wichita, which enjoyed a lucrative practice examining land titles for Eastern and Southern investors in the Wichita land boom. The boom suddenly collapsed, and Kane returned to his former occupation of railway telegraph operator. He worked for a time at Oklahoma Station which

Matthew J. Kane, who settled in Perry, O.T., became the second Chief Justice of the Supreme Court of Oklahoma. (Courtesy Archives and Manuscripts Division, OHS.)

made him one of the first residents of the community that became Oklahoma City.

He returned to the practice of law in Harper, Kansas, a few months before the April 22, 1889, opening of the Unassigned Lands, after which he settled in Kingfisher—as did some 40 other lawyers.[41] A conflict with gamblers, which Matthew Kane called his "most notable case," occurred shortly after he arrived in Kingfisher. He was retained as counsel by an industrious young man whose lot on Robberts Avenue, duly recorded by the provisional town government, was "jumped" by "Uncle" Jimmie Saunders, acknowledged leader of the town's gambling element. Kane brought an ejectment action before provisional Municipal Judge G. J. Keeney. Saunders and his cohorts were well represented by James Morris, a fiery, loud-spoken lawyer.

The case was argued the better part of one day in a small frame shack packed with gamblers. Despite Saunder's threats of bodily harm, Kane and his client refused to be intimidated. The verdict was in Kane's favor, but Saunders erected a tent on the lot and with several of his friends armed with Winchesters rebuffed the town marshal's efforts to remove them. Kane appeared be-

fore Judge Keeney and requested enforcement of the court's order. Unfortunately—as the judge pointed out—the court "was powerless in the premises," for the town had no jail in which to incarcerate lawbreakers. Undaunted, young lawyer Kane took upon himself the duty of building a jail to protect the dignity of the provisional court. He acquired a long stockade already under construction and installed iron bars and padlocks for the doors at his own expense. Then he informed Judge Keeney that the town had a jail

The judge deputized enough citizens to enforce his mandate. Judge Robert L. Williams, who later served on the Oklahoma Supreme Court with Matthew Kane, told how the episode ended: "The defendant, seeing that further resistance was apt to result in very serious consequences, gracefully surrendered, with the consoling and patriotic reflection that it is the duty of all good citizens to yield to the forms of law adopted by the people, no matter how unjustly they may be administered by the people's representatives. This was certainly the first jail established at Kingfisher—and probably the first in the territory of Oklahoma."[42]

Lawyers who had arrived in Oklahoma Territory with great expectations were frustrated not only by the absence of courts for normal law practice but also by the poor economic conditions brought on by the drought-plagued summer of 1889. Disappointed members of the Bar moved on to hoped-for greener pastures, and names prominent in the Territory's public affairs in 1889 and 1890 began to disappear from newspapers and public records. Most of the lawyers who remained represented clients engaged in land "contests"—disputes handled in the local land office which could be appealed to the Commissioner of the General Land Office in Washington, then to the Secretary of the Interior. According to one observer, land litigation "fattened the purses of hundreds of lawyers..."[43] James L Brown, who practiced law in Oklahoma City for more than two decades after the Run of 89, wrote that conditions eventually spawned "more litigation than was ever before known in the United States in the same length of time and over the same amount of land..."[44]

63

12

SUI GENERIS IN OKLAHOMA TERRITORY

Not until May 2, 1890, did Congress approve an Organic Act creating a government for the new Territory of Oklahoma. This Organic Act would serve as the Territory's "Constitution" for the next 17 years. The government thus created was republican in form and embraced the customary three departments—executive, legislative and judicial—with judicial power vested in a supreme court composed of a chief justice and two associate justices. Each justice drew an annual salary of $3000, a sum that exceeded the governor's salary by $400. The three justices were to carve out three judicial districts, and a justice was to reside in each district.

Presiding in both trial and appellate courts, the three justices had "authority for redress of all wrongs committed against the constitution or laws of the United States or of the Territory affecting persons or property." Up to six days at the beginning of each court term were to be devoted to federal cases. The Act adopted a large part of general Nebraska law, but those laws were subject to change by the Territorial legislative assembly.

General statutes of the United States now covered the sale of town lots. From the previous "Unassigned Lands," Congress provided for six counties which by popular vote were later named Payne, Logan, Kingfisher, Oklahoma, Canadian and Cleveland. A seventh county, Beaver, was formed out of what had been known as "No Man's Land," an area never before attached to any state. Beaver County was later divided into Beaver, Texas, and Cimarron counties. All county and township officials were to be appointed by the governor to serve until the first territorial election was held.[1]

To the disappointment of numerous Territorial residents who considered themselves well qualified for the political plums of a new government, President Benjamin Harrison chose eligible adherents of the Republican Party from outside the Territory for all top offices. For governor he selected a one-time practicing lawyer, George Washington Steele, an old friend from the president's home state of Indiana. Steele was a Civil War veteran, 50 years old, who had been elected four times to the United States House of Representatives. He accepted the governorship only on a temporary basis and remained for 17 months—probably three times as long as he expected to serve.[2]

Governor Steele relied on local recommendations for his appointment of county officials. One such appointment involved Frank J. Wikoff, later a successful Oklahoma banker. The governor had visited each of the other counties, and the time came to visit Payne County which had no railroad. Ready to lend assistance was the 23-year-old Wikoff, a recent graduate of law school in Cincinnati who was then city attorney of Stillwater in Payne County. Wikoff went to Guthrie, the Territorial capitol, hired the best carriage he could find, and brought Governor Steele, District Attorney Horace Speed, and Secretary of the Territory Robert Martin back to Stillwater.

Pleasant weather and good transportation helped the officials enjoy the trip, and the governor was ready to listen to young Wikoff's suggestions of names to fill county offices. Wikoff himself wanted to be county attorney, but the governor reminded him that, although the county could begin without a county attorney, it could not function without a county judge. He suggested that Wikoff first accept the latter office, then after the county was officially organized he could be county attorney.

The county judgeship was a position of local prestige, but Wikoff preferred the office of county attorney because, according to the Nebraska law extended to Oklahoma Territory, the county judge would be paid by the fee system. Fees were expected to be small during the county's first years. On the other hand the federal government paid monthly salaries to county attorneys—$90 a month for Payne County. Nevertheless, Wikoff accepted Governor Steele's suggestion and was appointed Payne's first county judge. A short time later he also became Payne's

From The Oklahoma Red Book, I, facing p. 80.

first county attorney after persuading a 27-year-old lawyer from Missouri, Sterling P. King, to move from Guthrie to fill the office of county judge.[3]

Governor Steele was not always as fortunate as he was in his Payne County appointments according to the following account (which one may hope is apocryphal). One aspirant to a county judge-ship could not meet the requirement to have been a lawyer in his home state, so he returned to his former home and arranged a meeting with the local Bar examination committee. The committee must not have been overly concerned with justice in Oklahoma Territory, for, as the story goes, "several kegs of beer" were consumed heartily and continuously," then they happily signed the appropriate documents certifying that their friend was a member of the legal profession. The name of the new judge and the county where he presided remain forever unidentified.[4]

The three justices President Benjamin Harrison selected for the Supreme Court of the Territory of Oklahoma were men well past middle age and of distinguished appearance. From Illinois came Chief Justice Edward B. Green, Associate Justice John G. Clark came from Wisconsin, and Associate Justice Abraham J. Seay was from Missouri. Frank H. Greer, editor of the *Oklahoma State*

Capital at Guthrie was ready with a thumbnail description of the new jurists after a week's observation:[5] "Chief Justice Green: pre-eminently a scholar, unquestionably a fine lawyer and apparently a friend of the masses. [Regarding the portly] Associate Justice Seay: Sufficient and efficient in mind and body. Associate Justice Clark: Logical in thought and routine in habits. Socially of plebeian sympathy. Mentally of patrician mold."

At eleven o'clock on the morning of May 29, 1890, the Territory's long-awaited Supreme Court held its organizational meeting in the court room of United States Commissioner W. M. Allison in Guthrie. Governor George W. Steele administered oaths of office, and the necessary court officials were appointed. The court adjourned after scheduling another session on June 10, 1890, for the admission of attorneys. United States Attorney Horace Speed left on a business trip to Norman the day after the court's organizational meeting. Just before leaving he made a brief announcement: "Our courts are now open and any proceedings which can be taken in the various states and territories can now be taken in Oklahoma Territory."[6]

Members of the bar who had tried to practice law in a land without local courts of competent jurisdiction for almost 13 months could look forward to a new day. Shortly after the first Supreme Court was organized professional advertising cards such as the following appeared in a Guthrie newspaper:[7]

> Practice in all courts and give experience and activity to all business. Overstreet & Flynn.
> Make specialty of Federal court business. Cavanaugh & Neill.

The great interest in land disputes was reflected by two ads. "…Will practice in all the courts of the Territory and before the U. S. Land Office at Guthrie in matters of final proof, contest, etc. Attention will be given to procuring titles to town lots and under the Oklahoma Town Site Laws. Williamson & Sealy." "Contests carefully prepared. We can locate homeseekers on a few choice claims. Rock, Clevinger & Hays."[8]

Territorial lawyers assembled in Guthrie on June 10, 1890, to attend the court session expressly designated for the admission of attorneys. James R. Keaton, who would be appointed to the

James R. Keaton, lawyer, jurist, president of the Oklahoma State Bar Association in 1930. (Courtesy Archives and Manuscripts Division, OHS.)

court six years later, provided an eyewitness account of the event. He described Judge Green as "a dignified, precise, scholarly gentleman..., always late and he never arrived in court on time and he was very slow when he got there." Keaton continued, "Well, the other two judges...opened court... After they got in session one of the two suggested that they didn't believe that they could adjourn that court without all the members being present, so they spent a half day looking at Indian Territory statutes and Nebraska statutes, and one of them says, 'I can find where we have a right to convene, but I don't find anything there where we can adjourn without the entire membership of the court being present,' but they finally did adjourn or took a recess anyway until the Chief Justice arrived."[9]

On that day, 115 lawyers were admitted to practice before the Supreme and District courts of the Territory. Each was required to possess a certificate of admission to practice before the highest court of any state, be in good standing there, and take the following oath: "I do solemnly swear that I will support the constitution of the United States and the Organic Act of the Territory of Oklahoma and that I will faithfully discharge the duties of an attorney and counselor according to the best of my ability, so help me God."[10]

The beleaguered legal profession so long without local government now faced a plethora of legislation. In its first three years the Territory endured three codes of civil procedure and two general revisions of the Territorial law.[11] Congress had provided that statutes adopted from Nebraska would be effective only until "the adjournment of the first session of the legislative assembly of said Territory."[12] When the legislators met in the latter part of 1890 they chose to copy the Indiana code of civil procedure along with a portion of the Dakota General Statutes.[13]

After many of the Territory's best legal minds studied the Indiana code, they concluded it failed adequately to address the Territory's problems.[14] Among those who disliked the code was the Territorial Supreme Court itself, as indicated by the role played in the code's replacement by the court's first clerk, Charles H. Filson. Stillwater's Freeman E. Miller, one of the first lawyers admitted to the Territorial bar, recalled the circumstances surrounding the Legislature's change from the Indiana to the Kansas code.

> Many wanted the Kansas Code...A hard fight followed the effort to adopt it, and the bill to that result was not passed until the last day of the session. It was quite voluminous, and there was no money to pay clerks for its enrollment so Mr. Filson and others procured its enrollment by private hands and without cost to the territory. They were, however, reimbursed by a later legislature.
>
> The bill was not enrolled until late in the night, and at three o'clock in the morning, Mr. Filson, then about 40 years old, wheeled the enrolled copy of the bill down the center aisle of the House Chamber to the Speaker's desk on a wheelbarrow. It was a novel and unusual sight and awoke mighty cheering from the galleries and members of the house as well.[15]

Chief Justice Green became well known for his frequent use of the phrase *sue generis*. In his "Preface" to Volume I of the *Oklahoma Reports* he explained:[16] "Never, before, in the organization of Territorial courts, were the same difficulties encountered as in the organization of the courts of Oklahoma. No other territory was opened to settlement in the same manner; and the conditions which confronted the courts at the very threshold of their work, were absolutely *sui generis*; and the innumerable questions which arose were entirely without precedent."

On one occasion Chief Justice Green blamed

sui generis as a reason for the court's delay in rendering a decision eagerly awaited by Guthrie attorney Harry R. Thurston. When someone asked him just what the Chief Justice meant by that expression, Thurston—who seems to have been the humorist of the Guthrie Bar—replied, "I don't know just what the English is of those two Latin words, but I know the American interpretation for it means he is in a hell of a bad fix."[17]

The newly created Supreme Court lost little time in meeting head on the legal condition "of its own kind" that Chief Justice Green deplored. Horace Speed represented the Territory in the court's first cases and cleared up two important questions of jurisdiction. The first concerned the jurisdiction of County Judge Charles A. Berger of Logan County under Sections 9 and 11 of the Organic Act. A "probate court" for the Territory was created with no mention of a "county court," although the latter court was referred to in certain provisions of the Nebraska code. The Supreme Court held that the probate court was not limited to probate matters but was essentially a "county court" with appropriate probate, civil, and criminal jurisdiction.[18] The second case affirmed the authority of the United States marshal and the United States commissioner to arrest and commit a prisoner accused of violating the Nebraska laws adopted for the Territory. Defense counsel had contended only "local territorial courts and officers" could arrest and commit the prisoner.[19]

Sui generis in Oklahoma Territory was most obvious in connection with land disputes. President Benjamin Harrison's proclamation of March 23, 1889, issued in accord with prior Congressional enactments for the opening of the Oklahoma country, had expressly warned that "no person entering upon and occupying said lands" before 12:00 o'clock noon on April 22, 1889, "will ever be permitted to enter any of said lands or acquire any rights thereto."[20] The phrase "enter upon and occupy" known as the "sooner clause" was, in the words of pioneer lawyer James L. Brown, "The one clause in the law that made more contention, I honestly believe, than any other statute that was ever written on earth."[21]

The clause had a direct effect on the efforts of four different classifications of settlers to acquire title to Oklahoma lands. The first of these was that great body of homesteaders who accepted the warning not to "enter upon and occupy" as meaning what it said and waited impatiently on the border of the Unassigned Lands until the designated time. Another classification consisted of "legal sooners"—railroad, government employees and others who entered under special permit and contended that inasmuch as they were legally within the forbidden territory they could acquire land so long as they did not "enter upon and occupy" until after 12:00 o'clock noon.

A third group established themselves, openly or secretly, prior to the designated time on land adjacent to the tract they desired. Not until 12:00 o'clock noon did they move onto the tract which they later claimed for their homestead. A fourth group relied on stealth and deceit to acquire their land before the prescribed time and held it by perjury—swearing they had complied with the law. It was especially the latter two groups who acquired the epithet of Sooners, having arrived "sooner" than the law had allowed.

The so-called "legal sooners" who settled on the choice lots in Oklahoma City quickly became objects of protest. A leader in the fight against legal sooners was the belligerent James L. Brown, a former Iowan and scourge of bootleggers while a county attorney in Kansas. Brown arrived in Oklahoma City one day after the Run and began the practice of law, always ready to speak out for what he believed was right. A month after his arrival Brown submitted a petition to the Secretary of the Interior inquiring as to the propriety of railroad and government employees acquiring title under the Homestead Act.[22]

More then 16 months later Secretary John W. Noble rendered his "doctrine of advantage" decision holding that a government employee who had resided in the Oklahoma District for five years and who had settled on a tract of land in Kingfisher eight minutes after the official opening could not take advantage of his position to the detriment of other homeseekers. However, Secretary Noble's opinion stated, "Each case must be determined upon its own merits and evidence."[23]

It remained for the United States Supreme Court to hand down a far-reaching "legal sooner" decision in the case *Alexander F. Smith, Appt.,* v. *Eddy B. Townsend*. Smith, a long-time railroad employee, had lived in a tent on railroad right-of-way in the vicinity of Edmond prior to April 22, 1889, and shortly after noon on that day had moved his tent about 150 yards to public land which he claimed for his homestead.

Abraham J. Seay, governor of Oklahoma Territory at the time, urged prompt disposition of the Smith-Townsend case in the belief that a Supreme Court ruling would "be the direct means of affecting settlement of ninety percent of all contest litigation over homestead claims in Oklahoma Territory." The Oklahoma Territorial Supreme Court considered the pending decision of such importance that in early 1893 it announced no opinions on Sooner cases would be rendered until the United States Supreme Court had passed on the "sooner question."[24]

In holding against Smith, the Supreme Court ruled that the phrase "enter upon and occupy" must be construed in the ordinary sense and left no doubt that any person who had acquired an unfair advantage by being in the Oklahoma District prior to noon on April 22, 1889, should be disqualified for homestead entry.[25]

Having resolved the "legal sooner" question, the courts now confronted the problem of perjury by the Sooners who had formed combinations and organizations to prove they had been outside the Oklahoma country at the appointed time.[26] Among these were: the Crutcho group, organized by members who had settled on rich land along the Crutcho tributary of the North Canadian River; the Lightning Creek Combination, whose land was in present-day Capitol Hill in south Oklahoma City; and the Bohemian Outfit, made up of naturalized citizens of the Mustang community.

These organizations had coached their witnesses thoroughly at regular meetings in order to support the whereabouts and actions of all members before, on, and after April 22, 1889. Men who under other circumstances would have objected to swearing falsely found solace in the erroneous opinions of a few lawyers that oaths required by the Land Office were not subject to the perjury statutes.[27] Others stretched the truth to rationalize their conduct. One group, for example, pleaded that at noon they were at the border of the Pottawatomie Indian reservation 15 miles east of Oklahoma City, usually referred to as the "Pott line." These "moonshiners", as they were known before the shorter and more inclusive "Sooner" appellation was applied, considered "Pott line" to be a camp in the woods several miles

inside the designated boundary where they had hung a cooking pot.[28]

One lawyer who dispensed an erroneous interpretation of the "enter upon and occupy" phrase was the distinguished General James B. Weaver. He had been a Greenback Party candidate for president of the United States in 1880 and in 1892 had received more than a million votes as the Populist candidate for that office. While an Iowa congressman, he had been an aggressive sponsor of opening the Unassigned Lands. When he arrived in the border camps a few days before the official opening, he drew large audiences whenever he chose to speak. Weaver insisted that as long as an individual did not "enter" as well as "occupy" the same piece of ground before the designated time he would not violate the law. He advised that a simple way around the prohibition was for a settler to arrive early on one claim then exchange it for the claim of another early settler. Relying on Weaver's advice, combinations of 50 to a 100 land seekers entered the country early. When the courts struck down Weaver's theory, the individuals—already bound together by a technical "loophole"—relied on perjury to support and protect their claims.[29]

Charles Colcord, sheriff of Oklahoma County, learned of another rationalization for perjury on one occasion when he took a carload of men convicted of that charge to jail in Guthrie. Colcord observed that most of the perjurers hailed from Butler and Chautauqua Counties in Kansas and asked, "What the devil is the matter with you Kansas fellows anyhow?" A prisoner replied, "I can tell you—that damned prohibition." He explained that in the 10 years that the sale of intoxicating liquor had been prohibited in Kansas, patrons of local bootleggers had formed the habit of lying when called on to testify against bootleggers. "Consequently," the prisoner told Colcord, "it got to where we did not regard an oath as anything. That prohibition law is the cause of my having these chains on today."[30]

In January of 1891 the first grand jury for the federal government indicted 75 individuals in the Territorial court for perjury before Judge John G. Clark in Oklahoma City. United States Attorney Horace Speed headed the prosecution, assisted by Special Agent John W. Scothorn, Assistant United States Attorney John F. Stone, and W. F. Harn.[31] Harn had only recently arrived

W.F. Harn, assigned to Oklahoma Territory to investigate perjury cases for the Department of the Interior, remained and acquired wealth through prudent real estate investments. (Courtesy The Daily Oklahoman.)

in Oklahoma Territory to undertake perjury investigations as a special agent for the Department of Interior. A graduate of the College of Wooster in Ohio, he had read law under private tutors and passed the Ohio Bar examination in 1881. He practiced law in that state although he was best known as a newspaper editor. His decision to settle in Oklahoma proved financially profitable. In later years the large fees earned in his law practice provided funds for real estate holdings that made his name appear frequently in Oklahoma City land records.[32]

For a year after his arrival in Oklahoma City Harn conducted secret investigations and obtained testimony to assist United States Attorney Speed in trying several hundred perjury cases.[33] The first trials required as much as four weeks for completion, with a day and night schedule characterized by vigorous prosecution and equally vigorous arguments by defense counsel. Threats

of assassinations were not unusual. A conspiracy to dynamite the courthouse and thereby dispose of Judge Clark, Speed, and Harn at the same time was discovered and barely averted in time. Agent Harn was a preferred target. On one occasion he narrowly escaped serious injury when alert action by a deputy United States marshal blocked an attempt by a defendant's son-in-law to plunge a knife in Harn's back as he left the courtroom. Another catastrophe was avoided when a bomb thrown under Harn's residence failed to explode.[34]

Conviction followed conviction, and the well-planned schemes of the various Sooner organizations began to crumble. Many defendants chose to flee the Territory either before indictment or after making bond. Some turned state's evidence and received leniency. One morning before Judge Clark, 11 defendants in rapid succession changed their previous pleas to "guilty as charged."[35] The "Bohemian Outfit" led by "Captain" Anton Caha was one of the most successful and highly publicized combines. According to W. F. Harn that organization finally made the mistake of exchanging witnesses with similar American combines, then when the testimony of certain American witnesses was shown to be tainted with perjury the cunning and "abundantly corroborated" testimony of the "Bohemian Outfit" was easily overcome. More than a hundred witnesses for the government helped the prosecution obtain conviction of 15 defendants in three days. They received sentences of one to four years at the penitentiary at Leavenworth, Kansas.[36]

Following convictions of the "Bohemian Outfit" the crime of "Sooner" perjury declined. Twenty years later, however, W. F. Harn noted that the government had not been totally successful in thwarting the claims of all Sooners. "There are instances where valuable claims were held by 'sooners'," he observed, "and all efforts to dislodge them proved of no avail."[37]

13

THE BENCH IN WESTERN OKLAHOMA TERRITORY

Abraham Jefferson Seay, 57 years old when appointed an associate justice, was to serve two years before becoming the second governor of Oklahoma Territory. Seay, more than six feet tall, had a problem of excessive weight and was handicapped as a public speaker by a high, falsetto voice. Nonetheless, his sense of humor and pleasant personality made him a popular trial judge and political figure. He was a 21-year-old farm boy when he arranged to work his way through an academy in Steelville, Missouri. He taught school, studied law, and at age 28 was admitted to the Missouri Bar just before the outbreak of the Civil War. He served four years with the Union forces and attained the rank of lieutenant colonel before returning to practice law at Union, Missouri. He had served a six-year term as circuit judge before his wartime friend, Secretary of the Interior John W. Noble, helped him gain the post of associate justice.[1]

All three justices received identical salaries, but Seay had hoped for the honor of being the first chief justice of the Supreme Court of Oklahoma. When he learned that President Harrison had picked Green to be chief justice, Seay reflected, "Well, after all the only advantage there is in being Chief Justice is the privilege of sitting in the middle upon the bench."[2]

At the first meeting of the Supreme Court the justices divided Oklahoma Territory into the three districts required by the Organic Act. Chief Justice Green held court for the first district at Guthrie and Stillwater, and the justices also convened in Guthrie for all appellate cases. Justice Seay in the second district held court at Kingfisher, El Reno, and Beaver City, while Justice Clark in the third district held court at Oklahoma City and Norman.[3]

The three justices were expected to convene court at least once a year at each location, so Justice Seay faced the greatest travel problem. The court term at Beaver, for example, required him to choose one of two routes from his headquarters at Kingfisher: (1) Take the train to Wichita,

then to Englewood, Kansas, and from there ride a stagecoach the remaining 50 miles, making a total trip of 300 miles from Kingfisher, or (2) Travel overland by wagon along the North Canadian River to Camp Supply, then along Beaver Creek to Beaver, a distance of 200 miles.[4]

Having resided in nearby Missouri, Seay may have been better fitted than the other two justices for the post of trial judge in that broad area that was to become known as Oklahoma's "short grass country," an area populated by "lawless and turbulent characters, government troops, cattlemen, Cheyenne and Arapaho Indians and United States Indian agencies."[5]

The Territorial courts had both original and appellate jurisdiction, and in the words of Justice Seay, they were "short on libraries and long on jurisdiction." However, according to Seay, "While our work was not perfect, it gave confidence, encouragement and support to the lawabiding people of the territory. Mine was known as a 'shotgun court' on account of my bluntness in rulings and decisions…"[6]

When Judge Seay and his successors traveled the broad "short grass country," an entourage of court officials accompanied them in hacks, buggies, wagons, or on horseback in an event which was both an excursion and a hunting trip. In addition to the clerk and stenographer, deputy United States marshals went along to take care of paying bills, serving summons and subpoenas, and making arrests. The marshals had charge of jury and witnesses during the first portion of the court term, which was devoted to United States business. The sheriff assumed those duties when cases of a local nature were tried. The same jurors sat for both federal and territorial courts.

Many respected lawyers joined the court party. Some already had clients along the way or had been retained to assist local county seat attorneys. Others were present to offer their services to anyone when the need arose. A "traveling court" of 27 people made the overland trip to hold the first term of court at Beaver. They feasted on deer,

Abraham J. Seay, Associate Justice of the Territorial Supreme Court and second governor of Oklahoma Territory. (Courtesy Western History Collections, University of Oklahoma Library.)

wild turkey, prairie chicken, and even an eight-pound black bass which the 360-pound deputy marshal, B. F. "Fatty" Smith, shot as it swam in a water hole near Woodward.[7]

When the party reached Fort Supply, the portly Judge Seay—tired of sleeping on hard ground—called on the fort's commanding officer, a colonel. Seay expected he would be invited to spend the night in a comfortable bed; however, as related by Cash Cade, "The colonel paid no more attention to a United States judge than to a common citizen." After the judge saw that the hoped-for invitation was not to be forthcoming, he took his leave with the parting words, "Good evening, Colonel—I used to wear the Eagle, but I earned mine by fighting with Black-Jack." After that reference to his Civil War career with General John A. Logan, the judge returned to his party to sleep on the ground. Liquid refreshments were available at the army canteen, and the judge told his friend, lawyer Robert C. Palmer of Kingfisher, "If you will buy some liquor and beer, the ground will feel like downy pillows." Whether the judge and friends slept on "downy pillows" the remainder of the night is not recorded.[8] Usually it was the assignment of the United States marshals to purchase food and supplies for traveling court officials. Marshal Chris Madsen once submitted

to Judge Seay for approval a bill for bread, $2.00; whiskey, $26.00. Judge Seay's reaction: "Why do they want so much bread?"[9]

The judges throughout Oklahoma Territory found that settlers on the quarter-section farms generally were law abiding although on occasion a dispute over land ended in bloodshed. In the villages, however, operators of gambling houses and unlicensed saloons sometimes tried to exercise undue influence on juries. At one term of Judge Seay's court a 12-man jury deliberated for several hours but could not agree on the guilt of the keeper of a gambling and bawdy house. In Seay's opinion the evidence proved him guilty "beyond a reasonable doubt." Seay finally withdrew all prior instructions and informed the jury the only question was "whether the defendant kept the house as charged." Another three hours passed and the jury asked for supper. Seay told them they would get no food until they reached a verdict. The judge then learned that one member of the jury, "a red-nosed man of some prominence in the town," had "hung" the jury by insisting the judge's instructions were erroneous.

According to Judge Seay, "I told him I declared the law; that the jury found the facts; that if he knew the law better than the court he should serve his friend as a lawyer and not as a juror. He was then discharged and the sheriff was instructed never to bring him into court again as a juror." During that court term Judge Seay encountered no further problem with suspicious "hung" juries, and several alarmed defendants even came forward and freely admitted their guilt.[10]

When George W. Steele resigned as governor of the Territory in 1891, Judge Seay—popular as a friend of the people and as a hard-working judge known for speedy trials and just verdicts—was mentioned immediately for the governorship. Political pressure on President Harrison demanded appointment of a "home man", and in the minds of most, Judge Seay after 18 months in the Territory was no longer a "carpetbagger." Two other candidates—both lawyers—were Acting Governor Robert Martin and Oklahoma City's Angelo C. Scott, but the president finally chose Seay upon the recommendations of such Republicans as Chief Justice Green and Secretary of Interior Noble.[11]

Matthew Kane, one of Seay's good friends from

his home town of Kingfisher, was on his feet pleading the case of *Kelly v. Courter* (1 Okla. 277) before the Supreme Court on January 5, 1892, when Guthrie attorney Henry E. Asp approached the Bench with telegraphed notification of Seay's new post. The appointment was expected so Kane guessed the contents of the telegram when Asp handed it to Seay. Kane recalled that Seay read it "without perceptible change of countenance" and passed it on to the other two justices. They too "read it with due judicial deliberation and seriousness…, exchanged faint congratulatory smiles and the regular business of the court was resumed."[12] Counselor Kane was proud to deem himself a participant—albeit a silent one—in that brief historical episode. The event would have been even more pleasant for Kane, he remembered, had the justices not proceeded to reverse the judgment Judge Seay had awarded him in trial court.[13]

The Democratic administration of President Grover Cleveland replaced Governor Seay with William C. Renfrow 15 months later, and the ex-governor returned to Kingfisher. Despite poor health he acquired wealth through banking, real estate, and mining investments. Dependent on crutches and wheel chair, he was staying at a San Francisco hotel at the time of the disastrous earthquake of 1906 but escaped injury and lived to the age of 83.[14]

Once Justice Seay's appointment to the governorship was assured, Republicans jousted for the vacated seat on the Territorial supreme court. President Harrison first offered it to Warren G. Sayre of Indiana, who declined it apparently because of the Territory's reported preference for a "home man."[15] His refusal cleared the way for the appointment of John H. Burford, then register of the land office at Oklahoma City.[16]

Burford was a graduate in law from the University of Indiana in 1874 at age 22.[17] For 14 years, a part of the time as prosecuting attorney, he had practiced law interspersed with politics. In 1889 36-year-old Burford contemplated the imminent settlement of the Unassigned Lands after the presidential victory of fellow Indianan Benjamin Harrison and decided his career should take a new direction. In his letter of March 13 to the president, he mentioned several positions he was interested in, including a Territorial judgeship. "I have made many personal sacrifices in the

John H. Burford, University of Indiana law graduate, for many years a popular Territory and state jurist and lawyer. (Courtesy OHS.)

past four years in politics to the detriment of my private business, and want to get back some of my losses," Burford informed the president.[18] But the best position available at the time was that of probate judge of Beaver County, an office to which Governor Steele appointed him in June of 1890.[19] His term as probate judge was brief, for on September 1, 1890, he accepted the office of register of the land office opened at Oklahoma City.[20] Eighteen months later he was promoted to the Territorial supreme court.[21]

Cowmen in the former No Man's Land saw little need for law and order at the time Judge Burford traveled to Beaver County to conduct his first term of court there. However, conditions were such that the new judge thought it advisable for everyone in the courtroom, except authorized officials, to surrender the guns they customarily carried. The court clerk issued receipts, and everyone could claim his property after court was adjourned.[22] The only place available for court to be held was over a saloon, and the customers of that establishment began to disturb court proceedings by their loud objections to the judge's ruling against guns in the courtroom. Burford was fortunate to have with him the legendary Deputy United States Marshal Chris Madsen, a Danish army veteran who was one of the Territory's famed deputy marshals called the "Three

Chris Madsen, Deputy United States Marshal, was Judge John C. Tarsney's "posse." (Courtesy OHS.)

Guardsmen." The judge sent Madsen downstairs to quell the disturbance. A few minutes later Madsen returned with the three principal troublemakers. "Judge, the rebellion is over!" he announced. He had subdued the three after pistol whipping two of them and shooting the other in the hand.[23]

Perhaps that episode in Judge Burford's first visit to Beaver initiated the respect that was said to have placed him "next to God" in Beaver County. He often traveled with a military escort. According to one veteran attorney, "They shined their shoes and changed their shirts when Judge Burford came to town."[24]

The annoyance and discomfort of service as a circuit-riding judge could have its lighter side as indicated in a story told by Judge Burford. He had arrived at a county seat town for a term of court after a dusty 20-mile ride on a cow pony in the scorching heat of the western Oklahoma sun. The defendant in the first case on the docket was accused of stealing a bathtub from Fort Supply, recently vacated by the military. Throughout the testimony Judge Burford's mind wandered as he pictured the stolen bathtub, remembered his hot, dusty ride, and thought about how much he longed to soak in cool water of the tub that awaited him at his home in Guthrie. Then, in the words of Judge Burford:

At last it came time to pass judgment and I made a speech beginning with the old phrase "Cleanliness is next to Godliness." I gave a long dissertation on bathing, on the Romans' love of the bath, on the fact that bathtubs were the mark of progress. All the while I was talking I kept noticing that the prosecution had a peculiar look on his face, that he was uneasy and looked as if he wished to interrupt me but I attributed it to the fact that he saw he was going to lose his case. At length, almost out of breath from enthusiasm on my subject I paused—the prosecution rose.

"Your Honor," he asked permission to speak. Reluctantly I granted it. "Your Honor, may it please the court, this man did not steal the bathtub to bathe in. He has no passion for cleanliness. He's using it for a horse trough."[25]

On April 19, 1892, a presidential proclamation opened 3 million acres in the Cheyenne-Araphoe country and allowed 25,000 people to rush for homesteads. Six more counties were added to Oklahoma Territory: Blaine, Dewey, Day, Roger Mills, Custer, and Washita. Day County existed only until Oklahoma's Statehood when the Constitutional Convention made it a part of Ellis and Roger Mills counties. Ioland was originally designated the county seat of that sparsely populated county, but most of the county officials appointed by Governor Seay lived near the village of Grand about 16 miles west of Ioland.

County Commissioners George Hastings, John Webb, and A. Blackstone and their constituents came to the conclusion that the water at Ioland was "bad," and that the location of the county seat was generally unsatisfactory to most of the county's inhabitants.[26] The term of court set at Ioland for November 7, 1893, was probably for the primary purpose of soliciting court approval of a plan to move the county seat to Grand. A shanty courthouse had been constructed at Ioland. Close to midnight on November 7, 1893, County Clerk H. I. Walck, who slept in his office there, was awakened by a pounding on the door. Walck answered, and a stranger asked where he could find a place to spend the night. In a foul mood from being awakened, Walck told him, "There is 160 acres of land round about the town for you to sleep on and that should be enough." The county clerk was embarrassed to learn that the late callers were Judge Burford and the court party, and he invited them in to spend the night on the court-house floor.

Just before retiring, Judge Burford remembered that the term of court was scheduled to begin that day, so he went through the formality of convening and adjourning court in order not to forfeit that term for Day County.[27] Most of the cases on the docket dealt with charges filed by United States marshals for illegal timber cutting and the fencing of government land. Trial of the defendants was set to begin November 9, so when the judge convened court on November 8 he found no business to be conducted that day. Court was adjourned, and Burford accepted County Clerk Walck's invitation to take part in a hunt in the "rough, wild country" northeast of Ioland.[28]

Once as they sat down to rest during the hunt, Walck asked the judge, "What would you do with such a country if you owned it." Perhaps the burden of traveling and holding court in a somewhat primitive environment influenced Burford's retort, "I would turn it into a cow pasture."[29]

By evening the defendants docketed for trial the next day began to arrive with their friends and entertainment seekers. The next morning the flat country around Ioland was covered with saddle horses, buckboards, "cow-camp chuck wagons," and a motley frontier assembly whose "Winchesters and 45's bristled."[30] The small courtroom could accommodate scarcely more than the court officials and parties involved in each case, so all other litigants waited outside for their turn. First on the docket was a cowman from Antelope Hills. He pleaded guilty both to cutting timber illegally and to fencing government land. Burford's leniency in that case—one dollar fine plus costs for the timber cutting and dismissal of the fencing charges—prompted all other defendants except one to plead guilty and receive similar mild punishment. County Clerk Walck observed that the judge's leniency may have stemmed from the opinion he expressed the previous day that the land was fit only for a "cow pasture."[31] Judge Burford ordered commitment papers to be drafted for the one defendant who refused to plead guilty. However, the judge had to set that defendant free also, for the county had no jail.[32]

Supporters of removal of the county seat from Ioland to Grand then submitted a petition in favor of removal signed by 30 registered voters—

Charles Swindall, Justice of the Supreme Court and district judge, derived practice expeperience in the rugged frontier law of western Oklahoma Territory. (Courtesy Archives and Manuscripts Division, OHS.)

only two less than the number who had voted in the last general election. Judge Burford explained that the court had no authority to permit removal of the county seat but on the strength of the petition, he said, "I'd just move." That was all the encouragement the county officials needed.[33] Oddly, the Ioland courthouse burned only two or three days after Burford's pronouncement, but not before all county records and equipment had been hauled to Grand in a lumber wagon pulled by a span of mules. A tent 18 x 28 feet furnished by County Clerk Walck served as a courthouse in Grand until a small wooden structure was built a few months later.[34]

When a vacancy occurred in the county attorney post at Grand in 1898, Charles Swindall, a young lawyer just out of Cumberland University, was appointed. That office had its hazards according to an account of one Swindall experience told by pioneer newspaperman Frank Smith of the Day County *Tribune*. Swindall was in his office in the frame courthouse one day when

Two tough citizens who faced a criminal charge in that county became offended and decided they did not like the way Charley [Swindall] parted his hair or something. They called upon him one day and started in to give him a sound thrashing. During the wild melee the stove was knocked down, the desk overturned and chairs smashed, but when the fracas was over interested and kind-hearted citizens came in, threw water in the two men's faces, gave them a little shot of hard liquor, and finally revived them so that they could mount their horses and hit the trail for home.[35]

Sturdy young lawyer Charles Swindall was later to become prominent in his profession, serving as a district judge from 1924 to 1929 and as a justice of the State Supreme Court from 1929 to 1935.[36] While district judge he received national attention for the severity of his sentences. In one case, later reversed, he decreed death in the electric chair for a participant in a bank robbery in which no shots were fired and no one was injured.[37]

In late 1893 Congress attempted to alleviate the caseload in western Oklahoma Territory by authorizing two more justices for the Territorial court. One appointment went to A. G. C. Bierer of Guthrie, who as a former resident of Garden City, Kansas, was already acquainted with Western customs. Less adapted to the rustic environment was the other new judge, John L. McAtee of Maryland.[38] Judge McAtee was to hold court twice a year in Grand, a community whose business district consisted of little more than a small, wooden courthouse, two stores, and two saloons.[39]

He was in the midst of a court session one afternoon at a time when one Duffy, a saloon keeper, imbibed too much of his own stock in trade. Duffy could not restrain his exuberance within the thin walls of his saloon, and the noise began to disturb McAtee's court a short distance down the street. The judge instructed the sheriff to arrest Duffy. Because Grand had no jail, he ordered the sheriff to keep Duffy at least a thousand feet away from the court until he sobered up. Duffy, handcuffed, was taken to the river bottom outside of town and chained to a tree where he spent the night. Brought before Judge McAtee the next day, he begged for a drink "to sober up on." The jurist finally sent him back to his saloon after an appropriate reprimand.[40]

After a few months of holding court in Western Oklahoma Territory, McAtee was so disenchanted with the primitive conditions and customs in that area that he asked for reassignment to counties farther east "for his comfort and feeling of personal security." In June of 1895 Judges Burford and Bierer accepted a re-arrangement

that left them with the western counties and assigned only Grant, Garfield, and Kingfisher to McAtee.[41] In the eight years he served as associate justice McAtee became known as something of a "czar" on a bench which was regarded as the "most autocratic on the circuit" by lawyers from outside Oklahoma Territory.[42]

He was indeed capable of unorthodox court behavior according to an account of the King-fisher trial of an alleged outlaw defended by Joe Wisby of Guthrie and prosecuted by Assistant District Attorney Thomas F. McMechan. Perhaps some political hostility existed between Wisby, well known in the Territory as a leader of the Democrats, and McMechan, an appointee of a Republican administration. In any event Wisby was a formidable adversary for McMechan, a former criminal lawyer in Illinois and Kansas and recently a prosecuting attorney in Oklahoma County. In the course of their courtroom combat they became increasingly personal in their arguments. Their animosity finally disturbed Judge McAtee to the extent that he turned to the clerk and declared, "A recess of this court is hereby ordered for fifteen minutes and the marshal is ordered to clear the space in this courtroom in front of the judge's desk in order that Tom McMechan, representing the United States government, and Joe Wisby, representing [the accused], may settle their differences." Judge McAtee may have attained his objective—the proposed fist fight did not occur; instead, the attorneys discussed their differences, shook hands, and the trial continued without further reference to personal shortcomings.[43]

The Democratic administration in the White House in 1896 decided good politics required replacement of Republican John H. Burford. Burford was off the bench less than two years, however, for in 1898 he was reappointed as Chief Justice, an office he retained until Statehood. During the period that Burford practiced law (from 1907 until his death in 1922) he served a term as president of the Oklahoma State Bar Association in 1911 and was a state senator from 1913 to 1917.[44] In 1914 as Republican nominee for the United States senate, he was defeated by Thomas P. Gore.[45]

To succeed Judge Burford in 1896, President Grover Cleveland selected John C. Tarsney, a Kansas City attorney and former congressman.

Cheyenne in the 1890s was perhaps typical of most of the court towns assigned to Territorial judges. (Courtesy OHS.)

Judge Tarsney had been on the bench about two and a half years at the time the *El Reno News* commented, "Judge Tarsney can imitate a cyclone before a grand jury better than any other man in Oklahoma."[46] The "cyclone" judge was remembered by E. E. Blake, an El Reno lawyer and one of the Oklahoma Bar's best story tellers, for his "slashing eyes" and "voluminous double chin."[47] Blake told of a court term in Washita County in the late 1890s when Judge Tarsney and his court party, dissatisfied with whatever hotel accommodations were available, were camping outside Cloud Chief, the county seat. A group of cowboys visited Cloud Chief one evening and caused considerable damage by "shooting up" the town during a drunken escapade.

Judge Tarsney instructed Deputy Marshal Chris Madsen to "take a posse and bring in those fellows." The deputy mounted his horse and prepared to gallop off. "Here," called the judge, "I told you to take a posse."

"I'm the posse. I git 'em," the deputy replied.

The next morning when court convened, Madsen had three cowboys ready for trial. The first cowboy took the stand, and the judge delivered his sternest lecture, "drew his chin down into its double," and assessed a sizeable fine. The cowboy quietly walked over to the clerk's desk, paid the fine, and was discharged. Out of the judge's hearing, he confided, "That damned old son of a gun can't pull his laprobe up over his face and scare me any."[48]

Judge Tarsney could have his tolerant moments, as demonstrated during a murder trial in Watonga. E. E. Blake remembered that the defendant's counsel, "a very noted lawyer" (probably Temple Houston), had too much to drink during the noon recess. He returned to the courtroom shortly before the appointed time, laid his head on the attorneys' table, and fell asleep. When court convened, the attempts to awaken him were unsuccessful. Judge Tarsney looked gravely at the attorneys seated before him and asked, "Gentlemen of the bar, what shall we do with him?"

Enid's Scott Denton, one-time Oklahoma Territory Bar president, arose slowly from his chair to the full height of his six feet and addressed the court: "I move the court order him poured back into the bottle."

"It is so ordered," Judge Tarsney declared.[49]

Tarsney, like his predecessor, Judge Burford, was uncomfortable in some of the county seat towns where most of the citizens carried firearms openly. When he arrived in Cheyenne in the fall of 1897, he issued an order forbidding carrying weapons on the streets during that term of court. On September 29, 1897, after court had been adjourned for the day, Judge Tarsney and County Attorney J. W. McMurtry sat visiting in front of the latter's office, which was across the street from a busy saloon.

Suddenly two men, Noy Aikins and one Johnson, argued in front of the saloon and began to fight. Johnson, the stronger of the two, was getting the best of Aikins when Bud Powers, a cattleman, emerged from the saloon and took advantage of "an opportunity to impress the judge." He used his pistol to break Aikins' nose and gave Johnson a severe beating. Rather than being impressed, Judge Tarsney was appalled. He ordered Powers arrested at once. The next morning he fined Powers $300 and ordered him jailed until the fine was paid. The judge noted that Powers could have been sent "hundreds of feet under ground to dig coal for years," but that fights occurred almost daily in the county and that Powers by "education and environment" had been taught "there is no law or that the arm of the law was powerless to protect itself." A Roger Mills County historian has recorded this incident as one that "threw a chill into pistol toting in Roger Mills County that has lasted down to the present day."[50]

One of western Oklahoma's most respected

Thomas Allison Edwards, lawyer and historian, provided eyewitness accounts of law practice in western Oklahoma. (Courtesy Archives and Manuscripts Division, OHS.)

lawyers—Thomas A. Edwards—was admitted to the practice of law by Judge Tarsney and retained a vivid recollection of the judge and a Bar examination which took place at a time when the Territorial judges made their own rules. The 24-year-old Edwards arrived in Washita County to teach school in March of 1898. He had taken some pre-law work at the University of Arkansas and had studied law in his spare time while teaching school in Arkansas. At a salary of $25 a month he taught at the Rainy and Little Hope schools for a few months, then located in Cloud Chief where he was fortunate enough to obtain shelter in a dugout—rent free.[51]

With a sparse library which included Blackstone's *Commentaries* and *Greenleaf on Evidence*, he isolated himself to prepare for the Bar examination. A large portion of Northwest Washita County was unsettled, and homeseekers were arriving regularly to establish claim to the land that was still available. They needed help in making homestead applications, and Edwards soon learned to prepare the necessary forms at the customary fee of one dollar per application.[52]

He felt ready to take the bar examination in September of 1898 after a period of study interrupted by a three-week bout with smallpox. Borrowing a horse and buggy, he set out on the three-

day round trip northwest to Cheyenne, one of the most remote sections of Oklahoma Territory, where Judge Tarsney was scheduled to hold a term of court.[53] A substantial part of the route was little more than a trail over canyons and across streams, and he had to spend much of the time determining where to cross. He camped on the prairie near what is now Elk City and had a satisfactory night's sleep after using his Colt pistol to frighten a pack of coyotes away. About noon the next day he arrived in Cheyenne.[54]

I went to the courthouse and entered an upstairs hall where court was in session. John C. Tarsney, a man of fine legal attainments and a most courteous gentleman, was presiding. A total stranger, I worked my way down the crowded aisle to the rail around the space reserved for lawyers and litigants. There I spoke to a lawyer who was not engaged, and told him I wanted to be examined for admission to the bar, and asked him to call my request to the attention of the Judge. In a few minutes, when there was a lull, he did so. Soon the Judge announced a recess until afternoon; then stated that he was informed an applicant for admission to the bar was present. He asked me to come forward. I approached the bench, and the Judge asked me a few formal questions, as to my age, place of residence, education, and the extent of my legal study. He said that he would appoint Mr. Temple Houston, of Woodward, Mr. C. O. Blake, of El Reno, and Judge McMurtry, of the local Bar, as a committee to examine; that the committee could use the court room as soon as those present had passed out."[55]

When only a few persons were left, a tall, rugged faced man came over to me, held out his hand, and said, "I am Temple Houston. This is Mr. Blake, and this is Judge McMurtry." We exchanged greetings, and conversed briefly. Houston then said, "Let's get through with this examination, I've got to get something to eat." He had remained standing—he then turned to me and asked abruptly: "What's the Rule in Shelly's Case?" I had been pouring over Blackstone for several years, and knew it almost by heart. That one was easy to state, but is considered really difficult to explain. My answer, in substance, gave the rule as announced by Lord Coke a long time ago. "Is that right, Blake?" Houston inquired. "Yes, I believe it is," Blake answered. "Well, that's all I want to know," said Houston, "I've been hearing of that damn rule all my life. I don't know yet what it is, and I don't know what that answer means, but if Blake says it's right, it is. I recommend we report this candidate for the Bar as well learned in the law and qualified for admission. Blake, you draw up the report. Let's go."[56]

When court reconvened, it developed that there was nothing more for trial that day. The judge said, "Gentlemen, the committee has recommended Mr. Edwards for admission. He will come forward." I did so, and was directed to take the witness chair. The Judge, I am sure, winked at the members of the bar as he announced that there were no matters requiring the attention of the court, so all the members of the bar present were added to the examining committee, and would further examine the applicant. They gleefully proceeded to do so. Each lawyer present had his favorite subject. If any had a question on which he was uncertain, he proceeded to recite the facts, and then asked for a statement of the law and the proper procedure. Among those present was John B. Harrison, much later, and for a long time, a member of the state Supreme Court and a Chief Justice. Also present, was Charles Swindall, who, himself, had been admitted to the bar only six months earlier. Later, he was a District Judge, and then a member of the Supreme Court. I was much relieved when this was over. Judge Tarsney smilingly informed me that the examination was satisfactory.[57]

Edwards returned to Cloud Chief and opened a law office. A little more than a month later he must have considered reentering the teaching profession when he wrote in his diary, "I am sitting in my office most of the time now, with a strong inclination to become discouraged at the present prospects."[58] Elected county attorney the next year, he moved to the new county seat of Cordell. In addition to his career as a practicing lawyer, before his retirement in 1945, he served 10 years as a district judge and 12 years on the Oklahoma Criminal Court of Appeals.[59]

If Temple Houston, son of the great Sam Houston of Texas and Western Oklahoma Territory's most famous trial lawyer, seemed to approach his duties as a member of the Edwards examining committee somewhat casually, he was even more so on a similar occasion related by Editor Dick Mitchell of the *Arapaho Bee*. Houston and his committee of Bar examiners had utilized the back room of a saloon for an all-night "examining" session of an applicant of questionable qualifications. The next morning Houston reported to the court that the committee had found the applicant "thoroughly qualified," although as Editor Mitchell pointed out, Houston failed to say what he was qualified for. Someone asked Houston how he could possibly recommend such an illiterate individual for the practice of law. Houston replied, "That fellow will make business for the rest of us lawyers. He'll get 'em into trouble and it will take a good lawyer to get 'em out."[60]

In February of 1899 President McKinley replaced Judge Tarsney with Clinton F. Irwin of Elgin, Illinois.[61] Judge Irwin was to remain on the Territorial bench until Oklahoma's Statehood, but he must have had second thoughts about his new post after his first visit to Cloud Chief, then the county seat of Washita County. He had been in the Territory only a few days when he notified the Washita County sheriff to prepare for a term of court in Cloud Chief for early March. The sheriff was apprehensive—a flimsily constructed store building was all that was available as a courtroom for the august judge, and it had no ceiling, cracks in the roof, cracks around the windows, no heat, and the weather was cold. Thomas A. Edwards, who had settled in Cloud Chief, described Judge Irwin's visit in an article for the *Chronicles of Oklahoma*:

The Sheriff did the best he could. He had a little platform built at one end of the room for the judge and clerk. Seats for those who might attend were prepared by laying planks across bases. He secured a small table for the judge and another for the clerk. Three small, smokey, kerosene stoves were found, one placed near the judge's table, one for the clerk, and one in the space provided for the lawyers. A real touch of luxury was a borrowed office chair for the judge. For the lawyers and officials, a dozen cane bottom chairs had been rented from the furniture store. In warm weather all this could be endured; but the weather was perverse and willed otherwise.

A hack from El Reno brought the judge and his retinue to Cloud Chief the late afternoon before the day set for the court to convene. The party put up at the Iron Hotel [so named after the sheets of corrugated galvanized iron installed on its outside walls.] The judge, fresh from Illinois, had never been in this particular section before. He didn't like it. He had never been in contact with these yokels from Palo Pinto, Van Zandt, and Jack County, Texas, nor their equally crude brethren from Izzard, Yell, and Polk County, Arkansas, nor their compatriots from the Chickasaw Nation. He didn't like them. He didn't like the hotel. He didn't like the backhouse out behind. He didn't like the food. In fact, he didn't like anything except the quart of monogram rye the proprietor brought him to soothe his jangled nerves.

The judge did not sleep much. All night long the wind blew. Loose sheets of iron on the hotel slapped, and rattled, and banged. The town dogs, a goodly number, barked and yapped and fought. Court was to convene at ten o'clock. It was a cold and backward spring, little remnants of snow still lingered in the shaded places. The wind was gusty, raw, and mean. Loose papers and tumbleweeds skipped across the square, down the streets, and piled up against houses and wire fences. The judge, with his overcoat buttoned and the collar turned up, came into the dreary place the Sheriff had provided. He proceeded to dress down the Sheriff, Neal Morrison, for not having made better arrangements. The Sheriff, however, convinced him that this was the best he could possibly do. So the Judge reluctantly sat down, with his overcoat on and the little oil stove at his feet, and ordered the court opened. As the call of the docket began, he cut short any attempt by the lawyers to argue any matter.

As persons came in or went out, the door was continually opening and closing. Dust sifted in and fell, like snow, on the tables and records. Now and then some extra strong gust of wind would shake the building. After court had been open for perhaps an hour, and as the door was opened, a strong gust of wind toppled to the floor a lamp which had been sitting on a table. The temper of the Judge had been rising, and this was the last straw. He jumped to his feet, and shouted, 'Bailiff, adjourn this damn court!' Then, turning to the sheriff, he said, 'Tell your infernal Board of County Commissioners there'll be no more court here until they provide a suitable place.' Within an hour he was on his way back to El Reno.[62]

John H. Cotteral, who years later was to become a federal district judge, then judge of the Circuit Court of Appeals, once experienced the sharp wit of Judge Irwin. Cotteral was representing a property owner in a condemnation suit opposed by John E. DuMars, counsel for the M. K. & T. Railway. Judge Irwin was sitting in the District Court at Guthrie in the absence of the regular presiding judge, John H. Burford.

Cotteral sought to introduce certain evidence in support of his case. DuMars objected to it as

Judge F. Hiner Dale's law office in Guymon, established January 1, 1907. L to R: Judge Dale's son, William, Judge Dale, fellow attorney John Gilson, and an unidentified client. Photo c. 1922. (Courtesy Judge John Dale.)

"Incompetent, irrelevant and immaterial, and not a proper measure of damages." Judge Irwin sustained the objections. Cotteral recorded an exception to the ruling and tried a different approach. Again DuMars objected, which was again sustained, and after repeated questions, objections, and adverse rulings, the record showed the following verbal exchange:

Mr. Cotteral: I don't understand the theory on which the court bases its ruling.

The Court: On the grounds on which they are made.

Mr. Cotteral: I've asked the same question several different ways, but he always objects, and the Court sustains him. I still don't understand the ground on which the Court sustains his objections.

The Court: Well, all I can do is to furnish you information, I can't furnish you comprehension.[63]

Successful removal of the county seat from Ioland to Grand, only one of several county seat controversies in Oklahoma's history, perhaps helped agitate a similar change in Washita County from Cloud Chief to Cordell. Through an injunction and other legal tactics engineered by long-time Washita County lawyer James W. Smith, Cloud Chief residents were able to forestall the move for four years.[64] However, in 1900 Cordell forced an election and received the majority vote for removal required by Territorial statute.

Cloud Chief adherents relied on the Washita county attorney who had replaced Smith to do the legal maneuvering that would delay the move once more. The county attorney temporarily enjoined the county commissioners from taking any action, and just before expiration of the injunction his constituents authorized him to appeal to the Supreme Court. Time was growing short, so he hurriedly drafted the motion for appeal. Realizing that the motion could not reach Guthrie in time by regular mail delivery, he made the mistake of delegating his son to travel to Guthrie to deliver the documents in person to the Supreme Court. The young man was sidetracked somehow and failed to reach the court in time. Certain outraged Cloud Chief people tarred and feathered him. The county attorney himself, in the face of ominous threats, took time to do little more than place his Winchester in his buggy and flee the county never to return.[65]

In an election held August 8, 1900, a majority of Washita County voters selected Cordell to be the county seat. Shortly thereafter the Board of County Commissioners arranged for wagons to move all county property to Cordell. The move was completed despite threats of violence from angry Cloud Chief partisans. Rather than leave the courthouse in Cloud Chief, the movers attached a log chain to it and in short order reduced the structure to a pile of cottonwood lumber. Then they loaded the lumber onto the wagons and transported it to Cordell where it was reassembled.[66]

Still unsettled was the question: which town was the legal county seat? Judges and lawyers could not agree as to whether a county seat established in Cloud Chief by Congress could be changed by a vote of the people. The Cloud Chief-Cordell fracas also emphasized dissension in the Territorial Supreme Court, then composed of John H. Burford, John L. McAtee, Clinton F. Irwin, Bayard T. Hainer, and B. F. Burwell. McAtee, appointed by Democrat Grover Cleveland, and Irwin, appointed by Republican William McKinley, had never liked each other personally or officially.

Irwin was the regular judge for the Second District. He chose Cordell as the county seat and proceeded to hold a term of court there. Chief Justice Burford took sides in the argument by assigning Judge McAtee of the Fifth District to hold court at Cloud Chief at the same time. For three days each judge presided in his respective court but each was careful to hear only uncontested cases. Finally Judge Irwin, disgusted, gathered his court party and headed his hack back to his home base at El Reno. On the way he swung by Cloud Chief and stopped at the Iron Hotel where McAtee was staying. There he instructed his bailiff, "Tell Judge McAtee to come out; I want to see him."

The bailiff returned with McAtee's reply, "It's as near from the hack to the hotel as it is from the hotel to the hack; if Judge Irwin wants to see me, he can come into the hotel." Judge Irwin ordered his driver to proceed to El Reno.[67]

The matter of the Washita county seat was not conclusively settled until 1906. Meanwhile a court decision had held that a county seat created by Congress, which was the situation with Cloud Chief, could not be changed by authority of Territorial statute. County Attorney Thomas A. Edwards and the county officials, who until then had considered Cordell the county seat, then prepared to move to Cloud Chief. However, a group of enterprising citizens quietly dispatched a committee of three to lobby their cause in Washington. On March 3, 1906, a special Congressional enactment ratified the election of 1900 that made "New Cordell" the county seat of Washita County.[68]

14

THE TUMULTUOUS TENURE OF JUDGE HENRY W. SCOTT

Section 14 of the Indian Appropriation Act of 1889 provided for a three-member commission appointed by the president to negotiate with the Cherokees and other tribes for the purchase of the remaining land west of that occupied by the Five Civilized Tribes.[1] Section 1 of the Organic Act for Oklahoma Territory provided that lands thus acquired were to be attached to Oklahoma Territory without further legislation. By authority of those two enactments, the Cherokee (or Jerome) Commission, appointed by President Harrison and headed by former Governor David H. Jerome of Michigan, was to play an important role in the growth of Oklahoma Territory.[2]

The commission's first agreement was reached on May 20, 1890, with the Iowas and was followed by agreements with the Sac and Fox tribes, the Pottawatomies, and the Absentee Shawnees. Acquisition of land from those tribes brought about another mad race on September 22, 1891, when 20,000 homeseekers rushed for 7000 homesteads of 160 acres each, which enlarged the counties of Payne, Cleveland, and Logan and created Lincoln and Pottawatomie counties as part of Oklahoma Territory.[3]

John Embry, who in 1916 joined the predecessor to the present Oklahoma City law firm of Crowe & Dunlevy, was one of the lucky 7000. A Kentuckian with the equivalent of a high school education, Embry had taught school while reading law in his spare time in the office of W. S. Taylor, later a governor of Kentucky. He was admitted to the Kentucky Bar in 1890, lived in Wayne County, Missouri, for a few months, then moved to Stillwater in Oklahoma territory.[4] He was 22 years old when he made the run into Sac and Fox country where he hoped to stake a claim near Chandler, which the government had designated as a townsite and county seat. M. M. Watson had located a choice claim in the vicinity Embry had in mind, and already had chased away a Sooner when Embry appeared. Fifteen years later, when Embry was appointed United States

Attorney for the Territory of Oklahoma, Watson wrote in rhyme of his first encounter with Embry:[5]

> The coast was now clear, until half-past two
> Then a bare back rider came tearing through
> He rode a coal black but he was so covered with red dust and foam,
> He would have made a good mate for Kane's strawberry roan,
> And he had run from the mouth of Bush Creek twenty miles away
> Where the Turkey Track Cowboys used to mow their hay.
> And as we approached he gave us to understand,
> That he had made settlement and was claiming the land,
> Says I, 'Young Man, you are all wet,
> While you came from the north we came from the east,
> And we beat you here an hour at least.

Watson continued his rhyme to say that he convinced Embry of his own prior claim and that "Gloom covered [Embry's] face," because, "This is the only chance in a life time to get a home..." Moved by the young man's disappointment, Watson confided:[6]

> I know of a claim that there is no one on
> And it has rich valley land that will grow big corn.
> Oak timber is plenty and there tall pecans grow,
> And across one corner the Dry Fork flows.
> Now this the claim that before us you see
> Here take this axe of mine, begin blazing some trees.

Embry had plenty of time to clear the land and cultivate the soil while he built his law practice in Chandler. Cora McCreary became his wife seven years later. She recalled that the first time she saw her future husband he was walking barefoot behind a plow.[7] Embry must have been satisfied with neighbor Watson's choice of a homestead for him, for he retained ownership of the land while

John Embry, who homesteaded a farm in Lincoln County on the day of the "Run" of September 22, 1891, served in several political offices, including Attorney for the Western District of Oklahoma. Later he headed the Oklahoma City law firm of Crowe & Dunlevy. (Courtesy Archives and Manuscripts Division, OHS.)

county attorney and county judge of Lincoln County, mayor of Chandler, United States Attorney for the Territory of Oklahoma, member of the lower House of the Territorial Legislature, Attorney for the Western District of Oklahoma, and eventually head of what is now Crowe & Dunlevy, one of Oklahoma's largest law firms. Nearly 65 years after the September 22, 1891, land opening, he still owned the homestead that his good Samaritan, M. W. Watson, had selected for him.[8]

Of the two counties created by the opening, Lincoln County was added to Chief Justice E. B. Green's First Judicial District, while Pottawatomie County became a part of Judge John G. Clark's Third Judicial District. Clark's district already included the busy Oklahoma and Cleveland counties. Even before Pottawatomie County was added to his caseload, Judge Clark was being criticized for "his extreme caution and slowness in the disposition of cases," or as one press comment suggested, "He was resolved to be legal if it took all summer."[9] Some 30 members of the Oklahoma City Bar in January of 1892 approved a petition asking Judge Clark to resign. A group headed by the respected Angelo C. Scott backed Judge Clark, however, and Clark himself stubbornly re-

fused to let local dissatisfaction force his resignation.[10] After Democrat President Grover Cleveland took office in 1893, he appointed Frank Dale to replace Clark, a Republican. Clark protested on the grounds that he had been appointed in 1890 for a four-year term and that the president had no power to remove him summarily.

Clark did not choose to pursue his objection by formal court action, so finally the other two justices—Green and John H. Burford—issued a written statement saying they had no alternative but to recognize Dale's May 1, 1893, commission as being *prima facie* proof that he held the office.[11] A few months later Chief Justice Green, himself a Republican, gave way to Dale as the president's choice to replace him in the First Judicial District and assume the post of Chief Justice.[12]

When President Cleveland replaced Green with Dale, he appointed Henry W. Scott to take charge of Dale's Third Judicial District headquartered in Oklahoma City. Scott, formerly of Kansas, was just past his mid-twenties. A handsome man of classic features and wavy black hair, he had already authored several books including a volume of biographies. He was said to have been an individual of outstanding intellect although one historian, Angelo C. Scott, no relation to the judge, attributed Judge Scott's appointment to the biographical work which was largely a eulogy of living American lawyers.[13]

Judge Scott's court, like other Federal courts with jurisdiction over the Indian population, faced a constant communication problem with non-English-speaking Indians. E. E. Blake was counsel in one case where the testimony of an Indian witness was interpreted in sign language to Comanche, then to the Kiowa language and back to English via the same route.[14] Judge John H. Cotteral once described the embarrassment of all concerned when an Indian witness assumed that the examining attorney meant "virginity" when he inquired as to the "veracity" of a squaw on the witness stand.[15]

One of the first Indian cases heard by Judge Scott required an interpreter and dealt with murder charges against three Shawnee Indians living in Pottawatomie County, only recently opened to non-Indian settlement. The defendants had encountered a problem early in the case when the attorney engaged for their defense collected his

Judge John H. Burford holding court in Chandler in 1902. At his right is J.B.A. Robertson, governor of Oklahoma 1919-1923. At his left is William M. 'Bill' Tilghman, famous Oklahoma peace officer. (Courtesy Western History Collections, University of Oklahoma Library.)

retainer fee and then departed the Territory. When located, he refused to represent the defendants without payment of an additional fee. Just before the trial, they engaged the more trustworthy firm of D. C. Lewis and Charles R. Reddick. The trial ended in acquittal for the Indians. The interpreter, Thomas Wildcat Alford, later indicated that the manner in which the trial was conducted helped allay the suspicions of the Shawnee Indians that their rights would never be protected in the white man's courts.[16]

Judge Scott had been on the bench less than a month when he convened the October 1893 term of district court in Oklahoma City and presided at the trial of a young black man, John Milligan, for the murder and robbery of an elderly farm couple and the wounding of their granddaughter. Milligan was defended by Amos Green, a brother of former Chief Justice E. B. Green, and

D. C. Lewis. The *Daily Oklahoman*, described Green and Lewis as "two of the best attorneys at the bar."[17] County Attorney J. H. Woods, assisted by J. W. Johnson, conducted the prosecution. Johnson, one of the most proficient of early Oklahoma City lawyers, had been an Assistant Attorney General of Illinois. Angelo G. Scott described him as "a truly wonderful political orator," an impressive figure with his "leonine head crowned with curling hair, large brown eyes, and a full and florid face."[18]

The defendant, Milligan, was found guilty, and after appeal to the Territorial supreme court his conviction was affirmed. Judge Scott sentenced him to be hanged on January 11, 1895, in what was to be the first legal hanging in Oklahoma Territory. However, opponents of capital punishment led by Dr. John R. Furlong banded together to prevent the hanging. They first attempted

John G. Clark, appointed Associate Justice of the Territorial Supreme Court in 1890. (Courtesy Archives and Manuscripts Division, OHS.)

Thomas Wildcat Alford (second from left), a Shawnee Indian, frequently served as court interpreter. (Courtesy Archives and Manuscripts Division, OHS.)

without success to persuade the Legislature to outlaw capital punishment, but they did convince Governor William C. Renfrow to grant a 60-day reprieve.[19]

In a mass meeting held at Guthrie's Hotel Royal, Dr. Furlong and his adherents secured Governor Renfrow's promise to commute Milligan's sentence to life imprisonment if the trial judge, Henry W. Scott, would make such a recommendation. At that juncture, a female contingent left the meeting and located Judge Scott, who was in Guthrie for a session of the Supreme Court.

United States Marshal E. D. Nix later observed that it was probably due to the young judge's "general respect for women" that he agreed to attend the meeting. When Judge Scott entered the meeting room, the chairman told him of the governor's decision. In silence the crowd awaited his reply, but the judge refused to change his decision. In a short speech he outlined the defendant's crime and the course of the trial. He concluded, "Everything has been done and legally done but the execution of the judgment. Therefore, I feel it my solemn duty to refuse to make any recommendation or in any way interfere with the executive department in this case." Despite the entreaties of the excited crowd, Governor Renfrow also refused to change his deci-

sion.[20] Subsequently, the first legal hanging in Oklahoma Territory took place in the yard of the Oklahoma County jail on a wet, dreary March 13, 1895.[21]

Judge Scott reached the height of public disapproval in two contempt of court cases. The first of these occurred early in his term when he was offended by references to his court in the *Times-Journal*, a predecessor to the Oklahoma City *Times*. After he sentenced the newspaper's editors, J. J. Burke and Elmer E. Brown, to a 10-day jail term and a fine of $250 each, an aroused citizenry held public meetings and passed resolutions of protest. One group proposed to raid the jail and remove the two editors by force, a proposal which the editors immediately rejected.[22] From outward appearances, however, the jail sentence must have been only a gesture. Each morning former Governor A. J. Seay and former United States Attorney Horace Speed, attorneys for the two editors, secured a writ of habeas corpus in the court of Probate Judge S. A. Steward because Judge Scott for some reason was unavailable. Nevertheless, each evening Judge Scott was available to order the editors returned to jail.[23]

E. E. Brown, Times-Journal editor, was sentenced by Judge Scott to 10 days for contempt of court. (Courtesy Archives and Manuscripts Division, OHS.)

Frank McMaster, a lawyer who established The Evening Gazette in Oklahoma City, was sentenced to five months in jail by Judge Scott for contempt of court. (Courtesy Archives and Manuscripts Division, OHS.)

Attracting even more attention was Judge Scott's confrontation with Frank McMaster, an editor, lawyer, scholar, and a Democratic Party leader. McMaster had been admitted to the Illinois Bar after service in the Civil War, and had once been an attorney for the Denver & Rio Grande Railroad. He practiced law in Kansas City before establishing *The Evening Gazette* in Oklahoma City after the opening of Oklahoma Territory.[24] Almost from the beginning of Judge Scott's term, he had been an object of Frank McMaster's criticism. At one point McMaster, exercising his alternate vocation as a lawyer, filed a petition in Oklahoma County's probate court, referring to an order made by Scott as being "issued willfully and corruptly...because of an immoral and dishonest conspiracy between the said Henry W. Scott, judge, and other parties..." The petition also accused Scott of other willful, corrupt and dishonest acts with the result that McMaster was brought into District Court on a contempt charge.

In the District Court proceedings before Judge Scott, McMaster continued his attack. In open court Scott reported, "[McMaster] was insolent, boisterous, contemptuous, anarchistic and defiant in the presentation [of his defense]." Scott suspended McMaster from the practice of law, fined him $500 and committed him to a five-

month jail term for contempt of court. Associate Justice John H. Burford honored a writ of habeas corpus that temporarily suspended the order for McMaster's commitment.[25] As in the Burke and Brown case, an aroused public entered strong protest against Scott's actions in resolutions that called on President Cleveland to remove him from the bench.[26]

Thompson B. Ferguson, editor of the *Watonga Republican*, had already called Scott "a bear greased, curly-haired Adonis" who had "made himself odious to the people of Oklahoma by his vindictive retaliation upon his critics." Ferguson now concluded, "The Press all over the territory has but one verdict, that Burford is the best lawyer on the supreme bench and Judge Scott the most extensively hated man in Oklahoma."[27]

County Attorney J. H. Woods applied to the Territorial Supreme Court for a modification of Burford's order. In an opinion rendered by Justice A. G. C. Bierer, the court ordered McMaster's recommitment to the Oklahoma city jail. The court found that McMaster had been guilty of "an absolute disregard for the highest and best offices that exist in our territory" and that Judge Scott had no other alternative than to rule the defendant guilty of contempt of court.[28]

In contrast to the situation in the Burke-Brown

85

James L. Brown, an outstanding Oklahoma City attorney, was once temporarily disbarred by Judge Scott. (Courtesy Archives and Manuscripts Division, OHS.)

case, McMaster while confined to jail was released only once, to vote in the city election. Reports denied by McMaster's friends declared that at one point he tried to take his own life. His confinement was of short duration, however, for after he repented and wrote Judge Scott a note of apology he was released.[29]

Another less publicized dispute took place between Judge Scott and J. L. Brown. In November of 1894 Brown had been elected County Attorney of Oklahoma County, but the following month William A. Wallace filed disbarment charges against him. At a disbarment hearing three weeks later, Judge Scott suspended Brown from practice pending trial of the disbarment charge. During his suspension, the time came for Brown to assume his new duties as County Attorney, but the incumbent, with the support of Judge Scott, refused to relinquish the office while Brown was under suspension.[30] Brown was later reinstated, and for many years he was one of Oklahoma City's outstanding lawyers.

After a little more than three years on the bench, Judge Scott resigned and was succeeded by James R. Keaton. Some doubt exists as to whether Scott resigned of his own accord or was asked to do so by President Cleveland. At the Fifth Annual Meeting of the Oklahoma State Bar Association in 1911, J. L. Brown, in an extem-poraneous talk, told of his experience with Judge Scott. The question of the recall of judges was receiving a great deal of attention at the time, and United States Senator Robert L. Owen delivered an address at the meeting on the subject. Following Owen's address, the chairman recognized Brown, who said:[31]

I wish to support my friend, Senator Owen, by giving in our city here a history of one of these removals. You may call it a recall. It had to be done, through the president.

Now let me tell you, when you undertake that thing, when you undertake a recall, you undertake one of the most difficult things in the world. We [had] a judge here—I will not tell all that he did—but step by step he became practically a monster. When it came to having somebody to step forward and attempt that man's removal there were only two members found in the bar who were willing to step into it. It cost one of those members worry, trouble, etc., until he soon went to his grave. Another, who is now addressing you, had to go through the thing of being disbarred by that same powerful judge, and had to be thrown out of office after being elected, and all that...

Now, gentlemen, I will tell you what it is; that is the way it went. The man [was] imprisoning fellows without right and without law, directing witnesses off the stand right in the middle of a trial, when persons were fighting for their liberty to keep out of the penitentiary, and telling the jury right in their presence that that witness had been guilty of perjury, and confining them in the jails over night until the witness would come back in the morning and admit that they were wrong...

Editor J.J. Burke reminiscing of his early days in Oklahoma City once told of seeing Judge Scott again many years after his own contempt of court experience. "Some years ago," Burke wrote, "before prohibition went into effect, he [Scott] settled down in Norman, and I took him into Jerry McCarty's saloon and slung a couple of big slugs of whiskey into him. He was 'all in' and surely needed the slugs. Last I heard of him he had braced up and was a leading light in Tammany in New York City."[32]

In 1929 while Scott was in St. Louis on legal business, he visited with his friend of Oklahoma Territory days, United States Marshal E. D. Nix, and subsequently wrote a four-page "Introduction" to Nix's book, *Oklahombres*, dealing with early Oklahoma Territory outlaws.

15

OKLAHOMA TERRITORY: DIVORCE MECCA OF THE WORLD

Judge Scott's court in the Third Judicial District, probably the busiest in the Territory, aptly exemplified the *sui generis* condition alluded to by Chief Justice Green. Along with numerous suits involving railroad rights-of-way, Indian lands, and the ever-present whiskey and robbery cases, Scott granted hundreds of divorces during a territorial "divorce boom" that spanned most of his three years on the bench.[1] The boom began after the Oklahoma Territorial Legislature in 1893 changed the residency requirements for divorce from two years to just 90 days.[2]

Heretofore South Dakota had been the nation's divorce Mecca, but thereafter Oklahoma Territory attracted a host of dissatisfied marriage partners who severed the bonds of matrimony with little regard for the requirement of "good faith" residence in the Territory. Some wags insisted that decrees were granted while applicants stopped off between trains just long enough for a divorce.[3]

At the time the new divorce law was passed, the Panic of 1893 was in full swing, and the future looked gloomy for the ample supply of attorneys-at-law in Oklahoma Territory. Thus the 65 lawyers among Oklahoma City's 5000 residents welcomed the new law with enthusiasm, as did lawyers in Guthrie, Perry, Kingfisher, and other county seat towns.[4] Established divorce lawyers reportedly acquired wealth in only a few months.[5] One of these was Guthrie's Volney Hoggatt, a former South Dakotan who perhaps encouraged the legislature to adopt the more liberal divorce legislation of his home state.[6]

Hotels, court clerks on a fee basis, and to some degree the Territory in general shared in the prosperity of the legal profession during the easy divorce era of about three years. Certain members of the Bar did not hesitate to advertise this new attribute of Oklahoma Territory. In a nationwide campaign one Kingfisher lawyer praised the merits of a quick and easy divorce in the Territory. His advertising circular listed 10 different grounds for divorce, emphasizing that the all-inclusive allegation, "gross neglect of duty," was available. The probate court was always in session, the circular announced, and could grant divorces without the delay encountered in a district court, and happily only three months residence in the Territory was necessary. "Persons coming to Oklahoma," the circular said, "will find the city of Kingfisher, with its 4,000 inhabitants and all modern improvements, a very pleasant place to live in."[7]

"Runners" employed by divorce lawyers boarded passenger trains 50 to 100 miles from Oklahoma City to become acquainted with the passengers. They extolled the legal abilities of their employers to those passengers contemplating divorce. Fees were negotiable. When several runners courted the same prospective client, the case often went to the lowest bidder.[8] Angelo C. Scott, who handled his share of divorces in Oklahoma City, could not remember a single client who stayed a day after the divorce decree was granted. These temporary residents, usually the wealthy and better known set who wished to avoid publicity, freely swore they were "good faith" residents of the Territory.[9]

A well known novelist of the day, Helen Churchill Candee, fulfilled the 90-day residential requirements in Guthrie while working on her newest novel, *An Oklahoma Romance*. Local residents felt sure that a handsome young Guthrie attorney was the prototype for the novel's hero.[10] Even European noblemen journeyed to the Territory to take advantage of the Oklahoma law. One Carl Rydingsward, a native of Sweden and an accomplished musician with an outstanding bass voice, became a popular participant in Oklahoma City's musical activities. Oklahoma City residents learned he was of royal blood after he obtained his divorce and departed; a few days later large headlines in a Boston newspaper announced, "Baron von Rydingsward secures divorce in Oklahoma."[11] One beautiful temporary resident, Princess Yznega of Brazil, attracted considerable attention as she went about with her bevy of attendants. A famous wild animal trainer, Carl Hagenback, stayed two months in Guthrie while he contemplated divorce, then changed his mind and left. New attachments, however temporary, were formed. In one instance, an attractive young female newcomer received her divorce, married her attorney, then divorced him and married the judge.[12]

Divorce seekers did not always receive the verdict they sought. Judge Frank Dale once refused to grant a divorce to the wife of a prominent San Diego merchant. He branded her divorce petition "heartless" because it contained no demand for custody of the children or, as Judge Dale expressed it, for "whatever fruits the union may have had."[13] Another unexpected result occurred when a young couple used the husband's homestead rights to settle on a farm near Watonga, then decided to get a divorce, intending to remarry after the wife used her separate homestead rights to acquire a quarter section of land adjoining their farm. Without consulting his wife, the husband alleged in the divorce petition that his wife was "a dirty housekeeper, a rotten cook and had a bad disposition." After the divorce was granted, the wife, angry over her husband's unflattering description, refused to remarry him. She chose to marry a bachelor neighbor instead.[14]

At the June court term in 1894 Chief Justice Frank Dale wrote an opinion in the case of *Irwin* v. *Irwin* that interpreted the somewhat ambiguous divorce legislation enacted in 1893. To the disappointment of most divorce lawyers the court held that the legislative intent was to eliminate the jurisdiction of probate courts in divorce proceedings.[15] At that time almost a year had passed since the new law's effective date of August 14, 1893. The *Guthrie Daily Leader* noted, "…Some thousands or more divorcees throughout the country, who have since re-married will find themselves with an extra husband or wife, as the case may be…"[16] That bigamous state of affairs was not cured until the legislative session of 1895 declared that all divorce decrees previously granted by the probate courts were legal.[17]

The 90-day residence provision received a severe blow in the Supreme Court term of June 1896. Charles F. Beach, Jr., an author of legal textbooks, was a New York City lawyer with a lu-

Oklahoma County Courthouse from about 1904 until the present courthouse was occupied in 1938. The old courthouse was demolished in 1951. (Courtesy The Daily Oklahoman.)

crative practice. His wife had been prominent socially in Philadelphia. When Beach decided to sue for divorce on grounds of extreme cruelty and neglect of duty, he filed his petition in the District Court at Norman, Cleveland County. Judge Scott granted the divorce. The decree was immediately appealed by Mrs. Beach on the grounds that her husband was not a *bona fide* resident of Cleveland County.[18] By the time the Territorial Supreme Court ruled on the appeal a year later, Beach had remarried and was on a European honeymoon. The opinion, written by Judge Tarsney, reversed Judge Scott's decision and found that Beach had made little pretense of becoming either a resident of Oklahoma Territory or of Cleveland County. He had apparently resided in Perry as a somewhat transient guest and visited Norman only when necessary for court proceedings. Judge Tarsney went on to state:[19]

An unenviable fame has already attached to this Territory by reason of the inducements which her laws have in the past offered for obtaining a dissolution of the status of marriage. The liberality of the law has been taken advantage of and has been abused. A large portion of the divorces asked

The house in the foreground was built by Judge Frank Dale about 1904. Of revived Georgian architecture, it was recognized as one of Oklahoma's finest homes at that time. (Courtesy OHS.)

for in our courts were brought by citizens of other states, who came into this Territory for the mere purpose of obtaining a divorce, and imposed upon the courts by perjury and fraud, not only as to the facts of residence, but also with respect to the procedure; thus occasioning injury to morals, reproach to the law, as well as obloquy to the

judicature which must administer the laws. This court, as a conservator of society, of the family, upon which society is founded, of the morals of the people, of the good name and fame of the Territory, owe it to all these that the laws shall not be administered with such laxity and disregard to the intention of the lawmakers as to bring reproach and dishonor upon the people of the Territory, and upon their judiciary.

An Edmond newspaper noted that under the Territorial court's ruling "three-fourths of the divorces ever granted in the territory" could be held invalid.[20]

Public sentiment encouraged Oklahoma Territory's representative in Congress, Dennis T. Flynn, to support legislation that would lengthen the 90-day residence requirement. On the other hand, opponents of any change in the law claimed it was "a scheme of Dakota lawyers, whose business has been lessened by the increased advantages of Oklahoma as a divorce haven."[21] Some members of the Territorial Bar and other interested individuals sent an attorney to Washington to lobby against any revision of the law. Nevertheless, Congress approved a bill on May 25, 1896, that required applicants for divorce in any Territory to maintain a one-year residence.[22] Thus ended the era of Oklahoma Territory as the home of liberalized divorce.

16

BENCH AND BAR IN THE CHEROKEE STRIP

Since the Civil War, cattlemen had fattened their livestock on the lush grass that covered land owned by the Cherokee Nation stretching along the southern border of Kansas. Properly identified as the "Cherokee Outlet" but also known as the "Cherokee Strip," this area consisted of more than 6 million acres and was some 60 miles wide and slightly more than 200 miles long. The Cherokees at first were able to collect rent from the cattlemen in only small sums fluctuating from 25 cents to a dollar a head. By a determined effort in 1882 they increased their total rental income to about $41,000 for the year.[1]

The cattlemen saw the need for an organization to promote their mutual objectives, and the following year they met at Caldwell, Kansas, to form the Cherokee Live Stock Association.[2] In addition to its own staff of attorneys, the Association employed as special counsel an intermarried citizen of the Cherokee Nation, John F. Lyons, of Fort Gibson. Historian Edward Everett Dale described Lyons as a lawyer of "rare tact and ability who of course practiced influence rather than law." Perhaps largely owing to the influence of Lyons, the Association accomplished its first objective a little more than two months after its organization: the consummation of a long-term land lease with the Cherokee Nation for $100,000 annually.[3]

Even before the cattlemen banded together into The Cherokee Strip Live Stock Association, they had agreed to boundaries established under their own common law, called "cow custom."[4] The Association became an important factor in Oklahoma history. Operating through a Board of Arbitration, it brought stability to an area otherwise without formal law or courts until the United States government completed purchase of the Cherokee Outlet in 1893.[5] The Association's existence ended soon after the Jerome Commission reached a purchase agreement with the Cherokee Nation in 1891, and the claims of the Tonkawa and Pawnee tribes to lands in the Cherokee Outlet were settled in 1893. In August of that year

President Cleveland proclaimed that the Outlet would be opened to settlement under the homestead laws by a land run to begin at noon, September 16, 1893.[6] Guthrie attorney Henry E. Asp is accorded much of the credit for provisions in the presidential proclamation that benefited Oklahoma's future development as a state. Asp, a native of New Boston, Illinois, had studied law in the office of William P. Hackney in Winfield, Kansas, before being admitted to the Kansas bar in 1878 when he was 22 years old. Hackney and Asp formed a partnership and moved to Guthrie shortly after the creation of Oklahoma Territory.

Legislation for previous land openings had reserved two sections in each township for public schools, but Asp, along with University of Oklahoma president David Ross Boyd, thought land should also be reserved for higher education and public buildings. They spent time in Washington, and ultimately they succeeded in including such legislation in the presidential proclamation despite strong Congressional opposition. The precedent thus established paved the way for similar provisions in the enactment that opened the Comanche, Kiowa, and Apache lands eight years later.[7]

At the direction of the president, the Secretary of the Interior took steps to prevent abuses prevalent in land runs of the past. Any person interested in making the race into the Outlet was required to register at booths located at principal points of entry. Qualified registrants were issued certificates that allowed participation in the race. However the registration system seems to have been generally regarded as ineffective for preventing fraud and deception. The safeguards amounted to a farce, in the opinion of Enid lawyer W. S. Whittinghill, who with some sarcasm insisted that the only useful purpose of a certificate was to confirm where the settler was. According to Whittinghill, "Every time a homesteader wondered whether he was actually in the Cherokee Strip or back where he used to live among his wife's people, he would carefully draw from his pocket the precious booth certificate, and prove to himself he was yet in the Strip."[8]

Disgruntled homeseekers accused government employees of accepting bribes to favor certain people. Inspector Alfred P. Swineford was a government official sent to Guthrie two months before the opening to locate county seats and land offices and to recommend sites for registration booths. He charged that forged certificates, illegally obtained from the Orlando booths, were sold in Guthrie during registration week. He blamed Guthrie attorney Volney Hoggatt for playing a major role in the scheme.[9]

On September 16, 1893, at high noon more than 100,000 pioneers—twice the number in the Run of 89, raced from points along the northern and southern borders of the Outlet beneath a blazing sun and buffeted by hot, dry winds. Some rode horseback, others drove wagons, and a few rode bicycles. Passengers jammed the trains that were permitted to travel at 15 miles per hour. Popular destinations for the homeseekers were land office and county seat settlements such as Perry, Enid, Woodward, and Alva. Counties eventually formed from lands of the Cherokee Strip added to northern Oklahoma Territory were Woods, Woodward, Garfield, Grant, Kay, Noble, and Pawnee.

Some lawyers in the race were destined to make their marks as leaders in the Oklahoma legal profession, several as judges and Supreme Court justices. Others reached the forefront in politics. Such was William Miller Jenkins, a lawyer from Arkansas City, Kansas, soon to be governor of Oklahoma territory. Jenkins was governor in 1901 when arrangements were made for opening the Kiowa-Comanche and Wichita-Caddo Indian land. Remembering his own experience as a hot, tired homeseekers who raced into what later became Kay County to stake a claim and build a dugout home, he strongly supported a change to a lottery method for subsequent land openings.[10]

Establishing his law office in Perry was a future governor of Oklahoma, Henry S. Johnston. He was a studious 23-year-old graduate of Baker University in Kansas who had studied law in offices at Erie, Kansas, and Denver, Colorado, before admission to the Bar in 1891. Except for the years 1926 to 1929, when he served as governor of Oklahoma, Johnston practiced law in Perry for more than 70 years, until his death in 1965. His

Henry S. Johnston, Perry lawyer for more than 70 years, prominent in the Constitutional Convention, and governor of Oklahoma 1927-29. (Courtesy OHS.)

tenure as governor ended during a political upheaval in which he was impeached and removed from office.[11]

Centers of potential business for lawyers were the land offices, where all homestead claims for the Cherokee land had to be filed. Thus, according to one account the acre of land around the land office in Perry was covered with the tents of individuals claiming to be lawyers. There the reputation of the legal profession suffered from the activities of "sharks, Jacklegs," and "Pettifoggers."[12] Nine days after the opening, Inspector Alfred P. Swineford complained that the business of land offices would proceed smoothly except for the interference of "a few jackleg land shysters calling themselves lawyers, who will be satisfied with nothing short of the privilege of running land offices to suit themselves exclusively..."[13]

Milton Cline Garber, 26 years old and a recent law graduate of the State University of Iowa, made the Run into the Outlet from the boundary line near Marshall in a wagon drawn by a span of mules especially trained for the occasion. Garber staked his claim near what was to be the present town of Garber and hurried to the Enid land office, 20 miles away to file his claim. At Enid Garber was appointed a member of a committee to investigate slow movement of a long line in front of the tent where numbers were being issued to admit homesteaders to the filing office in an orderly manner. The committee found that through bribery certain individuals were being allowed to enter the tent from the rear to obtain numbers. Garber, in company with a few other bold men, rushed the tent and routed a group who had just entered from the rear entrance. Thereafter the line moved in proper numerical sequence.[14]

Young Garber started his general law practice in the newly settled town that adopted his family name. But he still had time to work regularly behind a walking plow that tilled the virgin sod on his wheat farm. He also helped run a general store and drove a wagon to haul farm products to Enid and Perry. Nine years later he began a judicial career as probate judge of Garfield County. While a Territorial judge he presided over a variety of murder cases and won the especial acclaim of members of the Bar by his decision requiring a prisoner to pay his victim's family any excess money earned from his prison labor. Garber was elected to Congress from Oklahoma's Eighth District and served five terms until he retired in 1933.[15]

Another lawyer-farmer was James B. Cullison, who once had been an Iowa schoolteacher. Cullison had settled first in Kingfisher, but later at the age of 36 decided to make the race into the Cherokee Outlet. He staked an excellent claim near Enid, cultivated his land, and started a law career at the same time, often walking the six miles to and from his office in Enid. Cullison served as both probate judge and district judge before his election to a six-year term on the State Supreme Court in 1928 when he was 72 years old.[16]

Percy Constance Simons, a 23-year-old University of Kansas graduate, was one of the lawyers who rushed into the Outlet but failed to find a satisfactory claim. He returned to his law practice across the boundary in Caldwell, Kansas, and waited for someone to relinquish a desirable location. Before long he obtained a satisfactory claim in Grant County and moved his office to Pond Creek. Appointed Attorney General of Oklahoma Territory in 1904, he was praised for his vigorous prosecution of illegal medical practitioners and his support of effectual health legislation. After two years in the Attorney General's office, Simons resigned to enter private practice in Enid. Never hesitating to work 10-hour days

This view of Perry on October 3, 1893, shows law office tent of Thompson & Logan (second from left). (Courtesy Western History Collections, University of Oklahoma Library.)

92

and seven-day weeks, he became one of the Territory's and State's most respected lawyers. His long career ended with death at age 92 in 1962.[17]

Arriving by Santa Fe train at the designated county seat town of Alva on the eventful day of September 16, 1893, was Jesse James Dunn, destined to be one of Oklahoma's first Supreme Court justices and one of the ablest attorneys to make the race into the Outlet. Dunn's first trip within the boundaries of present Oklahoma had occurred five years earlier when he visited the scene of the "Hay Meadow Massacre" just across the Kansas state line in what was then known as "No Man's Land." A Kansas sheriff and three members of his posse had met death there in a gun battle that climaxed a dispute between the Kansas towns of Hugoton and Woodale over the location of their county seat. Twelve men subsequently were indicted in what was one of the most publicized and costly federal court cases up to that time. Public sentiment for the defendants and donated funds for their defense kept the case in the courts for five years. In the meantime most of the defendants met tragic deaths, so the case was finally stricken from the docket.[18]

Jesse Dunn's involvement as a witness in the "Hay Meadow Massacre" case and his admiration for Samuel N. Wood, a Kansas politician who assisted in the prosecution, perhaps whetted his interest in the law as a career. Dunn was a 21-year-old grocery store manager in Voorhees, Kansas, at the time of the "Massacre." He began to read law in the office of George Lynn Miller, later his brother-in-law and law partner in Alva. He was 26 years old and had recently completed a two-year law course at the University of Kansas when he made the race into the Outlet from Garden City, Kansas.[19] Dunn and Miller opened their office in a tent on Alva's public square. Dunn later wrote, "Every lawyer about the town was busily engaged in making out filing papers and filing contests and were [sic] earning all the way from $5.00 to $15.00 a day. This was more money than I had ever expected to earn as long as I lived and I was most assiduous in my attention to it."[20]

Dunn served two terms as county attorney, then formed a partnership with Francis M. Cowgill. While he waited for clients, he studied law, read the classics, and developed into an eloquent public speaker, effective story teller, and excellent trial lawyer. Always liked and respected by

Woodward County Courthouse, built in 1901-02. (Courtesy Western History Collections, University of Oklahoma Library.)

his peers, he was elected president of the Oklahoma Territory Bar Association in 1903. At Statehood in 1907, he was elected justice of the Oklahoma Supreme Court and then reelected in 1910 for a six-year term. He served a year as chief justice, then in 1913, despite a bright political future in Oklahoma and to the surprise of most Oklahomans, he resigned his office and moved to Oakland, California, to form a law partnership with his wife's uncle. Reasons for his departure are conflicting—whether for his family's health or, as some have said, to get away from Oklahoma politics.

Judge Dunn retained affection for Oklahoma, and his office in Oakland was a popular gathering place for Oklahomans visiting California. His reputation grew in that state while he earned the admiration of his colleagues, both as a public speaker and advocate. In 1919 he declined to be considered for the deanship of the law school at his alma mater, the University of Kansas. After his death in 1926, his partners continued the firm name of Dunn, White and Aiken until the partnership was dissolved 12 years later.[21]

Sidney B. Laune, late of Denver, was one of the horde of Cherokee Outlet homeseekers who arrived in Woodward in a Santa Fe railroad box car on September 16, 1893. Laune, one of the better-educated lawyers of that time, was holder of a Bachelor of Science degree from Wesleyan University of Ohio and a law degree from the University of Michigan. Only a short time before the Cherokee land opening, he had joined an established firm of Denver lawyers. In his words, "I had my nice new swivel chair tipped back and my feet on my shiny new desk" when one of the country's worst depressions, the Panic of 1893, arrived in Denver. Any legal business that transpired went to the experienced lawyers, so young Laune had to look elsewhere. He joined the Denver-Cherokee Outlet Colony, was elected its president, and soon led the colony to Woodward.[22]

On September 16, 1893, Laune staked a lot alongside that of J. R. Dean, a middle-aged lawyer who had been county judge in Smith County, Texas.[23] As soon as Laune and his new acquaintance pounded their stakes into the ground, they prepared to practice law, a process that consisted of removing office supplies from suitcases. Then they sat on their suitcases to wait for clients and took turns standing guard over their claims and belongings. The formation of the partnership, "Dean & Laune, Lawyers," was the logical consequence. In less than a week they had erected a 12 x 14 foot wooden shack for a combination home-office. Its center rested squarely on the line that separated their lots. The well-trodden earth made a satisfactory floor. Each partner's bed was constructed in the accepted frontier manner—a wooden frame filled with prairie hay.

Laune, young and unmarried, pondered a way to meet the attractive girls flitting among the tents and shacks and decided that a Sunday School was a necessity for the newly settled community. On the second Sunday after the Run, the Dean & Laune home-office overflowed with "weary-eyed men and women, big-eyed children," and "rosy-cheeked girls." Laune led in singing hymns, and Dean made an inspirational talk—he was careful not to call it a sermon. Woodward's first Sunday School class ended with a recitation of the Lord's Prayer.[24] But none of the "rosy-cheeked girls" caught Laune's fancy. Three years later, near Wellington in the Texas Panhandle, he found the girl he sought, a young schoolteacher, Seigniora Russell. More than 60 years later she wrote of her life in the Oklahoma Panhandle with Laune, in her book, *Sand in My Eyes*.[25]

17

TEMPLE HOUSTON: OKLAHOMA FOLK HERO

Arriving in Woodward in the same Santa Fe box car with Sydney Laune and other pioneers was Temple Houston, late of Canadian, Texas.[1] Houston, 33 years old, was already a well-known criminal lawyer. Although his death at age 45 occurred in 1905, he has become an Oklahoma folk hero, and tales of his eccentricities, courtroom antics, and frontier oratory have lived to the present. In the late 1920s Edna Ferber made him the model for her hero in the popular novel, *Cimarron*, twice made into a motion picture. In 1963 Houston was the principal character in a television series bearing his name.[2]

The youngest son of the venerable Sam Houston of Texas, Temple attended Baylor University, then read law and was little more than 21 years old when he was appointed District Attorney for the sprawling Texas Panhandle country. His popularity soared in the Panhandle where the rough-and-ready plainsmen accepted "Old Sam's son" as a "man's man" and a capable criminal lawyer. Already he was becoming a folk hero. One tale, probably more fiction than fact, told how he outshot both Billy the Kid and Bat Masterson in a marksmanship contest one hot afternoon in the town of Tascosa where he was attending a court session.[3]

He left the District Attorney post and enjoyed a good law practice as a defense counsel. His relationship with the Texas Court of Criminal Appeals deteriorated after a series of unfavorable decisions, and he began to criticize the court in state newspapers.[4] His reason for leaving Texas in 1893 is a matter of conjecture—whether to remove himself from the jurisdiction of the Texas Court of Criminal Appeals, to avoid comparison with his father, or for the more practical purpose of finding a larger clientele for his law practice. In any event, by late September of 1893, he was a citizen of Woodward, Oklahoma Territory, where he lived the rest of his life.

A successful Woodward lawyer, Sidney Laune, often found Houston on the other side in legal battles. This was especially true during the two years after Laune was elected County Attorney in 1900. An incident that has become a part of the Temple Houston folklore dealt with the horse thief who to his chagrin was captured astride the animal he had stolen. He had no funds to engage counsel, so the county provided him free board and room in jail for several days before county officials tired of the expense. County Attorney Laune, the judge, and the sheriff talked with Houston and persuaded him to undertake the man's defense.

"You may rest assured that any advice I give this unfortunate good fellow will be good advice," Houston told them. He asked for a private office to confer with his new client. Some time later an official decided to check on the two individuals conferring behind the closed door. He found the lawyer sitting quietly alone in the room, the window wide open. Temple smiled broadly. "Well boys, I gave him some good advice," he explained.[5]

Governor William C. Renfrow appointed as first probate judge of Woodward County the well-traveled J.D.F. Jennings who had been practicing law in El Reno. Born in 1831 in Virginia, Jennings was educated at Emory and Henry College, and had been a Methodist minister before he studied medicine and served as a surgeon in the Civil War. After the war he became a lawyer, was elected county attorney in Illinois, then practiced in Ohio, Missouri, and Kansas. He served two terms as probate judge in Coldwater, Kansas, before moving to Trinidad, Colorado, in 1888. From there he took part in the 1889 land run and acquired a claim southeast of Kingfisher. He moved to El Reno two years later.[6]

Three of Judge Jennings' sons—John D.F., Jr., Edward E., and Alphonso J. "Al,"—joined him in El Reno. John and Edward were admitted to the Bar after studying law in their father's office, but apparently Al had the advantage of formal legal training—one account makes him a law graduate of the state university in West Virginia while another refers to him as a graduate in law from the

University of Virginia at age 20. Al was elected County Attorney of Canadian County in 1892.[7] The slightly built Al Jennings, underweight even for his five feet two inches in height, had "red-ripe strawberry blonde" hair with a complexion to match. Twenty-nine years old in 1892, he was a flowery-tongued orator of the William Jennings Bryan school with unusual personal magnetism. His ability as conversationalist and story-teller may explain how he later capitalized on a short outlaw career to make a comfortable living for several decades.[8]

A year after Judge Jennings assumed the probate judgeship in Woodward, Ed and John Jennings moved there to practice law. Hard feelings arose between Temple Houston and the Jennings family apparently due to Houston's disapproval of some of Judge Jennings' court decisions.[9] Then in October of 1895, when Houston and Ed Jennings opposed each other in Justice of the Peace Court, a violent argument ensued over a point of law, and bloodshed was prevented only by the intervention of onlookers.

The two lawyers encountered each other that night in a Woodward saloon. A gun battle followed and when the smoke cleared Ed Jennings was dead and the arm of his brother John was shattered. In the trial seven months later, County Attorney B. B. Smith, assisted by Shannon Mc-

Cray, prosecuted Houston for first degree manslaughter. Houston was defended by a quartet of well-known members of the Territorial Bar: Henry E. Asp, D. P. Marum, Robert J. Ray, and Roy Hoffman. None of the Jennings family appeared in court to press the case, and the verdict of "not guilty" on the grounds of self defense was welcomed by Houston's many friends in both Texas and Oklahoma Territory.[10]

Hot-tempered Al Jennings claimed a miscarriage of justice in the Houston trial and embarked on a career of outlawry, vowing revenge against Houston. He was joined by his brother, Frank, two years his senior, who had been a lawyer for 10 years. Despite Al's boastful threats, the Jennings gang never confronted Houston, although the latter was a highly visible figure pursuing his law practice throughout all of Oklahoma Territory.[11]

The Jennings' newly chosen profession, comical at times, can be documented over a period of less than six months. Their attempts at train robbery were only partially successful. Twice they failed to blast train safes open because they failed to prepare the dynamite "soup" properly. Another time they piled railroad ties on the track to stop a passenger train, but the engineer raced the train through the barricade and scattered splintered ties in every direction.

Temple Houston in 1885. (Courtesy Western History Collections, University of Oklahoma Library.)

Temple Houston (second from left) with friends. (Courtesy Western History Collections, University of Oklahoma Library.)

Publicity photo of lawyer-outlaw Al Jennings during the Oklahoma gubernatorial race of 1914 in which he finished third in the Democratic primary. After serving less than five years in jail, Jennings returned to law practice in 1907 after he was granted a full pardon by President Theodore Roosevelt. In later years he was primarily an entertainer. (Courtesy Archives and Manuscripts Division, OHS.)

In November of 1897 Al, Frank, and another gang member, Pat O'Malley, managed to escape when they were attacked at the Spike S Ranch house near Sapulpa in the Creek Nation. Al suffered wounds in both legs. Six days later Frank was driving a wagon laden with straw on the way to Arkansas when a fallen tree across the roadway forced him to stop. He cursed. Al and O'Malley stuck their heads out from under the straw only to stare into the muzzles of guns held by four deputy marshals. An informer had told the officers of the gang's escape route.[12]

In the May of 1898 court term at Muskogee, Al Jennings was tried for attempting to kill a deputy marshal at the Spike S Ranch. He was found guilty and sentenced by Judge W. M. Springer to five years hard labor in the penitentiary at Fort Leavenworth, Kansas.[13] Then he was tried at Ardmore for a train holdup near Minco, and in February of 1899 Judge Hosea Townsend sentenced him to a life term in the Columbus, Ohio, penitentiary.[14] His brother Frank was sentenced to five years at Fort Leavenworth.[15]

After Temple Houston killed Ed Jennings in the Woodward saloon brawl, nobody questioned

reports from the Texas Plains that Houston was a dangerous man with a gun. Houston's reputation as a "man of few words and much action" worried Attorney General Harper S. Cunningham for a moment on the day the renowned Panhandle lawyer appeared at a Guthrie court session to apply for admission to practice before the Territorial Supreme Court. Cunningham, unaware that Houston was in the courtroom for that purpose, submitted the name of a black applicant ahead of Houston's. That was a cardinal error because racial prejudice of that day dictated that blacks should be subservient to whites at all times. Cunningham learned of his mistake a few minutes later. To his relief Houston graciously accepted his humorous apology in which he offered "to buy either a cigar factory or a brewery or both" in exchange for Houston's forgiveness.[16]

Houston's intemperance in the use of intoxicants was well known. In 1896 when he attended the national Democratic convention in Chicago, he was dubbed "The fair flower of the Oklahoma Delegation," and became a popular figure at the convention. Word came back to the Territory, however, that after being appointed to the "Notification Committee," he engaged in so much "notifying" that he missed part of the convention.[17]

Walter Ferguson was a boy in Watonga in the late 1890s who took full advantage of the Houston intemperance. Watonga, as a court town, attracted court notables from all over the Territory, including Temple Houston. With an eye for business, young Ferguson arranged that he alone was to get all of Temple's empty whiskey bottles, said to have been "legion in number." Sale of the "empties" for one to five cents each netted Ferguson a tidy sum.[18]

Two anecdotes about Houston always brought a chuckle when a group of lawyers recounted courtroom experiences. Once Houston became impatient with an Oklahoma City lawyer who assumed a haughty attitude toward local lawyers in a Western Oklahoma court case. "Your honor," said Houston turning to the judge, "this is the only man I've ever seen that could strut while sitting down."[19] At another time Houston was disgusted with the testimony of a state witness. After the witness was excused, Houston told the judge, "He sat there manufacturing perjury as gaily as a mockingbird ever sang his lay."[20]

Houston had no liking for the details of the law.

Legal questions and office paperwork he left to partners or associate counsel. He seldom represented a client in court without the assistance of a lawyer more learned in the law than he was, but he was always generous in praising his associates' contribution.[21] Among his partners during the years he practiced in Woodward were Robert J. Ray, David P. Marum, and T. M. Grant.[22] As associate counsel he often recruited such skilled criminal lawyers as A. R. Garrett and A. M. Thacker of Mangum, Watonga's Seymour Foose or Enid's W. S. Denton.[23]

Houston excelled as a jury lawyer. When all elements of a case were against him—the facts, questions of law, public sentiment—he relied on natural eloquence and knowledge of human nature to influence one or more jurors and obtain a hung jury. If the case had to be tried again and again, no matter, he could always rely on the adage, "Time will beat any criminal case."[24]

Space at the hitching racks around the courthouse was scarce whenever Houston was defense counsel in a murder trial.[25] Study of the classics and familiarity with the Bible combined with a flair for drama made his courtroom oratory an exhibition that attracted spectators from miles around.[26] He was in demand as speaker for public occasions, even if the reactions of his frontier audiences were like that described by Texas journalist T. C. Richardson. After hearing "the silver-tongued orator of the Plains" at a Mangum July 4th celebration, Richardson wrote, "I don't remember a word of what he said, but he said it in a manner to lift you out of your boots."[27]

Judge Burford, a personal friend of the Woodward lawyer, understood and appreciated Houston's idiosyncrasies as did most of Houston's colleagues. At a court term in Guthrie, Burford substituted for Judge Dale in some special cases. In one of these Houston was a defense counsel. One morning he appeared in court wearing a conspicuous tie made of rattlesnake skin. All that morning Judge Burford was unable to take his eyes off the rattlesnake tie while Houston pleaded his case, his swift steps taking him back and forth to the witness chair, the judge's bench, and the jury box. Time came for noon recess, and the judge could restrain himself no longer. He summoned Houston to the bench and said, "Colonel Houston, I wish you would change that tie at noon. I have been deathly afraid of snakes since

I was a kid, and that thing gives me the willies." Houston apologized. When he returned to the courtroom after lunch he wore a bright green tie.[28]

The trial of Alfred Son was perhaps Temple Houston's most difficult case. Son was charged with the murder of Fred Hoffman, a United States Commissioner and county treasurer of Dewey County, who was killed as he rode horseback from his home to Taloga, the county seat. Typical of Houston's conduct in a murder case, he had the help of at least six associates in the course of three separate jury trials in El Reno and one appeal to the Territorial Supreme Court.[29] At the first trial before Judge Burford, the jury could not agree—the count was 11 to one for conviction. Judge Tarsney presided at the next trial about a year later. This time the Houston magic failed, and Alfred Son was convicted and sentenced to life imprisonment. Houston turned the case over to John W. Shartel of Asp, Shartel & Cottingham, to file an appeal. The Territorial Supreme Court found that the prosecution had relied only on circumstantial evidence and failed to show that Son had a motive for murder. The cause was remanded to El Reno for a new trial.[30]

The courtroom was crowded to suffocation on November 16, 1897, nearly three years after Hoffman's murder. At Alfred Son's side sat Temple Houston together with associates R. B. Forrest, John Pitzer, and W. H. Grigsby. Grigsby had once been Houston's partner in Texas.[31] Across from them sat the prosecution, County Attorney William Black, John Stone, and J. C. McKnight.[32] Testimony showed Alfred Son had left Taloga on the morning of the murder to provide transportation into Taloga for his girl friend who lived on a farm.   Houston began his closing statement to the jury by emphasizing the prosecution's failure to show a motive, then he appealed to the jury's sense of the romantic: "Gentlemen, as I told you in the beginning, the territory has shown no motive for the commission of such a crime, and we have given you a reasonable—a true—explanation of every act and utterance of the defendant—even for his trip in that fatal direction. He went only to woo (and win) one of the daughters of the land, tender eyed, and fair to look upon, and how like a boy [with the intent] to take the shortest route to see his sweetheart and seeing her, to take her back by the longest route."[33]

Rather than remind the jury of an obvious verdict—guilty with life imprisonment—Houston offered only two alternatives: freedom or the death penalty, when he exclaimed:[34]

> This brave boy asks me to say to you that, to him, honor is dearer than life, and as the old exemplar of purest patriotism thundered in the ears of his country's oppressors, he says in this, his hour of trial, 'Give me liberty or give me death.' He demands that you free him or inflict the death penalty. Rather than that you should fix on his boyish brow the brand of felon, he would prefer to walk from your presence with his body polluted with the scales of white leprosy.

Houston reminded the jury of the value of a clear conscience, saying at one point:[35]

> You came into that box with light hearts and consciences clear. Oh, may you leave there thus! Untortured with the curse of having wrecked the life of him whose life you hold in the hollow of your hands. And he is so young, too. Boyhood's down still softens upon his childlike face. You will not be here long now. Your homes where loved ones are even now watching, waiting to greet you, and when you clasp them to your manly breasts may the rapture at that moment be not embittered by the memory of having wrecked the life of yonder boy, whom all law and righteousness plead with you to save.

Houston always preferred to have as many former Texans as possible on a jury—in a close case his own Texas heritage and the memory of old Sam Houston, his father, might sway the verdict.[36] In his closing statement to the Alfred Son jury, he reminded those from Texas that the defendant was also a Texan, saying, "He has a Texas home far across the southern prairies, where the skies wear a deeper purple, where the dawn has a brighter glow, and the sunset wears a softer gold; where midnight stars look down upon us in a more unspeakable splendor."[37]

His oratory reached a dramatic conclusion when he reminded the jury that others, too, would be affected by their verdict: "His loved ones, like yours, are waiting—No! No! not like yours—for his life is darkened even now by the awful shade of death and who shall tell what he feels? Gentlemen, break that suspense; dry those tears; bind up these almost broken hearts for now no power but you can do so. This noble duty done and each hour of life thereafter will grow proud with this recollection."[38]

At three o'clock the next afternoon the jury brought in a verdict of acquittal.[39]

Houston's most publicized defense oration was delivered in Woodward in 1899 at the trial of Minnie Stacey accused of prostitution. Judge Burford determined she had no funds to hire an attorney so he chose young Frank Swindall as the court-appointed attorney to defend her. On the morning of the trial, Swindall happened to encounter Temple Houston in the courthouse, and persuaded him to take the case. Houston had only a few minutes before the trial began and his defense plea was entirely extemporaneous. The following is a condensed version of what was later called his "Soiled Dove" or "Plea for a Fallen Woman" oration:[40]

> Gentlemen of the jury: You have heard with what cold cruelty the prosecution referred to the sins of this woman, as if her condition were of her own preference... Gentlemen, one of our sex was the author of her ruin, more to blame than she, then let us judge her gently... You know the story of the prodigal son, but he was a son. For the prodigal daughter there is no return... Oh, consider this when you come to decide her guilt, for she is before us and we must judge her... The Master, while on earth, spoke in wrath and rebuke to kings and rulers, yet never reproached one of these. One he forgave. Another he acquitted... And now looking at this friendless outcast, who of you can say to her, "I am holier than thou" in the respect which she is charged with sinning?

He referred to the accused adulteress Jesus Christ had saved from stoning and continued, "If the prosecutors of the woman whom you are trying had brought her before the Saviour they would have accepted His challenge and each one gathered a rock and stoned her. Gentleman, do as your Master did twice under the same circumstances that surround you. Tell her to go in peace."[41]

Needless to say, the all male jury by unanimous verdict declared Minnie Stacey "not guilty."[42] After the speech was reported throughout the nation, the court stenographer was besieged with requests for copies.[43] Novelist Edna Ferber dramatized the event into a moving scene in her novel *Cimarron*.[44]

In the early 20th century, Statehood was in the

offing for Oklahoma, and Temple Houston ranked high among potential candidates for governor.[45] He personally indicated interest in a judgeship and said that he would especially like to attend the Constitutional Convention for no other reason than "to abolish the office of Justice of the Peace."[46] This was not to be, however, for after a long illness he died at age 45, two years before Oklahoma became a state. Jesse J. Dunn said in a touching tribute at the next meeting of the Territorial Bar, "Temple Houston belongs to the ages."[47]

18

LAWYERS' LAST FRONTIER: SOUTHWESTERN OKLAHOMA TERRITORY

When Texas was admitted to the Union in 1845, it and the United States agreed to designate the Red River as the boundary between what had been the Lone Star Republic and Indian Territory. A dispute later arose as to whether the North Fork or the South Fork was the main channel of the river. One of the most important law suits in Oklahoma's history resulted. The United States Supreme Court, after considering 1400 pages of printed record in 1896, held that the South Fork was the correct boundary.[1] Thus an area of about l.4 million acres that formerly had been Greer County, Texas, was added to Oklahoma Territory and eventually became the counties of Harmon, Jackson, and a portion of Beckham.[2]

Greer County, Texas had been a part of the Texas Thirty-First Judicial District, known as the "Jumbo District" due to its great size and irregular shape. The District boasted more towns inhabited by prairie dogs than people, so someone dubbed its members of the Bar "Prairie Dog Lawyers."[3] Because of travel difficulties and the problems of perfecting a proper record, the district's lawyers rarely appealed their cases. The day came when a young newcomer from Tennessee violated this custom by appealing a decision he had lost. A grizzled "Prairie Dog Lawyer" protested, "Now the devil is to pay. This fellow has learned how to appeal cases, and we are going to be worked to death."[4]

When court terms for old Greer County were held in Mangum, jurors and witnesses traveled there by wagon and horseback and set up camp with their bed rolls and chuck boxes. In later years they enjoyed the comparative luxury of accommodations in the local wagon yard.[5] One of the town's first lawyers was Jarret Todd, a former schoolteacher and Confederate Army veteran. Todd was 38 years old and had just been admitted to the Missouri Bar when he opened his law office in a tent on the Mangum town square. He then joined the lawyers in the "traveling court" of Judge Frank Willis, "the law North of the Red River."[6]

"Civil cases were few and criminal cases tough," Todd recalled. "We would follow Judge Willis across his district over Greer, Wheeler, Wilbarger, and other counties at each term of court to get our business."[7] Another pioneer Magnum lawyer was future justice of the Oklahoma Supreme Court Charles M. Thacker. He was 23 years old at the time he settled there in 1889 and began to teach a class in bookkeeping to supplement his meager law income.[8]

That same year G.A. Brown, dubbed "God Almighty" Brown by Temple Houston, succeeded Judge Willis as District Judge in the Greer County area.[9] Joseph L. Sweet had just built a new home in Mangum when Judge Brown arrived to hold a term of court. Sweet's home had the only vacant room in town, so court was held there.[10] Judge Brown soon encountered Mangum's legendary John Rose, an eccentric, middle-aged, powerfully built man who operated a wagon yard and freight line in the 1880s and 1890s. Their acquaintance began when Rose walked barefoot into Judge Brown's courtroom. The shocked judge ordered the clerk to fine Rose $25 for offending the dignity of the court. Rose's friends convinced the judge that Rose intended no offense—he always went barefoot in the summertime.[11] The townspeople elected Rose justice of the peace. He held court first in a dugout and later in his wagon yard's camp house where the furniture consisted of a pine table and a few chairs. Court officials usually sat on the chairs while "the jury sat on sacks of feed, bales of hay, nail kegs, spring seats off wagons, or anything available."[12]

Judge Brown was holding court in Mangum in March of 1896 when a messenger from Quanah, Texas, brought word of the Supreme Court's decision that made Greer County a part of Oklahoma Territory. The judge carefully read the message, raised his head, removed his glasses and announced, "Gentlemen of the Jury, Members of

G.A. Brown, the "hand-shaking judge" of Mangum, was elected to the State Supreme Court in 1914. (Courtesy Western History Collections, University of Oklahoma Library.)

the Bar, Fellow citizens, visitors to this court. Court is adjourned. There will never be court held in Mangum, Greer County, Texas, again, for there is no such place on the map. By the decision of the Supreme Court this is Mangum, Oklahoma Territory. You are dismissed."[13] Judge Brown held the office of Texas' Forty-fourth Judicial District until 1903 when he moved to Hobart, Oklahoma Territory, and then to Mangum that same year. At Oklahoma's Statehood election in 1907, he was elected judge of the Eighteenth Judicial District and re-elected in 1910.[14]

During a general discussion at the annual meeting of the state Bar in 1913, E.G. McAdams of Oklahoma City blamed District Court trial delays on those "hand-shaking" judges who spent half of their time "electioneering." "[They] ought to be on the justice [of the peace] bench instead of the district bench," McAdams said. Brown, then a district judge, took the opportunity to explain his own "hand-shaking" proclivity and tell the convention why he moved from Hobart to Mangum in 1903:[15]

> It has been said that I am a professional hand-shaker, and it may be true. I love to shake hands with my friends. I came from Texas where it was customary and I remember I first landed in Hobart and opened up an office there and I did very

well. Men there come in and employed me and paid me my fee and came back and employed me again. I would go out on the streets and meet one of my clients and I would approach him intending to recognize him and shake hands with him, and sometimes if he was not from Texas before he got to me he would look up or down or look off, and I wanted to hand him one as I passed by him. That was not my way of doing. That man did not mean anything or harm by it. They had not been accustomed to my way of living and of hand shaking with your friends, and when I met them and recognized them they were not accustomed to that. I told some of my friends that I would not live anywhere that a man would pay me for working for him and then pass me by and I picked up and went over to Greer County where every one was from Texas and where if they met me expected to shake hands with me and I expected to shake hands with them and recognize them.

Judge Brown was elected to the bench of the State Supreme Court the next year, but died in less than a year, at age 67.[16]

After Greer County was added to Oklahoma Territory, five years passed before the next great expansion of the Territory based on the Jerome (Cherokee) Commission's agreements with Indian tribes concluded in the early 1890s. In negotiating for the purchase of Indian land, the Jerome Commission preferred to deal directly with tribal leaders unimpeded by the presence of legal counsel. But the Indian representatives realized their inadequacies at the bargaining table and often insisted on having the advice of counsel. That was the attitude of Chief Towaconie Jim, a Wichita Indian who was spokesman for the Wichita and affiliated tribes when the Commission began negotiation in May of 1891 at Anadarko for land that eventually became part of the Oklahoma counties of Caddo, Canadian, Blaine, Custer, Washita, and Grady.[17]

Towaconie Jim had visited briefly with the commissioners at Fort Reno the previous fall and had mentioned the names of two lawyers whose presence he desired at the negotiations. One of the lawyers was Luther H. Pike of Washington, D. C. Pike's father, Albert, had formed a friendly relationship with the Wichitas and affiliated tribes when he concluded a treaty with them for the Confederacy during the Civil War. Luther himself was the adopted son of the Wichitas and knew the tribe well. Eight years before he had prepared a

Chief Towaconi Jim, a Wichita Indian who recognized the importance of legal counsel. (Courtesy Archives and Manuscripts Division, OHS.)

631-page brief of their history and claims against the government to submit to the Office of Indian Affairs.[18]

At the May, 1891, meeting, Chief Towaconie Jim's opening statement, through an interpreter, expressed his displeasure that counsel was not present:[19]

He [Towaconie Jim] supposed that you would remember that we had a talk about two lawyers and when you came we looked around and did not see these two lawyers. You can look around and see these Indians and see they are not fit to do their business with a Commission; you can see they are sitting around smoking and the lawyers are not here and there is no use talking. About these two attorneys that we have, we want them to be present and there is a telegraph office and you can telegraph them and if they answer that they will come then they [the Indians] will be here; and that they have already lost two days by being here and when you hear from those two men they will

go on with the council and till then they can go on with their farming. It is time to plant sweet potatoes.

Chairman Jerome tried to convince the chief that retention of attorneys would be a needless expense, citing the case of the Pottawatomies who had retained counsel at a cost of $30,000 and fared no better than the Absentee Shawnees who had bargained without benefit of counsel.[20] Chief Towaconie Jim replied that an attorney "could use that book" and "stand up and talk better."[21]

A major item of disagreement was the price offered for the land. The Wichitas refused to consider a price of about 50 cents per acre offered by the Commission. After two weeks of negotiations, Chief Towaconie Jim told the Commissioners, "We don't understand all, and all do not understand, and the more you say the worse it is and now we won't know what to do and if we get attorneys we can go on with this council but the way we are if we raise nothing to eat we will be poor sure enough. We can't afford to lay around here like we been doing…, and if we were getting paid like you Commissioners we could stay here, too."[22]

Chairman Jerome finally relented, and Luther H. Pike was invited to the conference.[23] The Commission would not accept Pike's counter offer of $1.25 per acre but acquiesced to Pike's suggestion that "the conscience of Congress" should determine the amount to be inserted in the purchase agreement.[24] Chief Towaconie Jim's insistence on employment of counsel was rewarded on March 972, 1895, when Congress approved $1.25 per acre for the land.[25]

The opening of the Wichita and affiliated tribes reservations to settlement had to await purchase of adjoining lands owned by the Kiowas, Comanches, and Apaches. The Cherokee Commission concluded an agreement with the latter tribes in the fall of 1892, but Indian leaders alleged signatures to the agreement had been obtained by "fraudulent misrepresentation and concealment" and were able to delay Congressional approval for almost eight years. Congress approved the agreement in June of 1900.[26]

Chief Lone Wolf and a group of his fellow Kiowas refused to concede defeat and retained William M. Springer, the former United States Judge in Indian Territory, and his associates to pursue their objections through the courts. Springer during his 20 years in Congress had worked for opening Indian Territory to settlement and had authored the Springer Amendment in 1889 that opened the Unclaimed Lands and created the Cherokee Commission. He now led the fight to defeat the efforts of that Commission and block the last great opening of Indian lands. Lieutenant Colonel James F. Randlett, United States Indian Agent to the Kiowas, was exceedingly critical of what he called the "sedition" of the Springer-Lone Wolf combine and certain "unemployed attorneys of Anadarko, Okla." interested in large legal fees for litigation that could not succeed.[27]

Springer lost in both the Supreme Court of the District of Columbia and in the United States Supreme Court.[28] After the lower court's ruling of June 26, 1901, President McKinley on July 4, 1901, issued a proclamation that opened for settlement the lands of the Wichita and affiliated tribes, as well as the lands of the Kiowas, Comanches and Apaches. Territorial Delegate Dennis Flynn had recommended and secured the ap-

proval of Congress for a land lottery system to open those lands in an attempt to avoid the inequities and disorder of previous land openings.[29] Only 13,000 homestead tracts of 160 acres each were to be awarded, but 165,000 homeseekers registered at Fort Sill and El Reno for the drawing to begin on July 29, 1901. Many returned to their homes after registering, but thousands remained with the intent of settling in Oklahoma Territory even if their names were not drawn in the lottery.

Lawyers from near and far camped at Fort Sill and El Reno ready to offer their services. They were most frequently needed for preparation of registration papers, and business was especially good for those who held notary commissions. One notary public earned $70 by 3:00 p.m. in one day by filling out the simple registration forms at 25 cents each and impressing his notary seal. A man who falsely claimed to be a notary public narrowly escaped lynching. Another was arrested when the authorities learned his notary commission had expired.[30]

Lawyers who set up their tents near the regis-

Scene in El Reno where homeseekers registered for the land drawing in 1901. (Courtesy OHS.)

tration building at Fort Sill had not bothered to ask permission to locate their tents on government property. When told to move the tents, they failed to function with the speed the military had in mind. Without warning a detachment of soldiers rushed up and down the rows of tents flattening them while the surprised lawyers were inside. The lawyers accepted the incident with good humor and re-established their offices on land farther removed from the registration office.[31]

After 13,000 names had been drawn, the government began on August 6, 1901, to sell to the highest bidders the land previously reserved for town lots. More than $700,000 were received for lots at Lawton, Hobart, and Anadarko. One of the most enterprising of the Lawton lawyers was A.H. Cobb. He had practiced in Kansas City, but also had worked as a "chain man" on the crew who surveyed the Kiowa-Comanche country some time before. From his careful notes describing the topography of each quarter section of land, he prepared a map that netted him several thousand dollars from sales to those who needed help in locating the land they had won in the lottery or who wished to find desirable land to purchase.[32]

When map sales began to taper off, Cobb formed a law partnership with Charles C. Black, a practicing lawyer from Winfield, Kansas.[33] Cobb and Black opened their office in quarters similar to that of other lawyers in Lawton at the time, a tent with a wooden floor and enclosed by boards about three feet high. Office furniture consisted of a former spool cabinet, which they used for storing paper and blank forms, and a table three feet by 10 feet covered with an oil cloth with benches on each side. Their only book was the *Oklahoma Territorial Code.* They employed a law clerk at a salary of $40 a month plus the privilege of making his bed on the wooden floor. All legal papers were drafted in longhand.[34]

If one adhered to the adage, "Beware of the man with one book," he would have been wary of most of the Lawton Bar. However, the absence of a law library seemed to present no problem at the time. Bert M. Parmenter, appointed Assistant United States Attorney General by President Coolidge 24 years later, arrived at the Lawton townsite in a lumber wagon. He painted his name and profession on a narrow strip of muslin and placed it on the front of his tent, which served as

The oratory of Thomas P. Gore, a blind lawyer and later United States senator, impressed Lawton settlers in August of 1901. (Courtesy OHS.)

his office and the home for himself, his wife, and two children.[35] "We needed no law books, and had none. At that time there were no property rights to be litigated, there was, however, a large criminal practice, to be had, but it was not necessary to know any law in order to engage in the practice."[36]

Several lawyers who were to become well known in Oklahoma history settled in Lawton at the time. Scott Ferris, later a Congressman, brought his one law book to the partnership he formed with Z.I. Holt, who like Ferris was from Missouri. Their combination law and real estate office was in a tent, 10 by 12 feet. Unlike the tent occupied by Cobb & Black, it could not boast a wooden floor. A necessary employee of the firm of Ferris & Holt was one "Shorty" Crane, the owner of a team of white ponies and a four-seated hack. His responsibility was to transport homeseekers and help them select their claims. The lawyers' fee for assisting lottery winners and processing the necessary papers in the land office was $10.[37]

Two future United States senators hastened to Lawton to take part in the opening, Thomas P. Gore and Elmer Thomas. Gore, handicapped by the loss of his eyesight in two boyhood accidents, was a graduate of the law school of Cumberland University in 1892. He had practiced law in Mississippi and Texas. Assisted by his father, Gore was one of the first to settle at the Lawton townsite.[38] The Democrats, who held their first party meeting a few days after the Lawton townsite was opened, were impressed by the blind lawyer when he presented a two-page resolution recited from memory.[39] Only six years later Gore was selected United States Senator from the new state of Oklahoma.

Elmer Thomas had been a resident of Indiana and was a recent honor graduate of DePauw University in law, pedagogy, and elocution. He first became aware that Oklahoma City could be reached by railroad when he saw a faded poster in a country railway station in Indiana advertising a reunion of the Spanish-American War Rough Riders to be held in Oklahoma City. Next to that poster was one advertising a one-way homestead excursion to Oklahoma. Thomas borrowed the cost of the one-way ticket and on November 16, 1900, arrived in Oklahoma City to practice law while waiting for the Kiowa-Comanche country to be opened.[40] He shared a tent with a group of friends from Indiana on the night of August 5, 1901, the night before the official opening of the new land. The tense atmosphere of that night in a city of tents inhabited by adventurous pioneers, cowboys, soldiers, United States marshals, and Indians seemed to call for extra precaution, so Thomas and his friends took turns at guard duty. The future United States Senator was standing guard shortly after midnight when an excited man rushed by in search of a doctor to attend a wounded hold-up victim. However, the need for a doctor vanished moments later when another man dashed by in search of an undertaker.[41]

A county government took form promptly the next day with Leo McBryan as County Judge and W.C. Stevens as County Attorney. Lawton's first City Attorney was Jake L. Hamon. A quarter of a century later Hamon, as a wealthy oil man and maker of politicians, was to meet a violent death at the hands of his mistress in Ardmore.

By nine o'clock on the morning of the opening, a temporary courthouse and jail were located on Lawton's present courthouse square. The courthouse was a wagon, and the jail was the wagon's wheels where the prisoners were chained.[42] A group of progressive attorneys met one evening and by the light of the moon organized the Comanche County Bar Association.[43] Judge John

L. McAtee visited Lawton some time later and administered the oath of office to more than 200 lawyers.[44]

The trial docket of the District Court at Lawton was soon so far behind that the local Bar devised a novel way to dispose of civil cases. The members elected an "Assistant Judge" and by agreement of the parties assigned him 160 cases for trial before a jury drawn by the clerk in the customary manner. The Assistant Judge held court in a separate room, and his decisions and all other journal entries were signed by the regular trial judge. More than a hundred civil cases, indistinguishable from other matters on the judgment docket, were handled in this manner at nominal expense.[45]

Robert J. Ray described the Comanche County plan at the 1904 meeting of the Oklahoma and Indian Territory Bar Associations. He suggested the 18- to 24-month backlog in the Territorial courts could be handled in a similar way and accomplish a relatively clean docket for the advent of Statehood, which was anticipated in the near future.[46] The Oklahoma Legislature in 1911 and later years adopted a somewhat similar arrangement in the form of a Supreme Court Commission. Robert J. Ray himself served on the Commission from 1923 to 1927.[47]

The story of the settlement of Lawton was duplicated on a smaller scale in the two county seat towns of Anadarko and Hobart. In Anadarko funds from the government's auction of town lots enabled construction of a courthouse and jail along with a light and water system. Anadarko's courts overflowed with litigation, although as one writer said, "Decisions and verdicts in many cases were as uncertain as the shifting sands of western Kansas." Even though robberies, pickpocketing, prostitution, and an occasional murder occurred, the first case that required a jury of 12 dealt with a man accused of trapping fish in the Washita River. Few new residents met the residence requirements for jury duty, so Judge Crumm's Court impaneled a jury made up of Indian Agency officials, missionaries, Indian traders, and intermarried Indian citizens. Louie McKnight, a recent college graduate, prosecuted the case. The accused was found guilty and fined $250—five dollars for each fish caught illegally. The most convincing testimony took place in the jury room where juror John Cragg announced,

Tent offices at the Anadarko settlement in 1901. (Courtesy Western History Collections, University of Oklahoma Library.)

"He is guilty, for I saw him myself when he was trapping the fish."[48]

The opening of the Kiowa-Comanche reservation brought a peaceful solution to a problem that had nagged the Department of Interior for eight years: the illegal settlement of a 2700-acre strip of land in a bend of the Washita River called the "Neutral Strip" which later became a part of Washita County. The authorities had delayed eviction of the settlers due to political pressure and probably because they thought the land would soon be acquired by the federal government. The settlers, encouraged by the absence of governmental interference, organized the town of Oakdale in May of 1899 and renamed it Mountain View a few months later.[49] One of Mountain View's new residents was 21-year-old Richard A. Billups, a native of Mississippi and recent law graduate of Cumberland University. "I knew I had to work for a living and felt that I would like to make a name for myself in some new field," Billups later explained. "I had heard and read a great deal of the opening of Oklahoma, so I

packed my few belongings and my law books and came to Washita County August 20, 1899..."[50]

Billups set up his law practice in a small box building.[51] A few months later local residents sent him to Washington to lobby for legislation favorable to the "Neutral Strip" people. He persuaded Territorial Delegate Dennis Flynn to sponsor a clause in the bill opening the Kiowa-Comanche reservation that gave "Neutral Strip" settlers preference rights for 30 days to lands they had occupied and improved.[52]

The voters of Washita County expressed their approval of Billups at the polls a year after he arrived there by electing him probate judge, an office he held for four successive terms. He was under the statutory age during his first two terms in office and served only by the special approval of the legislature. He moved to Cordell in 1906 and was elected to Oklahoma's first state senate. He is best known in Oklahoma history for authorship of the "Billups Booze Bill"—the state's first measure for enforcing prohibition and establishing liquor dispensaries.[53]

Governor Haskell signing the Oklahoma prohibition law, "Billups Booze Bill," on March 24, 1908. Senator Richard A. Billups, the bill's sponsor, is at the governor's right. (Courtesy OHS.)

19

THE BAR STRUGGLES FOR STATEHOOD

On December 18, 1889, while the new occupants of the Unassigned Lands were deploring the lack of Territorial government, Congressman William M. Springer of Illinois was looking even further into the future. That day he introduced a bill that would have created the state of Columbia out of a portion of Indian Territory.[1] This was only the first attempt at Statehood in the 17 years of Statehood agitation led by lawyers of both Oklahoma and Indian Territories.

Differing conditions in the Twin Territories produced divided sentiment where Statehood was concerned. Over the years five different approaches to the question were considered:[2] (1) Single (joint) Statehood, a combination of Oklahoma and Indian Territories. (2) Separate (double) Statehood, each Territory to become a state. (3) Immediate Statehood for Oklahoma Territory and "piecemeal absorption" of Indian Territory when circumstances warranted. (4) Statehood for Oklahoma Territory only. (5) Statehood for neither Territory.

Conventions, held in both Territories, sometimes advocated separate Statehood but more often favored single Statehood. When resolutions were adopted and memorials sent to Washington the more serious and financially able conventions dispatched their own delegates to argue in the halls of Congress. Heated debates took place in the Committee on Territories and in the Committee on Indian Affairs in both houses.[3] Before Statehood was finally approved, the Congressional committees had considered 31 different Statehood bills.[4]

Many of the lawyer principals in the Statehood controversy were to become prominent in the Territories and the future state, while others appeared briefly then disappeared from the scene.

Oklahoma City in December of 1891 initiated the first organized Statehood convention, and the question of separate or joint Statehood arose immediately. John H. Burford, whose appointment to a Territorial judgeship occurred the following March, challenged a single Statehood report presented by the Committee on Resolutions headed by pioneer Sidney Clarke, dubbed the "Statehood evangelist."[5] Burford argued that any attempt to join with the Five Civilized Tribes would be wasted effort that would only delay Statehood for Oklahoma Territory. Horace Speed, the United States Attorney, described as the "youthful and brave young Knight of Statehood," opposed Burford, as did William P. Hackney, the senior partner of Henry Asp. Hackney insisted that the people were exhausted from "being bulldozed and murdered by Indian outlaws." His solution was "to bring the Five Civilized Tribes within the pale of civilization by means of laws, to protect themselves against outlawry."[6]

The convention adopted the committee report and selected a non-partisan executive committee to accumulate the necessary statistics and prepare a single Statehood "enabling act." Sidney Clarke was chairman of the executive committee, and other lawyer members were William P. Hackney, Frank J. Wikoff, and Samuel H. Harris. Harris in 1906 became president of the Oklahoma-Indian Territory Bar Association and in 1909 served on the first commission authorized to codify state laws.[7] The report prepared by the executive committee set out the basic arguments for joint Statehood with the Five Civilized Tribes. Those arguments were to be reiterated over the next 14 years: adequate population, fertility of soil, minerals, and favorable business, educational, religious, and social conditions.[8]

Clarke sent the report to David A. Harvey, Oklahoma Territory's first delegate to Congress, who introduced a joint Statehood bill in the House along the lines recommended by Clarke's committee.[9] Harvey was a Civil War veteran who had studied law at Miami University in his home state of Ohio and was admitted to the Bar in 1869 at age 21. While serving as City Attorney and Probate Judge in Topeka, Kansas, he had worked for the opening of the Unassigned Lands. He settled in Guthrie on the day of the opening.[10]

The House Committee on Territories allowed

Clarke, W.P. Hackney, and Horace Speed to speak during a series of hearings on the so-called "Harvey Bill." An effective argument against the bill was the provisions in existing treaties which prohibited the inclusion of Indian land within a state without the consent of the Indians themselves. Hackney agreed that such provisions were "public policy" at one time, but he said that the Indians for all practical purposes had nullified the policy by encouraging more than 200,000 whites to settle in Indian Territory.[11]

Horace Speed, like Hackney, argued that nothing in prior treaties kept Indian land from being included in a new state. Drawing on statements made by Judge Parker at Fort Smith and his own experiences as a United States Attorney, Speed stressed the open hostility to federal authority in Indian Territory. More crimes occurred there, he told the committee, than "in any other agricultural section of the United States of equal size and population," a situation that could be improved by local government and courts.[12]

The committee invited rebuttal from representatives of the Five Civilized Tribes. Roley McIntosh, a full-blood Creek, contributed a classic presentation of the Indian attitude toward Statehood.[13] Speaking through an interpreter, McIntosh referred to the previous speakers: "Many of them seem to be lawyers, men of fine address," he told the committee, but he himself was not "a trained lawyer," so they could expect no "hair-splitting arguments." With reference to the treaties against including Indian lands within a state he said, "I am an old Indian and I only know one way; and when you make a contract with me, I expect you to stand by it." In reply to charges of lawlessness in the Territory, he pointed out that lawlessness has always existed: "If we had no lawlessness there would be no need of laws." In his opinion the lawbreakers were intruders that the United States had agreed to keep out of the Territory.

McIntosh directed another blow at the lawyers: "There is some lawlessness down there, and the lawyers...are having a dearth of business and are anxious to get at these people down there." The location of federal courts also bothered McIntosh. He told the Committee, "Texas wants to take us down to Paris, Texas, and Kansas wants to take us to Wichita, and Arkansas wants to take us to Fort Smith, and now here is Oklahoma Terri-

Roley McIntosh, a Creek Indian representative in Washington for the Five Civilized Tribes during the Statehood controversy. (Courtesy OHS.)

tory holding us on this side."[14] Again referring to Speed's charge of lawlessness, McIntosh said:[15]

We have your deputy marshals all over our country—United States deputy marshals. We see them every day. And in all the little towns of the Creek Nation we have officers appointed by the Interior Department, who are known as Indian police, and who are also conservators of law and order. There are so many of those United States deputy marshals, and Indian policeman there, under appointment from the Government of the United States, that they hardly have criminals enough to catch. Sometimes these deputy marshals have trouble among themselves. One will say, "I had a writ for that fellow and you have gone and caught him."

The argument by McIntosh and others against Statehood was effective in the defeat of the Harvey Bill; however, the practical matter of a tax structure to finance state and local government played a prominent role in the bill's defeat. Homesteads in Oklahoma Territory were nontaxable only until the homesteader had satisfied government requirements, but Indian lands were expected to be non-taxable and inalienable for a period of years.[16]

At least four separate Statehood conventions were held in 1893. At a convention in Purcell, the influence of the legal profession was most evident

110

in the criticism of court conditions contained in a lengthy petition submitted to Congress in behalf of joint Statehood. The petitioners referred to "five ambiguous and conflicting court jurisdictions" composed of:[17] (1) The Indian courts "with their barbarous whippings and executions by shooting." (2) The Indian agent and the Indian police. (3) The Federal court at Fort Smith, and (4) The Federal court at Paris, Texas "with power of life and death…" (5) The Muskogee Federal court, "little more than a big justice court, that smacks strongly of the police court."

The petition explained, as Roley McIntosh had already indicated to the House Committee on Territories, that "We have so much law that we can't tell where one court's jurisdiction leaves off and another's begins." Inadequacies of the Indian Territory court system were to be repeated frequently while the fight for Statehood continued.[18] A week after the Purcell convention Delegate Dennis Flynn, who had succeeded David A. Harvey, introduced a joint Statehood bill that failed to receive favorable consideration.[19]

For the next several years a quick solution to the Statehood problem seemed out of the question, and citizens of the Twin Territories turned to other matters. The Five Tribes of Indian Territory anxiously followed the land allotments undertaken by the Dawes Commission. The Spanish-American War commanded attention from both Territories in 1898. The depression of the mid-nineties, crop failures, and Territorial and national politics were popular subjects in Oklahoma Territory.[20]

Indicative of the hard times for lawyers in the middle 1890s was the scramble for the City Attorney post in El Reno after John Schmook resigned. The "president of the late territorial council," and "a prominent applicant for a supreme court judgeship," as well as most of the local bar were reported to covet the office. After the town council selected W.W. Bush, a reporter for the *El Reno News* called on a few of the candidates to "express sympathy." In a jocular mood all indicated surprise that they had not been chosen, inasmuch as each had been assured that "six out of the seven councilmen were for him." J.J. Cane commented, "I'm going to quit having friends… Six out of seven is less than a majority." E.T. Marsh contemplated leaving the legal profession to enter the ministry, while one an-

C.B. Ames (left) with Judge Robert L. Williams. Ames, an active Statehood supporter, became chairman of the board of directors of the Texas Company (Texaco) in 1933. (Courtesy Archives and Manuscripts Division, OHS.)

nounced he had already resigned from the Bar but had not decided whether to "go to farming or get married."[21] Despite the shortage of paying clients, the town's legal profession still attracted new converts. The *El Reno News* reported in February of 1900 that "Tom Whistling Eye, a wild Indian youth, went to the Carlisle Indian School four years ago. He has returned dressed in the highest style, and announces that he will practice law."[22]

The turn of the century brought renewed interest in Statehood, and the names of a new generation of lawyers began to surface. Among these was C.B. Ames, one of the most capable lawyers ever to practice in Oklahoma. Ames was a graduate of Emory and Henry College and the law school of the University of Mississippi. In 1897 he was nearly 30 years old and already prospering as a Mississippi lawyer when he first visited Oklahoma Territory. Two years later he established a law partnership with H.H. Howard of Oklahoma City. His legal practice flourished while he earned a national reputation that in 1933 led to the chairmanship of the Board of Directors of the Texas Company in New York City.[23]

Early in his career Ames adopted a creed, pertaining to a lawyer's role in government, which he expressed as follows, "No lawyer can really understand the sacredness of a court, the true import of the Writ of Habeas Corpus, or the many other factors upon which law and legal procedure are based, if he does not know and understand government. Government cannot be disassociated from law." In accord with that concept, Ames became involved in Territorial politics the year after he arrived in Oklahoma. Appointed chairman of the Resolutions Committee at the Democratic Territorial Convention held in Enid, he wrote the convention platform. Later, due to his acquaintance with an influential Democrat, he was instrumental in inserting a "single Statehood" plank in the national platform of the Democratic party.

He wrote the platform for two subsequent Territorial conventions, at Claremore and Oklahoma City.[24] In February of 1902 he was the author, along with Ralph E. Campbell, later United States Judge for the Eastern District of Oklahoma, and Frank Wells, president of the Oklahoma State Bar Association in 1908, of a single Statehood resolution that the Oklahoma City Commercial Club presented to the Fifty-Seventh Congress. That resolution strongly objected to the political considerations that hindered prospects for Statehood.[25]

In 1901 the single Statehood movement gained support in the Indian Territory press, and the people themselves seemed more interested in the single state approach to their problems. The *Wetumka Herald* called for local self government, and complained that the 400,000 people in Indian Territory were governed only by marshals, judges, and postmasters.[26] A meeting at Oklahoma City of the Inter-territorial Executive Committee in October of 1901 appeared to be one of the most productive of Statehood efforts up to that time. Two lawyers, Robert E. Wood of Shawnee and Thomas C. Humphrey of South McAlester, played prominent roles.

Wood, 34 years old, was a member of the Oklahoma Territorial Legislature and a former County Attorney of Garfield County. He had been admitted to the Bar in 1888 after receiving his law degree from Washington University in St. Louis.[27] The professional career of T.C. Humphrey had taken an unusual turn. After he graduated from Missouri Medical College at age 23 in 1869, he began to practice medicine and engage in the drug business. A term in the Arkansas Legislature must have encouraged him to begin the study of law in 1876. He had already been admitted to the Bar before he enrolled in the University of Louisville where he obtained a law degree in 1879. Thereafter he practiced law, and in 1898 he moved his office from Fort Smith to Cameron in Indian Territory.[28]

Both Robert E. Wood and Humphrey proposed prompt action to convince Congress that the Twin Territories insisted on Statehood. Wood suggested a Statehood convention to memorialize Congress for an Enabling Act, while Humphrey pressed for stronger action that would convene 50 delegates from each Territory, frame a Constitution, present it to Congress, then demand immediate Statehood.[29] As a result the Executive Committee at the Oklahoma City meeting voted to hold a Statehood convention in Muskogee in November of 1901 to be attended by 300 delegates and alternates from each Territory with no specific requirement as to race, politics, or religion but all with a common objective—single Statehood.[30]

Humphrey later appeared before the Committee on Territories in both houses of Congress on behalf of single Statehood. After Congress voted four additional judges for Indian Territory in 1904, Humphrey—an enthusiastic Republican supporter of Theodore Roosevelt—received an appointment as judge of the Central District. His insistence on fairness for the Indians of that area earned him the sobriquet of "square deal judge."[31] Perhaps Humphrey's salary as judge diminished his desire for Statehood to the effect that he was only half joking when he told C.W. White, owner of the boarding house where the Judge stayed when he was in Durant, "I'm not ready for Statehood because I haven't been at the pie counter long enough."[32]

Territorial delegate Dennis T. Flynn recalled of the Statehood movement, "If a particular town didn't favor single Statehood, the next Statehood convention would be held in that town for public effect and to win them over to the cause."[33] Appropriately, the Inter-territorial Executive Committee voted to hold a Statehood meeting at Muskogee, a city believed to be strongly in favor of separate Statehood for Indian Territory. There was little doubt that Muskogee's size and location made it the logical choice for state capital if Indian Territory gained separate Statehood.[34] Statehood delegates were agreeably surprised at the enthusiastic welcome they received from Muskogee residents at the November, 1901, convention. At the railroad station a brass band greeted the approximately 1000 delegates, the largest of any Statehood meeting to date. The courtroom where they met was decorated with flags and banners.[35]

Lawyers were in the forefront as the meeting began. William T. Hutchings of Muskogee was immediately chosen temporary chairman. Hutchings, a Virginian, was a graduate of Yale College in 1881 and had been one of the first attorneys to settle in Muskogee in 1889.[36] Other lawyers, who spoke early in the meeting, were Judge John R. Thomas and D. C. Lewis, an Oklahoma City lawyer active in the Statehood movement for several years, along with Freeman E. Miller of Stillwater.[37] Miller was a native of Indiana where he was admitted to the Bar in 1886. He received a master of arts degree from DePaul University in 1890 and started his law practice in Stillwater that same year. Thirty-seven years old in 1901, he was one of the most versatile pioneer lawyers in Oklahoma Territory. Throughout his career, not only was he a criminal lawyer but also

he found time to be poet laureate of Oklahoma, an author, newspaper editor, legislator, and educator.[38]

The Muskogee convention delegates passed resolutions in support of single Statehood for the two Territories according to existing boundaries and with representation based on population. They favored allotment of Indian lands in severalty and, except for homesteads, no restrictions on disposal of the land.[39] Thomas H. Doyle of Perry was chosen chairman of a delegation selected to go to Washington, to present the convention's resolutions to Congress. Doyle, then 38 years old, was appointed to the Oklahoma Criminal Court of Appeals seven years later and, with the exception of one six-year term, served on that court until 1946 when he was 83 years old.[40] He had attended the University of Kansas for a short time, read law and in 1893 after being admitted to the Kansas Bar had moved to Perry in Oklahoma Territory.[41]

Doyle's selection as one of the Muskogee convention's Washington delegates marked the beginning of a six-year period that he regularly represented Statehood interests in Washington. He was an able delineator of the Statehood movement and was especially effective when he ap-

The versatile Freeman E. Miller of Stillwater—criminal lawyer, poet laureate of Oklahoma, newspaperman, legislator, and educator. (Courtesy Archives and Manuscripts Division, OHS.)

Thomas H. Doyle (standing) with "Alfalfa Bill" Murray. Doyle represented Statehood supporters in Washington, D.C., for six years and later served five terms on the Court of Criminal Appeals. (Courtesy Archives and Manuscripts Division, OHS.)

Photo made when G. W. Raymond was Chief Justice of the Court of Appeals in Indian Terrirtory. (Courtesy Western History Collections, University of Oklahoma Library.)

peared before the House Committee on Territories on January 26, 1904. There he made a lengthy statement for Statehood and subjected himself to questioning by Committee members. He outlined the history of the Twin Territories, described the various land openings, and detailed the usual arguments for Statehood along the lines of population, resources, and geography.[42] At one point in response to a question from Congressman Thayer of Massachusetts, Doyle had an opportunity to comment on the ability of Indian Territory lawyers, saying, "You find men just as brainy in every respect, following the profession of the law before those courts as we do in your State of Massachusetts.[43]

The ongoing drive for Statehood continued into July of 1905 when Oklahoma City hosted 10,000 people at a gala occasion supporting single Statehood. Among well-known lawyer delegates were Roy Hoffman, Robert L. Williams, W.A. Ledbetter, John Embry, Thomas H. Doyle, Jesse J. Dunn, W.B. Johnson, and two United States judges from Indian Territory, Joseph A.

Gill and Charles W. Raymond.[44] Convention leaders were eager to put forth a united front for single Statehood, but friction in the Muskogee delegation occurred between Clarence B. Douglas, editor of the *Muskogee Phoenix*, and Judge Charles W. Raymond, successor in 1901 to John R. Thomas in the post of "roving judge"in Indian Territory. Douglas denounced Judge Raymond at the Oklahoma City convention for having sent a special delegation under his control to the Oklahoma City convention. Raymond had ignored Muskogee Negroes, and disharmony prevailed when the Negroes sent their own separate delegation to the convention. A "prominent attorney" from Ardmore, probably W.A. Ledbetter, was quoted as saying, "While it must be admitted that Judge Raymond's methods are tyrannical, it is not the best policy to incur his enmity. He is the protege of Congressman [Joseph G.] Cannon of Illinois, who is in a position to do the Statehood cause much good or more harm as he may elect."[45] Douglas later wrote in his *History of Tulsa* that Judge Raymond had been unhappy with the extensive traveling involved in his new post of "roving judge"and through his powerful political influence caused Congress to divide Indian Territory's Northern District and thereby create for Raymond a Western District composed of the Creek and Seminole Nations.[46]

A spirit of cooperation overcame the disharmony at the beginning of the Oklahoma City convention, and the delegates united in a resolution asking approval of immediate joint Statehood at the Congressional session scheduled to begin in December of 1905.[47] However, one more important Statehood convention was to occur in Muskogee before Congress finally approved a Statehood bill.

In 1902 Indian leaders apprehensive of the Oklahoma Territory Statehood movement had begun a series of meetings in behalf of separate Statehood for Indian Territory. William H. Murray was appointed to represent the Chickasaw Nation at the meetings. He wrote in 1931 that those attending the meeting of Five Civilized Tribes leaders in Eufaula in November of 1902 had indicated a "great dread" of the fate of the Indian race if they were joined with the whites of Oklahoma Territory, a fear arising from the Pottawatomie County incident in 1898 when two

Seminole youths had been burned to death by a mob of white men.[48]

Indian leaders continued their regular meetings with no specific results until July of 1905—just before the great single Statehood meeting in Oklahoma City. James A. Norman, a Cherokee citizen, had been a Washington lobbyist, and his familiarity with the Statehood movement convinced him that the Five Tribes must act quickly if they were to avoid joint Statehood with Oklahoma Territory. Upon his own initiative but with the approval of Chief William C. Rogers of the Cherokee Nation and Chief Green McCurtain of the Choctaw Nation, he issued a call on July 5, 1905, for a separate Statehood convention for Indian Territory.[49]

Weary from three years of regular conferences, preceded by decades of threats of dissolution of their way of life, Indian leaders felt little disposed to take an active role in the Indian-sponsored convention. But they now received encouragement from Charles N. Haskell, lawyer turned railroad builder. Haskell, 45 years old in 1905, had been born and educated in Ohio. From age 17 he supported himself as a schoolteacher, but in his spare time he studied in the law office of J.H.L. Long in Ottawa, Ohio. On December 6, 1880, he passed an examination conducted by a committee of the Ohio Supreme Court, and three months later he began to practice law in Ottawa.[50]

The typical law office in Ottawa at that time was unpretentious—with well worn furniture on a bare, wooden floor and a box of sand that served as cuspidor and resting place for a stove. Haskell departed from local custom and outfitted his office with pleasant, comfortable furnishings.[51] Prospective clients took notice of him through his frequent appearances at public gatherings and his readiness to speak on almost any subject.[52] One of his first fees was $120 paid by a wholesale grocery company when he collected a $680 past due account owed by a local merchant. The merchant derived the $680 by mortgaging his farm to Haskell for a loan of $1,200. Word of Haskell's innovative and forceful collection methods reached other creditors, and he became a leading collection attorney in a six-county area.[53] His first important legal battle found his former mentor, J.H.L. Long, as opposing counsel when they confronted each other before a public meeting at the neighboring town of Leipsic. Their arguments turned into a shouting match verging on fisticuffs before they were separated by onlookers. At the conclusion of the meeting, the two lawyers were observed returning home to Ottawa on the friendliest of terms in the buggy that brought them to Leipsic.[54]

In a little more than six years the articulate and personable Haskell was an outstanding lawyer in Ottawa, but his agile mind searched for a quicker way to financial success. In 1887 he formed a corporation to construct a railroad through his home town. Thus began a career in railroad construction, interspersed with the building of telephone plants, that made him wealthy by the year 1900 when he was 40 years old.[55] His interest in telephone construction took him into Texas, and owing to his wife's health he established a winter home in San Antonio. He was returning by train from Texas to Ohio in April of 1901 when he engaged in social conversation with John R. Thomas, the United States judge in Indian Territory who resided in Muskogee. Judge Thomas persuaded him to visit Muskogee. Later that year Haskell entertained at a public dinner in Muskogee and announced plans to construct three railroads through the town. He also established his permanent residence there.[56]

When Haskell heard of the separate Statehood conference called by James A. Norman, he arranged a meeting with all five chiefs of the Five Tribes. He offered to support separate Statehood and pay all incidental expenses of the proposed separate Statehood conference if the chiefs would agree to support joint Statehood in the event the separate Statehood movement failed.[57] By accepting Haskell's proposal, the Indian leaders approved what was to be named the "Sequoyah Convention," and subsequently, when Congress denied separate Statehood, they remained true to their promise to support joint Statehood for the Twin Territories.

Although the Sequoyah Convention was doomed to failure, it developed into an excellent training school, and the constitution it produced provided a model for the Oklahoma Constitutional Convention the following year. The Sequoyah delegate roster contained the names of the strongest figures—all trained in the law—who were to dominate both the subsequent state convention and the first state legislature. Two future governors of Oklahoma were present: Charles N.

Haskell, possessor of great organizational ability and practical business knowledge reinforced by a legal background, and William H. Murray, a practicing lawyer who in anticipation of Statehood had familiarized himself with state constitutions and constitutional problems.

At the Sequoyah Convention the delegates approved a constitution of some 35,000 words for the proposed state of Sequoyah. They followed the format of the United States constitution with a preamble and a bill of rights and they established legislative, executive, and judicial branches of government. They embraced progressive ideas of the day in the realm of child labor law, female labor regulation, purity of food and drugs, and safety in the mining industry. The Populist leanings of William H. Murray and others were reflected in a provision for a strong corporation commission, laws against land ownership by aliens and corporations, and a requirement for the teaching of agriculture and domestic science in public schools. In line with a national trend, the proposed constitution included prohibition of alcoholic beverages, already a requirement of federal law in Indian Territory. Women's suffrage failed to win the delegates' approval.[58]

The lawyers disagreed as to whether the state should furnish accused criminals an abstract of evidence against them. A.S. McKennon, a former Dawes Commission member who had resigned in 1901 to accept an appointment as tribal attorney for the Seminole Nation, concurred with John R. Thomas that such a provision would be undesirable and would unduly prolong a trial.[59] Robert L. Owen, S.M. Rutherford, and James S. Davenport argued in defense of the provision, but all finally accepted a suggestion by Albert Gallatin "Cheesie" McIntosh that the state should provide the defendant with an abstract of only the evidence introduced to a grand jury.[60]

McIntosh was a popular Creek lawyer who had graduated from law school in Lebanon, Tennessee, and practiced in Carthage, Tennessee, before moving to Checotah, Indian Territory, in 1901. Chief Pleasant Porter appointed him superintendent of all schools of the Creek Nation, a position which was no detriment to a successful law practice that expanded into Oklahoma Territory and to the federal courts in Washington.[61]

A prominent Cherokee lawyer at the convention was W.W. Hastings, who used his experience in the courts of the Cherokee Nation to urge successfully that decisions in civil cases could be determined by a simple majority of jurors rather than the two-thirds majority supported by other lawyers present. The delegates agreed that only three Supreme Court justices were sufficient for the new state.[62] The convention attacked another Territorial problem, the political influence of railroads. According to one authority on the history of the late nineteenth and early twentieth century in the United States, "Judges, juries, and state officials were recipients of the largess of the railroads; the [free] pass was the least of the common evils indulged in."[63] Twin Territory jurists were apparently not immune to railroad influence, according to Perry attorney and later Oklahoma Governor Henry S. Johnston. Speaking at a reunion in 1932 of the living delegates to the Oklahoma Constitutional Convention, Johnston stated that in territorial days every Supreme Court justice carried a railroad pass in his pocket, and his family could be assured of spending each summer at the seashore.[64]

Oklahoma Territory judges also received criticism for other reasons. Certain lawyers claimed that the judges frequently exchanged districts so they could be assured of endorsements from lawyers of more than one district when the time came for reappointment.[65] Frank McMaster, lawyer-journalist, indulged in criticism of jurists and legislators in his *McMaster's Magazine*. The issue of March, 1898, noted that railroads had won every case that reached the Territorial Supreme Court in the last seven years.[66] An issue in August, 1899, referred to railroad lawyer Henry E. Asp as one "who while ostensibly managing the Santa Fe railroad makes judges, runs legislatures and dictates the religious frenzy of colored Sunday Schools."[67] The Sequoyah Constitution countered the railroad pass problem by prohibiting the acceptance of railroad passes by most public officials.[68] Criticism of railroad influence grew so strong in the Territories that after the Sequoyah Convention the politically ambitious Robert L. Williams declined to accept a renewal of his appointment as local attorney for the Missouri, Kansas, and Texas Railway.[69] Also, according to William H. Murray, noted Ardmore lawyer W.A. Ledbetter made "a bonfire of his railroad free pass."[70]

Two months after the Sequoyah Convention adjourned, the citizens of Indian Territory ratified the Sequoyah Constitution on November 7, 1905, by a vote of 56,279 to 9073. A committee appointed to present the constitution to Washington officials was received cordially by President Theodore Roosevelt. It was evident, however, that he disapproved of two separate states for the two territories.[71]

Although Congress also showed little interest in Sequoyah as a separate state, it seemed intent on passing an Oklahoma Statehood bill from the first day of the session beginning in December of 1905. Five single Statehood bills were introduced in the first four days.[72] Pawnee lawyer Bird S. McGuire, as the official spokesman for Oklahoma Territory, exerted his influence in favor of single Statehood wherever possible and was a frequent advisor to the Committee on Territories for both houses.[73] A Statehood bill introduced on January 22, 1906, by Chairman Edward L. Hamilton of the House Committee on Territories was finally approved on June 14, 1906, and President Roosevelt signed it two days later.[74] At long last the struggle for Statehood ended with the merger of Oklahoma and Indian Territories into the new state of Oklahoma.

20

THE BAR DRAFTS A CONSTITUTION

By passage of the Enabling Act of 1906 Congress created a basic legal structure for the new state of Oklahoma. The Act provided for a Constitutional Convention composed of 55 delegates elected from each of the Twin Territories and two from the Osage Nation, which also was to become a part of the new state. Guidelines were established to assure that the new government would conform with the United States Constitution.[1]

Congress placed two requirements in the Enabling Act that were subjects for argument: (1) the sale of intoxicating liquor in the Indian Territory portion of the new state was to be prohibited for 21 years, and (2) the capital of Oklahoma was to remain at Guthrie until 1913. Texas Senator Joseph W. Bailey protested, "No state ever came into the Union more qualified in any respect than does Oklahoma yet Congress has put upon her the badge of incompetency by refusing to let her select her own capital and denying her the right to regulate her own affairs by forcing prohibition."[2]

By forbidding the sale of liquor, Congress had merely continued a ban already in effect in Indian Territory, but Henry E. Asp was credited with making Guthrie the state's capital. Asp, well known as attorney for the Atchison, Topeka, and Santa Fe Railway Co., had his law office in Guthrie with James R. Cottingham but had spent most of the past seven months in Washington lobbying for Statehood. At the same time Asp, a Republican, used his political influence to assure the capital's location in his home city.[3] Residents of Guthrie's Twenty-Fifth District subsequently chose him to be their delegate to the Constitutional Convention.[4]

Results of the election of delegates to the Convention reflected a Democratic landslide. Of the 112 delegates elected, only 12—the Democrats dubbed them the "twelve apostles"—were Republicans. Henry Asp, a favorite target of the Democrats, was generally considered to have contributed to the Republican debacle by personifying two situations the citizens of the Territories found objectionable: the power of the railroads,

and the rule by government employees located in the city of Guthrie.[5] Nevertheless, Democrats William H. Murray and Charles N. Haskell in later years praised Asp as one of the most highly qualified delegates.[6] Murray, not overly prone to compliments, wrote: "His word was always true; and although he was roundly abused by the Democratic press and sometimes abused by the people, I trusted him as I did no other man in the Convention."[7]

Background studies show that the 112 delegates to the Constitutional Convention included 47 farmers, easily the most numerous occupation represented. Second in number was the legal profession with 27 practicing lawyers and four non-practicing. The practicing lawyers included: Henry E. Asp, Guthrie; Jesse A. Baker, Wewoka; John J. Carney, El Reno; J.H. Chambers, Atoka; J. Clint Graham, Marietta; Samuel W. Hayes, Chickasha; George A. Henshaw, Madill; Philip B. Hopkins, Muskogee; W.B. Hudson, Henryetta; W.C. Hughes, Oklahoma City; W.D. Humphrey, Nowata; Henry S. Johnston, Perry; Chamberlayne Jones, Ryan; Matthew J. Kane, Kingfisher; Joseph F. King, Newkirk; Wade H. Kornegay, Vinita; J. Howard Langley, Pryor Creek; T.J. Leahy, Pawhuska; Walter A. Ledbetter, Ardmore; William C. Liedtke, Eufaula; James H. Maxey, Shawnee; Charles L. Moore, Enid; Flowers Nelson, Tulsa; Charles H. Pittman, Enid; David S. Rose, Blackwell; J.W. Swarts, Chelsea; and Robert L. Williams, Durant.[8]

Two former practicing lawyers were most prominent—Charles N. Haskell, then a railroad builder with various business interests, and William H. "Alfalfa Bill" Murray, a "scientific farmer" who included his own name in his list of Convention lawyers.[9] Two other delegate-lawyers in the non-practicing category were Charles H. Bower of Cement who had been a lawyer in Virginia until he moved to the Chickasaw Nation in 1891 to engage in farming and ranching,[10] and John B. Harrison, a lawyer temporarily in the insurance-abstract business.[11] Harrison had been admitted

Henry Asp, pioneer Guthrie lawyer and Republican leader of the "twelve apostles" at the Constitutional Convention. (Courtesy Archives and Manuscripts Division, OHS.)

Wade Kornegay, learned Vinita lawyer, was always ready to expound his views during the Constitutional Convention and at meetings of the Bar Association. (Courtesy McFarlin Library, University of Tulsa.)

to the Greer County Bar in 1888 and would be elected to the Supreme Court of Oklahoma in 1918.[12]

There had been organized opposition to the election of lawyers to the Convention.[13] At one juncture Clement V. Rogers, a Cherokee Indian delegate from Claremore, remarked, "It would be a Godsend to this convention if there wasn't so damned many lawyers here."[14] However, as the work of the Convention progressed, some delegates seemed to recognize that the presence of even more lawyers would have expedited the handling of the numerous legal technicalities.[15]

The fiery, 41-year-old Wade H. Kornegay, with his Master of Arts Degree from Wake Forest College, a year of law at the University of Virginia, and an LL. B. degree from Vanderbilt University, had little patience with those unfamiliar with the intricacies of the law. To any obviously defective measure introduced for the delegates' consideration, his typical reaction was, "Mr. President, I don't think we should take up the time of the delegates with such nonsensical foolishness."[16]

From the time the Convention assembled at Guthrie's Brooks Opera House on November 20, 1906, there was little doubt that men trained in the law—especially those from Indian Territory—were in control. According to plan, Oklahoma Territory's Henry S. Johnston, who had

been mentioned as a candidate for president of the Convention, received instead the chairmanship of the Democratic caucus. For president, Durant lawyer Robert L. Williams nominated William H. Murray, who easily defeated a Muskogee lawyer, Philip B. Hopkins. The only high-ranking convention official from outside the legal profession was Peter Hanraty of McAlester, a favorite of Labor and coal miners. Hanraty was elected vice president after being nominated by Haskell. Lawton attorney John M. Young was elected secretary.[17]

Nominated by Walter A. Ledbetter and elected sergeant at arms was W.A. Durant, a Choctaw Indian graduate of Arkansas College at Batesville in 1886.[18] He had studied law in Paris, Texas, and was one of the City of Durant's first attorneys.[19] Haskell received the office he wanted, Democratic floor leader. After President Murray appointed a committee of seven, headed by Robert L. Williams, to survey the work to be done and the committees required to accomplish it, the domination of the Convention by Indian Territory lawyers was assured.[20]

The Convention relied on its "Judiciary and Judicial Department Committee" to resolve the difficult constitutional law questions that arose. W.A. Ledbetter, an avid student of the law, was well

Moman Pruiett, Oklahoma criminal lawyer. 'Moman County' could have been his namesake. (Courtesy OHS.)

qualified to chair that committee and was largely responsible for writing Article 7, Judicial Department. He was one of the Bar examiners for many years before Statehood and continued in that capacity after Statehood—always a "terror" to Bar applicants.[21] Although Ledbetter seemed to lack great political ambition, he apparently would have welcomed a seat on the Supreme Court and the title of Chief Justice. Until the day of his death in 1934, he was prominent in state Bar activities and in state government, but the goals he coveted in the early days were lost to a rival, Robert L. Williams.[22]

Williams, like Ledbetter, was an able lawyer practicing in the southern part of the state. However, in his climb to the Supreme Court, the governor's office, and the bench of both federal District and Circuit courts, he exhibited aggressiveness that was foreign to Ledbetter's nature. Williams is given credit for writing Article IX, Corporations, which is second only to Article XII, Counties, as the longest in the Constitution.[23] In the opinion of William H. Murray, Williams was a competent lawyer but "not a good English scholar—he circumlocutes when writing something."[24]

President Murray appointed a non-lawyer, Royal J. Allen, to chair the County Boundaries committee. He soon observed that Allen, exhausted from numerous battles with lobbyists

seeking county seat status for their communities, was in need of expert assistance. Just before the Christmas recess in 1906, both Charles N. Haskell and Murray worked for three days at almost a 24-hour pace to set the boundaries for 54 new counties.[25] Their active participation in the County Boundaries committee placed them in an excellent position the following March to prevent the naming of "Moman" County in honor of a lawyer they both disliked, Moman Pruiett of Pauls Valley.

Pruiett, probably the best-known criminal lawyer ever to practice in Oklahoma, was born in Indiana in 1872 and had little more than 19 months of formal education. From age 11 to 14 he worked in Arkansas as a bootblack, then sold newspapers on a train.[26] At age 16, while working for a railroad company, he was convicted of forgery in connection with a freight bill scheme and served six months in prison.[27] He later worked as a janitor for two different lawyers—first for about seven months with Phil D. Brewer of Hackett City, Arkansas, then 15 months with J.C. Hodges, a criminal lawyer in Paris, Texas. He showed an interest in the study of law, and both lawyers allowed him to use their libraries.[28]

He was hotheaded, restless, and a regular customer of local joints"—gambling houses and saloons.[29] Chiefly on circumstantial evidence, he was convicted at age 18 of robbing a drunk man. When the verdict was announced, he startled the judge and jury by proclaiming his innocence and shouting, "As sure as I live I'll make you sorry. I'll empty your damned jails, an' I'll turn the murderers an' thieves a'loose in your midst. But I'll do it in a legal way."[30]

Pruiett was paroled after serving two years of a five-year sentence and returned to Paris, Texas, to work in a cotton warehouse. During the next few years he spent most of his spare time reading law in the library of his friend, Stilwell Russell.[31] Russell and J.C. Hodges discussed with Federal Judge David E. Bryant, Pruiett's unusual ability to remember legal citations and opinions. Too, Hodges expressed doubt that Pruiett had been guilty of the robbery charge.[32]

In the autumn of 1896 Judge Bryant was in Paris, Texas, for a court term and invited Pruiett to take a day off from his warehouse job to observe proceedings in the court. Just before noon recess Judge Bryant surprised Pruiett by calling him to the bench, administering the lawyer's oath, and enrolled him as a member of the Bar.[33] The 24-year-old lawyer successfully defended his first two clients, one indicted for robbery and the other for murder.[34] After practicing only a short time in Paris, he decided opportunities were better a little farther north, and in November of 1896 he moved to Pauls Valley on the Washita River in Indian Territory.[35] There his reputation as a criminal lawyer flourished, and by the early 1900s his courtroom antics, coal black hair, and roaring voice had earned for him the title "Black Stud of the Washita."[36]

At the time of the Constitutional Convention Pruiett was a member of the Democratic Executive Committee. In appreciation of the time he had spent in Washington lobbying for Statehood at the expense of his lucrative law practice, Constitution delegates voted to name "Moman" County after him.[37] However, Pruiett was a bitter enemy of the other Chickasaw Nation attorney, "Alfalfa Bill" Murray, and no doubt Murray had approved the county name with reluctance.[38] Pruiett was also known to be a supporter of Lee Cruce of Ardmore, Haskell's principal Democratic opponent for the governorship.[39]

Both Murray and Haskell must have been pleased with subsequent developments. In March of 1907 the county seat fight between Sapulpa and Bristow brought an accusation that someone had offered Pruiett $1000 to favor Sapulpa as the county seat of his namesake county. Pruiett, irate, appeared before the committee himself and charged that "a prominent citizen" had offered him $5000 in behalf of Bristow.[40] No one pressed charges, but not long after that incident the boundary committee changed the name of "Moman County" to Creek County in honor of the only nation of the Five Civilized Tribes that had not heretofore been honored by a county or city name. The original handwritten parchment enrollment of the Constitution filed in the office of Oklahoma's Secretary of State reflects for posterity the change of mind on the part of the delegates—in the alphabetical listing of counties, Creek County does not appear between Craig County and Custer County; instead it was placed between Mayes County and Murray County where "Moman County" would have been.[41]

County seats and boundaries were of great importance to the delegates as well as to the general public, but the so called "Jim Crow" segregation questions also commanded attention. The delegates doubtless would have voted Jim Crow provisions to require separate railroad coaches and waiting rooms had they not feared President Roosevelt would retaliate by rejecting the entire Constitution.[42] Unusually outspoken in behalf of his race and against discrimination at the time was lawyer-newspaper editor William H. Twine, the first black lawyer admitted to practice in the United States Courts in Indian Territory.[43]

Twine had taken part in the settlement of Oklahoma Territory in 1889, then had moved to Muskogee in Indian Territory. As editor of the *Muskogee Cimeter*, a newspaper for blacks, he philosophized during the Constitutional Convention that "When white men speak out in praise of their race they are applauded and called patriots, but when a black man speaks in defense of his, he is called a demagogue."[44] He ridiculed the anti-Negro sentiments of William H. "Alfalfa Bill" Murray and the other delegates when he wrote, "If the Savior of mankind should come to Oklahoma today and go before the constitutional Convention and the color of his cuticle should show the dark tinge of one who had lived in the tropics, the cusses would crucify Him anew and Alfalfa Bill would provide the crown of thorns."[45]

Questionable provisions in the Constitution—such as a stipulation to prevent men in military service from voting, discrimination against foreign corporations, and changing the county boundaries set by Congress in the Organic Act—caused Republicans and others to complain that the president would refuse to approve the Constitution.[46] Murray appointed a committee of three lawyers—W.A. Ledbetter, Charles L. Moore, and Samuel W. Hayes—to visit President Roosevelt for the purpose of getting his reaction to their work.[47]

The Convention had early discovered the talents of Hayes, a 31-year-old resident of Chickasha. The son of a Texas tenant farmer, Hayes had attended the University of Virginia for two years, then studied law while he taught school and sold insurance in Ryan, Oklahoma Territory. He passed the Bar examination in June of 1900 and formed a partnership with E.E. Morris. Two years later he moved to Chickasha to become the law partner of R.D. Welbourne. Hayes was on several Convention committees, but his most important assignment was chairmanship of the Schedule

121

Committee, whose function was to facilitate the procedure for changing the form of government in the two Territories. Later he was elected to the state's first Supreme Court and served seven years before resigning in 1914 to race unsuccessfully against Thomas P. Gore for the United States Senate. Subsequently he practiced law in Oklahoma City and for many years was general counsel for the Marland oil enterprises.[48]

After Ledbetter, Moore, and Hayes returned from their visit with President Roosevelt and Attorney General Charles J. Bonaparte, the delegates followed the committee's recommendations and made numerous changes in the Constitution. Among these was a complete revision of Article IX dealing with corporations. Article V, the Initiative and Referendum section, also was revised, and Article III, Section 2, was amended to extend the right to vote to Oklahoma residents in the armed forces.[49]

While Murray and the delegates pushed for completion of the Constitution and its submission to a vote of the people, they faced a series of law suits. The county commissioners of Woods and Greer Counties objected to splitting their two large counties into several smaller ones and began actions against the Convention, Governor Frank Frantz, and other officials. The suits would have postponed approval of the Constitution and returned the two counties to their original boundaries.[50]

Murray pocketed the temporary restraining order served on him, and to the dismay of his lawyer advisors he refused to recognize the Supreme Court of Oklahoma Territory as having any jurisdiction over the Convention.[51] The Convention delegates adopted a different approach and selected six lawyers to represent them: Ledbetter, Charles L. Moore, Hayes, R.L. Williams, George A. Henshaw, and J.F. King.[52] Sitting on the Supreme Court of Oklahoma Territory at the time—all of whom were deposed at Statehood—were Chief Justice John H. Burford and Associate Justices Bayard T. Hainer, B.F. Burwell, Clinton F. Irwin, Frank E. Gillette, J.L. Pancoast, and Milton C. Garber.[53] Murray consulted the Convention lawyers from time to time but criticized their hesitancy in dealing with the Court. "Higher courts often make cowards of lawyers...," he later wrote.[54]

While the court deliberated the Woods and Greer County cases, Murray received a telegram from Ledbetter saying, "I believe the court will dissolve its order if you will send the court a telegram of respect so they can." Murray's wired reply to Ledbetter said, "I have no respect for arbitrary power. Give my regards to the court and tell them to go to Hell!"[55] On that same day the court held that neither the Convention nor its officers and delegates could be enjoined from exercising their rights and duties.[56]

The Convention adjourned on July 15, 1907, by a resolution that permitted it to remain an official body until after Statehood was assured. Governor Frantz issued a proclamation setting September 17 as the date for a vote to approve or disapprove the Constitution and elect state officers. A bitter partisan battle prevailed during the ensuing two months. William Howard Taft, future president of the United States and Chief Justice of the Supreme Court, visited the Territories to fight ratification and to describe the document as "a code of laws, not a Constitution." It was a "zoological garden of cranks" that needed complete revision, he told listeners at an Oklahoma City meeting.[57]

Not to be outdone, the Democrats brought their champion, the "Great Commoner," William J. Bryan, to the Territories. "Adopt the Constitution now," Bryan pleaded, "because it is the best Constitution in the United States."[58] On September 17, 1907, the people of the Twin Territories accepted the opportunity for home rule that had so long eluded them and approved the Constitution by a vote of 180,333 to 73,059. Two months later President Theodore Roosevelt signed the proclamation that made Oklahoma a state. The next day William H. "Alfalfa Bill" Murray issued his own proclamation that adjourned *sine die* what he always insisted was the greatest governmental body ever assembled in Oklahoma.[59]

The Constitution written in large part by Oklahoma lawyers found acceptance as far away as China a few years later. The Right Reverend James W. Bashford, a Methodist Episcopal Bishop residing in Peking, announced that the Oklahoma document had been adopted almost in its entirety by the state of Foo-Chou in the Republic of China. Opium was substituted for intoxicating liquors in the Prohibition section. Other Chinese governmental entities were said to be including parts of the Constitution in their statutes.[60]

21

THE BAR GOVERNS A NEW STATE

In preparation for Statehood the Democratic Central Committee sponsored a gubernatorial primary election in June of 1907 in which Charles N. Haskell defeated lawyer-banker Lee Cruce of Ardmore by approximately 3500 votes. Haskell then went on to defeat Territorial Governor Frank Frantz, the Republican candidate, in the general election and became the first of 15 law-trained men of the 21 who occupied the governor's chair in Oklahoma from 1907 to 1989. Jack C. Walton was admitted to the Oklahoma Bar after serving as governor. The lawyer-governors were:[1]

Charles N. Haskell, 1907-1911
Lee Cruce, 1911-1915
Robert L. Williams, 1915-1919
James B.A. Robertson, 1919-1923
Martin E. Trapp, 1923-1927
Henry S. Johnston, 1927-1929
William J. Holloway, 1929-1931
William H. Murray, 1931-1935
Ernest W. Marland, 1935-1939
Leon C. Phillips, 1939-1943
Robert S. Kerr, 1943-1947
Johnston Murray, 1951-1955
Howard Edmondson, 1959-1963
David Hall, 1971-1975
David L. Boren, 1975-1979

Oklahoma's 1907 Legislature, under the leadership of "Alfalfa Bill" Murray, Speaker of the House of Representatives, and Henry S. Johnston, President Pro Tempore of the Senate, attacked the formidable tasks of vitalizing the state Constitution, creating essential state agencies, and drafting all other legislation required to "breathe life" into a newly born state. The Enabling Act (34 Stat. 267) that authorized Oklahoma's Statehood provided for transferring all pending Territorial legislation to the appropriate courts. Files pertaining to property rights, formerly maintained by the federal government, were transferred to the Registers of Deeds in the counties where the records previously had been kept.[2]

The state's five-member Supreme Court assumed most of the duties previously performed on appeal by the justices of the Supreme Court of Oklahoma Territory and the Court of Appeals of Indian Territory, along with matters arising from the new state's constitution and statutes. Three lawyer-delegates to the Constitutional Convention had been elected to the court: R.L. Williams of Durant, Matthew J. Kane of Kingfisher, and Samuel W. Hayes of Chickasha. Jesse J. Dunn of Alva had defeated W.W. Snoddy, also of Alva, for a seat on the bench from District No. 5, and John B. Turner of Vinita had been elected over Republican Ralph Campbell (who would soon be appointed federal judge). Turner, a Tennesseean, had completed his junior year at the University of Tennessee before leaving school to study in the law office of Rowsey Stephens in Linneus, Missouri. Forty-seven years old at the time of his election to the Supreme Court, he had practiced in Vinita for 12 years.[3]

Numerous cases of first impression were appealed to the court. They often required interpretation of the state's liberal constitution and decisions as to the constitutionality of laws enacted by the first Legislature. The five original justices were all able, energetic men who approached their duties in a remarkable team effort that lasted nearly six years before Justice Jesse J. Dunn resigned to move to California in 1913.[4] The court had existed only about three years when a national publication, the *State Reporter*, praised it as "the hardest workingest court in the world."[5]

On its "First Judicial Day," November 16, 1907, the court elected Robert L. Williams Chief Justice. The duration of each justice's term was then determined by lot. Williams and Hayes were to serve until January 1, 1909, Kane and Dunn until January of 1911, and Turner until January of 1913.[6] After the justices had enrolled attorneys, fixed court terms, and selected the official court seal,

Four former Oklahoma governors at an "'89er Day" celebration. L to R: J.B.A. Robertson, Lee Cruce, Martin E. Trapp, Jack Walton. (Courtesy The Daily Oklahoman.)

Members of the first Supreme Court of Oklahoma. L to R: Samuel W. Hayes, Jesse J. Dunn, Chief Justice Robert L. Williams, Matthew J. Kane, John B. Turner. (Courtesy Archives and Manuscripts Division, OHS)

they took up the question of rules of practice. Until their own rules could be formulated, they decided the simplest procedure was to adhere as closely as possible to the rules everyone had been accustomed to in the highest courts of the Twin Territories. The court's own rules were approved and adopted on March 12, 1908.[7]

On November 19, 1907, the court adopted rules for admission to the Bar. A "State Bar Commission" was to administer semi-annual oral and written examinations, and applicants were required to score an average of 75 percent on the written portion. At least a high school education and three years study of law were necessary. The State Bar Commission was composed of Walter A. Ledbetter, Ardmore; H.B. Martin, Perry; Benjamin Elder, McAlester; George S. Ramsey, Muskogee; Thomas D. McKeown, Ada; Charles J. Wrightsman, Tulsa; Benjamin F. Williams, Jr., Norman; Charles H. Parker, Enid; Nestor Rummons, Hobart; John W. Scothorn, Guthrie; and Louis Davis, Lawton.[8]

A prominent Republican who had seized every opportunity to denounce the new Oklahoma constitution both publicly and privately was Abraham J. Seay, the second Territorial governor and one of Oklahoma Territory's first Territorial judges. He had engaged in many heated arguments with Robert L. Williams, a staunch supporter of the constitution. Under the "Schedule" of the constitution Seay met the requirements for admission to the Bar but had not chosen to apply for admission. On one occasion several months after Statehood, Seay—curious to see the new Supreme Court of Oklahoma in action—entered the courtroom while Chief Justice Williams was presiding.

Williams noticed the former governor when he approached the front of the courtroom to find a seat and addressed him with the sharp command, "Governor Seay, you will raise your right hand." In what was almost a reflex action Seay complied. In the next moment the Chief Justice administered Seay the attorney's oath of office that bound him "to support, protect and defend" the Oklahoma constitution whose provisions he had so hotly criticized during the preceding 12 months. Governor Seay apparently appreciated the Chief Justice's gesture; the friendship between the two strong-willed bachelors was strengthened thereby, and thereafter Seay seemed to have

Judge C.J. Blinn settled in Oklahoma City in 1909. He was a county judge for 40 years and was honored as "Probate Judge of the Year 1971." (Courtesy Barbara Blinn Vandenburgh.)

more tolerance for the constitution he once had demeaned.[9]

Two famous Oklahoma cases, one dealing with the "Grandfather Clause" amendment to the constitution and the other with removal of the state capital, had their origin in 1910 and involved some of the state's outstanding members of the Bar. The legal acumen of Julien C. Monnet, dean of the University of Oklahoma's new School of Law, contributed to the arguments against the "Grandfather Clause" and in support of removal of the state capital.[10]

State voters approved the "Grandfather Clause" in August of 1910 as a constitutional amendment. It was intended, in essence, to limit Negro suffrage by preventing any person from voting if he could not read or write any section of the Oklahoma constitution unless he was a lineal descendant of one who had the right to vote on or before January 1, 1866.[11]

Two election officials, Guinn and Beal, were convicted in federal district court of barring Negroes from voting in reliance on the "Grandfather Clause." Chief Justice Robert L. Williams, seldom one to let his judicial office interfere with personal beliefs, raised funds for defense of the two officials.[11] When the case reached the United States Supreme Court on appeal, in the forefront for defendants Guinn and Beal were three Oklahoma legal stalwarts: C.B. Stuart, A.C. Cruce, and W.A. Ledbetter. The Supreme Court had little difficulty in finding against them, however, and ruled that Oklahoma's Grandfather Clause was a discriminatory violation of the Fifteenth Amendment.[12]

Since Congress had passed the Oklahoma Territory Organic Act in 1890, lobbyists from Oklahoma City and Guthrie had wrangled over the location of the Territorial and state capital. Even back East in the small town of New Brighton, Pennsylvania, in 1909 the railway ticket agent knew of the rivalry between the two cities. When 22-year-old C.J. Blinn, just graduated from the law school at Yale University, prepared to buy a ticket to Guthrie, a prospective location for his law practice, the ticket agent urged him to go to Oklahoma City instead. "Guthrie is the capital all right," the agent told Blinn, "but Oklahoma City is the place that's on the boom." Blinn accepted the ticket agent's advice and settled in Oklahoma City where he practiced law for 25 years, then throughout the next 40 years handled 50,000 probate cases while county judge.[13]

A year after Blinn chose Oklahoma City, state voters in a special election on June 11, 1910, selected Oklahoma City for their state capital in preference to Guthrie and Shawnee. Oklahoma City's population at the time was 64,205, Guthrie's 11,654 and Shawnee's 12,474.[14] Governor Haskell in an unexpected maneuver moved the seat of state government from Guthrie to Oklahoma City the day after the election.[15] Guthrie supporters took the capital removal issue to the United States Supreme Court on appeal in the case of *Coyle* v. *Smith*. By a seven to two decision that court upheld removal on the theory that the provision of the Enabling Act making Guthrie the capital until 1913 was an unreasonable restriction imposed on the state.[16]

The decision must have been especially gratifying to W.A. Ledbetter, author of the initiative petition voted on at the special election. From the time the Constitutional Convention began, he had protested the capital feature of the Enabling Act and had defended capital removal in the courts along with Attorney General Charles West, C.B. Stuart and B.F. Burwell.[17]

The business of the Oklahoma Supreme Court continued apace, but not until 1917 did the Leg-

Oklahoma's first Criminal Court of Appeals, now the Court of Criminal Appeals. L to R: Thomas H. Doyle, Henry M. Furman, Henry G. Baker. (Courtesy Oklahoma Department of Libraries.)

islature increase the number of justices from five to nine. By 1911 the court was inundated with cases on appeal to the extent that the Third Legislature authorized assistance by a six-member Supreme Court Commission with the commissioners to serve two-year terms.[18] One commissioner, Philip D. Brewer, former judge of the Superior Court at McAlester, wrote an opinion that established the validity of common-law marriage in Oklahoma in a memorable case with an appropriate title—"*In re: Love's Estate, Love v. Love.*" Emma Love was deemed the common-law wife of Albert W. Love despite the arguments of an able team of lawyers consisting of Seymour Foose, Robert A. Lowry, and R.C. Brown.[19]

The constitution makers by Article VII, Section 2, provided for a Criminal Court of Appeals, an inappropriate name later changed to Court of Criminal Appeals. That court was vitalized by House Bill No. 397 introduced in Oklahoma's first legislative session by 26-year-old Robert M. Rainey, the youngest member of the House of Representatives at the time and a future Chief Justice of the Supreme Court of Oklahoma. Rainey had attended Cumberland University and worked for the Dawes Commission before entering into a law partnership in Atoka with John H. and David H. Linebaugh.[20]

The act creating the Criminal Court provided for three members with the same qualifications as Supreme Court justices. Legislators apparently had some misgivings about creating a new court at the time, for they decreed its termination on

January 1, 1911. It was made permanent, however, in 1909.[21] Governor Haskell appointed to the court from the Southern District 58-year-old Henry M. Furman of Ada, who had finished second to R.L. Owen but ahead of Thomas P. Gore in the preferential Democratic primary for United States Senate in 1907. That appointment was Haskell's opportunity to reward Furman for abiding by a "gentleman's agreement" that had promised each of the Twin Territories a United States senator at Statehood. Owen and Furman were both residents of Indian Territory, so Gore became a senator because of his residency in Oklahoma Territory.

Furman had read law in Louisiana and Texas before his admission to the Texas Bar in 1874. He practiced in Fort Worth and Denver, then moved to Ardmore in 1895 before settling in Ada in 1904. Twice elected to the Criminal Court, he was serving there at the time of his death in 1916.[22] Governor Haskell chose his friend and fellow Ohioan, Henry G. Baker, as the first member of the Criminal Court from the Eastern District. Baker was then 50 years old and had been a lawyer for nearly 28 years. Since settling in Muskogee a few years previously, he had devoted most of his time to oil and railroad transactions. He and his associates were reported to be the first to find paying quantities of oil in the Creek Nation.[23] For the Northern District's representative on the court Governor Haskell selected Thomas H. Doyle of Perry, the lawyer who had argued the case for Statehood so expertly before Congress. Doyle was to make a lifetime career of service on the Criminal Court bench except when he failed to be reelected in the Hoover landslide of 1928. He served until John A. Brett defeated him in 1946 when Doyle's age of nearly 83 was a major issue.[24]

The new Criminal Court, convened for the first time on September 16, 1908, elected Henry M. Furman presiding judge and accepted 115 cases referred to it by the state Supreme Court.[25] The court early took a stand against unethical conduct by members of the Bar. Judge Furman wrote an opinion in 1911 that threatened disbarment of disreputable lawyers and stated, "No lawyer has a right to make a criminal out of himself in order to succeed in the trial of any case... Lawyers should be held more strictly accountable for their conduct than any other class of people..."[26]

One of the state's most unyielding disagreements between executive and judicial departments occurred between the Criminal Court of Appeals and the lawyer turned banker, Governor Lee Cruce. Due to his aversion to capital punishment, Governor Cruce commuted at least 19 death sentences during his term of office.[27] "The ground I take is that the infliction of the death penalty by the State is wrong in morals, and is destructive of the highest and noblest ideals in government," he told the Fourth Legislature.[28] In an opinion sustaining the death sentence of one Newton Henry, Judge Henry W. Furman criticized Cruce and discussed the "infinite harm done to the administration of law in Oklahoma." Said Furman, "No governor has the right to substitute his own view for the law on capital punishment or any other question."[29]

Cruce had another disagreement with the court because of Lieutenant Governor J.J. McAlester's inclination to pardon convicted criminals any time the governor left the state. While Cruce was out of the State at a three-week governors' conference in 1912, McAlester granted 55 pardons. The next year during Cruce's two day absence, he granted five more. The infuriated governor attempted to revoke all pardons issued by McAlester, and the question of a pardon for George Crump serving seven years in the penitentiary for fraud reached the Criminal Court of Appeals. The court held that the lieutenant governor assumed all powers of the governor, including the right to pardon, any time the governor left the state.[30]

When Governor Cruce was unable to attend a governors' conference in Colorado, because he feared more pardons by the lieutenant governor, he unloaded his feelings in a highly publicized letter to the governors, accusing the court of joining with the lieutenant governor to "raid" the state's prisons. The letter was made public before the Crump opinion was officially published and prompted Judge Thomas H. Doyle, one of Cruce's opponents in the 1907 gubernatorial campaign, to append a special statement to the opinion. He reprimanded the governor and expressed regret that the constitution prevented a citation for contempt of court. "The spectacle of a governor publicly assailing a high court of this state is without precedent in the annals of the republic," Doyle said.[31] The Court and Governor

Oklahoma's first Attorney General, Charles West. (Courtesy OHS.)

The Charles West home in Guthrie, built in 1891. The state's finest wine collection was said to be stored in its basement.

Cruce remained at odds throughout the rest of his term. He refused to change his attitude toward capital punishment and was careful never again to give the lieutenant governor an opportunity to exercise his pardoning power.

A few years after formation of the Oklahoma Criminal Court of Appeals, Theodore Roosevelt wrote in *Outlook* magazine that the Oklahoma court was "the most progressive and outstanding court in the nation." Also complimentary of the court was distinguished law professor John H. Wigmore of Northwestern University who once said that "The Criminal Court of Appeals of Oklahoma, by its decisions has become the greatest criminal court of the age." The court's high standing grew largely from the decisions of Thomas H. Doyle, an acknowledged champion of human rights during his early years on the court. He was especially effective during the Prohibition era as a staunch protector of individual rights in "search and seizure" cases.[32]

Charles J. West, Oklahoma's first Attorney General, had become known in the Twin Territories after his friend, Territorial Governor Frank Frantz, retained him to prosecute a series of railroad rate cases on behalf of Oklahoma Territory.[33] West, born in 1872, had studied at Johns Hopkins University and the University of Leipsig before settling in Kingfisher to edit a newspaper in 1894. He studied law and was admitted to the Territorial Bar.[34] Just three years before he was elected Attorney General, he had been a prank-playing young lawyer in Enid where on April 1, 1905, he was a principal in an April Fool joke that gave birth to Enid's famed "Sucker's Convention." The "Convention" had its origin when Tom Cannon, the local jailer, spied an empty beer bottle—a "dead soldier"—on the street in front of the jail. He called his friend West and told him the sad tale of a young soldier who lay dying in the jail. The soldier had asked for West, the only lawyer he would trust, and was ready to pay him a $50 fee to prepare his last will and testament.

Ambitious young attorney that he was, West lost no time in stuffing the necessary forms into his brief case and rushing to the jail. Jailer Cannon met him at the entrance to extend a solemn greeting, and they walked in silence to the bunk in the last cell. He pulled back the covers to reveal the "dead soldier" and cried "April Fool." West resolved not to be the only "sucker." Within minutes, using telephone numbers supplied by West, the jailer summoned about 40 business and professional men to the jail. To lawyers the soldier was in urgent need of professional advice; doctors were needed to treat a soldier wounded in a fight; and newspapermen and photographers were needed to report the whole tragic story. As each "sucker" arrived, the jailer accompanied him in a solemn trek to the "dead soldiers" cell. Before the episode was over, all the participants posed for a group photograph of the "Sucker's Convention" of April 1, 1905. Included, besides West himself,

128

L to R: Oklahoma Senator Josh Lee, former Senator Thomas P. Gore, former Senator Robert L. Owen, Senator Elmer Thomas, photographed in the late 1930s. (Courtesy OHS.)

were Houstin James, who was the lawyer-father of author Marquis James, Judge W.S. Whittinghill, Judge W.O. Cromwell, H.G. McKeever, James B. Cullison, Charles Moore, W.S. Denton, and other unidentified lawyers of Enid.[35]

After his election as Attorney General, West purchased the Guthrie home of Henry Asp. There he was known to have the state's finest wine collection stored in his basement behind barred windows. Ironically, one of his most important duties at that time was to see that state officials enforced the new prohibition law.[36] Soon after he took office, West assumed the role of "trust buster" and filed 48 suits in McAlester to break up the so-called "coal trusts."[37] A frequent source of newspaper copy during his two terms as Attorney General, he returned to his law practice after finishing next to last among six candidates for the Democratic gubernatorial nomination won by Judge Robert L. Williams in 1914.

In accord with Section 21 of the Enabling Act, the state Legislature elected Oklahoma's first two senators—Robert L. Owen and Thomas P. Gore. Of the 15 men who have served in the United States senate from Oklahoma during the period 1907 to 1989, 10 have been lawyers: Owen, Gore, J.W. Harreld, Elmer Thomas, Josh Lee, E.H. Moore, Robert S. Kerr, J. Howard Edmondson, Fred R. Harris, and David L. Boren. Non lawyers have included W.B. Pine, Mike Monroney, Henry Bellmon, Dewey F. Bartlett, and Don Nickles.

Owen, long a successful lawyer in Indian Territory, had been special counsel for Indian tribes from 1890 to 1907. He had already obtained

judgments from the government totaling several million dollars before conclusion of his most recent case in May of 1906 in which the Eastern Cherokee faction of the Cherokee Nation was awarded $5 million.[38]

Senator Gore, the blind lawyer from Lawton, attracted an avalanche of unwanted national publicity in 1913 and 1914 when one Minnie Bond sought damages of $50,000 from him for assault and defamation of character in a suit filed in district court at Oklahoma City. Mrs. Bond retained "an array of six competent and high-priced attorneys" led by E.J. Giddings, a dynamic, highly sensitive lawyer thought by many to be an orator unrivaled in Oklahoma. He was assisted by Ross N. Lillard, a 31-year-old former Tennesseean who had recently made headlines in Oklahoma City as a vocal councilman and assistant county attorney.[39] Giddings had indicated he planned to make the race for Attorney General in the election scheduled later that year.[40]

Senator Gore's selection of defense attorneys indicated he did not take lightly the threat to his political future. Heading the list was the brilliant criminal lawyer, Moman Pruiett, along with Charles B. Stuart, the former judge in Indian Territory, A.C. Cruce, able attorney and brother of Oklahoma's current governor, and William I. "Bill" Gilbert, the 36-year-old attorney destined in future years to be a lawyer-consultant to Hollywood movie stars.[41] From reports of the Gore-Bond trial in the *Oklahoma News* one may get an impression of the manner of delivery of Charles B. Stuart, whose name is always listed among Oklahoma's greatest lawyers. Describing Stuart's address in defense of Gore, the *News* said:[42]

> A deep voice, a fine physique, incisive gestures, and exact enunciation were bundled together in this plea, as weapons, hurling an ammunition of precise and sonorous and classical English. The broad fields of literature and history were gleaned for a few choice figures and comparisons, in this Stuart masterpiece. And the effect was a more thrilling drama than commonly comes on the plotted stage.
>
> So aside from the bearing that this oration had on the speed of the jurors—maybe they would have taken a minute or two longer in bringing back their verdict if they hadn't been urged on by this oratory—it furnished to some several hundred in the court room the feeling that it isn't

S. Prince Freeling, Oklahoma's second Attorney General. (Courtesy Archives and Manuscripts Division, OHS.)

such a hardship after all not to have lived in the days of Demosthenes.

State newspapers almost unanimously supported the blind senator, and from the beginning most observers believed he was the victim of a political conspiracy.[43] After eight days of testimony the jury left the courtroom and returned in a matter of seconds with its verdict in favor of Senator Gore.[44]

E.J. Giddings, Mrs. Bond's counsel, placed fourth in a field of six in the 1914 Democratic primary election for Attorney General.[45] The new Attorney General replacing Charles West was S. Prince Freeling. Freeling, not quite 41 years old, was a Harvard graduate who practiced in Shawnee following admission to the Oklahoma Bar in 1900 and had served three terms as county attorney of Pottawatomie County.[46] Attorney General Freeling defended the state in the "Alter Wine Case," a confrontation that involved the Catholic Church and for a time in 1918 endangered the drive for national prohibition. The problem arose from Oklahoma's "Bone-Dry Law" of 1917 that made it "unlawful for any person in this state to possess any liquors received directly or indirectly from a common or other carrier."[47]

Attorney General Freeling issued a formal opinion that held the statute must be applied to sacramental wine. "We do not make the law; we merely construe it," he explained.[48] Railway companies relied on Freeling's opinion and refused to accept shipments of wine for Oklahoma. The Catholic Church formulated a test case on October 4, 1917, when Father Urban de Hasque of the Catholic Diocese in Oklahoma tried to ship eight quarts of wine to a church in Guthrie. After the Santa Fe Railroad refused the shipment, de Hasque filed suit in Oklahoma County district court against the railway company alleging interference with the entire Catholic dogma, including freedom of religion, as set forth in Article 3 of the Louisiana Purchase Treaty of April 30, 1803.[49]

The controversy involved lawyers on both sides capable of "profound argument and great oratory."[50] For the plaintiff were two Catholic lawyers, W. Frank Wilson and Mont F. Highley, and a Lutheran lawyer, John H. Shirk. Samuel Hayes, recently the Chief Justice of the state Supreme Court, and J.R. Cottingham defended the Santa Fe Railway. Attorney General Freeling participated in behalf of the State.[51] District Judge George W. Clark rendered his decision on Christmas Eve, 1917, holding that the "law means what it says and says what it means," and that the transportation of fermented wine into Oklahoma, even for sacramental purposes was illegal. In view of Clark's decision, national dry leaders feared that the national prohibition amendment would be defeated by the opposition's argument that even sacramental wine would be prohibited.[52]

However, the justices of the Oklahoma Supreme Court found a way to approve plaintiff de Hasque's contention. The opinion was written by Justice Thomas H. Owen, a former Muskogee lawyer who had been appointed to the Criminal Court of Appeals by Governor Haskell in 1909 and to the State Supreme Court in 1917 by Governor Williams. Owen wrote that the Legislature intended to suppress only "the evil of intemperance," and the prohibition of sacramental wine thus was not "within the intention" of the makers of the prohibition law.[53] Justice Owen's opinion received international attention.[54]

Attorney General Freeling appeared before the United States Supreme Court several times in behalf of the state. Probably his most complex case was *Oklahoma v. Texas*, the Red River boundary case which he filed in 1919. Oil had been discovered in the Burkburnett Field in Texas, and the field spread to the Red River where the valuable deposits raised the question of ownership of the river bed. *Harlow's Weekly* reported that the lowest valuation placed on the disputed property had been $250 million.[55] Both Texas and Oklahoma claimed ownership of the river bed. Because each state granted drilling rights, disputes between the oil operators developed, and for a time armed conflict threatened. Oklahoma brought suit against Texas, then the federal government intervened with an ownership claim. The United States Supreme Court assumed original jurisdiction and appointed a receiver to manage the disputed area.[56]

The court named Frederick A. Tyler, an attorney of Washington, D.C., to take testimony that in 1924 comprised nine printed volumes of some 5,500 pages.[57] Several of the best-informed authorities in the country testified. Hearings were held at county seats on the Oklahoma side of the Red River, extending from Idabel to Hollis, and on the Texas side from Texarkana to Quanah, as well as at Oklahoma City, Austin, Texas, and Washington, D.C. Each litigant—Oklahoma, Texas, and the United States—furnished a court reporter and typist to take testimony at each location. Jim Feagin, a Texas court reporter, estimated the transcript consisted of about 20,000 pages with four carbon copies.[58]

Names familiar in Oklahoma legal circles were prominent in the trial of the "Red River cases." John A. Fain, pioneer Lawton attorney, was retained by the federal government; former Judge Frank Dale represented oil interests; Henry Asp protected the interests of certain Indian allottees; Herbert M. Peck, later a United States District At-torney, represented the state; and W.A. Ledbetter and H.L. Stuart were among attorneys representing other interested parties.

By 1924 the United States Supreme Court had rendered three formal opinions and three decrees in addition to 28 orders. In brief the court held that Oklahoma's boundary extended to the south bank of the Red River, with title in riparian owners, but the United States government held title and ownership to the south half of the river bed.[59]

While the *Oklahoma v. Texas* case was in the United States Supreme Court, Attorney General Freeling resigned his office early in 1922 with the understanding that the State of Oklahoma would retain him as a private attorney in the case after he had relinquished his duties as Attorney General. He then joined the firm of Lydick and Hood.[60] By the year 1921 Freeling's appearances before the United States Supreme Court had made him a widely known figure among members of the national Bar. After the death of Chief Justice Edward D. White in May of that year, Freeling was selected to represent the nation's lawyers at the memorial services for the Chief Justice.[61] He was best known to the Oklahoma religious community for his 8000-word lecture, "The Trial of Jesus Christ," which he frequently delivered at church gatherings.[62] His political career ended, however, when he finished last among five candidates for the Democratic nomination for United States senator in 1924.[63] He continued to practice law in Oklahoma City until his death in 1937 at the age 64.[64]

22

THE FEDERAL BENCH AFTER OKLAHOMA STATEHOOD

Republicans Ralph E. Campbell and John H. Cotteral both met defeat in their bid for seats on Oklahoma's first Supreme Court, but it was their good fortune that a Republican administration reigned in Washington. On the advice of his friends, especially Territorial Governor Frank Frantz, President Theodore Roosevelt chose Campbell and Cotteral for the federal judgeships in Eastern and Western Oklahoma at an annual salary of $6000.[1]

A cartoon that appeared in Guthrie's *Weekly Oklahoma State Capital* on the day Oklahoma became a state was reminiscent of Indian Territory Judge Thomas C. Humphrey's remark a few years before, "I'm not ready for Statehood because I haven't been to the pie counter long enough."[2] The cartoon pictured Oklahoma's two new federal judges, Cotteral and Campbell, each with fork in hand ready to devour his piece of pie while President Roosevelt admonished, "Now, take your time boys, you've got a lifetime to eat them."[3]

Cotteral, 43 years old in 1907, had earned consideration for the federal post by his vigorous support of President Roosevelt while chairman of Oklahoma Territory's delegation to the 1904 National Republican Convention. Summoned to Washington for an interview after Matthew J. Kane defeated him for a seat on the Supreme Court, Cotteral passed "screening" by Secretary James R. Garfield. Garfield told him to be present with other visitors the next morning in the presidential reception room. At the reception President Roosevelt dominated a jovial, informal conversation with all his visitors as a group for a few minutes while they remained standing. Suddenly he stopped talking, and pointed to one of the men, "I want to see you," he said. He turned to another man, "I want to see you." He continued to single out each man until he came to Cotteral, "I don't care to see you further," he told Cotteral.

Surprised and hurt by the President's manner, Cotteral returned to his hotel where he decided

Federal Judge Edgar S. Vaught, Western District of Oklahoma, April 26, 1956. (Courtesy OHS.)

to remain one more day. The next day a reporter called and told him the White House had announced his appointment as federal judge of the Western District of Oklahoma. He later learned that President Roosevelt had wanted to meet him just to see if he looked the way the president thought a federal judge should look. Satisfied with Cotteral's appearance, the president deemed further conversation unnecessary.[4]

Judge Cotteral was still on the federal District Court in 1928 when the death of Walter H. Sanborn left a vacancy on the United States Circuit Court of Appeals for the Eighth Circuit, which included Oklahoma at that time. President Calvin Coolidge accepted the endorsement of Republican leaders and appointed Cotteral to fill the vacancy. He served there until his death in 1933.[5] To replace him in the Western Oklahoma District, the President chose Edgar S. Vaught.

Vaught, a graduate of the Carson-Newman College in Mossy Creek, Tennessee, in 1899, had accepted a position as principal of Irving High

The Urschel kidnapping trial in 1933, Judge Vaught at the Bench, jury at left, media correspondents at tables at far right. (Courtesy Archives and Manuscripts Division, OHS.)

School in Oklahoma City in 1901. After a few months he was promoted to Superintendent of Oklahoma City schools. Encouraged by lawyer friends, he began to "read law," primarily under the tutelage of C.B. Ames. He passed the Oklahoma Territorial Bar examination in 1905 at the age of 32.[6]

Within a few years after changing from public education to law as a profession, Vaught became a busy trial lawyer in partnership with J.H. Everest and R.P. Brewer. In one year he won 57 out of 63 jury cases.[7] His sense of humor made him so popular as an after dinner speaker that during the time he was being considered for the federal post one journalist remarked, "Ed Vaught is too funny to make a good U. S. Judge and in the second place we can't afford to lose him as our official toastmaster."[8]

Judge Vaught once singled out the sensational kidnapping case of wealthy oil man Charles F. Urschel in 1933 as perhaps the most important case he ever tried as far as the general public was concerned. At that trial, spectators, communication equipment, and journalists from all over the nation filled Vaught's Oklahoma City courtroom to capacity. The judge relaxed camera restrictions to allow photographs and motion pictures during the trial, which ended with 13 individuals sentenced to imprisonment. Among them was George "Machinegun" Kelly whose reference to government agents as "G Men" when he was captured, added that term to the nation's vocabulary.[9]

Judge Vaught assumed inactive status in 1956 after 28 years on the bench.[10]

President Roosevelt's other choice for federal judge at Statehood, Ralph E. Campbell, grew up in Kansas where his family moved from Pennsylvania in 1869 when he was two years old. He received a good education for that era, a bachelor's degree from Northern Indiana University in 1892 and a law degree from the University of Kansas two years later. He practiced in McAlester and Little Rock, Arkansas, and after four years in Oklahoma City he returned to McAlester. Campbell, at age 40, attended the first Republican state convention, held in a large circus tent in Tulsa, in the summer of 1907. His close friendship with Oklahoma Territory's Governor Frank Frantz was said to be like that of "Damon and Pythias," which perhaps influenced President Roosevelt to approve him for the judgeship without the scrutiny applied to Judge Cotteral.[11]

In Judge Campbell's 11 years on the federal bench, he made decisions in varied types of litigation that formulated Oklahoma law. Addressing the annual meeting of the Oklahoma State Bar Association in December of 1917, Campbell described his docket. It included the customary bankruptcy matters and a preponderance of criminal cases, which he attributed to the liquor problem among the Indians of his district. Foreign corporations, entering the state to participate in profits from oil, gas, and other mineral resources, brought litigation based on "diversity of citizenship" jurisdiction. He also admitted many cases to his court because of the "federal question" involved. Much of the court's business arose from the role of the federal government in instances where it sought to protect the rights of Indian citizens.[12]

Judge Campbell's tenure on the bench was not a peaceful one. He received threatening letters for his part in the trial of leaders in the Industrial Workers of the World Labor movement, and during World War I both his home and that of United States Attorney W. E. McGinnis were dynamited.[13] About six months after he addressed the 1917 Bar Convention, he announced his resignation effective July 15, 1918, to accept a position with the Cosden Oil Company in Tulsa.

Judge Campbell died in his law office on January 9, 1921, by what was reported to be the accidental discharge of a revolver he had purchased

Ralph E. Campbell, first Federal Judge for the Eastern District of Oklahoma. (Courtesy Western History Collections, University of Oklahoma Library.)

the day before. A contemporary jurist commented, "Judge Campbell was one of the most popular trial judges on the federal bench. He resigned from the bench partly because he did not like the restrictions and the rigid formalities, which he often referred to as 'straight jacket' in character… He was deliberate in his judgement, quiet and unassuming in pronouncing sentence and never became contaminated with the tendency to autocracy which the position sometimes entails."[14]

Robert L. Williams, 50 years old when his term as governor ended in January of 1919, had already applied for the federal judgeship vacated by Ralph E. Campbell the previous year. According to some critics, Oklahoma's congressional delegation supported the Williams candidacy only because a seat on the federal bench would eliminate him as a future political opponent.[15] Lawyers already familiar with the "biting tongue and arbitrary manner" that Williams later displayed as a federal judge, feared him as a potential "Czar on the Bench." But friends like Judge Robert L. Rainey insisted that personality quirks had not kept Williams from being a great judge on the Oklahoma Supreme Court and that he could be depended upon to render "an intelligent, honest, and quick decision."[16]

In December of 1918, while still governor, Wil-

liams addressed a national governors' conference in Annapolis, Maryland, and three days later called on Attorney General Thomas W. Gregory in Washington to discuss his application for the judgeship. Although the visit was made at the Attorney General's request, the Oklahoma governor sat for three hours, while later-arriving callers were admitted to the Attorney General's office ahead of him. Williams suspected his composure was being tested in view of charges that he lacked "judicial temperament." Consequently, he exhibited his best behavior in 20 minutes of friendly conversation with his host, and the interlude ended with the Attorney General's casual announcement that the Williams name would be sent to the Senate for confirmation.[17]

Senator Gore's influence expedited Senate approval and on February 19, 1919, Williams was placed in charge of a 40-county district in Eastern Oklahoma with seven court towns. He was soon exposed to the congested docket and frequent travel that had perhaps encouraged the resignation of his predecessor. Nevertheless, traveling at first by train and later by automobile, he began to make progress in clearing his docket. But the liquor cases that followed passage of the national prohibition act congested the federal courts, and in Judge Williams' opinion turned them into police courts.[18] Aided by lawyers and litigants, Williams sought assistance from his friends on the Oklahoma congressional delegation in an effort to secure the approval of a second federal judicial post for his district.[19] Although the additional judgeship was approved in 1922, rivalry in the Republican Party delayed appointment of a new judge until February of 1924, when President Calvin Coolidge appointed Franklin E. Kennamer.[20]

Kennamer was born in Alabama in 1879 and studied in the office of a leading Alabama lawyer before moving to Indian Territory in 1898 to teach school. He continued law study, was admitted to the Bar in 1905, and formed a partnership in Madill with Charles A. Coakley in 1908. The firm was active in Indian land litigation, criminal law, and as railroad attorneys. Kenammer himself was well known in southern Oklahoma as a trial lawyer at the time of his election to the Oklahoma Supreme Court in 1920.[21] At one time Kennamer and his brother, Charles B., of Alabama were the only brothers serving as federal district judges in different states.[22]

Actively supported for the judgeship by other Republican factions were Frank Lee, the United States District Attorney, James Harris, the national committee-man, and Bird McGuire, a former Congressman.[23] Kennamer as a compromise candidate, had the support of Senator W.B. Pine, while the other senator, John W. Harreld, would have preferred Tulsa lawyer John B. Meserve.[24]

The 54-year-old Meserve's experience included service as a county prosecutor and state legislator in Colorado before moving to Tulsa in 1906, five years as Assistant United States Attorney, and two years as Tulsa's municipal attorney. He had a busy law practice and was active in the Tulsa County Bar Association, the State Bar, and the American Bar Association.[25] Two years after Judge Kennamer's appointment, Tulsa's popular Charles O'Connor, who was elected to Congress in 1922, spoke at the Oklahoma State Bar meeting and criticized those "political lawyers and political clients" who opposed Meserve in behalf of "their own private gain and profit."[26] Judge Kennamer showed his own respect for Meserve by appointing him as special master to hear testimony, examine evidence, and report the facts in the famous Ullie Eagle case in which 200 claimants vied for the $26 million estate of a murdered Creek Indian child.[27]

The unusual situation of two federal judges—Williams and Kennamer—in the same district created patronage problems. A dispute first arose when Kennamer tried to name the United States Commissioner at Hugo. Then a more serious wrangle occurred because the two judges could not agree where they would hold court. Five months after Kennamer's appointment, Walter H. Sanborn, Senior Judge of the Eighth Circuit, settled the argument by himself designating the jurisdiction for each judge. He placed Williams over the Muskogee , Vinita, McAlester, and Hugo courts and Kennamer over the courts at Tulsa, Ardmore, Chickasha, and Ada.[28]

Dissension between the two federal judges presented an opportunity for Tulsa, the burgeoning "petroleum capital of the world," to achieve its ambition of becoming the headquarters city for a federal court. For years after Elijah G. Tollett, Jr., moved his Commissioner's court to Claremore from Tulsa in the late 1890s, lawyers and other Tulsans had argued that their town was entitled to court status. But they were handicapped by the town's geographical location on the dividing lines of the Creek, Cherokee, and Osage Nations.[29]

In anticipation of forthcoming Statehood, a progressive element of Tulsa's 7,000 citizens had recognized that in the new state their city would benefit from court town status and as a center for recording deeds and other conveyances. The local Commercial Club placed those objectives alongside admission of Oklahoma to Statehood at the top of its agenda for 1905 and 1906. The Club voted to send as its representative to Washington, 41-year-old attorney William J. Gregg. Gregg had been reared in Kansas where he received only an elementary school education, which he supplemented by self study. In 1892 at age 28 he was admitted to the Kansas Bar. He moved to Tulsa from Kansas City in January of 1905 and went to Washington for the Commercial Club in December that year.[30]

A few months later Gregg and other Tulsa boosters succeeded in adding a provision to the Indian Appropriation Bill of 1906 that made Tulsa one of the new recording districts and court towns along with Wilburton, Bartlesville, and Duncan. A large portion of the Northern judicial district was added to the Western district, and Tulsa was made a permanent United States Commissioner's headquarters. A court for the Western District of Indian Territory was to be held there three times annually.[31] The first United States judge assigned to Tulsa was William R. Lawrence, a Civil War veteran considered one of the leading lawyers of Eastern Illinois.[32] Williams J. Gregg was rewarded after Statehood by appointment as the first United States District Attorney for the Eastern District of Oklahoma.[33]

By 1920 Tulsa's population of more than 72,000 was twice that of Muskogee and was destined to almost double its own 1920 population in the next decade. Heretofore, Tulsa boosters had been forced to acknowledge Muskogee's judicial supremacy as headquarters for the Federal Court in Eastern Oklahoma, but now they argued that the increased population in the booming oil rich counties of the Tulsa vicinity would sustain a new court district. To be a division of the Eastern District was not enough. Certain Muskogee Lawyers, unhappy with the reign of "Czar of the Bench" Robert L. Williams, looked forward to moving to

Tulsa if it acquired headquarters status in a new Federal district.[34] Ardmore and McAlester were also in the running for a new court headquarters, but diligent work by the Tulsa Bar and others culminated in 1925 with Tulsa's selection as the headquarters for the new court of the Northern District of Oklahoma under Federal District Judge Kennamer.[35]

Other court towns in the new district were to be Pawhuska, Bartlesville, Vinita, and Miami.[36] Removal of the "fat oil counties" from the Eastern District was intended, according to one account, to make Judge Williams "an interior town Police Magistrate."[37] The thriving Tulsa area became an attractive place to practice law, but the removal of several leading firms from Muskogee to Tulsa could be at least partially attributed to their desire to move from Judge Williams' jurisdiction.[38] Williams for years had complained of overwork, but under the new arrangement he still had to travel from Muskogee to the widely scattered court towns of Ada, Okmulgee, Hugo, McAlester, Ardmore, Chickasha, Poteau, and Pauls Valley. After the addition of Durant in 1929, his district was nearly 200 miles long and 175 miles wide.[39]

Judge Kennamer—President Coolidge's "Harmony" selection—before long adopted the aggressive manner of his associate, Judge Williams. In the 1924 presidential contest between Republican Coolidge and Democrat John W. Davis, Kennamer feared Coolidge stood in danger of losing the Oklahoma black vote. He charged that a "state capitol conspiracy" existed and that the colleagues he had sat with on the State Supreme Court a few months before were guilty of dishonesty in their interpretation of election laws involving Negroes.[40] A grand jury investigation did not sustain the Kennamer allegations.

Not long after the newly organized Northern District court began operation, Judge Kennamer made a speech that disturbed opponents of the prohibition amendment in his district. The gist of his talk was that his "territory would immediately be so dry that by comparison the Sahara desert would look like the fertile valley of the Nile." True to his word, the judge began to sentence squads of bootleggers to Leavenworth Penitentiary. Some disgruntled lawyers studied the bill that had created the new district and decided Kennamer was not the Northern District judge after all. They concluded that Congress, in forming the

new district, had appointed Kennamer as judge contrary to the constitutional requirement that federal judges must be appointed by the president.[41] That argument failed, however, and Judge Kennamer continued his campaign to stamp out the sale of illegal liquor in his domain.

Oklahoma's public relations sustained a blow in September of 1925 when federal and city prohibition officers raided Tulsa's Mayo Hotel at the time the national convention of the Veterans of Foreign Wars was in session. Irate convention delegates prepared to depart the city posthaste. They agreed to remain only after a valiant conciliation effort by their organization's state officials.[42]

Talk of impeaching Judge Kennamer in early 1928 emphasized his uncalled for severity with liquor traffickers. The judge's friends rushed to his defense to combat the more serious charges of bribery and favoritism involving certain Tulsa attorneys, one of whom was said to be his relative. Twenty-six impeachment charges were filed by Henry Stroud, a former Department of Justice agent. The charges were answered by the judge's attorneys, C.B. Stuart and George Ramsey, and subsequently dismissed after an investigation by a House sub-judiciary committee.[43]

Even though Judge Kennamer survived the attack on his public role, he suffered a personal tragedy when his 19-year-old son, Phillip, on Thanksgiving night, 1934, killed John F. Gorrell, a member of Tulsa's fast-moving young social set. W.F. "Dixie" Gilmer, a 1923 law graduate of the University of Oklahoma, as Tulsa's assistant county attorney gained a state-wide reputation in the prosecution of young Kennamer. The latter, through Chief Defense Counsel A. Flint Moss, pleaded self defense in a bizarre tale of Gorrell's plan to kidnap a wealthy young debutante said to be the object of Kennamer's unrequited love.[44] Phillip Kennamer was sentenced to 25 years imprisonment for manslaughter by District Judge Thurman S. Hurst, but Judge Kennamer continued to battle for his son.[45] Twice the state Criminal Court of Appeals denied a new trial, and Governor E.W. Marland announced, "No clemency for Kennamer during my administration."[46] In November of 1938, after Phillip Kennamer had served about 32 months of his sentence, Judge Kennamer made his strongest appeal for a parole. The numerous political enemies he had made as federal judge should be ignored, he pleaded; his son should receive the same consideration that was accorded ordinary citizens. Governor Marland was apparently convinced that the young Kennamer was mentally deficient and paroled him to three Tulsa oil men over the objections of "Dixie" Gilmer.[47]

Governor Marland's term ended in January of 1939, and the new governor, Leon C. Phillips, returned Kennamer to the state prison the following June. In the midst of World War II, after another clemency hearing, Governor Robert S. Kerr released him to join the armed forces. He maintained a good military record and died in the line of duty as a paratrooper.[48] Grief over his son's misfortunes contributed to Judge Kennamer's physical disabilities and led to his retirement. To replace him, President Roosevelt appointed Royce H. Savage.[49]

Savage graduated with an outstanding record from the University of Oklahoma Law School in 1927, when he was 23 years old. Just graduated and in need of immediate employment, he crammed all his belongings into a Gladstone bag and rode the interurban railway from Norman to Oklahoma City. There he obtained a position in the office of Insurance Commissioner Jess G. Read. Two years later he accepted a salary of $200 monthly to work in the Tulsa law office of Eugene O. Monnet, son of the dean of the University of Oklahoma Law School.[50] Savage decided to return to Oklahoma City in 1938 to join the firm of Cantrell, Savage and McCloud headed by John H. Cantrell, president of the Oklahoma Bar Association in 1942. After having been active in Josh Lee's successful senatorial campaign in 1936, he was rewarded by appointment to the federal judgeship for the Northern District in October of 1940 following the resignation of Judge Kennamer.[51] Judge Savage served more than two decades on the federal bench, then resigned in October of 1961. In the same career adjustment adopted by Judge Ralph E. Campbell, he accepted a position as head of the legal department of a large oil company.[52]

In 1979 Joseph W. Morris became the third Tulsa federal judge to resign in favor of a position in the oil industry. Judge Morris had left the deanship of the University of Tulsa Law School five years before to accept the judicial appointment for the Eastern District.[53] Due to the vacan-cies that developed because of Judge Morris's resignation, the death of Judge Allen E. Barrow, and the creation of two new judgeships by Congress, Senator David L. Boren in 1979 had the unusual responsibility of recommending four new members for the federal District Court. He first considered naming his recommendations from a list prepared by the Oklahoma Judicial Nominating Commission but later decided to appoint his own 13-member nominating committee.[54] From more than a hundred applicants he selected Lee R. West, Thomas R. Brett, James O. Ellison, and Frank H. Seay.[55]

Four Oklahomans have followed John H. Cotteral to a seat on the United States Circuit Court of Appeals, the highest judicial post attained by an Oklahoman. Like Judge Cotteral, two of these—Robert L. Williams and Alfred P. Murrah—went directly to the higher court from Oklahoma's Federal District courts. From the time of his appointment to the federal bench in 1919, Judge Williams had looked ahead to further advancement in the judicial hierarchy and worked hard to keep his political fires burning.[56] But as years went by Williams was passed over for younger men until Senators Elmer Thomas and Josh Lee joined to support him for the Tenth Circuit Court of Appeals in 1937. He was then 68 years old, and to gain the appointment he had to promise to retire at age 70.[57]

On the Circuit Court Williams never departed from his customary gruff, unorthodox courtroom manner and procedures, interspersed with homespun philosophical discussions, all generally resented by lawyers and other court participants. His 70th birthday arrived in December of 1938. With reluctance he relinquished active duty on March 31, 1939, seemingly under pressure from as high an authority as President Franklin D. Roosevelt himself.[58]

Alfred P. Murrah was appointed to the federal District Court in 1937 with the endorsement of Senator Josh Lee. Born on October 27, 1904, the 1927 University of Oklahoma law graduate was only 32 years old—the youngest federal judge in the nation—when he took the oath of office in March of 1937. As the first of Oklahoma's "roving judges," he was available for duty in all districts of the state.[59] He was named to the Tenth Circuit Court of Appeals in 1940 and after 30 years service took senior status to direct the Federal Judi-

Alfred P. Murrah, appointed Oklahoma's 'Roving Judge' for the Federal District Court in 1937, was named to the Circuit Court of Appeals in 1940. (Courtesy OBA.)

Tulsa lawyer Stephanie K. Seymour was appointed to the Circuit Court of Appeals in 1979, the first woman to serve on that court.

cial Center in Washington, D. C.[60] With his nickname of "Fish," Murrah was one of the best-known judges in the United States within the legal profession.[61]

Oklahoma's next two appointees to the Circuit Court went directly from their private law practices. William J. Holloway, Jr., of Oklahoma City, son of the former governor of Oklahoma, received his Bachelor of Law degree from Harvard University in 1950. He practiced law for 18 years before appointment to the court in 1968.[62] Stephanie Kulp Seymour of Tulsa, also a Harvard Law School graduate, Class of 1965, was selected for the court by President Jimmy Carter in 1979. In addition to becoming one of Oklahoma's five highest ranking jurists in history, she has the distinction of being the first woman to serve on the Circuit Court.[63]

Judge Kennamer was not the only Oklahoma Federal judge to be burdened with unfavorable publicity. Stephen S. Chandler, described by one writer as "the embattled personification of judicial independence," feuded with other federal judges and has been criticized for both his personal and official conduct.[64] Also, Judge Allen E. Barrow was at odds with his associates on the bench and incurred criticism for being too lenient

with white collar criminals before his death in 1979.[65]

The federal jurist whose name has been most familiar to the average Oklahoman is Luther L. Bohanon, appointed in 1961 upon the recommendation of his good friend, Senator Robert S. Kerr. Judge Bohanon's decisions leading to school busing in the early days of racial desegregation in Oklahoma City were denounced, as were his sweeping orders for Oklahoma prison reform. However, in July of 1979, five years after he assumed senior judge status, he received citations from both the Oklahoma Senate and the House of Representatives in recognition of courageous service while on the federal Bench.[66]

The judges appointed to the Federal bench in the state from 1907 to 1987, are:

Judge	District	Year Appointed
Ralph E. Campbell	Eastern	1907
John H. Cotteral	Western	1907
Robert L. Williams	Eastern	1919
Franklin E. Kennamer	Northern	1924
Edgar S. Vaught	Western	1928
Alfred P. Murrah	All Districts	1937
Eugene Rice	Eastern	1937
Royce H. Savage	Northern	1940

L to R: Judges Stephen S. Chandler, Luther Bohanon, and Fred Daugherty, who have all assumed the status of senior judge. (Courtesy OBA.)

Judge	District	Year Appointed
Bower Broaddus	All Districts	1940
Stephen S. Chandler	Western	1943
William R. Wallace	All Districts	1950
Ross Rizley	Western	1956
Luther L. Bohanon	All Districts	1961
Frederick A. Daugherty	All Districts	1961
Allen E. Barrow	Northern	1962
Edwin A. Langley	Eastern	1965
Luther B. Eubanks	Western	1965
Joseph W. Morris	Eastern	1974
H. Dale Cook	All Districts	1974
Ralph G. Thompson	Western	1975
Lee R. West	Western	1979
Thomas R. Brett	Northern	1979
James O. Ellison	Northern	1979
Frank H. Seay	Eastern	1979
David L. Russell	All Districts	1982
Wayne E. Alley	Western	1985
Layn R. Phillips	Western	1987

Judges Chandler, Bohanon, and Daugherty have assumed senior status. Judge Eubanks at first assumed senior status and was replaced by Judge Phillips; he later retired from the Bench. Judge Alley was appointed to the new judgeship for the Western District created by Congress in 1984. The last nine judges listed above were those actively serving on the Bench in February of 1989.[67]

23

THE LAW AND THE INDIAN

The monetary value involved in proceedings before the United States District Court for the Eastern District of Oklahoma in the early days of Statehood was said to exceed that of any court in the United States. A lawyer's practice in that busy region in only a short time could encompass land titles and contract and corporate law as well as honest misunderstandings, trickery, fraud, collections, insurance, injuries, and damages. The impact of the petroleum industry was great. Lawyers willing to study and solve that industry's unique problems were liberally compensated for their services.[1] Some lawyers acquired great wealth through investments in that fast-paced business.

Land title practice required the Oklahoma lawyer to be familiar with the general laws of conveyancing, administration and guardianship proceedings, tax titles, sales under execution, and probate of wills. He applied his knowledge to various classifications of land: Homesteads, school land, town lots in Indian Territory and the Osage Nation, land purchased from Indian tribes or individuals, land held by individuals of the Osage Nation, land held under trust patent by members of scattered Indian tribes, and land held by individual members of the Five Civilized Tribes.[2]

The last five of these classifications arose largely from allotments of Indian land by the Dawes Commission. Indians of the Choctaw and Chickasaw tribes had received the largest individual allotment, a comparative value equivalent of about 320 acres to each member, while the Cherokees received 110 acres each, the Creeks 160 acres, and the Seminoles 120 acres. Negro freedmen of the Choctaw and Chickasaw tribes were allotted 40 acres each, but freedmen of other tribes shared equally with tribal members.[3] The Indian allottee was fair game for investors interested in the land for agricultural and mineral purposes. Generally for a period of years the land was "restricted" as to alienation of the land set aside for a homestead. Otherwise surplus land was alienable under complicated legislation based on the Indian tribe, and degree of Indian blood possessed by the allottee.

Between the years 1899 and 1904 Robert L. Williams began the accumulation of his land holdings of about 7000 acres by the acquisition of Choctaw and Chickasaw land mostly through leases with option to purchase. If the land was restricted as to sale, he relied on the Indians' honesty for reasonable assurance that the option to purchase would be honored when the land became alienable.[4] Large Indian landholders, such as Cherokee lawyer Robert L. Owen, whose land and its improvements had been divided among other tribal members by the Dawes Commission, were able to maintain control of the land by a similar lease-purchase arrangement.[5]

Proponents of removal of Indian restrictions on alienation of land gained a significant victory on May 27, 1908, by a Congressional enactment that removed restrictions on certain classes of Indians of less than full blood.[6] Oklahoma probate (county) courts were given almost complete control over Indian administration. Later developments showed that these courts were perhaps more diligent in protecting the Indians' right than their predecessor federal courts had been. But judges were oftimes generous with fees and costs applicable to estates owned by both children and adults. Although most guardians were honest, others embezzled and dissipated funds entrusted to them. The Oklahoma courts were ill-equipped to handle the tremendous volume of business, much of which came to them from a backlog of federal cases.[7]

The *Daily Oklahoman* in 1911 attempted to reform probate court conditions by promoting corrective state legislation. The newspaper published an article under the headline: "Protection against Guardians Sought.—Indian Minors Being Systematically Robbed in Many Instances.—Aid of Legislature will be Invoked.—Some Charges Already Preferred." The article discussed instances where Indian minors had been defrauded and told how Attorney General

W.W. Hastings, Cherokee tribal authority and Oklahoma congressman from 1914 to 1932 (except years 1920 and 1921). (Courtesy Archives and Manuscripts Division, OHS.)

Charles West had tried without success to remove from office the County Judge of Seminole County, Thomas S. Cobb. It quoted from the Attorney General's brief charging Cobb, the guardians he appointed, and land appraisers with a conspiracy to defraud Seminole Indians and freedmen of their inherited land.[8]

Cobb was a Texan, born in 1873, who had been admitted to the Texas Bar at Gainesville in 1896 after studying law while employed by the railway mail service. He practiced in Gainesville and in Lawton before establishing a permanent residence in Wewoka. He was elected the first County Judge of Seminole County at the Statehood election in 1907.[9] Attorney General West was unsuccessful in his ouster proceedings against Cobb, and the latter brought suit against the Oklahoma Publishing Company for damages based on libel. In what became one of Oklahoma's most publicized libel actions, George W. Clark, Judge of the Oklahoma County District Court, ruled for the defendant publishing company. The decision was affirmed by the Oklahoma Supreme Court under Oklahoma's "Privileged publication" statute (Section 2340, *Comp. Laws* 1909). The court ruled that the Attorney General's brief was a privileged publication from which the newspaper published fair and true excerpts without malicious intent and without falsely charging the defendant with a crime.[10]

In 1912, W.W. Hastings, Cherokee tribal attorney, made a special effort to correct practices of forgery, perjury, bribery, and conspiracy in Adair County where Indians constituted about one-third of the population. A County Judge and three attorneys were disbarred. Oklahoma Supreme Court Justice Robert M. Rainey ordered the disbarment of two of the lawyers convicted of criminal conspiracy in an opinion that described their conspiracy against minors and incompetent Indians as "repellant to every sense of right and justice." Rainey wrote, "The true lawyer has ever been the champion of the weak and the oppressed, and we have no sympathy whatever for those whose conduct often creates an unjust prejudice against worthy members of the profession."[11]

M.L. Mott, an attorney for the Creek Nation, used funds provided by the Department of Interior in 1912 to investigate guardianship records of eight counties in the former Creek Nation. His report alleged "bad management and great waste," insolvent bondsmen, loans based on inadequate security, and loans made to the guardians themselves or members of their families. He blamed a large part of the unreasonable expenses on extravagant attorney fees.[12] Soon after publication of the Mott report, six of eight county judges affected by the report retired.[13] The widely publicized allegations aroused both houses of Congress. The Oklahoma Congressional delegation dispatched a lengthy wire to Governor Lee Cruce and the Legislature informing them that unless the state initiated improved probate procedures, "it may be extremely difficult to retain such probate jurisdiction as we now have.[14] However, the Legislature paid little heed to the recommendations of Governor Cruce or the Oklahoma delegation.[15]

Lawyers were unusually outspoken in regard to probate problems later that year at the 1913 convention of the Oklahoma State Bar Association. W.V. Thraves, former County Attorney in Nowata, observed, "If I had one percent of the money the Indian minor citizens have been robbed of since Statehood, I would be the richest fellow in Oklahoma." Well acquainted with the situation was W. W. Hastings of Tahlequah, who said, "[There have been] thousands upon thousands of estates of minors and deceased persona destroyed in Eastern Oklahoma, or practically stripped of all property, and the violators of the law have not been prosecuted."

Hastings reminded his listeners, "You, of the western side of the state, do not understand the heavy amount of probate cases there are in every county in the eastern part of the state." It was his understanding that Muskogee County alone had 4000 to 5000 probate cases, far more than the court system and the few probate attorneys could handle. C.B. Ames, who became president of the Association three years later, expressed his opinion that "It is a disgrace to this state that white people be permitted to rob Indians."

The Association unanimously approved a resolution prepared by the Committee on Jurisprudence and Law reform, headed by C.B. Stuart, that favored radical reform in probate procedures to reduce the cost of administering estates and to protect the property of descendants, especially minors.[16] Six months later, with the encouragement of Cato B. Sells, newly appointed Commissioner of Indian Affairs, the Supreme Court of Oklahoma officially adopted rules for application in state courts that required close supervision of guardians, adequate notice to interested parties, hearings in open court relative to major transactions, and regulation of attorney fees.[17] However, the Oklahoma Legislature in 1919 abrogated the Supreme Court's rules and instructed each County Judge to formulate his own probate policies in conformity with state law.[18] Five years later the Legislature in its "Protection of Estates Act" attempted to correct probate abuses by limiting guardianship and attorney fees, forbidding transactions between judge and guardian, and placing limitations on investment of estate funds.[19] Congress in 1926 enacted legislation supported by the State Bar Association that included a significant provision requiring Indian land conveyances to be approved in open court.[20]

Indian minors of the Five Civilized Tribes shared equally with adults in allotment of tribal land. Thus their inheritances could range in value from whatever an ordinary farm was worth as agricultural land up to untold riches from oil deposits. Valuable allotments in the Glenn Pool Oil Field were owned by two Creek children who in March of 1911 were killed by a dynamite ex-plosion. Fred S. Cook, a special agent for the Department of Labor, assembled evidence that led to the indictment of William Irvine and others for murder and a criminal conspiracy to obtain the allotment of one of the children.[21]

The Bureau of Indian Affairs retained Samuel Morton Rutherford as special prosecutor, a departure from his usual role of defense counsel. Rutherford, then in his early fifties, was a graduate of Emory and Henry College in Virginia where he had been an outstanding scholar. He was admitted to the Bar after study in a Fort Smith law office. He had served as United States Commissioner at Atoka and had been a United States marshal, credited with placing 65 outlaws in the Fort Smith jail within six months after his appointment. In 1898 he entered into a law partnership with two former federal judges, C.B. Stuart and Yancey Lewis, in Muskogee, where he was elected mayor in 1903.

The trial of William Irvine and the other defendants lasted six weeks, in which Rutherford and two associates were opposed by 13 lawyers for the defense. Rutherford's biting sarcasm was demonstrated at one point in the trial when a defense attorney admitted that he personally was not "a finished criminal attorney." Rutherford retorted, "That is self-evident and apparently you are willing to obtain money under false pretenses." The trial ended with Irvine sentenced to life imprisonment. The circumstances in the Creek children's death prompted the Oklahoma Legislature in 1915 to enact a statute that prevented an individual from sharing in the estate of a victim for whose death or disablement he was responsible. Rutherford was to become one of the most popular of Eastern Oklahoma lawyers. During a criminal trial in Tahlequah a few years before his death in 1922, he was greeted by applause every time he entered the court room.[22]

Almost from the time the Dawes Commission began allotment of Indian lands, many investors found it to their advantage to deny the power of Congress to restrict alienation of land. Land conveyancing continued unabated in the face of legislation that was admittedly obscure and complicated until the United States Supreme Court's 1912 decision in the famous "Thirty Thousand Land Suits."[23] That action, which involved a variety of specialists in Indian Law—S.T. Bledsoe, Robert J. Boone, George C. Camp, H.H.

Rogers, J.H. Maxey, J.H. Miley and B.B. Blakeney—was filed by the Attorney General of the United States against 16,000 defendants to cancel more than 30,000 conveyances of allotted lands made by members of the Five Civilized Tribes in violation of restrictions. The United States Supreme Court accepted as a test case, *P. E. Heckman and Robert L. Owen, Appts., v. United States*, to cancel 3715 conveyances of Cherokee land. The opinion written by Charles Evan Hughes sustained the government's position by cancelling deeds that had clouded title to millions of acres. The decision permitted no refunds of purchase prices because the laws against sale of allotments were matters of common knowledge.[24]

Not only had certain individuals in Eastern Oklahoma been inclined to disregard laws that forbade sale of Indian land, but the Muskogee area in particular had become notorious for its handling of probate cases involving Indians and freedmen. The Muskogee Bar was embarrassed in May of 1914 when Robert J. Boone, one of its leading members and prominent in Muskogee social life, was sentenced to three years imprisonment for embezzlement from minors.[25] Mrs. Boone "haunted the state capitol" seeking pardon for her husband. Supported by bankers, lawyers, judges, a United States senator, and the publishers of two newspapers, she persuaded Governor Robertson to pardon Boone after he had served seven months of his sentence.[26] He then withdrew from the legal profession and went into the oil business in Tulsa.[27]

At about the time of Boone's difficulties, the Muskogee Bar Association lodged a complaint with the Bar Association against six Muskogee attorneys after a grand jury asked their disbarment for improper activity in connection with the large estates of two Creek freedmen.[28] Four of the attorneys were suspended from the practice of law for six months.[29] Disbarment proceedings against J. Coody Johnson were dropped because the principal witness against him died after the proceedings began.[30]

Edward Curd, attorney for the large Sarah Rector estate, was not so fortunate as the other five attorneys. While on retainer as the estate's attorney, he had accepted fees from individuals selling land to the estate and from others who borrowed money from the estate. Referee P.D. Brewer refused to agree with Curd's contention that accepting separate fees was common practice in Muskogee County. Brewer stated that even if there were such a custom, "Its inherent vice and immorality would prevent its being operative or affording a shield for the attorney acting under it." No man could serve "two masters at the same time whose interests are diametrically opposed to one another." Accepting Referee Brewer's recommendation, the Supreme Court of Oklahoma decreed that Curd would be disbarred from the further practice of law in the state.[31]

Numerous cases dealing with oil-rich Indians followed the discovery of petroleum in Eastern Oklahoma. In one such case, Barney Thlocco, believed to have died just before the citizenship rolls were opened, rested unmourned in his grave for 13 years. Then, after oil valued in the millions of dollars was discovered on his allotment, more than 85 people claimed him as kin. At a federal hearing on one aspect of the Thlocco matter in Muskogee early in 1919, a reporter commented, "Something like 50 lawyers and most of the Snake tribe of Indians are trying to prove to the court that Barney left more descendants than any man since the days of Brigham Young, and that each of them was his nearest and dearest relative."[32]

In one of the early Thlocco cases, involving such noted attorneys as C.B. Stuart, A.C. Cruce, George S. Ramsey, and Malcolm E. Rosser, the United States Supreme Court held that the accuracy of the Dawes Commission citizenship rolls could be impeached only by fraud or gross mistake.[33] Federal Judge Franklin E. Kennamer in 1929 was confronted with another phase of the Thlocco controversy in a case that considered Creek heirship laws and customs relative to the reputed $26 million estate of Ullie Eagle. Ullie was a 10-year-old Creek child who in 1902 was hanged by persons unknown less than six months after she was allotted a 160-acre tract in the northwest corner of present Creek County. Longtime Indian Territory attorney John B. Meserve was appointed by Judge Kennamer as special master. In the course of his fact-finding assignment Meserve grouped the 200 litigants into 15 groups by the manner of ascent and descent through which they claimed relationship to Ullie Eagle. The 50 attorneys involved included Joseph A. Gill, N.A. Gibson, and Charles Rogers of Tulsa and Creekmore Wallace of Sapulpa.[34]

Oil companies themselves entered heirship lit-

Jackson Barnett, the "World's Richest Indian." (Courtesy The Daily Oklahoman.)

igation to protect contractual agreements as in the estate of Thomas Atkins, where oil man Charles Page obtained control of the famous "Tommy Atkins" oil lease in the Cushing Field.[35] Page had discovered Minnie Folk, formerly Minnie Atkins, and supported her claim that Tommy was her illegitimate son in opposition to five living "Tommys" and relatives of three deceased "Tommys."[36] The United States Supreme Court ruling in favor of Charles Page and his associate, R.A. Josey, increased Page's net worth to some $20 million, making him one of Oklahoma's wealthiest men and eventually one of the state's best known philanthropists.[37]

The winning lawyers in the Atkins case were Benjamin F. Rice and Thomas D. Lyons, whose Tulsa law firm was one of the first to acquire expertise in oil and gas law. Rice, a University of West Virginia law graduate, moved to Tulsa in 1904 after oil and gas were discovered in that vicinity.[38] Lyons a graduate of Notre Dame and holder of a law degree from the University of South Dakota, joined Rice in 1907. They later opened an office in New York City.[39]

Probably the most famous of the Indian oil land cases involved Jackson Barnett, once heralded by newspapers as the "World's Richest Indian." Until about 1912 Barnett was a smiling, unkempt, eccentric character often seen standing against a wall on the sidewalks of the town of

Henryetta. Perhaps his smile broadened after oil was discovered on land allotted to him in Creek County. For the next 35 years his name was connected with various proceedings in the courts of Oklahoma, California, Kansas, New York, and the District of Columbia.[40]

News of Barnett's wealth spread around the country soon after discovery of oil on his land, and the mail received by his guardian, Carl J. O'Hornett, a Henryetta lawyer, was filled with requests for donations and offers of marriage.[41] Eastern Oklahoma Baptists sought a gift of $200,000 for their denomination because, according to one Baptist minister, "if we do not get this money the lawyers and the department [of Interior] will get it as they have always done."[42] In 1920 Anna Laura Lowe, a Kansas widow, whisked the 70-year-old Barnett away and attached herself to him in two marriage ceremonies, first in Kansas then in Missouri. The new Mrs. Barnett then took charge of the Barnett millions.[43] For years Barnett was subjected to mental examinations and at least 21 major court trials where the rhetoric of competing counsel often lulled him into a restful nap.[44] He was finally adjudged mentally incompetent to enter into a marriage contract and his 14-year marriage was annulled by a federal court in California.[45]

Barnett's death in 1934 signaled a new round of court fights with 115 lawyers and nearly a thousand claimants seeking a share of his estate. Attorneys were accused of contacting "Barnetts" all over the United States to inform them they were related to the deceased Indian and offering their services.[46] District Judge Robert L. Williams assumed jurisdiction. At times all the space in his courtroom was occupied by lawyers representing their numerous clients.[47] Most of the better-known attorneys in Eastern Oklahoma participated, the youngest being the 29-year-old Dick Jones of Okemah. N.A. Gibson complained after one particularly slow day, "The way the trial is going I predict that Dick Jones and Harry Parris (of Eufaula) will be the only lawyers who will live long enough to receive any fee."[48]

Judge Williams delivered a 521-page opinion in favor of 34 claimants on December 16, 1939, five years after Barnett's death.[49] A year and a half later, when the case was appealed to the United States Circuit Court of Appeals, after six years of litigation more than one third of the attorneys for the winning claimants were deceased. One winning attorney, Leon C. Phillips, was then governor of Oklahoma, and Dick Jones was a judge of the Criminal Court of Appeals.[50]

Due to the complex nature of the Barnett case, Judge Williams remained connected with it after his elevation to the bench of the Circuit Court of Appeals and on special assignment after his retirement.[51] After a final decision by the United States Supreme Court, the matter of attorney fees was under consideration for another four years. Judge Williams fixed the fees at 25 percent of the amount recovered, and all fees were finally paid on May 11, 1945. Dick Jones received $55,345, the largest received by any lawyer.[52] The Barnett case eventually culminated in a voluminous file of 7000 pages of depositions and 20,000 pages of trial record, and in all its diverse phases remains one of the most representative cases of Indian litigation.[53]

Somewhat different legal talents from those usually required in Indian probate proceedings evolved after 1924 when Congress designated the Court of Claims, "notwithstanding the lapse of time or statutes of limitations," to be the proper forum to hear and adjudicate contests growing out of agreements and legislation affecting the Indian tribes.[54] Tribal officials lost no time in retaining counsel. Soon 59 suits had been filed against the United States government.[55] Nearly a quarter of a century later, two Oklahoma lawyers, Congressman William G. Stigler and Grady Lewis, a lineal descendant of a Choctaw chief, helped draft provisions incorporated into the Indian Claims Commission Act of 1946. This was intended to adjust claims on an equitable basis without regard to "technical defenses of Government."[56]

Persevering attorneys, after diligent research and endless delays, have won millions of dollars for their Indian clients. Grady Lewis won a $3.5 million judgment in the Court of Claims in 1951 after 25 years of research and study.[57] The complexity of such suits once prompted Assistant Attorney General Perry W. Morton to remark, "You have never seen difficult cases until you have seen one of the Indian claims cases."[58]

Counsel undertaking an Indian claims dispute on a contingent fee basis could expect a sizeable expenditure of funds from his own resources. Earl Boyd Pierce, a 1928 University of Oklahoma

(Courtesy J. Douglas Mann.)

law graduate, had to let his other law practice decline and was forced to mortgage every piece of property he owned during the years spent in pursuing one claim for the Cherokees.[59] He became a specialist in Indian law and was instrumental in winning two landmark lawsuits for his Cherokee clients; one recovered a $14 million judgment and the other returned Arkansas River Bed land to the Cherokees reported to be worth $100 million.[60]

One of the most protracted Indian claims cases was won by Washington Attorney J. Roy Thompson Jr., son of a secretary to Oklahoma's Senator Thomas P. Gore. After the senator lost his reelection bid in 1936, he set up a law office in Washington. In 1938 he agreed to handle a Comanche, Apache, and Kiowa additional compensation claim for 60 million acres of ancestral land deeded to the federal government in 1865 and 1867. While Thompson was attending night law school, the senator employed him for part-time work on the claim, and after his admission to the Bar Thompson adopted that litigation as his full-time project. He finally settled it in 1975 for $35 million and a 10 percent contingent attorney fee.

The settlement and fee were reported to be the highest ever approved in Indian claims litigation. In Thompson's 95 page petition for legal fees, which he subheaded "Hazards Arising from Shortness of Life," he noted, "To receive the compensation to which one is entitled in an Indian case one must manage to live longer than the litigation… This is a hazard which gives pause to all who contemplate the assumption of a professional obligation which may take decades to complete." By Thompson's calculation he had spent 36 years on the project while foregoing all other professional opportunities. He had outlived two of the government's four attorneys as well as Senator Gore and two other Oklahoma colleagues, Frank Miskovsky and W. C. Lewis, Sr.[61] He could well attest to the axiom that "An Indian lawyer should live to be as old as Methuselah, have the patience of Job, and the wisdom of Solomon."[62]

WHITE LAW SCHOOLS—BLACK LAWYERS

In 1907, C.B. Ames, with the assistance of Henry G. Snyder, organized a Department of Law at Epworth University, the predecessor of Oklahoma City University, offering a three-year course of evening study preparatory for the state Bar examination.[1] Also in operation at that time was the Capital Business College in Guthrie which taught commercial law courses that included contracts, agency, bailments, and legal forms.[2]

At the first meeting of the Bar Association for the new state of Oklahoma in 1907, the members discussed the need for a state law school and approved a resolution encouraging the legislature to provide for a law department in connection with the state university at Norman.[3] Nearly two years passed before the University of Oklahoma School of Law began operation in September of 1909. Epworth University's Department of Law merged with the University's school after the spring semester of the following year.[4]

Lee Cruce and J.D. Lydick of the University Board of Regents, together with a committee of the Bar Association, approved the employment of Julien C. Monnet as first dean of the school at a salary of $4000 annually, the same amount paid Governor Haskell and the University's president.[5] Monnet, then approaching 41 years of age, held an LL.B. degree from the State University of Iowa and had practiced law 11 years before enrolling as a freshman in Harvard Law School to prepare for a teaching career. He was graduated cum laude in 1908. His 32 years as dean at the University of Oklahoma parallel the story of the organization and growth of the University's law school.[6]

Monnet first attended a Bar Association meeting in February of 1910. When asked to speak, he stressed the pressing need for higher standards for admission to practice law and outlined plans for development of the new law school. He explained that the "case study" method then in use by leading institutions would be adopted at the University. For the next two decades at annual Bar meetings Dean Monnet, as a member, and often chairman, of the the Committee on Legal Education and Admission to the Bar, took advantage of every opportunity to speak in favor of higher admission standards. Over the years the requirements for admission to the University law school increased from only a high school education for most students to the four years of college currently required.[7]

Of the several proprietary law schools operated by lawyers in Oklahoma, one of the largest was Mills Law College in Oklahoma City, which had 35 graduates admitted to the Bar in the years 1924 to 1932 while administered by Clarence M. Mills, later a District Judge.[8] The Mills College was followed by Oklahoma City College of Law, another evening school, which in 1952 merged with Oklahoma City University and continued night classes until 1972 when its curriculum was expanded to include both day and evening classes.[9]

A young law clerk, E.E. Hanson, initiated the idea of a night school for Tulsa, which was organized in 1923 with 18 students. Dean of the school was Washington E. Hudson, a state senator who had studied law at Vanderbilt University.[10] On March 12, 1925, the school was merged with the University of Tulsa as a three-year law school, and a little more than a year later the Oklahoma Supreme Court granted it the same privilege as that accorded the University of Oklahoma School of Law—admission of its graduates to the practice of law without examination.

By 1926 the Tulsa school had a faculty of 18 attorneys, and although the University of Tulsa terminated its affiliation in early 1927, the school continued to operate.[11] It joined once more with the University of Tulsa in 1943, mainly through the efforts of John Rogers, Tulsa philanthropist and civic leader who served as dean without pay from 1949 to 1957.[12]

Oklahoma's most recently organized law school, opened in August of 1979, was the O.W. Coburn School of Law affiliated with Oral Rob-

Monnet Hall, University of Oklahoma law building from 1913 to the mid 1970s. (Courtesy Western History Collection, University of Oklahoma Library.)

The University of Oklahoma Center, built after a fund-raising campaign spearheaded by former Law Dean Earl Sneed in 1974.

erts University (ORU) in Tulsa. Its stated objective was to "fulfill a national demand for Christian lawyers." Claiming not to be "just another law school," the ORU aimed to provide students with: (1) a quality education in law, (2) a Christian value-centered environment, and (3) a cross-pollination with other professional fields.[13] The American Bar Association, whose policies disapprove of religious discrimination, considered denying academic accreditation to ORU on the grounds that it practiced discrimination by requiring an oath of religious faith from faculty and students. However, that issue was resolved after the Association voted to grant an exception to schools "having a religious affiliation and purpose." The institution had about 100 students, and its 164,000 volume law library was 17th in size among 168 law schools accredited by the American Bar Association. Effective June 1, 1986, Oral Roberts University terminated its law school and transferred its law library to CBN University at Virginia Beach, Virginia.[14]

A pattern of racial segregation in the Oklahoma school system had been established by the constitution, Art. 13, Sec. 3, and subsequent statutes. Consequently Ada Lois Sipuel, a black honor graduate of Langston University, a school for blacks in Oklahoma, was denied admission to the University of Oklahoma Law School when she sought to enroll in January of 1946.[15] Leaders in the National Association for the Advancement of Colored People retained Amos T. Hall, a black attorney practicing in Tulsa, to represent Sipuel in a test case against Oklahoma's segregation laws. Thurgood Marshall, later a justice of the United States Supreme Court, came to Oklahoma to assist Sipuel in his capacity as chief counsel for the NAACP.[16]

After defeat in the lower courts, the Sipuel case was appealed to the United States Supreme Court. That court reversed the judgment of the Oklahoma Supreme Court in January of 1948 and ordered the state to provide Sipuel a legal education equal to that received by white students under the equal protection clause of the Fourteenth Amendment.[17] The State Regents for Higher Education undertook immediately to furnish "separate but equal" facilities by creating Langston University School of Law at the state capitol building in Oklahoma City. Within a week the regents arranged for a faculty of three, headed by Jerome E. Henry of Oklahoma City along with Randall S. Cobb and Arthur Ellsworth.[18]

Only one student, T.M. Roberts, ever attended the Langston school. Walter M. Harrison, the white former managing editor of the *Daily Oklahoman* and *Oklahoma City Times*, applied for ad-

The Gold Star Building, home of the Oklahoma City University School of Law. (Courtesy Oklahoma City University.)

Home of the University of Tulsa School of Law as it appeared about 1953. (Courtesy W.R. Grimshaw, Jr., and S. Erickson Grimshaw.)

mission, which was denied because he was not of Negro blood.[19] Mrs. Fisher, the former Ada Sipuel, refused to enroll in the institution which Thurgood Marshall labeled a "Jim Crow" school.[20]

Mrs. Fisher was again refused admission to the University of Oklahoma. Her attorneys, Hall and Marshall, filed a motion in the District Court of Cleveland County in March of 1948 contending that the Langston law facilities were not "substantially equal" to those at the University of Oklahoma.[21] After the court denied the motion, a Fisher appeal to higher courts was deferred while the NAACP turned its attention to admission of another black, George W. McLaurin, to the University of Oklahoma Graduate College.[22]

In October of 1948 McLaurin was admitted on a segregated basis to take graduate courses not offered at Langston University. The Legislature in May of 1949 amended Oklahoma statutes to allow all qualified blacks to attend white schools, although on a segregated basis, in order to pursue programs of instruction not offered at black institutions.[23] The Langston University School of Law was scheduled to close effective June 30, 1949, so Mrs. Fisher was permitted to enroll at the University of Oklahoma for the summer term 12 days prior to that date.[24] The United States Supreme Court in 1950 reviewed the McLaurin case

and ruled that black students should be permitted to attend the previously white schools on a non-segregated basis.[25]

Mrs. Fisher completed her law course at the University of Oklahoma in the summer of 1951. Previous Bar policy had allowed prospective summer school graduates to take the June Bar examination prior to graduation rather than wait another six months for the February examination. In the past, however, students had been known to take the examination, receive their licenses to practice, then forego the summer courses that led to a law degree. Consequently University and Bar officials agreed in 1951 that in the future all students must have their degrees before sitting for the examination.

Mrs. Fisher applied for special permission to take the June, 1951, examination rather than wait for summer graduation as required by the new rules. Permission was granted—no doubt Bar officials wanted to avoid another controversy like the one that accompanied her admission to law school. However, they turned down a request for similar dispensation made by Robert W. Blackstock, a white senior law student. When Blackstock learned Sipuel's request had been granted but his had been refused, he pondered the matter. Perhaps words like "reverse discrimination" crossed his mind and encouraged him to make a

Dedication of John Rogers Hall, University of Tulsa College of Law, 1974. L To R: William H. Bell, 1978 OBA President; Dr. William Wiseman, Pastor, First Presbyterian Church, and member of University of Tulsa Board of Trustees; Robert Parker, member of Board of Trustees; J. Paschal Twyman, President, University of Tulsa; the speaker, present Chief Justice of the Supreme Court William H. Rehnquist; Joseph W. Morris, Dean of the College of Law; Dr. Robert Kelly, Chaplain, University of Tulsa. (Courtesy College of Law Library, University of Tulsa.)

William H. Bell, 1978 OBA President (left) with John Rogers at the dedication of John Rogers Hall, University of Tulsa College of Law, in 1974. (Courtesy of Sharon Bell.)

bold decision. On Friday, June 15, 1951, the weekend before the examination scheduled to begin the following Tuesday, Blackstock, destined to be president of the Oklahoma Bar Association only 12 years hence, typed his petition. He filed with the Supreme Court of the State of Oklahoma a case styled *Robert W. Blackstock v. The Oklahoma Bar Association*, pleading his right to sit for the examination. The next day, Saturday, he received a telephone call at his Norman residence from Justice John E. Luttrell informing him he could take the examination. Just as Allan Bakke's well-publicized 1978 "reverse discrimination" suit was to end happily for Bakke in the United States Supreme Court, so had Blackstock been victorious in his "reverse discrimination" suit in the Oklahoma Supreme Court. At summer's end, in addition to having won his first law suit Blackstock had both his law degree and a license to practice.[26]

Ada Lois Sipuel Fisher passed the Bar examination and joined the firm of Bruce and Rowan in Oklahoma City.[27] That firm's J.J. Bruce, whose name is perpetuated in the "J.J. Bruce Society," an organization of black lawyers, was in the active practice of law for more than 60 years. His daughter, Shirley Darrell, in 1982 became the first black as well as the first woman to be elected to the office of Oklahoma County Commissioner.[28] Another long-time black practitioner, B.C. "Ben" Franklin of Tulsa, was born in Indian Territory in 1879 and practiced in the Territory and state for about 50 years. His son, the noted historian John Hope Franklin, was inducted into the Oklahoma Hall of Fame in 1978.[29]

In 1955 the United States Circuit Court ruled unconstitutional an Oklahoma law that required every non-white candidate's race to be shown after his name on the election ballot.[30] Nearly another decade passed, however, before Oklahoma blacks in 1964 achieved significant success in politics by electing four of their race to the state legislature. Three were lawyers: E. Melvin Porter and Archibald B. Hill, Jr., of Oklahoma County, and Curtis L. Lawson of Nowata County.[31] Porter,

Amos T. Hall (left) with Thurgood Marshall, present Justice of the United States Supreme Court, and Ada Lois Sipuel Fisher in 1948. Dr. Fisher retired in 1985 as assistant to the Vice President for Academic Affairs at Langston University. (Courtesy The Daily Oklahoman.)

Four judges active in the Oklahoma City Association of Black Lawyers (L to R): Municipal Judge Albert Alexander, Judge Ozella Willis of the Workers Compensation Court, Special Judge Emilykaye Lonian for Oklahoma City Municipal Courts, and Special Judge Susan Bragg for the Oklahoma County District Court. (Courtesy OBA.)

a 1959 graduate of Vanderbilt University School of Law, became the first black member of the Oklahoma Senate. Hill, a graduate of North Carolina Law School, and Lawson, who had his law degree from the University of Arkansas, went to the House of Representatives.[32]

Another black lawyer, Charles L. Owens, in 1963 was appointed Assistant Attorney General of Oklahoma by Attorney General Charles Nesbitt. Owens had earned a law degree at the University of Tulsa while working for the Tulsa Police Department. Governor Dewey Bartlett appointed him Oklahoma's first black judge after Boston W. Smith resigned the judgeship of the Seventh Judicial District.[33] Amos T. Hall, a counsel in the Sipuel case, was a veteran of 44 years as a Tulsa lawyer, having studied in the office of B.C. Colbert after moving from Louisiana in 1921.[34] He was admitted to the Oklahoma Bar in 1925. Appointed Associate District Judge in February of 1968, he defeated three Tulsa County opponents in the primary election of the following year and became the first black judge to take office by winning an election.[35]

25

WOMEN OF THE LAW

Like the feminist movement in general, women lawyers were slow to win popular approval in the United States. The wife of a lawyer, Elizabeth Cady Stanton, led the fight for women's rights beginning in 1848, but not until 21 years later was the first woman licensed to practice. At that time Belle Mansfield of Iowa was admitted to the Bar after she convinced a judge that the words "male" and "men" in the state admission statutes also meant "female" and "women."[1]

Women admitted to practice in Oklahoma and Indian Territories were so rare as to merit special newspaper attention. In February of 1893 Mrs. Minerva K. Elliott, a government employee connected with the Indian school at Shawnee, passed an examination conducted by a committee of lawyers and was reported to be the first woman admitted to the Oklahoma Territory Bar.[2] Anabel Fleming was the subject of national notice in 1899 by *Munsey's Magazine* and *Harper's Bazaar*, as one of the few women west of the Mississippi licensed to practice law. Miss Fleming had worked in the office of her father, J.T. Fleming, clerk of the federal Court at Pauls Valley. She was probably the first woman lawyer in Indian Territory when admitted by United States Judge Hosea Townsend on November 14, 1899. According to the *Philadelphia Record*, "Miss Fleming had been amusing herself with *Blackstone* and *Kent* since she was eleven years old, and would rather hunt up a case than go to a dance." *Harper's Bazaar* was impressed by her "association with the bloody justice of the frontier," and noted that on the day she was admitted to the Bar she attested the death warrant of a man sentenced to be hanged.[3]

A husband-wife law partnership began at Okarche in 1902 when Lillie C. Spink, already admitted in Illinois, joined her husband, George.[4] Four years later in Indian Territory, Judge Joseph A. Gill granted admission to Mrs. Margaret Gale of Bartlesville. Her unusual scholastic attainments included a law degree from the University of Michigan and post graduate work at the University of Chicago.[5] Another woman lawyer

In her law office with a client is Margaret McVean, who practiced law in Oklahoma City from 1903 until her death in 1938. (Courtesy Archives and Manuscripts Divisiosn, OHS.)

with excellent scholastic credentials, who like many of her male counterparts chose to pursue a legal career in a new land, was Margaret McVean. Thirty-four years old in 1903, the former Kentucky schoolteacher had attended Cornell University and Cincinnati Law School, then received a law degree from the University of Michigan. A male classmate remembered, "she was a very beautiful young lady."

Three days after her arrival in Oklahoma City in January, 1903 she was admitted to practice on the motion of J.R. Keaton, the former Territorial judge, also from Kentucky. While presiding as first president of the State Bar of Oklahoma at the annual convention a quarter of a century later, Judge Keaton recalled that a month after he had so proudly recommended his fellow Kentuckian, she sued him and a number of other defendants for a reason he did not disclose. "But I have even forgiven that," Judge Keaton hastened to add.[6]

McVean joined the voluntary Bar Association in 1920. That was the year of ratification of the women's suffrage constitutional amendment, and President George L. Bowman at the annual convention made a special point of introducing "our

Kittie C. Sturdevant, first woman member of the Bar Association. (Courtesy The Daily Oklahoman.)

three lady attorneys…, Miss Bessie Newson, Miss Margaret McVean and Mrs. Katherine Van Leuven."[7] McVean's practice consisted primarily of probate, real estate, and oil lease transactions, and she once remarked, "Inasmuch as so much of the charity work of this city has fallen to my lot, I am not one of the prosperous lawyers. I am just pioneering, and therefore the things that no one else is interested in come to my office."[8]

At the 1930 Bar convention she entered into a discussion of residence requirements for lawyers and observed that in Oklahoma one "has to wait twenty-five years to make a living practicing law."[9] When she died at age 69 in 1938, she was the oldest woman lawyer in point of service and had for years been counsel and confidante for the state's growing number of women lawyers.[10]

Another pioneer woman lawyer in Oklahoma City, Kittie C. Sturdevant, joined the voluntary Bar Association in 1913 and became its first woman member, seven years in advance of McVean. Almost 70 years later in Oklahoma City Sturdevant was past 90 years old and still in active practice specializing in probate, bankruptcy, insurance claims, and administrative law. A descendant of a family of lawyers, she had worked as a stenographer in the Shawnee office of Jesse D. Lydick after graduation from high school in 1908. She first impressed Lydick with having a "legal mind" on the day he finished dictating a pe-

tition in an important damage suit, and she asked, with some timidity, if he had possibly omitted the jurisdictional statement essential to the petition. Surprised and pleased, Lydick corrected his mistake, and thereafter he offered every encouragement in Sturdevant's study for admission to the Bar.

In Lydick's office she gained experience in Indian land matters, railroad damage suits, and the general practice of law. Like some other law students of the time she also took a correspondence course. In 1912 she passed the three-day state Bar examination which the State Supreme Court included in admission requirements after Statehood. The examiner's last question was a facetious one: "Is it lawful for a man to marry his widow's sister?" Their one female applicant responded, "It is unlawful for a marriage relationship to exist between a woman and the ghost of a man." Of the 125 participants, Sturdevant made the highest grade. W.H.L. "Swamp" Campbell, Clerk of the State Supreme Court, customarily presented a choice bird dog to the individual receiving the highest score; however, he substituted a $25 cash prize for the female winner who had no desire to own a bird dog.[11]

Edgar A. de Meules at the 1913 meeting of the Bar Association nominated Miss Sturdevant to be the organization's first female member and concluded with a poem:[12]

> They talk about a woman's sphere
>   As though it had a limit;
> There's not a place in earth or Heaven,
>   There's not a task to mankind given,
> There's not a blessing or a woe,
>   There's not a whisper, yes or no,
> There's not a life, a death, a birth,
>   Nor aught that has a feather's weight of worth,
> Without a woman in it.

Despite the de Meules tribute to womanhood, General Council Chairman R.A. Kleinschmidt's preliminary remarks at the meeting indicated that the novel question of admitting a female had caused a slight division in ranks. Said Kleinschmidt, "We have taken the precaution to fortify ourselves by securing the signature of at least every well known admirer of the opposite sex." But plain spoken W.H. Kornegay raised the question, "Is she eligible under our constitution?" President James H. Gordon replied, "I am unable to answer that question, for at the time we formed the organization we were not aware we had this danger to confront. Unless a point of order is made the report is open to discussion and consideration." G.C. Abernathy of Sturdevant's home town, Shawnee, moved for her admission. The motion was seconded, and after a vote by the raising of hands Sturdevant became the Association's first female member.[13]

The voluntary Bar Association seemed to hold little attraction for the few women lawyers. Tulsa hosted the annual convention in 1914, and Ethel K. Childers of that city joined Kittie Sturdevant as the only other female member. Childers' specialty was petroleum law, and *Harlow's Weekly* reported in 1921 that her salary was $5000 annually, a substantial salary for anyone in that day.[14]

After the first World War, a woman law student was still a rarity. Female lawyers often were criticized for taking a man's job, and parents feared spinsterhood for a daughter who attended law school.[15] Nonetheless, there was growing awareness of the distaff side of the law, especially after passage of the women's suffrage amendment. Muskogee's Frank Lee looked around the room at Oklahoma's 1921 Bar convention and remarked, "One thing, I think, is worthy of note; we have ladies present and I can see in the future the time when these chairs will be filled with ladies and gentlemen, and when the Bar will be composed of ladies and gentlemen…"[16] *Harlow's Weekly* announced that year, "The feminine attorney is coming into her heritage." Oklahoma could then claim 34 women lawyers and perhaps another dozen women engaged in the study of law. Women who took the Bar examination generally made high grades, but only a few entered private practice, choosing instead to do title and lease work as employees of oil companies. Others specialized in probate practice, and a few held political appointments.[17]

An appointment as City Attorney of the village of Pharoah went to Ethel Proffett, Okfuskee County's only woman lawyer, in 1923.[18] She later practiced in Tulsa under her married name of Ethel M. Stephenson and was believed to be the first Oklahoma woman admitted to practice before the United States Supreme Court.[19]

The women's suffrage amendment was prominent in the news in 1920 when Cato Sells, United

Florence Etheridge Cobb, Wewoka, came to Oklahoma about 1920 as probate attorney for the Commissioner of Indian Affairs. (Courtesy Archives and Manuscripts Division, OHS.)

States Commissioner of Indian Affairs, published a detailed account of his work in behalf of Oklahoma Indians. Sells pointed out, with a hint of pride, that one of the government's 20 probate attorneys was a woman. The woman attorney was Florence Etheridge Cobb, holder of a master's degree in law from Washington College of Law, where she had also taught before moving to Oklahoma. She settled in Wewoka, married Judge T.S. Cobb, and in addition to being city librarian, wrote poetry and practiced law. She also served terms as Justice of the Peace and Municipal Judge before her death in 1946.[20]

Oklahoma Attorney General S. Prince Freeling had won reelection in 1918 despite his well-known opposition to women's suffrage.[21] Two years later he appeased female critics by appointing Katherine Van Leuven, the widow of Ottawa County's first County Judge, to the office of Assistant Attorney General.[22] Described as "charming, energetic, resourceful," Mrs. Van Leuven had read law in her husband's office for six years and studied at the University of Chicago for 18 months before she was admitted to the Oklahoma Bar in 1913 at age 25.[23]

In 1921 a delegation of Tulsa women, declaring vice conditions were so bad in their city that it was unsafe for a woman to travel unescorted, petitioned Governor Robertson for help. Subsequently Attorney General Freeling dispatched Mrs. Van Leuven to Tulsa on what some described as the most responsible assignment ever entrusted to an Oklahoma woman to that time. However, the move was labeled a political ploy by Tulsa lawyer A.J. Biddison. He insisted Mrs. Van Leuven was in Tulsa only "because she must have something to do, and can do as little harm here as she can anywhere else."[24] Nonetheless she was credited with breaking up the Tulsa vice ring and soon became Oklahoma's best-known woman lawyer.[25]

Mrs. Van Leuven joined the Oklahoma City firm of Blakeney and Ambrister in 1926. Four years later, when her son Kermit graduated from the University of Oklahoma, they established what was reported to be the nation's first mother-son law partnership. She later achieved national recognition as a champion of women's rights and at one time served on a national welfare committee headed by Eleanor Roosevelt. In 1930 she finished seventh in a field of 10 Democratic candidates in the United States senate primary.[26] When Commissioner of Labor W.A. Pat Murphy appointed her to an attorney's post in the Unemployment Compensation and Placement Division in 1937, the Oklahoma State Bar *Journal* referred to her as the "first lady of Oklahoma law."[27] She was in private practice in Oklahoma City before her death in 1967.[28]

Approximately a hundred women belonged to the Oklahoma State Bar Association in 1934 when a group of Oklahoma City women formed the Women Lawyers' Club of Oklahoma, which evolved into the current Oklahoma Association of Women Lawyers. Norma Wheaton of Tulsa, a staunch advocate of women's right to serve on juries and hold any public office, edited *The Citator*, the Women Lawyer's monthly publication. Mrs. Wheaton's male colleagues recognized her competence as a lawyer and leader in 1946 when she was elected president of the Tulsa County Bar Association.[29]

Male delegates to the 1958 Oklahoma Bar convention learned with some surprise that their female counterparts had driven wedges in "for men only" political offices, particularly county judgeships where women then held offices in seven Oklahoma counties. Marie Dunn of Murray County in 1946 had become the first woman

Norma Wheaton, president of the Tulsa County Bar Association in 1946. (College of Law Library, University of Tulsa.)

judge of a court of record in Oklahoma.[30] Two county attorneys, Louise Bingham of Woods County and Mildred L. Miles of Harper County, were described by associates as "Feminine and lovely when they get into the courthouse." Judge Christine LeGate of Ardmore, interviewed at the 1958 convention, remarked with a smile, "When I ran for office, some men said they never would vote for a woman—and I am sure some of them didn't vote for me. Some of the stiffest opposition came from male lawyers."[31]

By the 1960s the career prospects for a woman lawyer remained greatly discouraging. Nancy Coats of Oklahoma City, a hard-driving, articulate lawyer elected president of the Oklahoma Bar Foundation in 1981, recalled that while she was one of the five women law students in her class at the University of Oklahoma in the early 1960s, someone asked, "Do you feel guilty about taking a position that should go to a man who would have to support a family in the future?" Her answer was an emphatic "No!"[32] After she received her degree, she was offended by lawyers who inquired during employment interviews,

"Do you type? Will you answer the telephone when the receptionist is at lunch?"[33]

More women could see a future beyond law school in the 1970s when societal factors encouraging them to seek full-time careers outside the home. In growing numbers they chose legal careers, aided by the widespread campaign for women's rights. At the University of Oklahoma female representation in the freshman class increased from 15 percent in 1972 to more than 40 percent in 1980. In 1979 nine of the top 10 in the entering law class were women, and two years later all three top-ranking law students were female.[34]

During the decade of the 1980s, more practicing lawyers were willing to interview and hire female applicants. By 1989 an estimated 40 to 50 percent of Bar applicants were women. More women held judgeships and served in leadership capacities with Bar associations.[35] Partnerships in prestigious law firms no longer were unattainable. In Oklahoma City, Brooks Smith Murphy, a 1975 law graduate of the University of Wisconsin, was elected to a partnership in Crowe & Dunlevy, a firm whose history dates from 1902. The Crowe & Dunlevy 63-member legal staff was second only to Hall, Estill's 80 members in Tulsa as the state's largest law firm.[36]

Stephanie Kulp, five-feet-two-inches tall, 22 years old, was one of 23 women along with 552 men when she entered Harvard Law School in 1962. She joined Baker and Botts in Houston a few years later, the only woman among 160 lawyers. In 1975 she achieved a partnership status in the Tulsa firm of Doerner, Stuart, Saunders, Daniel and Anderson where she met and married another partner in the firm, R. Thomas Seymour. Four years later President Jimmy Carter appointed her the first female jurist to sit on the bench of the Tenth Circuit Court of Appeals.[37]

A little more than two years following Seymour's appointment, another Oklahoma "first" occurred after the predominately male membership of the Judicial Nominating Commission included the name of Alma Wilson among those recommended to Governor George Nigh to fill a vacancy on the State Supreme Court. In February of 1982 Nigh appointed Wilson, a University of Oklahoma law graduate, to be the Court's first female member. Justice Wilson supplemented her qualifications, which included extensive experience as a Municipal and District judge, with the wry observation, "I have brought an entirely new viewpoint to the court, being the first daughter, wife and mother on the court in seventy-five years."[38]

The second woman to be on the Supreme Court was Yvonne Kauger, who had served on the

Jayne N. Montgomery, member of the 1988 Oklahoma Bar Foundation Board of Trustees. (Courtesy OBA.)

Alma Wilson, first woman Justice of the Supreme Court of Oklahoma, appointed by Governor George Nigh in 1982. (Courtesy OBA.)

Yvonne Kauger, appointed in 1984, the second woman Justice of the Supreme Court of Oklahoma. (Courtesy OBA.)

Sally Mock, Chairperson, 1989 Board of Bar Examiners. (Courtesy OBA.)

court's staff as judicial assistant to Justice Ralph Hodges. Her excellent academic credentials included being valedictorian of her Colony High School graduating class, a degree magna cum laude from Southwestern State University, and top student in her 1969 law class at Oklahoma City University.[39]

No woman has yet served on the Court of Criminal Appeals, but the six-member Court of Appeals has two female judges. Judge Patricia MacGuigan, first in her 1974 law class at Oklahoma City University, was a judicial assistant for Supreme Court Justice Don Barnes when elected to the court in 1982. Judge Carol M. Hansen, also a 1974 graduate of Oklahoma City University Law School, was marshal of the Supreme Court at the time she was named to the Court of Appeals by Governor George Nigh in 1985.[40]

26

THE TERRITORIAL BAR ASSOCIATIONS

The Muskogee Bar Association had been active since 1889, but by the turn of the century the influx of lawyers to 14 more court towns and other communities indicated need for a Bar organization of broader scope than the one in Muskogee alone. Several progressive lawyers took advantage of the expected attendance at a Territorial convention scheduled for South McAlester on February 23, 1900, and called a meeting for that date to organize a Bar Association for all Indian Territory.[1]

Most of the lawyers arrived at South McAlester on the evening of February 22, 1900, and met at the opera house to elect temporary officers, headed by Edgar Smith of Vinita as president. Smith appointed a committee on constitution and by-laws and one to recommend a plan for permanent organization. The next day the 133 lawyers in attendance elected Smith the permanent president of the "Indian Territory Bar Association," whose stated objective was "to advance the science of jurisprudence, promote the administration of justice, to scrutinize such proposed legislation in Congress affecting the jurisprudence of the Indian Territory as may be proper to uphold the honor of the profession of law, and to encourage cordial intercourse among the members of the bar."[2]

The constitution provided for committees on Jurisprudence and Law Reform, Legal Education, Publication, Grievances, and Banquet.[3] President Smith appointed a committee of three members residing in the various court towns to represent the Association in the examination of Bar applicants and to report professional misconduct. Annual meetings were to be in October on the first day of the session of the United States Court of Appeals in the Indian Territory.[4]

At "the first annual meeting," held in South McAlester in October that year, a paper on "Taxation in the Indian Territory" by W.O. Davis of Gainesville, Texas was read, and W.T. Hutchings of Muskogee spoke on "Cicero, the Pagan Lawyer." On the list of 152 members were well-known lawyers of the Territory such as Charles B. Stuart, Clifford L. Jackson, S.T. Bledsoe and Henry M. Furman, as well as the names of future politically important people such as R.L. Williams, William H. Murray, Robert L. Owen, and W.W. Hastings.[5]

As required by the constitution, President Smith opened the meeting with a review of current legislation affecting Indian Territory, of which the most important was the Indian Appropriation Bill that provided funds to continue the work of the Commission to the Five Civilized Tribes. Smith expressed the opinion that the government was treating the Indian Territory like a reservation occupied by a few Indians and an Indian agent, although the Territory had 400,000 people, along with newspapers, railroads, banks, businesses, and "fifteen places of holding United States Court, where four United States Judges, who would be an ornament to the judiciary of the proudest state of the Union, administer the Constitution and laws of the United States expressly put in force therein, together with the code of the State of Arkansas borrowed for this jurisdiction by Congress."[6]

Smith reminded the members that the Association's success was dependent upon their cooperation. "We are not always willing," he said, "to sacrifice our own personal convenience or devote the time necessary to the successful upbuilding of the organization."[7] The presidents elected in subsequent years were Charles B. Stuart, 1901; C.L. Herbert, 1902; Clifford L. Jackson, 1903; and Joseph G. Ralls, 1904.

In neighboring Oklahoma Territory the Oklahoma [Territory] Bar Association was organized on the morning of June 10, 1890—the day of the first official session of the newly organized Supreme Court in Guthrie. J.W. Johnson of Oklahoma City was temporary chairman. After 14 months of waiting for official recognition as lawyers, owing to the failure of Congress to provide for Territorial government, the approximately 200 lawyers present first concerned themselves

Oklahoma Bar Association Past Presidents, December 1988. Front row (L to R): Paul M. Vassar (1983), James D. Fellers (1964), G. Ellis Gable (1954), Wilson Wallace (1977), Joseph M. Culp (1967), Burck Bailey (1988). Back row (L to R): William G. Paul (1976), Jim F. Gassaway (1971), Robert J. Turner (1984), John E. Shipp (1985), John L. Boyd (1982), C.D. Northcutt (1975), Robert W. Blackstock (1963), James R. Eagleton (1986), Deryl L. Gotcher (1974), David K. Petty (1987), John R. Wallace (1973), Winfrey D. Houston (1969), Thomas R. Brett (1970). (Courtesy James D. Fellers.)

with procedure for admission to the Bar. Chairman Johnson appointed three lawyers from each of the six counties represented to summarize pertinent admission rules and regulations for presentation to the court that afternoon.[8] To give the admission committee time to prepare a report, the meeting adjourned and met again at 1:30 p.m., 30 minutes before the court was to convene. The committee report confirmed that ample provisions for admission to the Bar existed under United States statutes and under the Nebraska statutes adopted for the Territorial government by the Organic Act. By unanimous vote another committee of seven was selected to request ad-

mission of the applicants by the Supreme Court on that same day.[9] The court accepted the committee's recommendation and agreed to admit all attorneys who could prove they were members in good standing of the Bar of another state.[10]

The court had met at Guthrie 11 days earlier so that Governor George W. Steele could administer oaths of office, and court officials could be appointed. The lawyers may have been critical of the court for its failure to arrange for their admission at that time, which perhaps prompted the following curious comment in an account of the Bar meeting of June 10 reported by the *Oklahoma State Capital*[11] "The most interesting portion of

Harper S. Cunningham, first president of the Oklahoma (Territory) Bar Association. (Courtesy Western History Collections, University of Oklahoma Libraries.)

the above meeting is not published. The reporter not being up in profanity and pet names did not feel equal to the emergency of accurately drawing a pen picture of a hall full of intelligent gentlemen disguised as _____ _____ _____ _____ _____, well, let the matter drop; the bar met and the enemies are still alive." J.R. Keaton's account of the session of June 10 of the court, when Chief Justice Green was late and the other two justices could not find a law that said they could adjourn, would indicate the lawyers had found much to criticize in the court's actions to date.[12]

About 35 Territorial lawyers became members at the first meeting of the Oklahoma Territory Bar Association, which elected Harper S. Cunningham as president. Cunningham, then 44, was a Civil War veteran who had homesteaded in Kansas, found time to read law, and had been admitted to the Kansas Bar in 1876. While a member of the House of Representatives in the Second Assembly of Oklahoma Territory, he helped draft the Civil Code and the Territorial library bill.[13] He was appointed Attorney General in 1898 and held that office for two years.[14]

The constitution of the Oklahoma Territory Bar Association, unlike that of its counterpart in Indian Territory, originally placed no limit on the

number of terms an officer could serve; consequently the members elected Cunningham to the presidency each year from 1890 to 1897.[15] John W. Shartel followed Cunningham as president and served two years, 1898 and 1899. In 1900 he was succeeded by J.C. Strang of Guthrie, who later followed Cunningham as Attorney General for Oklahoma Territory, serving in 1900 and 1901. John H. Cotteral, future federal District Judge and Judge of the Circuit Court of Appeals, was elected president for 1901, and Scott W. Denton of Enid served in 1902. Jesse J. Dunn and Roy Hoffman were presidents in 1903 and 1904 respectively.[16]

Annual meetings were held in Guthrie in the first week of January each year, to correspond with the session of the Territorial Supreme Court. Like the Indian Territory Bar, the Oklahoma Bar at its annual meeting heard and discussed papers of general interest to the profession. Reports were heard from standing committees on Jurisprudence and Law Reform, Judicial Administration and Remedial Reform, Legal Education and Admission to the Bar, Commercial Law, and Law Reporting and Digesting.[17]

Needed legislation was regularly discussed. The Oklahoma Territory Bar was among the first organizations to lead the fight for Statehood, an objective greatly aided by the lawyers' friends and contacts in their home states.[18] The Association always sought to raise the standards for admission, and made the most progress in that regard with a legislative act of March 4, 1903.[19] President Jesse J. Dunn in reference to that measure said, "Many seek the profession, who for numerous reasons, are unfitted, and this new act which grants license only after an examination by a commission appointed by the Supreme Court, and then on its order, will correct many of the abuses heretofore existing."[20]

The Oklahoma Association had been in existence only a few years when the members addressed a proposal at one of the annual meetings to create a Circuit Court of Appeals with appellate jurisdiction over cases decided by the Territorial Supreme Court. Each member had his own idea as to which class of cases should be subject to appeal. Throughout the discussion everyone spoke deferentially of the "learning, ability and integrity" of the Supreme Court itself. Finally a member of the Logan County Bar, undaunted by the

Clifford L. Jackson, president of the Indian Territory Bar Association in 1903 and the Oklahoma State Bar Association in 1907. (Courtesy Gloria C. Bates.)

W.I. Gilbert, who argued against consolidation of the Indian Territory and Oklahoma Territory Bars. He became president of the Oklahoma State Bar Association in 1909, but later he moved to California where, as indicated by this picture with Aimee Semple Mc- Pherson, he became a well-known attorney for promi- nent California personalities. (Courtesy Western History Collections, University of Oklahoma Library.)

presence of the Supreme Court justices at the meeting, interrupted to say:[21]

> Mr. President: All members talk of the learning and ability of the Supreme Court, yet want to ap- peal their cases and prevent others from appeal- ing cases. Henry Asp wants to appeal the Santa Fe cases, but no other. Jerry Strang wants to appeal his cases, and no others. No one seems to want the cases I am interested in appealed, and so I must speak for myself.
>
> I also want to appeal my cases. I don't, however, want to appeal from the learning and ability of the Supreme Court. If it is so learned and able, why do you all want to appeal and review its judge- ment? I do not want, I say, to appeal from the learning and ability of the Supreme Court; I want to appeal from its damned ignorance.

Prolonged laughter, joined in by the Supreme Court justices, ended the subject of appellate ju- risdiction for that time.

Throughout the life of both the Oklahoma Ter- ritory Bar Association and the Indian Territory Bar Association, a foremost subject of the day was Statehood. The issue came before the June, 1904, meeting of the Indian Territory Bar when S.T. Bledsoe of Ardmore moved, "It is the sense of this meeting that a union be had of the Bar Associa- tions of the two Territories at once."[22] Most of those who participated in the discussion agreed

that single Statehood for the two combined ter- ritories was inevitable and that the Association would not be entering into a political controversy by agreeing to amalgamation with the Oklahoma Bar Association. The most vocal opponent of the motion was W.I. Gilbert of Duncan. "Instead of an amalgamation, it will be a swallowing," he in- sisted. "There are more lawyers in Oklahoma City than there are in the whole central district." W.A. Ledbetter of Ardmore disagreed, saying, "The Oklahoma Bar Association have but few more members than we have."[23]

Clifford L. Jackson of Muskogee led the argu- ment for consolidation of the two Bars. On the assumption that Statehood for both Territories would be expedited as soon as the two Territories could agree on single Statehood, Jackson said:[24]

> The lawyers of the two Territories are going to write the new constitution. There may be a hundred or more members of the convention, and there may be only five of them lawyers, but the lawyers who are there will write the new constitution...
>
> The bringing of the lawyers of these two Ter- ritories into one Association will create a good fel-

lowship amongst them;…and they will be better prepared to enter upon the work of preparing the constitution and formulating the government of the new state…My desire is to hasten forward the time when we shall have a state government over the Indian Territory…I want it before I die. That is all I hope for, and I believe it would be better for us to have one great state.

W.I. Gilbert showed his ability as an advocate (which he also used to advantage later as attorney for movie stars after moving to California) by his tenacity in opposing a combination of the two Bars. "I am like Mr. Jackson, only I am different," he said. "…We are certain to have trouble with Oklahoma Territory. The only way to be prepared to meet that is to preserve our individuality."[25] Later discussion brought out that Gilbert feared everyone would ultimately be forced to practice under the laws and procedures of Oklahoma Territory. Moreover, he had a low opinion of Oklahoma lawyers as individuals. "I have lived on the border of Oklahoma [in Duncan] for ten years," Gilbert said. "I know a number of lawyers there, and know their methods of practice; and I know a great many other things, for instance, the amount of fees they charge."[26]

W.A. Ledbetter did not share Gilbert's pessimistic view of amalgamation. "Now, though unwilling it might be of us," he said, "we are going to be forced into Union with Oklahoma. We have got to meet their conditions that seem to weigh so heavily upon Mr. Gilbert…I do not have the same opinion I am proud to say of the Oklahoma lawyers that my friend, Gilbert, seems to have…In all of the qualities that make up a good bar I believe they will stand side by side with the bar of the Indian Territory…I am willing to trust a member of the Indian Territory bar in any contest with the bar of Oklahoma, with full confidence that the Indian Territory will take care of itself."[27]

Jackson's motion, seconded by Ledbetter and approved by the membership, assured "the amalgamation or junction" of the two Associations.[28] Later development indicated that the lawyers of Oklahoma Territory must not have been overly disturbed by W.I. Gilbert's criticism. He was elected vice president of the first consolidated association, and a few years later he moved to Oklahoma City to practice among the lawyers he had scorned. He served as president of the Oklahoma

Bar Association in 1909. In 1913 he moved to California where he became a highly successful member of the Los Angeles Bar.[29]

The executive councils of the Bar Associations of both Territories met in Oklahoma City on September 17, 1904, and unanimously adopted a resolution "That the Oklahoma Bar Association and the Indian Territory Bar Association are amalgamated and consolidated under the name of and to be known as the Bar Association of Oklahoma and Indian Territory."[30] The new association held its first annual meeting in Shawnee on December 29 and 30, 1904. If a sectional controversy had occurred at that meeting, the Indian Territory delegation could have been easy victors because fewer than 25 percent of the 138 listed members were from Oklahoma Territory.[31]

A feature of the Shawnee meeting was the manner in which the assembled lawyers took for granted the future admission of the two Territories as only one state—18 months before Congress approved Statehood for Oklahoma. The "one new state" theme was carried out in papers read by W.T. Hutchings and Judge Frank Dale on a judicial system for the new state. Similarly, J.F. Sharp and P.C. Simons read papers that dealt with the new state's Code of Civil Procedure. Simon emphasized the advantage of adopting the Oklahoma Territory code which included a judicial system already in operation. He praised recent legislation to raise the standards of the profession in Oklahoma Territory by requiring comprehensive, written examinations for admission to the Bar.[32] The members approved a resolution that requested the President and Congress to admit the two Territories as one state.[33]

Prohibition of intoxicating liquors often received attention at the Association meetings. At the meeting of the Indian Territory Bar in 1904, C.L. Herbert denied newspaper reports that the Association wanted to move its headquarters to Oklahoma City where "liquid refreshments" were available.[34] After the Prohibition amendment passed in the new state of Oklahoma former Territorial Judge James R. Keaton wryly suggested that the annual meetings should be held in Arkansas, "where we can have all the necessaries of life."[35]

The Association met as "The Bar Association of Oklahoma and Indian Territory" in December of 1905 and 1906. But in December of 1907, a month after Statehood, due to an automatic name change already provided for in the Association's constitution, it met in Oklahoma City as the "Oklahoma State Bar Association." Of some 315 lawyers listed as members at that meeting, only about 40 percent were from Oklahoma Territory, thus continuing the dominance of Indian Territory membership. The larger cities of the state were represented as follows:[36]

Oklahoma City	56
Muskogee	35
McAlester	20
Chickasha	14
Ardmore	13
Tulsa	10
Guthrie	10

President Clifford L. Jackson, approached his duties with great seriousness as reflected in his comments when G.A. Brown of Mangum and W.E. Utterback of Durant were not present to read papers assigned to them:[37]

The next is one on Judicial Decrees by Judge G.A. Brown. Judge Brown is not here and hasn't his paper prepared, so he has advised us. With reference to that, I have this to say—that in preparing this program these papers were all assigned months ago, and I did not consider an assignment made until I had the written promise of each of the gentlemen to whom I made the different assignments that they would discharge the duty and prepare the papers on the subjects named.

Oklahoma City's S.H. Harris softened the criticism somewhat by his tongue-in-cheek observation: "Mr. President, in proceeding with the trial, wouldn't it be necessary to appoint counsel for the defendant?" But to Jackson the offense was unforgivable. His reply: "In such cases as these, the defendant is not entitled even to counsel"[38] Jackson's ability as a presiding officer no doubt had the approval of his colleagues. Before his election to the presidency of the Oklahoma State Bar Association, he had served several terms as president of the Muskogee Bar and once as president of the Indian Territory Bar Association.

BENCH AND BAR UNDER ATTACK

The Oklahoma State Bar Association, a voluntary membership organization, had existed for about six years when it began to receive misconduct reports with mounting frequency. Complaints charged attorneys with employing drummers to solicit business, and practitioners in the Indian land area were accused of solicitation as well as charging exorbitant fees to their trusting Indian clients. Very few complaints were directed at members of the Association itself, but President J.H. Gordon of McAlester probably spoke for most members at the 1913 convention when he said it was the Association's duty to protect and defend the reputation of the Bar in general.[1]

Later, growing dependence upon the automobile resulted in an increase in personal injury cases, and the Association received more complaints of "ambulance chasing" and use of "runners." Mont F. Highly spoke at the Bar's annual meeting in 1923 on "Legal Ethics—Active and Inactive." From his personal knowledge he told of a young man who had been injured in an automobile accident, and within an hour three runners for lawyers arrived at the home of the victim's father to solicit business. One runner offered the father a bonus for his son's signature on a contract. The father rushed to his son's bedside and learned two law office runners had preceded him there. One resourceful runner already had the son's signature on an agreement with a firm of Oklahoma City lawyers.[2] Other unethical conduct could be attributed to "police court" lawyers and criminal lawyers who enjoyed a comfortable income, not by pleading the client's case but by arranging his bond.[3]

The Bar's Committee on Grievances was always hampered by the absence of clear legislation for disbarment. It could not summon witnesses or try disbarment cases without first obtaining Supreme Court approval.[4] Also, year after year at the state Bar meetings the Grievance Committee had to report a lack of funds to conduct disbarment proceedings against even the most flagrant

Frank M. Bailey, Chickasha, elected president of the Bar Association in 1917 and again in 1938. (Courtesy Mary Bailey.)

offenders.[5] Too, local Bar were criticized frequently for failing to take part in filing and pursuing charges against errant lawyers in their vicinity.[6] On one occasion, however, Warren K. Snyder contributed weeks of his time and the Oklahoma City Bar Association paid necessary expenses to disbar J.W. Burns, a former minister. While practicing law, Burns had become so "energetic in acquiring business and taking fees, that he sometimes forgot to give his client his share of the recovery."[7]

Charges of unethical behavior were on the increase in 1919, but President John Tomerline of the Oklahoma City Bar Association was not unduly alarmed. In his welcoming address at the annual convention he commented, "The laity has long indulged in facetious remarks about our profession. The demagogue knows he can always raise an applause by disparaging remarks about the lawyer. The reason is obvious. The ethics of the profession are so high that the shyster attracts unusual notice and the laity are misled to point to him as an example; whereas he is the exception that proves the worthiness of the great body of the profession."[8] But members of the Bar like W.H. Hills of Enid blamed the profession itself for the public's criticism. "It is our fault that the bars are down," he told those present at the 1916 convention, "that our tribunals that have charge of passing on the qualifications of prospective and embryo attorneys are too lax and do not do their duty."

He cited the case of a lawyer from Maryland who settled in Enid, took the Bar examination, and was admitted. The amazed Hills was familiar with the lawyer's lack of legal ability, so he made a trip to the office of the Clerk of the Supreme Court in Oklahoma City to examine the man's admission records. He had practiced in Maryland for 16 years, Hills reported, but his score on the examination was "a general average in all subjects of about eighteen and a half below zero." One question on the application asked if he had ever been disbarred. "Yes, sir," he replied, "I was disbarred in Maryland for getting drunk in the court room and insulting the court." One of the examiners told Hills the man was admitted because "He was the only one that had the nerve to tell the truth, and…[we] felt sorry for him." Said Hills, "[Failure of examiners to perform their duty] is the reason why we are in disrepute." "That is why we are criticized in the streets and in the barber shops, and elsewhere. I say the power to stop that rests with us…"[9]

The practice of admitting applicants without adequate training in the law had been a problem in both Territorial and early Statehood years. A lawyer at the 1909 Bar convention stated that just before Statehood one United States district judge admitted 27 deputy marshals without examination knowing that they would automatically be allowed to practice in the new state under the "prior admission" clause in Section 33 of the "Schedule" of the constitution. Paul G. Darrough, longtime lawyer and Referee in Bankruptcy in Oklahoma City, recalled that immediately prior to Statehood Judges Joseph A. Gill and Luman F. Parker in the Indian Territory granted licenses to practice to many of their courthouse friends.[10]

During most of the period from Statehood until passage of the State Bar Act of 1929, a major prerequisite for taking the Bar examination was only two years of "regular and attentive law

Paul G. Darrough, longtime Oklahoma City attorney and Referee in Bankruptcy. (Courtesy The Daily Oklahoman.)

study." President Edgar A. de Meules observed at the 1927 convention, "This study may be in the office of an attorney with or without supervision or it may be at home without supervision or it may be through the aid of a correspondence school."[11] As early as 1910, the Bar Committee on Legal Education and Admission to the Bar implied that the longtime custom of reading law in a law office was unsatisfactory. Apparently some attorneys were careless in certifying that applicants had "regularly and attentively studied law."[12] Committee member Vern E. Thompson stated the problem in 1928 when he spoke in favor of high school completion and at least three years of study in an approved law school:

> The Oklahoma requirement that an applicant for examination must present a certificate that he has studied law two years signed by some attorney in the state is a pure farce. Our local Bar has been much embarrassed by illy prepared attorneys who have been admitted on examination by the State Bar Commission on a certificate of either some disreputable member of the Bar or one who has not the moral courage of refusing to sign such a certificate when he knows that the applicant has not consistently studied law for the required period of two years.[13]

The Bar Association's suggestions for strengthening admission standards and improving dis-

(Courtesy Shirk, Work, Robinson & Williams.)

166

barment procedures received little consideration by the Legislature and Supreme Court.[11] Moreover, the Supreme Court always retained the right to admit candidates on motion. The court exercised that prerogative in 1923—perhaps due to political pressure—to the extent that lawyers at the annual convention recorded strong objections. In his president's address, N.A. Gibson of Muskogee spoke of "flagrant exhibitions of ignorance" that degraded the courts in the eyes of the people, and he went on to say:[15]

> Even our highest court has not escaped criticism. In recent years, men not even pretending to have studied law, but who were friends of some influential politicians, have been admitted to the Bar, on motion and without examination, and when thus badged with the right to practice, have joined in the plunder-bund of pardon peddlers, and political pirates, and besmirched the reputation of the Profession.

W.A. Ledbetter agreed and noted that during the last year some 32 applicants had been admitted on motion by the Supreme Court. Kathryn Van Leuven spoke in support of a resolution, later adopted, asking the court to eliminate the 32 members from the rolls and thereafter discontinue admission on motion without approval of the State Bar Commission.[16] The Supreme Court disregarded the State Bar's resolution, and newspaper attention to the court's admissions practice provided only a slight deterrent. The *Muskogee Times-Democrat* gave front page space in 1924 to a discovery by members of the Coal County Bar Association that Bert Thornsborough, a legislator-coal miner who had supported impeached Governor Jack Walton, had been admitted on the motion of Chief Justice J.T. Johnson. Walter A. Lybrand, then president of the State Bar, filed a vigorous protest, and the court rescinded Thornsborough's admission.[17] Nevertheless, 11 months after the newspaper publicity, Thornsborough was readmitted.[18]

A.E. Kull, a columnist for *Harlow's Weekly*, made an interesting discovery in January of 1926. "I never knew until a few days ago," Kull wrote, "the wonderful advantage of just being admitted to the bar on motion made by somebody. The old, somewhat obsolete methods of putting in five or six years of the best part of your life attending college certainly cannot be compared with this new motion idea." Kull told of an "Attorney at

W.E. Crowe, OBA president in 1947, in his Enid law office about 1921. (Courtesy Mrs. W.E. Crowe.)

Law" recently admitted by motion who was now passing out cards together with a large display advertisement describing his specialties. Kull himself had always wanted to be a lawyer, he explained to his readers, but he had no desire to spend the "five or six years," or " a lot of jack." He concluded, "But now if I can just find out who it is that has the say so, I am sure going to have somebody make a motion that I be made an 'Atty at Law' pronto. If attys can be made that way, why can't we get 'Hand-me-down' doctors and dentists in the same manner?"[19] Ridicule of the Supreme Court's admission policy continued to be ineffective. On Christmas Eve, 1928, the 47-year-old impeached governor, Jack Walton, showed he still possessed political potency by obtaining a "courtesy permit" to practice law. Justices of the Supreme Court declined comment.[20]

Since Statehood, criticism of higher courts—usually avoided by other state Bar associations—had been a favorite form of recreation by pioneer Oklahoma lawyers at state Bar meetings.[21] Tulsa's Charles O'Connor said in 1927, a year before he was elected to Congress, "The first, and most distinct, shock that my country-boy soul received when I came here some ten years ago, was to hear the common custom of the lawyers cussing the court."[22] Criticism was especially sharp at the 1915 Bar convention. Vinita's veteran Indian Territory lawyer, W.H. Kornegay, flayed tribunals ranging from the United States Commissioner's court in Indian Territory to and including the United States Supreme Court.[23] Kornegay expounded at one point, "We need more individuality in our judges, we need more intelligence in our judges, we need more industry. Why did the wise men and the prophets in the olden times retire to the mountains? For the purpose of what? To think. Why do the judges go to the mountains now? Is it to think? No, I apprehend it is to drink."[24]

Kornegay's remarks disturbed several of the lawyers as being unfair criticism. The motion of E.G. McAdams the next day to expunge the Kornegay comments from the record provoked a discussion of free speech. The irate A.J. Biddison of Tulsa arose to object to the McAdam's motion and exclaimed,[25]

> Mr. President, if it is the purpose that we come here annually to see a bunch of castrated and castigated geldings jump through the hoops, then lets take our demits and go home. If it is not going to be possible for the members of this Bar Association to express in this meeting their ideas concerning the actions and activities of the Courts of the officers of the Government, State and National, we will serve no good purpose by coming here. I am against this motion and every element of it. I did not approve much what was said and read on yesterday relative to the courts and their decisions, but I do believe and I do approve of free speech. There is one thing that a lawyer cannot stand for "and that is muzzling anybody.

George Ramsey, then president of the Association, also took the floor to champion free speech, saying, "If we cannot come here and review, criticize and analyze judicial decisions we will abandon this Association and go home."[26] Kornegay himself denied that he had made specific reference to any single judge and assured those present that, "Whenever I am called on to answer for what I have said by the court whose dignity has been offended I will make good..." R.J. Shives asked, "What about what you said about the judges retiring to the mountains to drink and not to think?" Kornegay replied, "I know. What I meant to say was that during the summer time they go to the mountains of Colorado, drink of the pure waters of mountain streams, regardless of 'Sunny Brook,' or take your choice."[27] W.A. Ledbetter accepted Kornegay's statement

as constituting an apology and suggested the latter's speech of the day before never be literally put in cold type."[28] His suggestion was disregarded. Likewise, E.G. McAdams motion to expunge the speech from the record was tabled. Consequently, more than 30 pages in the printed proceedings of the 1915 convention record the entire "free speech" discussion, which lasted more than an hour and a half.[29] Kornegay's expression, "going to the mountains to drink and not to think" became a standing joke at future Bar meetings.[30]

Later Kornegay himself joined the court system he had criticized so much, by accepting Governor Murray's appointment to the State Supreme Court in 1931 after J. Howard Langley resigned because of poor health.[31] Kornegay contended that under the state constitution his term lasted until the next election of state officials, so he refused to file for the post at a 1932 special election.[32] A State Supreme Court decision proved him wrong, and the seat went to the winner of the election, Wayne W. Bayless.[33]

At the 1927 Bar convention, Horace G. McKeever, destined to be the Association's president the following year, deplored the "reprehensible conduct" of any judge who listened to a lawyer or litigant in the absence of the opposing side. He explained the practice was what old time lawyers labeled "horse shedding the court," a stratagem by which a lawyer arranged to be the first to arrive at the office of a country justice so he could call him out to the horse shed to discuss the case before the trial began.[34]

At the time McKeever described "horse shedding," an angry Tulsa oil man, O.O. Owens, was fighting what he might have termed another version of the practice: exercising undue influence on the courts. Oklahoma citizens had witnessed during the 1920s a legislative-executive struggle that ended with the removal of Governors Jack C. Walton and Henry S. Johnston from office. They were also spectators to an upheaval in the state's higher courts spawned largely by the stubborn persistence of Owens, a disgruntled litigant. The episode began in 1925 after minority stockholders of Riverside Oil & Refining Company won a money judgment from Owens while he was operating manager of the company.[35] The Oklahoma Supreme Court ruled against Owens in all subsequent proceedings.

In the course of the litigation, Owens charged

the court with judicial misconduct.[36] Not content with fighting his private war through the courts, Owens also sought help from the Oklahoma electorate and the Legislature. His first approach was to announce his candidacy for a seat in the House of Representatives and to attack the State Supreme Court in a full-page political advertisement published in the *Tulsa Daily World*. The advertisement implied that the justices had condoned "alleged corruption in political matters," and that certain members had been accused of making the court "a tool for use in private controversies." Owens closed his advertisement with, "It is for the purpose of eliminating, if possible, the contempt for law, facts, evidence, precedent, equity and justice, heretofore exhibited by certain members of the Supreme Court, that I am a candidate for election as a state representative."[37] By January, 1927 Owens, loser in all battles to date against both courts and lawyers, nevertheless had won his campaign for a seat in the House of Representatives.[38]

On January 7, while Owens prepared to renew his attack through the Oklahoma Legislature, Attorney General George F. Short filed an information against him for contempt of court based on the newspaper advertisement and on accusations Owens had made during previous court proceedings. Prosecution of the contempt charge was delayed because of Owen's legislative immunity, but after the Legislature adjourned the State Supreme Court sentenced him to a year in jail and a $5000 fine. He was jailed within a few minutes after his sentence was announced, but his attorneys, H.B. Martin and A.F. Moss, filed an application for writ of habeas corpus with James S. Davenport, then a judge of the Criminal Court of Appeals.

Judge Davenport, by approving Owens' bond and releasing him from custody of Oklahoma County Sheriff Ben B. Dancy, initiated a conflict between appellate courts that was unique in the history of American jurisprudence. The angry Supreme Court responded with an alternative writ of prohibition against Davenport and the Criminal Court of Appeals. Chief Justice Frederick P. Branson's opinion denied the authority of the Criminal Court and termed it a court "with special and limited jurisdiction."[39] Presiding Judge Thomas Doyle of the Criminal Court re-

taliated with a 127 page opinion that again released Owens.

Sheriff Dancy was caught in the middle between the two courts. He consulted Attorney Edgar S. Vaught who asked the State Supreme Court for a writ of certiorari to review the Criminal Court's judgment. In response, Chief Justice Branson described the Criminal Court proceedings as an "attempt to decapitate the judicial system of Oklahoma" and ridiculed Doyle's opinion. Branson affirmed that the Supreme Court's role was indeed "Supreme" under the constitution and threatened to use more stringent means, if necessary, to keep the Criminal Court within its authority.[40]

At the time Chief Justice Branson issued his opinion, H.B. Martin had previously made arrangements for an Owens' appeal to the Circuit Court of Appeals. That court refused to overturn the State Supreme Court's decision and agreed that the Criminal Court was in fact a subordinate court with limited jurisdiction. The United States Supreme Court denied a writ of certiorari on May 5, 1930; however, the Owens attorneys were ready with an application to Governor Holloway for a pardon, which the governor granted on June 3, 1930. Owens had already served 3 days of his one year sentence in the Oklahoma County jail. The governor considered the time served was "sufficient to vindicate the law and sustain the dignity of the court of the state..." He also cancelled the $5000 fine and court costs.[41]

While the Owens matter tarried in the courts, the nine members of the State Supreme Court disqualified themselves, and a special court appointed by the governor tried H.B. Martin for statements made in a petition for rehearing relative to the Riverside stockholder judgment against Owens.[42] Martin was a graduate of the University of Kansas in 1885 and had been counsel in numerous Oklahoma civil and criminal cases.[43] The court found him guilty of direct contempt for exercising bad faith by "adopting uninvestigated statements of his client" that alleged dishonesty and misconduct by the judges. He was fined $1000.[44]

After both Owens and Martin were cited for contempt, M.A. Breckenridge entered the controversy. Breckenridge, attorney for the *Tulsa Daily World*, had been Tulsa's first County Attorney and Superior Court judge.[45] His opinion of

Maurice A. Breckenridge, Tulsa's first County Attorney and Superior Court Judge. (Courtesy College of Law Library, University of Tulsa.)

the contempt actions was published in the *Tulsa Daily World* on May 1, 1927, when, in substance, he argued that the court should not have suspended the writ of habeas corpus in the Owens case and insisted the Criminal Court was superior in all criminal matters. The State Supreme Court then cited Breckenridge for contempt due to his publishing a "contemptuous, scurrilous, defamatory, false and malicious article" that deliberately inpugned the court's actions. In a subsequent hearing, Breckenridge admitted to misinforming the reading public since he had not adequately researched the law on the subject of "contempt." He was suspended from the practice of law for 30 days.[46]

A more serious disbarment penalty was assessed against H.A. Ledbetter who had practiced in Ardmore nearly 30 years and had served as Vice President of the Oklahoma State Bar Association and Chairman of its Grievance Committee. He had been an attorney in both the Owens and Martin cases. He was accused on eight counts and convicted upon his own admission that he had falsely stated on several occasions that he paid a $750 bribe to J.W. Clark of the State Supreme Court. He pleaded that, due to a serious physical affliction, he had resorted to the excessive use of intoxicating liquor and while under the influence of liquor had made the statements

attributed to him. Although Ledbetter was disbarred in the state courts, he continued to practice in federal courts by special order and was finally reinstated to the Oklahoma Bar in February of 1933.[47]

The Legislature tried to call a special session for December 6, 1927, "to investigate the conduct of state officials" as authorized by Initiative Petition No. 79 approved by the voters in 1923. Despite an opinion written by Chief Justice Branson in the case of *Simpson v. Hill, et al.*, holding that the petition was invalid because only the governor could call a special session, the House of Representatives voted to proceed with the impeachment of Governor Johnston and Harry B. Cordell, president of the State Board of Agriculture. The House also voted to impeach Chief Justice Branson because of his opinion in *Simpson v. Hill*. When the Senate called on Branson to preside at a court of impeachment to try Governor Johnston, he appeared before the Senate to explain further his opinion in *Simpson v. Hill*. In an almost humble manner he declined to preside over the impeachment proceedings because to do so would violate his oath of office. The Senate agreed that any action at that time would be unlawful and adjourned to await the next regular session of the Legislature in 1929.[48]

Meanwhile Representative Owens took time to impede the appointment of Edgar S. Vaught as federal judge of the Western Oklahoma District. No doubt in part because of his displeasure with Vaught for his advice to Sheriff Dancy in the Supreme Court-Criminal Court controversy, Owens filed charges during Vaught's Senate confirmation hearing accusing him of being "a member of a ring of lawyers [that] maintained an improper relationship with the Oklahoma State Supreme Court..." The general belief was that if Vaught had been present to answer Owens' charges, he would have received confirmation without delay and that his absence as well as Congress' hectic rush to adjourn prevented his confirmation. In the meantime, however, President Coolidge began Vaught's 28-year career on the federal bench with an interim appointment which was made permanent by Congress a few months later.[49]

After the impeachment and removal of Governor Henry S. Johnston in the first months of 1929 on a charge of "general incompetency," the Oklahoma Legislature proceeded with the busi-

Fletcher S. Riley, Justice of the Supreme Court, 1924-48. (Courtesy Western History Collections, University of Oklahoma Library.)

ness that most interested Representative Owens. The House of Representatives on March 27, 1929, voted 11 impeachment articles against Chief Justice Charles W. Mason and Justice J.W. Clark and nine against Justice Fletcher S. Riley. The charges involved the integrity of court decisions and the influence of "specially favored" lawyers. The *Simpson v. Hill* case was mentioned and indications were that Frederick P. Branson might have been impeached also had he not been defeated in his reelection campaign.

The Senate Court of Impeachment tried Justice Clark first for his purported bribe by H.A. Ledbetter.[50] The trial, recorded in two volumes totaling 4125 pages, ended with his acquittal on each of the 11 counts.[51] O.O. Owens assumed the role of chief prosecutor throughout the trial and made no attempt to conceal his dislike for members of the Supreme Court. At one point he was rebuked by Senator W.C. Austin for going too far in the examination of witnesses.[52]

Justice Mason was acquitted after a vote taken on the single charge of accepting an automobile as a bribe.[53] The Senate court then dismissed all charges against Fletcher Riley.[54] Riley in 1927 had sued O.O. Owens and the *Tulsa Daily World* for libel based on the Owens political advertisement. That 14-day trial ended with a $100 damage verdict for Riley and costs assessed to Owens.[55]

Justice J.W. Clark sued Owens and the World Publishing Co. in the court of District Judge P.L. Gassaway in Atoka for $200,000 damages for libel.[56] Clark won a $50,000 verdict, but it was reversed by a specially appointed Supreme Court three years later on the grounds that the newspaper advertisement was not libelous per se, the plaintiff had failed to prove special damages, and, further, the statute of limitations had been tolled.[57] Five years later Owens and the World Publishing Co. succeeded in reversing a part of Judge Gassaway's decision regarding court costs and were awarded $365.95 by the State Supreme Court.[58]

Thus closed a bitter fight lasting over a decade in what essentially began and ended with the O.O. Owens war against members of the State Supreme Court. The Oklahoma electorate, although not familiar with ramifications of the attack on the court, must have decided a fresh start was in order. Of the nine justices who sat on the court in 1928, seven (C.W. Mason, E.F. Lester, James I. Phelps, John B. Harrison, Albert C. Hunt, Fred P. Branson, and J.W. Clark) lost their bids for reelection. Robert A. Hefner declined to run again when his term expired in 1932. Only Fletcher S. Riley was reelected.[59]

Justice Riley, a former county attorney of Comanche County, was a University of Oklahoma graduate admitted to the Bar in 1917.[60] Thirty-one years old when first elected to the Supreme Court in 1924, he was destined to become a controversial member of that body and exhibited somewhat unorthodox behavior during the latter years of his 24-year tenure on the bench. He caused some confusion in 1942 when he left to join the armed service without resigning from the court. After Riley's absence for about two months. Governor Leon C. Phillips appointed Oris L. Barney of Anadarko to fill the court vacancy; however, Riley returned to reclaim his office shortly after Barney's appointment.[61]

On one occasion Justice Riley, annoyed by differences with the other justices, submitted for their consideration a revised opinion written entirely in Latin.[62] His actions in 1948 required a landmark interpretation of Oklahoma law when he filed for reelection to the Supreme Court, then on the last day of the filing period filed as a candidate for the United States senate. The State Election Board rejected his candidacy for the latter post, so Riley initiated proceedings in the State Supreme Court for a writ of mandamus that would compel the Election Board to accept his application as a candidate for both offices.

All justices except Chief Justice Thurman S. Hurst and Ben Arnold disqualified themselves to hear the case, so Governor Roy J. Turner appointed seven special justices. The nine justices agreed that a writ of mandamus should issue to require the Board to place Riley's name on the ballot for United States senator. They also held that by filing for that post he had withdrawn his candidacy for the Supreme Court. Justice Riley returned to the private practice of law after finishing eighth in a field of 10 candidates for the senatorial nomination.[63]

28

THE STATE BAR ACT OF 1929

The legislative-executive conflict of the 1920s, which developed into a legislative-judicial battle during the O. O. Owens affair, directed attention to the imperfections of the state Bar. Layman and lawyer alike criticized the Bar in general for unethical conduct attributed to either practicing lawyer or jurist. However, President Edgar A. de Meules argued eloquently in his address at the 1927 Bar Association convention that criticism of the entire profession because of the incompetence of court personnel was unfair. Lawyers comprised only a small fraction of those who voted the judiciary into office, he pointed out, and for the most part laymen were inclined to vote against candidates endorsed by the Bar. But de Meules, like other responsible members of the voluntary Bar Association, agreed that any substantial reform in the administration of justice and the conduct of lawyers must come from the Association—the only organized, state-wide group among the legal profession.[1]

The Association's president in 1930, former Territorial Judge J.R. Keaton, listed the following shortcomings of the Oklahoma Bar setup which Bar officials had tried since Statehood to correct:[2] (1) Lack of adequate educational requirements (both academic and legal) as a prerequisite to an applicant's taking the examination for admission to the bar; (2) The custom or practice of admitting to the bar certain applicants on motion, without examination, who possessed neither the legal nor literary educational qualifications therefor; (3) Lack of any officer, board or commissioner, whose specific legal duty was to enforce the disciplinary provisions of the old statute relating to "Attorneys at Law"; and (4) Lack of proper cooperation among members of the bar and between them and the courts in the important matter of bringing about a more efficient and expeditious administration of justice in this state.

The problem of regulating the legal profession was not unique to Oklahoma. The American Bar Association approached the problem by preparing a model State Bar Act to create a unified, self-governing Bar that required compulsory membership and had the power to control and discipline a state's lawyers. The model Act had the approval of leaders in the profession such as Elihu Root, William Howard Taft, and Roscoe Pound.[3]

The Oklahoma State Bar Association appointed a committee in 1921 to draft a unified Bar Act along the lines recommended by the American Bar Association.[4] Subsequent failure to adopt the act in Oklahoma could be traced in part to disagreement among the lawyers themselves; however, in 1927 President de Meules also blamed the Legislature. The Association's repeated recommendations for remedial legislation had received "less consideration than the tramp at the back door," de Meules said.[5] When asked why the Legislature paid so little attention to the Association's proposals, one young state senator replied, "The Bar Association is just a selected coterie of more or less successful lawyers who simply have a family reunion once a year, but it is not representative of the rank and file of the Bar."[6]

Eventually the Association's Committee for a Self Governing Bar found the right formula in 1928 for obtaining membership approval when it recommended, with only slight revision, the act already adopted in California.[7] Lawyer-legislators helped guide the measure through the Oklahoma Legislature. Weary after a six-month marathon in which it removed Governor Johnston from office and considered impeachment charges against three Supreme Court justices, the Legislature passed the State Bar Act in special session on June 22, 1929.[8] Association members had followed the advice of such lawyers as W.C. Austin, chairman of Senate Judiciary Committee No. 1, along with Mac Q. Williamson and R.L. Wheatley, who advised against introducing the act in the regular session because of the possibility of unfavorable publicity during the impeachment trials. Strong supporters in the House of Representatives were lawyers Chamberlayne Jones, R.H. Stanley and Clay M. Roper.[9]

William J. Holloway, governor of Oklahoma, 1929-31. (Courtesy OHS.)

For the first time in months Oklahoma's three departments of state government acted in complete harmony. They even approved the emergency clause that made the act effective immediately. Lawyer-Governor William J. Holloway called it "one of the most constructive pieces of legislation" by the Twelfth Legislature. He felt there would no longer be "any monkey business" by certain men admitted to the practice of law in the last decade without proper qualifications. He attributed passage of the bill to the honorable members of the profession and emphasized, "Frankly there were sinister influences seeking to defeat its passage. *They know I know it, and you know.*"[10]

Under the new act all state lawyers were required to belong to the State Bar of Oklahoma, administered by a Board of Governors of 13 members elected by the membership. One member was elected from each judicial district and four from the membership at large. The Board of Governors prescribed rules and regulations binding on all members of the Bar in the areas of admission to practice, disbarment, and other disciplinary measures. However, the Board's broad actions were always subject to approval by the State Supreme Court.[11]

The twenty-third and last annual meeting of the voluntary Oklahoma State Bar Association was held on February 21, 1930, with John R.

Kane as president. The next day J.R. Keaton, elected president by the Board of Governors, presided at a special meeting of the new statutory "State Bar of Oklahoma." Kane described the Bar act as "a new broom, as well as a rainbow."[12] But other lawyers doubted the Act would endure. One of these was Atoka's Joe Ralls, whose years as an attorney dated back to the organization of the first Muskogee court. He accurately predicted that lawyers in the legislature would eventually repeal the Act.[13]

Charles W. Mason, Chief Justice of the Oklahoma Supreme Court, was invited to speak at the special meeting. He was unable to attend, so his address was read by Justice Albert C. Hunt. The Chief Justice praised the new legislation as "the dawn of a new day,"but used the occasion to direct a blow at the old voluntary group that had so freely criticized the courts in times past when he said:[14]

The Bar Association of this State, prior to this time, has been a voluntary organization and while some good has been accomplished, the state conventions have been very largely social affairs. The lawyers have come together, giving each other the glad hand, renewing old comradeships, extending felicitations to each other and that is about all that has been accomplished, except to give some lawyer who had recently lost a case an opportunity to cuss the court while his opposing counsel sat by and enjoyed his vilification and vituperation without uttering a word and little realizing that such procedure was eating out the very foundation of government itself by shaking the confidence of the uninformed layman in the judiciary.

The Chief Justice noted that under the new compulsory State Bar Act the Association should follow the example set by the American Bar Association and transform itself from "largely a social association"into an organization interested in the "serious questions"of the day. A "serious question" the new Association addressed immediately was the problem of lawyer discipline. At the time the Bar Act was adopted, the Legislature appropriated $14,000 for prosecution of lawyers named in complaints against the profession. The Supreme Court accepted the Board of Governor's recommendations for 12 specific causes for disbarment, which included willful violations of one's duties as an attorney, boasting special influence with the courts, solicitation of business, and improper division of fees with laymen.[15]

Under the new disciplinary procedures, the Board of Governors and various Administrative Committees devoted most of their time to hearings and disposal of complaints. During the prior 22 years of Statehood only 58 disbarment proceedings had been initiated, resulting in 21 disbarments. After the new Bar Act, the Board of Governors was confronted with 95 complaints carried over from prior years and 59 new complaints. In a little more than a year the Board disposed of 63 complaints: 32 by dismissal, 15 by reprimand, three by suspension, and 13 by disbarment recommendations to the State Supreme Court.[16]

Julian C. Monnet, dean of the University of Oklahoma Law School who chaired the Committee on Legal Education and Admission to the Bar, reported major admission changes at the December, 1930, meeting. Since passage of the unified Bar Act the following three reforms, long advocated by the Committee, had been placed into effect:[17] (1) The lengthening of the period of required study before eligibility to pass examination for admission to the Bar from two years to three years; (2) A registration system by which every student of the law in this state must not only give proof afterwards but also give proof in advance of his study of the law by being compelled to register officially as a student with the State Bar so that it may be known that he is in good faith pursuing the study of the law; and (3) The abolition of all privileges of entering the Bar without an official examination by a competent committee appointed by the State Bar itself.

The new Bar Act assessed annual dues of five dollars to finance the first official legal publication, the *Oklahoma Bar Journal*, that went to all lawyers in the state. Some lawyers objected to the dues and the new Act in general on the theory that the act was an unconstitutional infringement

In 1977 Chief Justice Ralph B. Hodges of the Oklahoma Supreme Court conducted this symbolic swearing in of the University of Oklahoma's law class of 1927 on its 50th anniversary. Prominent in this class were Federal Judges Luther Bohanon and Royce H. Savage and Dick Jones of the Court of Criminal Appeals. Lee B. Thompson, OBA President in 1972, was also in this class. (Courtesy David Milsten.)

Ernest W. Marland, governor of Oklahoma, 1935-39. (Courtesy OHS.)

of their rights since the practice of law was a matter of right rather than a privilege.[18] Governor Holloway had anticipated controversy and before signing the act received Judge Robert L. Williams' informal affirmative opinion that it was constitutional.[19] Two years later, however, the Oklahoma Supreme Court signified its own approval in an opinion written by Justice W.H. Kornegay.[20]

Compulsory Bar Association membership mandated by the 1929 Bar Act facilitated statistics reflecting the number of lawyers practicing in the state. Supreme court records had listed about 1800 lawyers admitted to practice at Statehood. The number of active lawyers reached about 3000 in the next decade. Membership in the voluntary Bar Association had never exceeded about 19 percent of the active Oklahoma lawyers until returning war veterans in 1918 boosted the total to 1412—not quite half of the lawyers in active practice. In that year the Oklahoma Bar claimed third place in membership among the states, exceeded only by New York and Illinois.[21] The increased membership was due largely to the enthusiastic leadership of President Edgar C. McAdams, who served five terms as Oklahoma City Bar president. He died in 1923 at age 47.[22] At the time of the 1929 act the Supreme Court rolls listed 8000 Oklahoma lawyers. That accumulation of names enrolled since Statehood was revised as of December 31, 1931, to eliminate names because of death, removal from the state, and failure to pay dues, leaving 3569 licensed lawyers.[23]

Ernest W. Marland, a law graduate of the University of Michigan, had promised during his successful campaign for the Oklahoma governorship in 1934 to initiate a businesslike approach to the conduct of state business. He fulfilled that promise early in his administration by using funds from voluntary contributions to engage the prestigious Brookings Institution of Washington, D.C., to study and make recommendations for improvements in state government. In the area of "Prosecution, Counsel, Representation, and Defense," only to the State Bar Act did the Brookings Institution extend its whole-hearted approval.[24] Conversely the report criticized Oklahoma's judicial system as being "second only to the Legislature in general disorganization and inefficiency."[25] The report also objected to the County Attorney system where inadequate salaries and insecurity of tenure attracted inexperienced young men and middle-aged men who had failed in private law practice.[26]

Despite praise from the Brookings Institution the State Bar Act was to last only from 1929 to 1939—the approximate period of the Great Depression. As will be seen, the rigors of earning a living by the practice of law in that unhappy decade may have contributed to the act's demise.

29

THE STATE BAR ACT OF 1939

The new Oklahoma Bar Act was scarcely under way when the stock market crash of 1929 preceded the Great Depression. A lawyer who remembered well the hardships of Oklahoma law practice during the next decade was John M. Holliman, state legislator and 1959 Bar Association president. A graduate of Ouachita College in Arkansas, Holliman was law secretary to James T. Shipman in Bartlesville until he passed the three-day Bar examination which he took along with 86 other applicants at Oklahoma City in 1921.

He began a solo practice in Bartlesville with a one-volume edition of *Oklahoma Statutes*, some *Oklahoma Reports* and the 40-volume *Cyclopedia of the Law*, his *Words and Phrases* of that day. His first years in practice were largely devoted to collecting accounts and preparing tax returns. Customary collection fees were 15 percent without suit, 20 percent if suit was filed, 33-1/3 percent if he had to try the case, and 50 percent of the amount recovered if the case went to the Supreme Court. From about the first half of 1930, Holliman recalled, "Law business ceased. Nobody had any money. Collection business was nil, because there was nothing to collect, unless you wanted a fellow's coat. I welcomed any business that came into my door but it had to be on a cash basis. I owed twenty-three months rent at one time—there just wasn't any law business."[1]

The first years of the Great Depression saw 5000 banks fail and erase the savings of nearly 9 million Americans.[2] The failure of Tulsa's Exchange National Bank and the liquidation of its successor, the Exchange Trust Company, made front page news in Oklahoma in 1933 and furnished temporary business for 31 lawyers. N.A. Gibson and Flint Moss headed a list of two dozen lawyers defending 28 directors. J.M. Springer of Stillwater led a prosecution staff of seven. Flint Moss highlighted the 10-day hearing with what a local newspaper described as a "masterful and vigorous" defense argument. On March 23, 1934, Judge Williams ruled the evidence showed no intent to defraud and sustained all defense demur-

Horace D. Ballaine, who began his law practice in 1931 during the Great Depression after graduating from the University of Oklahoma. (Courtesy College of Law Library, University of Tulsa.)

rers. Twenty-four pleased lawyers and seven not so pleased returned to everyday business, and the case faded from the newspapers.[3]

A general merchandise store failed in Wewoka and provided employment for young Robert L. Cox, recent University of Oklahoma law graduate, Class of 1931. Settling the store's numerous accounts receivable with Seminole Indians proved to be a difficult assignment. Many of the Indians were illiterate and lacked English names. Consequently, Cox was kept busy for weeks as he traced accounts on the firm's books that referred only to descriptions such as "Big Nose Jim" or which identified the debtor by number such as "Seminole Indian No. 1."[4]

Especially courageous were the law graduates of the Thirties who entered solo practice. Although Merton M. Bulla of the University of Oklahoma, Class of 1931, later enjoyed an outstanding oil, gas, and probate practice, he started as a lawyer in that bleak depression year so afraid he might miss a client that he often remained in his office rather than leave to eat a noon meal; however, the hoped-for client seldom appeared.[5] E.D. Hieronymus, 1968 Bar president, finished law school in Tulsa in 1930. Every Saturday morning he went to the courthouse to sit in the jury box during "motion docket." On occasional providential Saturdays one of the judges would notice him and ask "Are you a lawyer?" Hieronymus' affirmative reply could generate a fee for his services as a court-appointed defense counsel.[6]

University of Oklahoma graduate Horace D. Ballaine, future District Judge and long-time Tulsa lawyer, began his practice at Cleveland, Oklahoma in 1931 with a typewriter, a set of *Oklahoma Reports*, the two-volume set of *Oklahoma Statutes* and a form book. The $60 fee he received for an infrequent mortgage foreclosure was "big business", particularly when compared to the $15 or $20 he received for a divorce case or the five or six dollars for examining an abstract.[7] Alfred Stevenson, veteran of more than a half-century of law practice in Hughes County, recalled that during prohibition days small town lawyers could earn a respectable fee by defending against the most frequent criminal charge, bootlegging. Quite often a defense plea alleging lack of a proper search warrant would free the defendant.[8]

In 1933 a young lawyer, then secretary to a United States District Judge in Los Angeles, wanted to move to Oklahoma. His letter to Judge Robert L. Williams asked if the judge knew of "any small connection I could make so that I might sustain myself until I have passed the Bar examination there."[9] Judge Williams' reply by return mail offered no hope. "I know of no connection whatever that you could probably make now," he wrote. "I was talking to a young man the other day whose father for fifteen years was a member of the Supreme Court of Oklahoma; he has been admitted to the bar two or three years and he is working for a law firm on a percentage basis now and not making over $50.00 a month. My advice to you is to stay at Los Angeles if you can retain the position you now have. This is not the time to move."[10]

In 1933, the depth of the depression, a national survey showed the average income of lawyers to be $3868 annually—nearly $1000 more than a physician's income.[11] It appears doubtful, however, that the income of Oklahoma lawyers attained the national average. Some even had difficulty paying the five dollars annual dues. They were fortunate indeed who could face suspension for nonpayment of dues with the sense of humor shown by the lawyer who wrote the following rhyme to the Board of Governors in February, 1934:[12]

In Re: Application for Reinstatement
Gentlemen:
PETITION
My legal lights you've doused and ended;
   And sans a cent, I've been suspended,
By the bar: Excommunicate Recapiended:
   For dues delinquent I'm apprehended.

Oh listen to my last lament:
   My cash long since has all been spent,
For taxes, groceries and rent;
   I pray your honors to relent.

Restore to me again my shingle;
   Allow me with the courts to mingle;
For I have dunned my client single
   Who has responded; my pockets jingle.

Premises considered, I therefore urge thee;
   From my sins to forthwith purge me,
Eleven bucks I herewith slip ye
   And ask that you will readmit me.

Depression-caused reduction in tax revenues prompted some jurists to adopt innovative methods to keep their courts open. They asked lawyers to agree to a six-man civil jury at every opportunity to avoid drastically reduced court terms. Judge W.G. Long of Murray and Garvin Counties asked jurors to serve for $1.50 a day rather than the customary $3.00.[13] Judge C. Guy Cutlip of the Superior Court of Seminole County used two unpaid volunteer attorneys as triers of the facts when he could persuade the litigants to waive a regulation jury. According to Judge Cutlip this procedure saved taxpayer money and expedited the trial of cases while the lawyers themselves benefited by observing court proceedings from a judge's viewpoint.[14]

In Pontotoc County, County Judge Claude V. Thompson and County Attorney Truman S. Harrison made the "supreme sacrifice." They regularly returned 20 percent of their salaries in order to reduce court expenses. On the other hand, when county commissioners in an unnamed community sought to reduce the salary of an assistant

Retiring members of the 1934 Board of Governors. L To R: W.E. Utterback, OBA president, 1932; W.C. Austin, former state senator; A.W. Trice, OBA president, 1944. (Courtesy The Daily Oklahoman.)

County Attorney, he turned to the courts and won a decision affirming that his salary was fixed by law and could not be reduced.[15]

Unauthorized practice of law by individuals and companies deprived lawyers of business they sorely needed during the Depression. Banks, abstractors, real estate agents, collection bureaus, notaries, and justices of the peace routinely drafted wills, contracts, and conveyances and sometimes examined abstracts of title. Thus laymen failed to receive proper legal advice, and the legal profession was subjected to competition unrestrained by ethical considerations.[16]

Following organization of the Oklahoma State Bar Association in 1929, the Board of Governors took the lead in a campaign to end unauthorized practice.[17] A Committee reported some progress after conferences with a committee representing state banks and trust companies.[18] The State Supreme Court in 1934 handed down a decision that the Association as an arm of the court was a lawful entity that could maintain an action to enjoin unauthorized practice of law. This landmark decision provided the state and local bar groups the leverage needed to curtail the more flagrant violations.[19]

Bar officials with mounting frequency began to blame the profession's problems on a surplus of lawyers. The Bar examiner's report in 1931 called attention to figures showing 10,000 new lawyers were being admitted in the United States annually, twice the number deceased or retired each year. The report noted, "It is apparent, therefore, that competition is rapidly becoming more in-

tense, that there are or soon will be too many lawyers."[20]

In August 1933 the *Oklahoma State Bar Journal* reprinted a *Saturday Evening Post* editorial referring to the law as an "overcrowded occupation" and suggesting that Bar Associations, examiners, courts, and Legislatures should endeavor to limit "the number of unfit and unethical lawyers."[21] Four months later Albert W. Trice, destined to be president of the Association in 1944, presented the report of the Board of Governors at the Bar's annual meeting and said, "We are also concerned with the serious problems which confront the individual lawyer arising out of the grave overcrowding of the profession. It is an alarming fact that in the ratio of lawyers to population, Oklahoma stands at or near the highest of the States and as a corollary, the total property values in our State are near the lowest per lawyer in the Union."[22]

Many Oklahoma lawyers criticized the 1929 Bar Act as being excellent in theory but impractical because of the uncompensated leadership required and the likelihood that a small minority would be in control.[23] In view of the friction within the Bar itself, it is not surprising that the Legislature, in each session of the 1930s except 1937, contemplated repeal or modification of the act.[24] The Legislature in 1937 determined that a better approach was to have its members join the legal profession. Hence House Bill No. 461 decreed that three terms in the Legislature qualified a legislator to practice law in Oklahoma without examination.[25] Governor Marland agreed with the Board of Governors that the bill was not in the interest of the profession or the public. The governor vetoed the measure and is said to have told members of the Legislature, "I would be willing to sign such a bill if you also submit one providing that anyone who has had a venereal disease three times will be allowed to practice medicine."[26]

According to Justice Denver Davison, who was on the State Supreme Court in the late 1930s, the Legislature at that time seemed to want to take over the Bar and dictate admission to practice. As in the Twenties the court found itself again subjected to legislative pressure for admission of unqualified applicants on motion without examination.[27] One applicant admitted to the Bar on motion was immediately elected County

Oklahoma Governor Leon C. Phillips (1939-43), standing, watches election returns in the 1938 Democratic primary. (Courtesy OHS.)

Judge.[28] Lawyer A. Francis Porta served in the House in 1939, and a quarter of a century later he told of the antagonism toward lawyers: "When I was in the Legislature—and this in not a new thing—all they had to do to kill a bill was for Tom Kight [representative from Rogers County] to stand up and say, 'Why, this is a lawyer's bill,' and brother, she went out the window."[29]

When 34 of the 54 applicants who sat for the December, 1938, Bar examination failed to pass, they no doubt remembered the Bar leadership's frequent references to the oversupply of lawyers. A former state senator whose son failed the examination charged that the Bar examiners had "deliberately cut down on the number of new attorneys to be admitted to practice and competition."[30] An announcement that the State Supreme Court would review the examination papers fortified his argument. Governor Leon C. Phillips told a Tulsa audience, "There is a group making up about one-third of the bar of the state that is trying to maintain control so that the number of new lawyers is greatly reduced."[31]

The Legislature was in session at the time, and, because several Bar candidates from the University of Oklahoma law school had failed, students and alumni started a movement to have University graduates admitted thereafter without examination as had been the practice before the

1929 Bar Act. The House passed legislation to that effect with the support of Governor Phillips. The governor said in his Tulsa speech, "If these graduates are not properly qualified to practice law without examination, we should either close up the school or rejuvenate it." The governor, himself a graduate of the University law school, admitted he was not satisfied with the school and went on to say, "I advocate teachers in the law school who could make a living practicing law. I would even go so far, if I could get the regents to agree to it, as to employ a man who does not even have a law degree, provided he could properly teach law."[32]

When the House-approved measure reached the Senate, Thomas C. Waldrep, a Shawnee lawyer and University of Oklahoma law graduate, decided the time was ripe to abolish the Bar Association. He introduced an amendment for that purpose. Heated debates in the House and Senate showed strong disagreement among state lawyers which Senator Paul Stewart, an Antlers rancher-lawyer, termed a conflict between "cornfield lawyers" and "corporation attorneys" to gain control of the Bar. Discrimination and arbitrary control of the Bar by a few lawyers were argued in a three-hour Senate debate.[33]

After the Senate approved the Waldrep amendment by a vote of 24 to 17 and returned it to the House for further consideration, alarmed leaders of the Bar Association throughout the state joined members of the Board of Governors in a rush to the state capital. However, the telephone calls and telegrams that bombarded the legislators convinced then that a majority of state lawyers either openly or secretly favored an end to the Bar Association. What the press described as "tumultuous scenes" occurred during House debate in which House officers had to suppress one attempt at physical combat. Lawyer Don Welch, Speaker of the House, endorsed the bill and accused a "lawyer lobby" of threatening University of Oklahoma law student members of the Legislature who also supported the bill.[34]

On final roll call the amended bill passed in the House by a vote of 63 to 52. In its completed form the measure repealed the 1929 Bar Act and made the State Supreme Court the determinate authority over the practice of law and administration of the Bar except for a provision admitting "Grade A" law school graduates without examination. "Grade A" schools were defined as schools recognized by the Association of American Law Schools, National Association of Law Schools, the American Bar Association, or the Supreme Court of the State of Oklahoma.[35]

Bar leaders had been caught unaware of the legislative hostility that the results of the December, 1938, Bar examinations had brought to light, and until the final vote they thought the bill would be defeated. Those lawyers who believed repeal of the Bar Act had injured both the legal profession and the public in general went so far as to suggest referendum procedures and court battles to carry the matter into the next legislative session. Others felt it would be impossible to arouse sufficient interest for repeal of the bill and were willing to accept legislative action as final.[36]

While the bill awaited the governor's approval, an *Oklahoma City Times* editorial defended the Bar Association and warned that admission of "Grade A" law school graduates would "open the way for hundreds, denied the right to practice in their own states, to come in droves to Oklahoma and be admitted without sufficient test." The editorial condemned the new legislation and insisted that "It gives the unscrupulous element a renewed grip on the bar and a renewed entry into the courts, which the old law steadily was loosening and closing."[37] Unmoved by newspaper pressure Governor Phillips signed the bill, and in a speech at Clinton explained, "I would be in favor of re-enacting the bar act some of the newspapers have had so much to say about if the newspapers will agree to passage of a law setting up a committee of five to regulate and control the *Daily Oklahoman* and *Tulsa World*.[38]

While the Legislature debated repeal of the 1929 Bar Act and Bar leaders mourned its demise, the State Supreme Court reviewed the December, 1938, examination papers. According to then Supreme Court Justice Denver Davison, the justices concluded that the seven-member Board of Bar Examiners had been influenced by graduates of out-of-state law schools on the Board, and consequently had prepared questions unfair to graduates of Oklahoma law schools. The Supreme Court review awarded passing grades to 24 of the 34 applicants who had previously failed.[39]

The court set up a temporary executive council to control the Bar one month ahead of the July

Five Crowe brothers, including four lawyers and two OBA presidents. L to R: Raymond L., government employee; Robert D., Oklahoma City lawyer; W.E., OBA president, 1947; V.P., OBA presiodent, 1960; A.G., Oklahoma City lawyer. (Courtesy Mrs. W.E. Crowe.)

28, 1939, date the legislature had set for the legal death of the old Bar Association. On October 10, 1939, however the court declared that it held inherent power to regulate the practice of law under Article IV, Section 1, of the Oklahoma constitution without regard to legislative enactment.[40] The court proceeded to appoint a new Board of Bar Examiners and adopt new rules substantially the same as those in force under the old Association except for the following changes in three major areas of past dissension: (1) Appointment of the Executive Council by the Court rather than election by members of the Bar; (2) Revision of disbarment procedures; and (3) Reduction of membership fees from five dollars to three dollars annually.[41]

The justices in a positive display of their independence from the Legislature ruled that all law school graduates must take the Bar examination and thus nullified the Legislative "Grade A" law school exemption. In a case that came before the State Supreme Court the next year, the court ruled unconstitutional the legislative enactment for admission of "Grade A" schools on motion and affirmed its own inherent powers to regulate the requirements for admission to the Bar.[42]

The court also provided for formation of a State Bar that became the present Oklahoma Bar Association at an organizational meeting held in Oklahoma City on December 28 and 29, 1939, with a record attendance of more than 700 lawyers.[43] Justice Harrison L. Danner, a new member of the Supreme Court, had written most of the new rules and was invited to discuss them at the meeting. He explained the Court's decision to disregard the legislation that would have admitted "Grade A" law school graduates on motion:[44]

> Can you see where any control could be had by the Bar of Oklahoma or by the Court of Oklahoma over such a situation? I cannot help but believe that there might have been some little influence outside of the state in attempting to get that bill through. The result, to my mind, would have been devastating.
>
> All of you have known of the oil booms at Seminole, at Oklahoma City, and at Tulsa. If those provisions had remained the law, it would have meant that any graduate of these schools could have come in here without previous residence and be admitted on motion, and when the boom was over, move on.

Valjean Biddison of Tulsa, a "city lawyer," brought the country-city conflict into the open when he asked the assembled lawyers, "Will the affairs of this Association be controlled by the lawyers of the state generally, or will it be controlled by the Oklahoma City lawyers when the meeting is held here, or by the lawyers from Tulsa when the meeting is held there, because they have a majority in attendance at every meeting held? The idea back of the whole plan of delegates is that we will have representatives from every section of the state and from every county administering the affairs of the Association and deciding the important questions coming up."[45]

The members voted to vest control in a House of Delegates patterned after the American Bar Association. One delegate would be elected from each county and an additional delegate would be elected for each 50 members in a county, with a maximum of 10 delegates per county. Thus counties with metropolitan areas, such as Oklahoma City and Tulsa, were restricted to no more than 10 delegates. The reorganization plan was deemed a distinct victory for "country lawyers."[46] At the meeting's close, a spirit of cooperation prevailed. For the first time the State Supreme Court had exercised firm leadership of the state's lawyers under its constitutional powers. Although the court retained for itself a nucleus of control through appointment of an Executive Council, essentially it left to the Bar the right to govern itself. As the clouds of the pending war drifted toward the United States, the Bar Association seemed better structured than ever before to assume its obligation of service to the legal profession and to the general public.

THE NEW OKLAHOMA BAR

Conflict over the organizational structure of the Oklahoma bar had dominated the news about the legal profession throughout much of the year 1939; however, during 1940 more dramatic aspects of the profession captured front page headlines: the trial of Oklahoma City lawyer Orban C. Patterson, and County Attorney Lewis Morris' prosecution of the well-publicized "Communist Cases."

During the two decades of 1920 to 1940, when critics of the legal profession spoke of "shysters" and "fixers," better-informed Oklahoma citizens thought of Orban C. Patterson as undisputed "King of the Underworld." Patterson had received his law degree from the University of Oklahoma in 1914 and started his career in the office of Moman Pruiett, the Southwest's renowned criminal lawyer. Five years later his knowledge of the Oklahoma City vice world and its assorted characters earned him a behind-the-scenes partnership .with newly elected Mayor Jack C. Walton.[1]

Even after Walton departed for a brief reign in the governor's office before being impeached, the Patterson syndicate prospered and extended into the "upperworld," where effective contacts assured the continuity and growth of the Patterson influence. Patterson himself was a legendary figure, a "ghost in soft shoes" in 1938 when Charles E. Dierker of Shawnee was appointed United States Attorney for the Western District of Oklahoma.[2] Dierker had read law in the office of E.E. Hood, before he, like Patterson, started his law practice in 1914.[3]

After one of Oklahoma's most thorough criminal investigations, Dierker brought Patterson to trial before Federal District Judge Edgar S. Vaught on January 31, 1940, for income tax evasion. Dierker subpoenaed 54 witnesses but the testimony of only the first witness—Seth Stone—convinced Patterson he should enter a plea of *nolo contendere*.[4] For Judge Vaught's consideration in sentencing, Dierker outlined the sources of Patterson's unreported income: houses of prostitu-

Lewis R.Morris, Oklahoma County Attorney, considered one of Oklahoma's most brillian prosecuting attorneys. (Courtesy Archives and Manuscripts Division, OHS.)

tion, gambling, liquor traffic and car theft. But, said Dierker, "The extent of the defendant's nefarious activities can never be known." Judge Vaught sentenced Patterson to five years in prison and a $25,000 fine. He died in Utah in 1944 eight months after his release from federal prison at Leavenworth, Kansas.[5]

Later in the year, on the eve of World War II, the Oklahoma City "Communist cases" featured the oratory of County Attorney Lewis R. Morris and tested Oklahoma's Criminal Syndicalism Act. That act in general covered individual criminal conduct connected with attempted labor or political reform.[6] Morris, once a protege of Moman Pruiett, was serving his fifth term as Oklahoma County Attorney. Considered one of the most brilliant prosecuting attorneys in Oklahoma's history, he was frequently the recipient of page one newspaper publicity. Two years previously he had obtained the convictions of four defendants in the notorious Oklahoma City School Board bribery trials.[7]

Morris and his associates in the "Communist cases" convicted four individuals of advocating overthrow of the government. The heat of battle must have blinded counsel for both sides to the ban against indulging in personalities set out in the "Cannons of Professional Ethics" recently published by the newly formed Oklahoma Bar Association. District Judge Ben Arnold later admitted he had allowed both sides considerable latitude in their arguments.[8] Hearings in the pivotal case appealed to the Oklahoma Criminal Court of Appeals brought newspaper and magazine journalists to Oklahoma City from across the nation. *Amicus curiae* appeared for both sides, most of them convinced of the defendants' guilt; however, all four convictions were ultimately reversed.[9]

The conviction of lawyer Orban C. Patterson and his removal from the legal profession had been a major victory for the Oklahoma Bar Association (the OBA). But as the new Association concluded its first year under the revised Bar Act and the rules of the Supreme Court, President John E. Luttrell could also report that three primary administrative objectives had been achieved: County Bar Associations were in operation, a definite program of legal institutes was underway, and the weekly *Journal* had replaced the ten-year-old monthly *Bar Journal*. Also, the *Oklahoma Official Reports* which had cost five dollars per volume could now be purchased for the unheard-of-price of $1.90 each, the lowest price in the Nation for official reports. Other state associations besieged the Oklahoma Bar for its magic formula after officials at the American Bar Association's annual meeting called the Oklahoma Bar Association "the ideal pattern for bar integration."[10]

Two weeks before the Japanese bombed Pearl Harbor on December 7, 1941, newly elected Bar President John H. Cantrell outlined an ambitious 16-point program that forecast 1942 to be a year of unsurpassed Bar activity and achievement.[11] In less than a year, however, the Oklahoma Bar Association had become a "Gold Star" organization. The armed services claimed an estimated 30 percent of the state's 4500 lawyers.[12] The organized reserves, National Guard, and the Selective Service Act called many lawyers to active duty, but others were quick to volunteer, as did Lee B. Thompson, destined to be OBA president in 1972. Thirty-nine years old, married, and the father of three children, he could have declined active service; instead, he served from 1940 to 1946 in the United States Army, earning five campaign stars.[13]

On the home front OBA officials encouraged members to protect the practice of their colleagues in the service, and when the need arose, to substitute for them in unfinished legal matters without profit for themselves.[14] Conditions in many counties curtailed law practice to the extent that some attorneys could not earn a living. When possible the Bar's Executive Committee helped those attorneys find employment in other Oklahoma communities.[15]

The Bar Association limped through the war years in rented, inadequate quarters with a staff of three under the leadership of Presidents Cantrell, Ray S. Fellows, A.W. Trice and Charles E. France.[16] When President Fellows took office, the *Journal*, bulwark of the Association, was about to cease publication due to lack of funds, partly because lawyers in the military service were receiving it and all other membership privileges free of charge.[17] The *Journal* continued publication only after the Supreme Court's approval of a dues increase from five dollars to $7.50 annually.[18]

Bar committees secured lawyers to act as legal advisers for county and other local defense committees, furnished speakers to build and maintain public morale, and provided a clearing house for legal advice free of charge to impecunious service men and their families.[19] The War Department bestowed its highest rating, "Superior," on the Oklahoma Bar for the cooperation of the Committee on War Work and the contributions by individuals attorneys to the Department's Legal Assistance program.[20]

Unauthorized practice by laymen intensified during World War II years. At the Bar's annual meeting in 1945, Fred Spellman of Alva reported numerous complaints against accountants, auditors, bank clerks, and "lay counselors," such as estate planners, labor counselors, administrative tribunal specialists, and public relations counselors.[21] During the next year the OBA headed off encroachment by executing agreements for clarification of activities that constituted the practice of law with responsible organizations that included the Oklahoma Society of Certified Public Accounts, the Oklahoma Association of Life Un-

Former OBA presidents. L to R: LeRoy Blackstock (1966), Jim F. Gassaway (1971), Lee B. Thompson (1972). (Courtesy OBA.)

derwriters, and the Oklahoma Trust Companies Association.[22] The OBA in later years utilized similar methods for obtaining the cooperation of errant individuals and lay groups through conferences and the issuance of warning letters.[23] Two future OBA presidents, LeRoy Blackstock and Deryl Gotcher, with the assistance of District Judge W. Lee Johnson led the Tulsa Bar's fight against illegal practice by collection agencies and Justice of the Peace courts in the 1960s.[24]

The veterans who returned to their Oklahoma law practice after the defeat of Germany and Japan in 1945 found the OBA ready to help them adjust to their profession. Older lawyers conducted a series of "refresher" or "brush-up" seminars to survey changes since 1941 and to review certain areas of the law.[25] The *Journal* published special articles beneficial to veterans.[26] Many veterans were married students and former school teachers who returned to school under the G.I. Bill. The OBA arranged for correspondence study through the University of Oklahoma and for the first time in history the University offered a 12-week summer term to accelerate the legal instruction curriculum.[27]

One returning veteran was 37-year-old Carl Albert, a graduate of the University of Oklahoma and holder of a Bachelor of Civil Law Degree as a former Rhodes Scholar at Oxford University. Shortly after Albert started his McAlester law practice in 1946, the incumbent Congressman, Paul Stewart, informed him on the night before the filing deadline that he would not seek reelection. Albert raced to Oklahoma City the next day to file his candidacy for the post.[28] He won the Democratic run-off election by only 330 votes, but in later years he won easily, and for three decades he served in the United States House of Representatives, the last six years as Speaker of the House, the highest national office ever held by an Oklahoman.

Lawyer veterans returned to their practice and found that the "revising, digesting, and promulgating the statutes of the state," required every 10 years by the Oklahoma Constitution had finally been completed.[29] The work began under supervision of the Board of Governors of the old Bar Association, but had floundered in part owing to dissension among members of the Bar and confusion as to how far "revision" should go without

Young Carl Albert at a luncheon with the Oklahoma congressional delegation in 1947. L to R: Toby Morris, Glen D. Johnson, Mike Monroney, William G. Stigler, Preston E. Peden, George B. Schwabe, Ross Rizley (future Federal Judge), and Albert. (Courtesy The Daily Oklahoman.)

Photo made in 1949 when Chief Judge Orie Phillips (center) of the 10th United States Circuit Court of Appeals addressed the Tulsa Metropolitan Chamber of Commerce. L to R: Whit Y. Mauzy, United States District Attorney; Royce H. Savage, United States District Judge, Northern District of Oklahoma; G. Ellis Gable, then president of the Tulsa County Bar Association and OBA president in 1954; Judge Phillips; Alvin Richards, Oklahoma representative to the American Bar Association; William S. Hamilton, then OBA president; and an unidentified representative of the Chamber of Commerce and master of ceremonies. (Courtesy G. Ellis Gable.)

assuming prerogatives and powers of the Legislature.[30]

After most war veterans returned home by the end of 1945, Oklahoma had slightly more than 3800 lawyers in active practice. The three counties with the most practicing lawyers were Oklahoma with 1041, Tulsa 793, and Muskogee 128. Dewey County with only four had the least number of active lawyers.[31] Nine candidates sat for the Bar examination in January of 1946, one of the smallest groups ever to take the examination. However, the State Board of Bar Examiners reported in 1947 that 89 applicants had passed the Bar examination that year. Noting that the University of Oklahoma had enrolled 520 law students, the University of Tulsa, 130, and the Oklahoma City School of Law 227, the Board complained that:[32]

> For some reason, the public feels that to be a lawyer or a member of the bar, is to have found the tub of gold at the end of the rainbow. By the thousands they are flocking into the law schools of this country. They come to us from every walk of life without previous college training, seeking to be registered as a law student under our rules, which provide for two years college training or its equivalent.

Effective February 1, 1942, the State Supreme Court had adopted a registration requirement of two years of college work "or its equivalent." The Bar Examiners in 1945 recommended a revision of the rules to strike the words "or its equivalent" and to require at least two or three years of college study, if not a college degree, before registering as a law student. In 1947 the court accepted that proposal, and Oklahoma joined 36 other states that required at least two years of college. The court had already ruled that effective January 1, 1947, the traditional reading of law in a lawyer's office would no longer be acceptable to satisfy a requirement of three years study in a full-time law school or four years in a part-time or evening law school before taking the Bar examination.[33]

The old custom of reading law in a law office had one outstanding advantage: the opportunity to observe and experience the practice of law first-hand. A present-day variation of that custom, the legal intern program, was first tested during the OBA presidency of Hicks Epton in 1953 when the Association allowed eight University of Oklahoma law students to work in law offices as clerks during the summer before their senior years.[34] Further experimentation convinced the Committee on Student and Lawyer Placement and Internship in 1963 that internship benefited not only the senior law student but also the entire legal profession.[35] Thus the State Supreme Court in 1967 approved an OBA request for a two-year pilot program to begin with limited licenses granted to 24 legal interns for practice in approved law offices under the general supervision of experienced attorneys.[36] The following year, during the Bar presidency of E. H. Hieronymus, the Ford Foundation awarded the program a grant of $20,000.[37] By the middle of 1969 the legal intern program was acknowledged to be an outstanding success, and the OBA in 1970 received the coveted "Award of Merit for Excellence" from the American Bar Association for its innovative approach to practical training.[38]

The new profession of "legal assistants" or "paralegals" received the official approval of the American Bar Association in 1968. Employing a practice that had worked well in the medical profession, the Oklahoma lawyer found he could devote more of his own expertise to truly legal problems by drawing on the services of legal assistants trained by qualified instructors at such institutions as Oscar Rose Junior College or the University of Oklahoma. A professional organization for legal assistants located its national headquarters in Tulsa.[39]

The OBA's program of voluntary continuing education, mainly devoted to the veteran after World War II, expanded under the leadership of Howard Tumilty and in 1955 led the nation in the extent of subjects offered.[40] By the 1970s burgeoning malpractice suits emphasized the importance of continuing education to maintain the lawyer competency required by the Code of Professional Responsibility.[41] Thus more than 3600 state lawyers attended 34 continuing education institutes conducted by the OBA in 1979.[42]

A survey of the Bar membership in 1981 confirmed that a majority favored mandatory continuing legal education.[43] A special committee was appointed, headed by David K. Petty of Guymon, who in 1987 was elected OBA president. The committee prepared a proposed program requiring continuing legal education, which was approved by the House of Delegates and submitted to the Oklahoma Supreme Court. On January 17, 1986, the court sanctioned rules for mandatory legal education effective March 1, 1986, that required 12 hours of legal training each year for all practicing lawyers, with certain exemptions. Among those exempt were lawyers at least 65 years old and any members of the Oklahoma Bar not practicing within the state.[44]

Not long after the end of World War II the Bar Association was "pre-emptorily evicted" from its

Clee Fitzgerald of Stillwater, a leader in raising funds to construct the Oklahoma Bar Center. (Courtesy OBA.)

Edward H. Palmer, Executive Director and Secretary-Treasurer of the Oklahoma Bar Foundation. (Courtesy OBA.)

The Oklahoma Bar Center. (Courtesy OBA.)

Richard L. McKnight, 1989 president of the Oklahoma Bar Foundation. (Courtesy OBA.)

rented headquarters office, and President Gerald B. Klein faced the difficult task of finding suitable office space during a landlord's market. That experience convinced President Klein that the Bar needed its own permanent quarters. At a meeting in June of 1946 the Executive Council approved Klein's motion for the formation of the Oklahoma Bar Foundation whose first objective was to sponsor acquisition of a permanent Association home to replace "broom closet" quarters in Oklahoma City's American National Building. President Klein himself made the first cash contribution to the Foundation for that purpose.[45]

Although the Foundation was incorporated in 1949, it had to wait another decade before undertaking the formidable fund-raising campaign necessary to purchase or build a suitable facility. John M. Holliman took over the OBA presidency in 1959 and announced his administration's primary aim would be to build the Bar facility that had been discussed for so many years. Foundation leaders solved the problem of a suitable site by selecting the present Lincoln Boulevard location near the state capitol building in Oklahoma City in preference to a location on the Oklahoma

City University campus.[46] They also decided that Robert Blackstock, Clee Fitzgerald, Hicks Epton, and William S. Hamilton would undertake a pilot funding experiment in their home communities to ascertain whether Oklahoma lawyers were willing to support a sizeable building project.

Results of the pilot campaign were convincing. Blackstock reported the Foundation should be able to raise $400,000, a fanciful sum in the opinion of some committee members. Nevertheless, his optimism proved warranted after approximately $450,000 was collected. In September of 1962 one of the most attractive Bar centers in the United States was dedicated. Diamond-matched slabs of Colorado Yule and Walnut Travertine marbles were used on the exterior veneer of the structure. The Colorado Yule was obtained from the same quarry that provided white marble for the Lincoln Memorial and the Tomb of the Unknown Soldier.[47] Membership growth and the Association's expanded services necessitated a five-office addition to the headquarters in 1977 to house the Continuing Legal Education Department, visual aids, and a computer.

By 1983 the staff of six when the Bar Center

was completed had grown to 23 and provided services for more than 10,000 lawyers and judges. Additional office space was urgently needed. Furthermore, 21 years had taken its toll on the building; a need for extensive repairs was evident. The Oklahoma Bar Foundation in October of 1983 secured the services of Edward H. Palmer, a graduate of the University of Iowa College of Law and former Dean of the Oklahoma City University School of Law as Executive Director. Palmer was to head a fund-raising campaign to renovate the Bar Center, develop new programs "to assist in the administration of justice," and to administer funds in custody of the Foundation.[48] "The Bar Center Update Program" from 1984 to 1986 raised approximately $300,000, which was applied to the cost of major exterior improvements, carpeting, refurbishing, and construction of new offices.[49]

OBA President Burck Bailey in November of 1988 stressed the need for a membership dues increase. He noted, among other financial requirements, that "the Oklahoma Bar Center is overcrowded," and proper working conditions for the personnel were possible only by an appropriate dues increase.[50] The Oklahoma Supreme Court on December 9, 1988, approved an increase from $100 to $175 annually for lawyers admitted to practice for three years or more. Dues for lawyers in practice less than three years were raised from $50 to $87.50 per year.[51] In July of 1989, with 34 employees crowded into the original 15,000-square-foot structure, the Oklahoma Supreme Court authorized expansion of the Bar Center to approximately 41,000 square feet and approved the use of marble for the building's exterior. OBA President Anthony M. "Tony" Massad reported that the court had approved a total estimated cost of $2.2 million for the project[52]

31

JUDICIAL REFORM

The old voluntary Oklahoma State Bar Association, by committee reports and general discussion, during its lifetime regularly had proposed legislation to improve the state judicial system. Such distinguished lawyers as John H. Burford and C.B. Stuart early went on record in favor of a non-partisan Supreme Court, a stance that the salty W.H. Kornegay called "an irridescent dream"in 1906 at the annual meeting of the Oklahoma and Indian Territory Bar Association.[1] Lawyers at that meeting voted by a narrow margin for a state-wide District Attorney system, almost 60 years before a similar plan was adopted by the Oklahoma Legislature.[2] The Bar's Committee on Jurisprudence and Law Reform, Judicial Administration and Remedial Reform submitted one of its most comprehensive reports in 1921. The report acknowledged that lawyers were divided on proposals for court reorganization but recommended consideration of the following changes:[3] (1) Selection, tenure and retirement of judges.; (2) A Bar committee on Court Organization Procedures and Practice, composed of a permanent membership so far as practicable.; (3) A statutory "Judicial Council" to study court organization and procedure.; (4) An "Administrative Chief Justice"who would devote most of his time to administration rather than to deciding cases and writing opinions.; (5) Annual judicial conventions within the state to exchange ideas.; (6) "Courts of Conciliation" for small claims.; (7) Courts of record authorized to render declaratory judgements as to written instruments and statutes.; and (8) "Industrial Courts" to decide industrial controversies.

At the next legislative session, in 1923, the Legislature addressed major judicial reform only to the extent of temporary relief for a burdened Supreme Court docket by authorizing 15 Supreme Court Commissioners whose terms were to expire on December 31, 1926.[4] J.F. Sharp, a former member of the Supreme Court Commission, criticized the Commission system as being little more than "an opportunity for good lawyers to come to

Oklahoma City, and remain for a short time, and write a good lot of opinions, and…then accept employment from some oil company looking for a capable attorney, or become associated with some strong law firm."[5]

Sharp's criticism of the Supreme Court Commission could also have been directed at the Supreme Court, from which Sharp himself had resigned in 1919 to join the firm of Stuart and Cruce in Oklahoma City. *Harlow's Weekly* observed in 1927 that of 14 Chief Justices of the Oklahoma Supreme Court up to that time, all but three—Robert L. Williams, Thomas H. Owen, and Samuel W. Hayes—had been elected to the court, usually from a small town, had served until attaining the honor of Chief Justice and a state-wide reputation, then returned to the practice of law, usually in Oklahoma City.[6]

The Bar Association in 1925 appropriated $750.00 for expense involved in placing before the people a constitutional amendment to create a unified court system with election of judges on a non-partisan basis.[7] That effort failed to generate sufficient interest. The reason often given by legislators for their refusal to adopt the Association's recommendations was, in effect, "You lawyers are not in agreement among yourselves as to what needs to be done."[8]

Again in 1927 the Legislature approved a Supreme Court Commission of nine members whose terms expired on December 31, 1930. Once again responsible members of the Bar debated ways to relieve adjudication delays of two to five years that had plagued the Oklahoma Supreme Court since Statehood.[9] Chief Justice E.F. Lester, with the support of his associates, secured legislative approval for one law clerk at a salary of $3600 per year assigned to each justice. The law clerk system was an immediate success. In eight months the court disposed of almost twice as many cases at less than half the cost of those handled under the Commission arrangement.[10]

But the backlog of cases was still overwhelming. Chief Justice Fletcher Riley claimed in a speech before the American Bar Association in 1933 that "litigation is more voluminous in Oklahoma than elsewhere in the Union—in the English speaking world."[11] Attorneys in states included with Oklahoma in the *Pacific Reporter* series probably agreed with Riley. They resented having to purchase new volumes of the series replete with Oklahoma cases and containing a relatively few opinions from their own courts.[12]

The mass of litigation peculiar to Oklahoma was generally thought to be a consequence of: (1) The great diversity of traditions, customs and ideas in the citizenship of a new state.; (2) Questions arising from moulding Indian governments into one state.; (3) Discovery and development of the state's vast mineral wealth.; (4) The simplicity of the appeal process.; and (5) In more recent times, cases arising from activities of the Industrial Corporation Commission and the State Tax Commission.[13]

The Supreme Court of Oklahoma in 1933 requested legislative authority for use of lower court judges to assist in clearing its docket. The court also asked for an appropriation to pay the salary of a Referee, a post already created by statute. The Legislature refused to comply with either request. Chief Justice Riley reacted with a quotation from Scripture, St. Matthew 7:9, "Or what man is there of you, whom if his son ask bread, will he give him a stone?"[14]

The justices then paused to reexamine their own constitutional authority and by a resolution on January 5, 1934, designated District Judges to serve as aids to the court on a voluntary basis in an advisory capacity. Within a short time all but five of the state's District Judges had volunteered their services at no additional expense to the state and without apparent detriment to their own court business.[15]

The court, now confident that it could initiate improvements without awaiting legislative or executive action, decided to create a "Judicial Council." The Council was instructed to function "as a melting pot or coordinating agency for judicial reformation."[16] Following a recommendation of the Bar Association's Board of Governors, the Council resolved that its first objective would be to win a decisive victory over the Supreme Court's 2000-case backlog. The court and the Board of Governors accepted the Council's plan—subject to approval of the litigants—to use

150 lawyers to write advisory opinions in committees of three without compensation.[17]

Overcrowded state dockets were not peculiar to Oklahoma courts alone. A publication of the American Bar Association remarked that it would watch the Oklahoma effort with interest and sympathy. Dr. Edson R. Sunderland, a specialist in judicial reform on the University of Michigan law faculty, said, "I think the lawyers and judges of Oklahoma are showing more force, ingenuity, professional intelligence and public spirit than those of any other state at the present time."[18]

Although the contribution by lawyers and district judges was reported to have been substantial, in June of 1935 Edwin R. McNeill, Fletcher Riley's successor as Chief Justice, announced that advisory opinions would be discontinued. "I want to get the court's business back again in the court," McNeill said. Objections later ascribed to the advisory arrangement were the following: (1) Belief that lawyers chosen to submit opinions gained an advantage in attaining public office; (2) The justices thought they spent too much time discussing opinions with their authors and ofttimes had to rewrite the opinions.; and (3) The possibility that the advisory opinion could be "affected by local conditions."[19]

By the middle of 1937 all cases assigned for advisory opinions had been returned to the court. With the help of another law clerk authorized by the Legislature in 1937, the court was able to turn out an unprecedented number of opinions.[20] The justices announced in 1938 that "Every case briefed is assigned for opinion." The backlog had been reduced from more than 2000 cases to 808, and the docket was said to be as close to current as practicable.[21]

The state of Missouri by constitutional amendment in November of 1940 adopted a non-partisan court plan patterned after an American Bar Association recommendation. The plan allowed the governor to fill judicial vacancies from a list of candidates selected by a non-partisan judicial commission. The success of the Missouri plan encouraged the OBA House of Delegates to consider a similar plan for Oklahoma.[22] After months of study an OBA Special Committee endorsed a non-partisan judicial system to begin at the county court level and include district and appellate courts. Members of the committee undertook a state-wide educational campaign in 1946, convinced that they had the answer to the problem of judicial reform. They detailed the plan's essential features in a series of addresses before various Bar and lay organizations and enumerated the following objections to Oklahoma's method of judge selection: (1) Political influence overshadows and outweighs merit in the selection of judicial candidates; (2) Voters are provided with no criteria upon which to estimate the judicial qualifications of candidates in both state-wide and local elections; (3) Judges are embarrassed and intimidated by political leaders; and (4) Lawyers of high standing and judicial qualifications are not attracted to the bench when required to engage in a political campaign.[23]

Supporters of the non-partisan plan submitted it for the approval of the House of Delegates at the 1946 annual convention. To their dismay the Delegates by a vote of 40 to 31 tabled a motion asking the Legislature to submit the plan to a popular vote.[24] Then for a time the extensive judicial reform envisioned by the Special Committee gave way to a more urgent matter that concerned the practicing lawyer, the ever recurring dilemma of the overcrowded State Supreme Court docket. A case backlog of about 600 on the State Supreme Court docket in the early 1950s appeared small when compared to more than 2000 on the docket two decades earlier. However, the anxious advocate and his client whose case was among the 600 could be understandably critical of unreasonable delay in the disposition of the court's business. Bar officials saw ease of appeals as the reason for the court's heavy case load and more jurists on the appellate Bench as the solution.[25]

In 1951 a bill to create a new Court of Civil Appeals passed the Legislature, although not in the form recommended by an OBA legislative committee. Subsequently the bill was vetoed by Governor Johnston Murray. Apparently objections to details of the court plan by judges and Murray's lawyer friends contributed to the veto.[26] The Supreme Court, as a temporary expedient, again called on members of the Bar to check records and briefs and write advisory opinions as had been done in the 1930s.[27]

Two years later a bill to create a permanent Supreme Court Commission failed to pass the Senate. The Bar confronted the "dilemma of the docket" once again when G. Ellis Gable took office as OBA president in 1954 and appointed a Supreme Court Docket Committee headed by former Bar President John E. Luttrell. The committee report favored a permanent seven-member Supreme Court Commission. The OBA achieved at least a partial victory when the 1955 Legislature approved a three-member Commission with terms to expire in 1959.[28]

President G. Ellis Gable blamed the tremendous case load on the numerous judicial bodies feeding litigation to the appellate courts. He pointed out that at Statehood, appeals came from the courts of 22 District Judges, 77 County Judges, and a Corporation Commission. By 1954 appeals were originating from 21 more District Courts, five Superior Courts, six Common Pleas Courts, another County Court, 41 state boards, special courts or commissions, and Turnpike Authority.[29]

By the early 1960s the OBA could claim partial credit for improved trial court procedures, more satisfactory judicial salaries, and a measure of retirement protection for jurists by means of supernumerary legislation.[30] Nevertheless, major court reforms had failed as had efforts to replace the outdated County Attorney system with a District Attorney arrangement.[31] In the minds of most Bar officials a non-partisan plan for selection of judges still headed the list of needed judicial reforms.

The drawbacks to an elective judiciary emphasized by the Special Committee in the 1946 campaign for a non-partisan court had not abated. Also, to the uninformed layman, the organized Bar seemed largely to blame for the sins of any delinquent jurist. The decision in the 1950 case of *Chambers v. Central Committee of the Oklahoma Bar Association* reinforced the argument for creation of a "Court on the Judiciary" that could proceed against any jurist without resorting to cumbersome and inadequate statutory measures. In the *Chambers* case the Bar brought disciplinary action against a Tulsa Court of Common Pleas judge for unprofessional and unethical conduct while on the bench in open court. The opinion written by State Supreme Court Justice Earl Welch held that "A judge is not an attorney at law so long as he holds the judicial position."[32]

Jack N. Hayes, Jr., of Tulsa, the 1962 OBA president, told the Forum on Judicial Administration in an Oklahoma City speech; "The evils of our present system of partisan election of judges are

Hicks Epton (left), 1953 OBA president, with Lowe Runkle, lay member of the Judicial Nominating Committee. (Courtesy The Daily Oklahoman.)

Dean Earl Sneed of the University of Oklahoma, instrumental in Oklahoma's Judicial Reform. At the time of his death, he was OBA president-elect for 1979. (Courtesy The Daily Oklahoman.)

almost too obvious to be mentioned. We have many able, intelligent, dedicated men in our judicial system in Oklahoma. We honor them and appreciate them. But in my county we have at times had judges on the bench swept in by party landslides who literally could not tell the difference between plaintiff and defendant in contested matters."[33]

Two years later Deryl L. Gotcher, who was to be OBA president in 1974, showed concern at a Tulsa County Bar Association luncheon when, with "all the love and kindness I can muster," he urged Tulsa judges to "beware of the very appearance of evil," not to fraternize with questionable characters, and indeed to "be sober as a judge."[34]

A renewed drive for judicial reform in the 1960s emphasized the absurdity of a lawyer conducting an antiquated political campaign for a judicial office. During a lull in a solemn discussion of judicial reform at one Bar meeting, the veteran Wewoka lawyer Hicks Epton injected a bit of humor.

That reminds me of the time back in the early 1900s when three candidates ran for county judge in my home county. I was just a boy but I went to the political rally and heard all three of them speak. The first speaker was a Civil War veteran and he told of losing his leg in the Battle of Ma-

nassas. He waved his wooden leg and begged for the voters' support. The next speaker said he was a veteran of the Battle of Shiloh. He mourned the loss of his arm in that battle and implored the people to vote for him. The last speaker said he was too young to be in the war so he still had both arms and legs. But he did want everybody to know that he was the worst ruptured S.O.B. in the county."[35]

Judges, lawyers, and leading laymen attended a three-day conference on modern courts at Norman in late 1962 sponsored by the OBA, the Joint Committee for the Effective Administration of Justice, and the American Judicature Society, with the cooperation of Oklahoma's three law schools. Participants at the conference listed defects in the Oklahoma court system: The partisan political selection of judges, uncertainties in the matter of judicial retirement, lack of an adequate method of dealing with complaints involving the judiciary, and a minor court (Justice of the Peace) system suffering from lack of trained judges and the so-called fee system of justice.

Several court reform plans were considered, including the "Missouri Plan" and one submitted by Dean Earl Sneed of the University of Oklahoma College of Law.[36] An outgrowth of the conference was the Oklahoma Institute for Justice, Inc., organized with a goal of "sweeping reforms

193

for courts of justice in Oklahoma." The OBA House of Delegates approved a modernization plan for state courts at its July, 1964, meeting.[37] The first judicial reform measure submitted for approval by the people was State Question No. 415, supported by the Institute and the OBA, to create a Court on the Judiciary. In the form of a constitutional amendment, the measure was intended to eliminate the existing cumbersome method of removing judges only by impeachment through the Legislature. The proposed amendment was defeated at the November, 1964, general election.[38]

Although embarrassing to all Oklahoma courts and lawyers, the Oklahoma Supreme Court scandal of 1964 and 1965 provided the impetus for reforms sought by the OBA. On April 8, 1964, a Federal grand jury indicted State Supreme Court Justices Earl Welch and N.S. Corn for income tax evasion. Welch had served continuously on the court since 1932. Corn had joined him on the bench in 1934 and served 25 years before assuming semi-retirement status in 1959. Corn pleaded *nolo contendere* in July of 1964 to the five-count tax charge and was sentenced to 18 months in prison and a $11,250 fine. Welch pleaded innocent and his trial was set for the following October.[39]

At the time of Corn's conviction, United States District Attorney B. Andrew Potter avoided mentioning names, but he later told the federal court of evidence indicating Corn and "other members" of the court had been paid $150,000 for "campaign expenses."[40] Conviction of a Supreme Court justice and Potter's obvious reference to corruption by other justices shocked Oklahomans and attracted media attention in what has been termed "the worst black-eye Oklahoma ever had."[41] While traveling in Egypt, LeRoy Blackstock, who was to be OBA president 18 months later, picked up the Far East edition of the *New York Times* and learned of the Oklahoma catastrophe.[42] During the next three years Blackstock was among leaders of the Oklahoma Bar who worked for corrective judicial legislation.

United States Attorney Potter's reference to "other members" placed all Supreme Court justices under suspicion and impaired public confidence in Oklahoma courts and the legal profession as well. The aroused OBA president, James D. Fellers, called a special meeting of the Executive Council for July 7, 1964—six days after

the Corn *nolo contendere* plea. Despite Justice Earl Welch's 1950 opinion that placed a judge beyond the discipline of the Bar Association, the Council resolved to recommend Corn's disbarment and to undertake a complete investigation of the Supreme Court and the state Bar in cooperation with government agencies.[43]

Determined to obtain all possible information from the Bar itself, a special investigation committee made up of former OBA presidents placed the following one-page advertisement in the *Bar Journal*:[44]

BRIBERY?
You are a lawyer.
You know the difference between allegation and proof, and the difference between irresponsible charges and evidence.
If you have, or know anyone who has, any proof or evidence of bribery of any member or former member of the Supreme Court of Oklahoma, please get in touch with the Investigating Committee of Examiners.

Corn's trial and subsequent events resurrected the financial difficulties and bankruptcy of the Oklahoma City-based Selected Investments Corporation. The Oklahoma Tax Commission had sued that firm in 1953 for failure to pay income taxes construed to be dividends paid to investors. An Oklahoma District Court upheld the Tax Commission, but Selected Investments appealed to the State Supreme Court. Then in 1957 Chief Justice Welch wrote a majority opinion that saved Selected Investments almost $200,000 in back taxes and interest and assured a reduction in future income taxes.[45]

Selected Investments survived only until February of the next year when a petition in bankruptcy was filed against the corporation. During subsequent bankruptcy proceedings, future Federal Judge Luther Bohanon, in behalf of creditors, questioned Hugh H. Carroll, the corporation's president. In what Judge Bohanon has recalled as his "golden hour in the courtroom," he elicited vague testimony from Carroll that the firm had made a $150,000 cash "loan" to one Pierre Laval, identified by Carroll as a French-Canadian oil promoter. Carroll had little knowledge of Laval or his whereabouts, and finally admitted to Bohanon that in making the cash "loan" he had "bought the Brooklyn Bridge."[46] Carroll, his wife, and three associates were convicted and imprisoned for mail fraud and conspiracy.

The $150,000 disbursement had occurred at approximately the same time as the Supreme Court decision in favor of Selected Investments. Pierre Laval could not be located, and rumor persisted that he was "that G-D Supreme Court."[47] The names of Justices Welch and Corn kept recurring, leading to their indictment on April 8, 1964, after a grand jury investigation in which Carroll confessed that Laval did not exist and that he had given the $150,000 to Justice Corn for "campaign expenses." In November Justice Welch was sentenced to three years in prison and a $13,500 fine after a Muskogee federal jury deliberated one hour and 47 minutes following a two-week trial. Three weeks later the 80-year-old Nelson Corn gave officials a lengthy sworn statement acknowledging that he had received the $150,000 from Carroll and had paid $7,500 each to Welch and Justice N.B. Johnson. He recounted an arrangement with Oklahoma City attorney O.A. Cargill, Sr., that began in the 1930s. Cargill had created a Corn "campaign fund" to receive contributions each time Corn voted on a case in accord with Cargill's instructions.[48]

The OBA's Investigating Committee worked nights, weekends, and holidays without compensation for eight months to distinguish groundless assumptions from legitimate complaints against any lawyer or justice of the Supreme Court. The Committee and staff investigated 28 separate cases that had been decided by the State Supreme Court, heard the sworn testimony of 58 witnesses, and accumulated numerous unsworn statements.[49] On April 3, 1965, the Committee cleared all justices on the Supreme Court at the time except Corn, Welch, and N.B. Johnson. Corn and Welch resigned from the bench and Bar. Johnson was removed by the Oklahoma State Senate.[50] Disciplinary action recommended by the Committee was also taken against certain lawyers. One of these was Wayne W. Bayless, a Supreme Court Justice from 1933 to 1948. Bayless resigned from the Bar in February of 1966, charged with conspiracy to bribe one or more justices.[51] O.A. Cargill, Sr., was convicted of perjury in June of 1965 and resigned from the Bar the following month.[52]

"Why didn't you speak out and make your complaint sooner?" was the oft-repeated question by the OBA Investigating Committee to witnesses

Amos M. Pinkerton (center) chairman of the ABA's Bar Activities Section, awards OBA first place in the Award of Merit competition for 1964-65 for the entry, "To Whom Could We Have Told It?—The Bar Faces Up To Judicial Misconduct." L to R: Kenneth Harris, OBA Executive Director; James D. Fellers, 1964 OBA president; Pinkerton; and T.D. Nicklas, 1965 OBA president. (Courtesy Oklahoma Department of Libraries.)

who revealed instances of judicial misconduct. The reply was usually another question, "To whom could we or should we have told it?" To prevent a similar situation in the future, the Committee recommended that "steps be taken to establish a continuing tribunal or body to which persons could bring their complaints of misconduct against the judiciary."[53]

A short time later the OBA's House of Delegates sanctioned a reorganization of the state's court system, to consist of: (1) A court of the Judiciary; (2) Selection of judges as opposed to election; (3) General sessions courts to replace antiquated Justice of the Peace Courts; (4) A district attorney system to replace the present county attorney system; and (5) A Court administrator[54]

The American Bar Association at its 1965 annual meeting recognized the Oklahoma Bar Association with its "Award of Merit" for prompt action in the Supreme Court scandal and for formulating recommendations to prevent its recurrence.[55]

One OBA proposal—a change from the County Attorney system to one requiring a District Attorney to be assigned generally to each

District Court Judicial District—had first been introduced in the Legislature by Representative Hugh Sandlin of Holdenville 10 years previously. Governor J. Howard Edmondson also advocated such a change in 1959 and 1961. The legislative measure gradually gained support by county attorneys and was enacted into law in June of 1965.[56]

For the most part it was the past presidents of the OBA who drafted and sponsored another measure to create the Court on the Judiciary, capable of removing and compelling retirement of judicial officials for cause, which had failed as a constitutional amendment in 1964.[57] The Oklahoma electorate in May of 1966 approved Article VII-A which established such a court. Thus Oklahoma became one of only four states capable of dealing with an ineffective jurist in a forthright manner.[58] The Legislature in 1974 authorized a Council on Judicial Complaints, an investigatory

and accusatory agency where complaints may be filed.[59]

After the election that assured creation of a Court on the Judiciary, OBA officials hardly paused before initiating the most significant campaign to date, one intended to convince the people that effectual administration of Oklahoma justice required complete modernization of the Oklahoma court system. The 1966 OBA President, LeRoy Blackstock, joined with Earl Sneed, former dean of the University of Oklahoma College of Law, and Clark Thomas of the editorial staff of the *Oklahoma City Times*, to form a non-profit corporation called Judicial Reform Inc., to receive financial contributions on a tax exempt basis.[60] During the next year Judicial Reform Inc., worked with the Oklahoma Institute for Justice, and citizens groups to publicize the need for court reorganization along with merit selection and retention of jurists.[61] The voters rejected tra-

100th meeting of the Oklahoma Judicial Nominating commission on April 27, 1988, in Oklahoma City. Attending, front row, L to R: Howard Conyers, Administrative Director of the Courts; Dr. Gary Copeland, Norman; Sherman Floyd, Poteau; Vernon Roberts, Poteau; Ms. Mary Geasland, Tahlequah; John Dunn, Woodward; Alan B. McPheron, Durant; Juanita Mayfield-Holley, Office of the Courts, Staff Assistant to the Commission. Back row, L to R: Jim Bob Wright, Clinton; John Boydston, Tulsa; Russell Perry, Oklahoma City, Mark A. Ashton, Lawton, current Chairman; D. Kent Meyers, Oklahoma City; John A. Gladd, Tulsa, Ms. Joniece Frank, Sapulpa. (Courtesy OBA.)

The Supreme Court at work. L to R: Justices Yvonne Kauger, Robert E. Lavender, Rudolph Hargrave, Chief Justice John B. Doolin, Justices Ralph B.Hodges, Robert D. Simms, Alma Wilson, Hardy Summers. (Courtesy OBA.)

dition on July 11, 1967, and approved two constitutional amendments. Those amendments and implementation statutes enacted by the Legislature replaced Article VII of the constitution with an integrated state-financed court system that made district courts the successors to the jurisdiction of county courts, abolished Justice of the Peace courts, created a new intermediate appellate court to assist the Supreme Court, and provided for an Administrative Director of the courts. The governor was to fill vacancies on the Supreme Court and Court of Criminal Appeals from names chosen by the Judicial Nominating Commission of 13 members, including both lawyers and laymen. After a trial period the names of jurists on the two courts appear on a retention ballot every six years, subject to voter approval or disapproval by a "Yes" or "No" vote. All other judges were to be elected on a non-partisan basis and interim vacancies filled by gubernatorial appointment.

Legislation in 1987 placed appointment and retention of the intermediate appellate court (The Court of Appeals) on the same basis as that of the Supreme Court and the Court of Criminal Appeals. The number of judges on the latter court was expanded from three to five.[62]

At first, the Judicial Nominating Commission

selection process was confined only to the two highest courts. However, with some pressure from the legal profession, governors began to seek the advice of the Commission in filling judicial vacancies occurring on other courts. Public and legislative approval of the Commission's performance subsequently led to legislation requiring the governor to use the Commission's recommendation in filling all state judicial vacancies except that of Special Judge. During the decade beginning in June of 1971 the Commission processed 800 applicants for judgeships and sent the governor nearly 170 names for consideration.[63]

When the 1970s ended, the Oklahoma Supreme Court included five justices appointed after the revolutionary judicial reform campaign: Justices Don B. Barnes and Robert D. Simms, 1972; Justice John B. Doolin, 1973; and Justices Rudolph Hargrave and Marian P. Opala, 1978. Two justices—Ben T. Williams, elected in 1952, and Pat Irwin, elected in 1958—had not been implicated in the shake-up of the mid-1960s. Ralph B. Hodges had been appointed in 1965 to succeed Earl Welch, a victim of the court scandal. Robert E. Lavender was appointed on June 24, 1965, to succeed the impeached N.B. Johnson.[64]

After the death of Justice Williams in 1982,

The Supreme Court of Oklahoma in 1989. Front row, L to R: Justice Robert E. Lavender, Vice-Chief Justice Marian P. Opala, Chief Justice Rudolph Hargrave, Justice Ralph B. Hodges, Justice Robert D. Simms. Back row, L to R: Justice Yvonne Kauger, Justice John B. Doolin, Justice Alma Wilson, Justice Hardy Summers. (Courtesy OBA.)

Governor George Nigh appointed District Judge Alma Wilson, a law graduate of the University of Oklahoma, to be the court's first woman justice.[65] Pat Irwin accepted appointment to a United States Magistrate post in 1983.[66] Governor Nigh replaced him with Justice Hodges' political assistant, Yvonne Kauger, a 1969 Oklahoma City University Law School graduate. Justice Barnes left the bench to return to private law practice in 1985. His successor, also appointed by Governor Nigh, was District Judge Hardy Summers, a graduate of the University of Oklahoma College of Law in 1957.[67]

Constitutional and legislative enactments had made the legal profession largely responsible for selecting and maintaining an efficient court system. The decade of the 1980s presented a vexing problem not uncommon to all elective and appointive offices: the need to provide remuneration adequate to attract and retain the best-qualified applicants. OBA Executive Director

Marvin C. Emerson addressed that perplexing matter in October of 1984 when he cited a 50-state survey that placed Oklahoma district judge salaries 43rd from the top. Salaries of all other associate and special judges in Oklahoma were at the bottom of the 50-state list. Emerson's statistics revealed that in the preceding 27 months a third of the district judges and more than half of the special judges had resigned.[68] Salaries of appellate judges ranked approximately 30th in the nation.[69]

"The matter of judicial salaries in Oklahoma has created a crisis situation," Emerson stated. "It is time for the members of the legal profession to become actively involved in solving the crisis." The OBA Board of Governors encouraged all lawyers to publicize need for a 15 percent increase in judicial salaries by "aggressive discussions" with legislators, news media, and the Oklahoma citizenry.[70] That concerted effort apparently accomplished the desired result, for despite the state's depressed economic condition the 1985 Legislature and Governor Nigh responded with a 15 percent increase for all members of the judiciary.[71]

Unfortunately, as pointed out by OBA President John Shipp, even with the increase, Oklahoma salaries remained among the lowest in the nation. "We recognize that the battle to obtain fair salaries for all of our judges has just begun, not just ended," said President Shipp.[72] David K. Petty began his presidential term in 1987 with a reminder that "A top priority of the Oklahoma Bar Association must be to continue efforts to secure adequate pay and support personnel for our courts."[73] Preparations were made for further salary adjustments in the 1988 legislative session.[74] Bar officials advocated a raise of 10 percent, but legislation eventually approved in 1988 granted only five percent for appellate courts and district judges. Associate district judges and special judges received the recommended 10 percent.[75] In an era of unabated inflation, maintaining adequate salaries and personnel at both federal and state levels poses a never-ending challenge.

32

THE DILEMMA OF DISCIPLINE

In the eyes of the public the legal profession was largely responsible for the Supreme Court scandal of the mid 1960s. On the other hand lawyers could blame the public's past indifference to court reform and its inclination to disregard the Bar's recommendations for elective judicial offices. Bar members agreed, however, that circumstances called for a long-discussed updating of Bar Association rules and by-laws, especially with regard to what Hicks Epton had termed, "the dilemma of discipline."[1]

As far back as World War II Bar officials had felt the profession's inability to rid itself of unethical practices could be attributed to inadequate rules governing disciplinary procedures. The rules were "ambiguous and duplicitous," in the opinion of Bar President William S. Hamilton, who in 1949 appointed a "State Wide Disciplinary Committee" to study the problem. The committee submitted a set of revised rules, which the Supreme Court approved, placing more authority in the Executive Council and Central Committee to investigate and prosecute complaints.[2] The committee also recommended that all state law schools emphasize the subject of legal ethics, an approach Bar Association General Counsel Jeff Laird again recommended nearly 20 years later to combat an "alarming ignorance" of ethical standards.[3]

Even after the 1949 rules took effect, disciplinary procedures continued to break down for the same reason that had vexed officials of the old voluntary Bar Association and the State Bar of Oklahoma: the reluctance of lawyers to represent the Association in disbarment hearings.[4] The Association in 1953 employed Harry G. Foreman, a former United States District Attorney, to investigate and prosecute unauthorized practice of law as well as disciplinary complaints.[5] Lawyers remained hesitant to serve on Grievance Committees or as prosecutors and trial examiners, but Foreman, aided by a number of conscientious attorneys, within two years purged the Bar of some of the worst offenders.[6]

In the late 1950s the Bar contended not only with client grievances but also with lawyer complaints against ambulance chasing and fee-splitting. Tulsa County Bar President Jack N. Hays, Jr., told of "chasers" using runners to visit accident victims in the hospital and lawyers sending them flowers with business cards attached.[7] Ryan Kerr, a lawyer-state senator from Altus, informed his associates in the Senate, "You men who are not lawyers don't have any idea the bird dogging and shystering that is going on. Anyone who would do this is not entitled to be called a lawyer. And if we lawyers don't clean up our house no one is going to clean it up for us."[8]

The Executive Council had met infrequently in previous years, but in 1960 it convened monthly in order to devote more attention to disciplinary matters. General Counsel Foreman decided he could spend only part of his time with the Association, so the Council employed Wilson McCully as a full-time investigator.[9] McCully had retired from the Federal Bureau of Investigation after 17 years' service, and now he began a new career with the Bar Association that lasted until his retirement a second time in 1978.[10]

When Robert W. Blackstock assumed the Bar presidency in 1963, he resolved to clear the backlog of disciplinary cases on the Bar docket. In that year the Bar's Executive Council effected the disbarment of five lawyers and led the nation in disposing of disciplinary matters, despite continued reluctance of lawyers to sit in judgment of their peers.[11]

Under the leadership of LeRoy Blackstock in 1966, following the State Supreme Court debacle, the OBA undertook far-reaching changes in rules and procedures. Some lawyer-critics had long maintained the Bar's structure prevented participation by the average lawyer. One complaint charged that the State Supreme Court exercised unwarranted control under its right to appoint a majority of the Executive Council. Another common complaint accused the OBA's past presidents—there were 22 of them in 1966—of

Chief Justice John B. Doolin conducts the swearing in of new members of the Bar in May 1987. (Courtesy OBA.)

Jack N. Hayes, Jr., OBA president in 1962. (Courtesy Gable & Gotwals.)

having too much influence in the House of Delegates, which was the legislative body of the Association. Membership in the House was composed of past presidents with lifetime voting privileges along with members of the Executive Council and at least one delegate from each county, based on lawyer population, except that Oklahoma and Tulsa Counties were permitted a maximum of 10 delegates. The 10-member limitation was also a source of complaint.[12]

In a display of harmony the OBA adopted new rules and by-laws in 1966 by an overwhelming vote.[13] The State Supreme Court surrendered its right to appoint members of the Board of Governors, formerly called the Executive Council. Thereafter all members of the Board were to be elected by the House of Delegates.[14] After December 31, 1965, anyone who became a past president would be a member-at-large of the House of Delegates but after three years would serve as a non-voting member.[15] Stricter disciplinary rules were adopted. A full-time General Counsel was to have specific powers of investigation and prosecution to enforce the stricter rules. Dues were raised from $30 to $40 annually to support the new Bar program.[16]

The limitation on the number of delegates from Oklahoma and Tulsa Counties was increased from 10 to 15. Friction between "city" and "county" lawyers over that limitation remained in controversy, however, for another 12 years. In 1978, when Oklahoma and Tulsa County lawyers constituted 58 percent of the Bar's total membership but had only a 25 percent membership in the policy-making House of Delegates, the Tulsa Bar campaigned for a "one-man one-vote" approach to membership in the House.[17] The Tulsa Bar threatened to "dot their i's and cross their t's," and place the matter of reapportionment before the State Supreme Court if a satisfactory solution was not reached.[18] "Country" lawyer and future Bar President C.D. Northcutt of Ponca City led an 11th-hour compromise increasing the maximum Oklahoma and Tulsa County delegations to 30 members each.[19]

John G. Bonomi, chief counsel for the New York City Bar Association, visited the Oklahoma Bar Association in 1969 in his capacity as a member of a national committee studying lawyer discipline procedure in all the states. He described the Oklahoma program as "a disciplinary system unsurpassed by any in the county."[20] Nevertheless, discipline problems continued to increase while in-state active membership grew from 4424 in 1970 to 5144 in 1975.[21] President Northcutt noted in 1975 that the Board of Governors was spending one-half to two-thirds of its time on disciplinary matters and proposed establishment of

John M. Amick, elected District Judge in Oklahoma County in 1978, was the OBA General Gounsel who conducted former Governor David Hall's disbarment proceedings. (Courtesy OBA.)

New members of the Bar take their oath as attorneys at St. Luke's Methodist Church in Oklahoma City in the fall of 1988. (Courtesy OBA.)

a separate group to relieve the Governors of that function.[22] Two years later the Supreme Court approved formation of a Professional Responsibility Commission of seven lawyers to work with General Counsel John Amick in investigating and processing complaints.[23]

Persistent criticism that the seven-lawyer Commission tended to ignore accusations against fellow lawyers brought about a major change in 1981 when its membership was changed to five lawyers and two non-lawyers.[24] In addition, a 21-member panel of 14 lawyers and seven non-lawyers, called the Professional Responsibility Tribunal, was formed. From that tribunal a Trial Panel of two lawyers and one non-lawyer was designated to hear disciplinary charges and report its findings and recommendations to the Supreme Court for final disposition. In answer to charges of unnecessary secrecy in disciplinary matters, the new rules allow the proceedings to become matters of public record after the time for the Respondent's answer has expired.[25] Bar President Ben T. Owens observed, "The professional man has, up to a point, some right to privacy so that every petty complaint will not be aired publicly, but there's a point that they should become public and I think this process strikes a good balance."[26]

The Professional Responsibility Commission

and the General Counsel have observed that "both within the legal community and in the community-at-large, there is an increasing focus and sensitivity to the profession's ethical standards and their enforcement."[27] Annual reports prepared by the General Counsel show that about 500 complaints in 1981 almost tripled to 1426 in the year 1988.[28] By 1989 about half of annual membership dues was required to finance a staff of 11 in the General Counsel's office devoted in the main to discipline problems.[29]

Most complaints involved misunderstandings and lack of communication that might be easily resolved. In 1988, for example, 1014 grievances were processed on an informal basis. The remaining 412 constituted grievances involving 263 out of a total OBA membership of 11,988, with 8637 actively practicing in Oklahoma. "Neglect" was the most common complaint. The Supreme Court that year applied disciplinary sanctions to 25 attorneys.[30] From 1981 through 1988 the Court disbarred 21, suspended 51, and permitted 29 to resign from the OBA while disciplinary action was pending.[31]

As part of the OBA's ongoing effort to police its own profession, President Paul M. Vassar in 1983 appointed a committee to study a set of model rules of professional conduct recommended by the American Bar Association, to replace Oklahoma's Code of Professional Responsibility adopted in 1970. The proposed rules were subjected to intensive study by the Vassar committee, the Board of Governors, and the House of Delegates before their adoption by the Oklahoma Supreme Court effective July 1, 1988.[32] The format of the new "Oklahoma Rules of Professional Conduct" is intended to simplify the lawyer's quest for guidance. They incorporate several departures from the former Code, particularly in the areas of contingent fees, conflict of interest, candor to the court, and advertising.[33]

The Professional Responsibility Commission measures a lawyer's professional conduct by guidelines set out in the "Oklahoma Rules of Professional Conduct." On the other hand, as a representative of the legal profession—"a special fellowship"—the lawyer must also be guided by personal conscience. The so-called "uncivil practice of law" is characterized by disrespect for other lawyers and the courts—a disregard for the basic courtesies taught by the Golden Rule.

Attorneys have been more vocal in recent years in criticizing the decline of "professionalism" and, especially, the lack of professional courtesy. They acknowledge that the adversarial nature of the practice of law has always been a contributing factor, but they also blame lack of personal acquaintances and friendships, along with financial pressures intensified by an ever-expanding lawyer population.[34] The OBA presidencies of David K. Petty in 1987 and Burck Bailey in 1988 both emphasized that the administration of justice and the image of the profession would benefit from a renewed spirit of professionalism exhibited in a lawyer's conduct toward clients, opponents, the courts, and the general public.[35]

33

PUBLIC RELATIONS

A nation in travail found it easy to accuse the legal profession of feasting on the misery of the unfortunate during the depression days of the 1930s. Lawyer fees led the list when funds were disbursed after bankruptcies, bank failures, and mortgage foreclosures. Public opinion of the Bar was at low ebb. Improved relations between Bar and public were sorely needed early in 1932 at a time when, as the *Chicago Bar Association Record* observed, "The average lawyer is in the eyes of the public an unmitigated nuisance."[1]

To combat the Bar's public relations problem, the Oklahoma County Bar Association began a series of radio programs in April that year entitled "The Lawyer and the Public." Bar President Charles B. Cochran inaugurated the broadcasts with a 10-minute talk about Bar Associations. Weekly programs thereafter included "The Lawyer and the Public," conducted by Federal Judge Edgar S. Vaught, "The Starvation Period" by Coleman H. Hayes, and a talk by C.B. Stuart on "Selecting Judges." At the conclusion of each program the public submitted questions for discussion by the speaker.[2] The Oklahoma County Bar also attracted welcome publicity in May of 1934 when it initiated an annual secret ballot in which lawyers voted for county judicial candidates and made public the results.[3]

In Tulsa the Junior Bar Association in September of 1933 began to furnish free legal services covering almost every branch of the law to individuals referred by charitable agencies, the county attorney's office, the Ministerial Alliance, and members of the Bar. In a period of two years the young lawyers provided assistance to 400 applicants.[4] Another group of young lawyers in Oklahoma City led by James D. Fellers, future president of both the Oklahoma Bar Association and the American Bar Association, attained favorable publicity for the profession in 1938 by a drive against "Loan sharks" who charged usurious rates of interest to low-salaried workers.[5]

The Junior Bar Conference of Oklahoma in July of 1962 conducted the first "Bridge the Gap Institute" specially planned as a practical seminar for lawyers newly admitted to the Bar.[6] The new institute is now sponsored annually by the Young Lawyers Division (YLD) of the OBA, an organization open to any lawyer under 36 years of age or who has been admitted to practice less than three years. The YLD includes among its varied activities a mock trial program for high school students and discussions of the law held at senior citizen centers during Law Week each year.[7] In recognition of outstanding services being rendered by the YLD, the Oklahoma Supreme Court on January 9, 1989, expanded membership of the Board of Governors from 16 to 17—the new members to be the duly elected Chairman of the YLD.[8]

In November, 1941, on the eve of World War II, OBA President John H. Cantrell announced that one aim of his administration would be "the establishment within the association of a live and functioning committee, or bureau, of public relations."[9] The war delayed an active campaign to improve the profession's image; however, a few months after the war ended, the OBA supported radio programs that disseminated helpful information for the Oklahoma layman about the legal profession, clinics were held explaining a nonpartisan court plan, and a pamphlet on "The responsibility of the citizens as a juror" was distributed.[10] The Committee on Public Relations that President Cantrell envisioned came into being in the latter part of the 1940s and represented at that time, in the words of President William S. Hamilton, a "comparatively new concept of the organized Bar."[11]

One of the OBA's most effective public relations programs has been the observance of "Law Day," an idea Oklahoma lawyers generally credit to Hicks Epton of the Seminole County Bar Association. The latter organization sponsored a "Know Your Courts—Know Your Liberties" program at Wewoka on May 1, 1946,[12] in accord with Epton's suggestion that special events on May Day of each year should pay tribute to the American

This photo, representative of the Brett family's years of contribution to the Oklahoma legal profession, depicts Judge John A. Brett, Sr. (left), Judge of the Court of Criminal Appeals from 1946 to 1963, swearing in his brother, Judge Tom Brett, who has served on that court since 1965. Hanging on the wall (fourth from left) is the picture of their father, Rutherford Brett, who has the unusual distinction of having served on Oklahoma's three highest courts: the Supreme Court, the Supreme Court Commission, and the Court of Criminal Appeals. Thomas R. Brett, Federal Judge for the Northern District of Oklahoma since 1979 and OBA president in 1970, is the son of Judge John A. Brett, Sr. Seated at the Bench are Judges Hez J. Bussey (left) and Kirksey Nix of the Court of Criminal Appeals.

system of justice and counterbalance Communist celebrations held annually on that day.[13]

In 1948 the OBA Public Relations Committee, with the encouragement of Epton and other members of the Seminole County Bar, presented a 55-minute "Oklahoma Lawyers' Forum" in Wewoka, the first of its kind in Oklahoma. Albert Trice acted as moderator; Howard T. Tumilty discussed "Who is a Lawyer?"; Gentry Lee spoke on "What Does a Lawyer Do?"; and Denver Davison of the Oklahoma Supreme Court answered the question, "How Can a Lawyer Help You?" The presentation was so well received by an overflow crowd of more than 150 Rotary and Lions Club members, newspaper publishers, civic leaders, and attorneys that similar programs were conducted before large crowds in Ada, Ardmore, and Lawton.[14]

While chairman of the OBA Committee on Public Relations, Epton promoted a celebration of Law Day at the University of Oklahoma in 1949. With the cooperation of Dean Earl Sneed,

"Law Day" became an annual event at the University and evolved into a state-wide celebration to climax the Oklahoma Bar Association's "Know Your Courts—Know Your Liberties Week," usually shortened to "KYC-KYL Week."[15] A panel of United States Supreme Court justices and civic leaders screened hundreds of entries in 1954 before awarding the Freedom Foundation's "George Washington Honor Medal" to the Oklahoma Bar Association for its KYC-KYL Week of the previous year.[16]

Since 1957 the American Bar Association has sponsored "Law Day" as a special day set aside by Congress and presidential proclamation for Americans to celebrate their liberties by a variety of special events: addresses by Federal and state leaders, lawyers, and judges; courthouse tours; town meetings; and nationalization ceremonies.[17]

A popular newspaper feature has been "It's the Law in Oklahoma," presenting legal subjects of common interest to the layman with a "preventive law" theme. The feature—at one time carried by

A mock trial sponsored by the Young Lawyers Division of the OBA in 1986. High school students from Clinton won first place; Sapulpa placed second. (Courtesy OBA.)

The OBA'a Annual Law Day Program, "Ask a Lawyer," was televised on Oklahoma's Educational Television stations on April 26, 1989. More than 500 attorneys assisted in answering more than 4000 telephone calls. (Courtesy OBA.)

276 state newspapers—originated in Enid in 1953 and won the American Bar Association Committee on Merit award as the outstanding public relations program in America for a non-metropolitan area.[18] Winfrey Houston, OBA president in 1969, was indoctrinated into State Bar work by devoting his Saturdays to writing that column.[19]

Outside public relations assistance in the early 1960s developed the newspaper features, "The Family Lawyer," "Legal Problems," and "OkLaw Oddities." The latter, a believe-it-or-not cartoon series, depicted noteworthy events and facts about the law and was published in 164 newspapers in 64 Oklahoma counties. It won the "National Award" from the American Society of Association Executives in 1964.[20]

From time to time throughout the years the OBA has aired radio and television programs with a public service theme. Television had been in Oklahoma a scant three months in September of 1949 when the Association used the facilities of WKY-TV in Oklahoma City to televise a dramatized law case conforming as closely as possible to legal procedures.[21]

The leap from annual membership dues of $40 to $100 voted by the membership in 1974 allowed an expanded Public Relations program with a full-time Director of Information.[22] Stepped-up radio and television announcements and program followed. One of the most popular of these has been in a question-and-answer format called, "Ask a Lawyer."[23] As a part of the 1980 observance of Law Day, lawyers on the two-hour "Ask a Law-yer" production, carried over Oklahoma educational television stations, answered nearly 3000 questions ranging from what to do about barking dogs, to complex estate problems.[24]

Oklahoma Bar Presidents Hicks Epton and G. Ellis Gable in the early 1950s encouraged a formal program of free legal aid to the needy, not only as a part of the lawyer's ethical responsibility but as a tool of public relations.[25] The only organized legal aid program had been in Tulsa where, since the Great Depression days of the 1930s, the Tulsa County Bar had led all local Bars in rendering legal aid to the poor.[26] Every law firm in Tulsa assigned one lawyer to the project, and two members of the University of Tulsa Law faculty were also available to help.[27]

Experience with Tulsa's accomplishments encouraged President Gable in 1954 to take special interest in establishing Legal Aid programs in other communities of the state. Conferences with the American Bar Association's Committee on Legal Aid and Lawyer Reference Service convinced Gable and Harry Dyer, chairman of the OBA committee, that the most successful legal aid bureaus existed in connection with local Community Chests. The Tulsa County Bar reached an agreement with the Tulsa Community Chest and on January 3, 1955, organized a corporation that became the state's first Legal Aid Society.

The next year the Oklahoma County Bar Association formed a similar organization called the Legal Aid Society of Oklahoma County, and the Duncan Bar also started a Legal Aid program.[28]

During the presidential administration of James D. Fellers in 1964, the House of Delegates endorsed formation of Legal Aid Societies by all local Bar Associations throughout Oklahoma.[29] Federal aid legislation has lessened need for assistance from local attorneys; nevertheless, local Bar groups must still volunteer free legal services at times due to the heavy load carried by government agencies.[30]

A Nowata County lawyer in 1981 tested the legal profession's responsibility to represent indigent defendants in criminal cases. The State Criminal Court of Appeals rejected the lawyer's contention that District Judge Arthur J. Boose's order appointing him counsel for an indigent defendant constituted the involuntary servitude abolished by the 13th Amendment. Judge Hez J. Bussey's opinion noted that the lawyer was entitled to statutory compensation and also observed, "It has been determined to be unethical for lawyers to refuse to represent indigents in criminal matters without a justifiable excuse when they are appointed by the court."[31]

The busy administrations of OBA Presidents Epton and Gable in 1953 and 1954 not only promoted free legal assistance but also advocated a "lawyer referral" or "lawyer reference" program on a state-wide basis to place laymen in touch with lawyers qualified to handle specific legal problems.[32] This public relations expedient that could also benefit the individual lawyer had to wait over a quarter of a century before beginning state-wide operation. Bar President C.D. Northcutt in 1975 recommended the program and told state lawyers, "Actually, there are many people throughout the state who do not know a lawyer and really do not know how to find one."[33]

Four years later, in the administration of President John M. Luttrell, the Board of Governors approved an operating plan submitted by the Special Statewide Lawyer Referral Committee. By December 1, 1979, the program was in statewide operation omitting only the counties that had their own systems such as Oklahoma, Tulsa, and Cleveland. The plan, modeled after those in surrounding states, permitted any state resident to place a free telephone call to the Bar Center in Oklahoma City and arrange an appointment with a lawyer located as near the client as possible.[34]

A survey team from the American Bar Association had recommended establishment of the Lawyer Referral Service in a critical evaluation of the Oklahoma Bar Association conducted in 1977. The team revisited the OBA in 1981 and, in a glowing report, termed the organization "exceptionally well-run, well-organized and financially sound." In addition to praise for the Lawyer Referral Service, the team cited "a well-run and adequate" grievance procedure and an "excellent" Continuing Education Program.[35]

Almost entirely due to the insistence of OBA President Epton, the House of Delegates in 1953 considered a measure to establish a "Lawyers Indemnity Fund" as a good will gesture to protect the public against defalcation by lawyers.[36] The measure failed by an overwhelming 150 to 7, but President Epton wryly admitted his defeat could have been worse. He told a reporter, "Five of the folks who voted for it told me afterward they opposed the fund, but they didn't want me to be without any votes."[37] Nevertheless Epton's proposal surfaced again 11 years later following the unfavorable publicity for the legal profession caused by the indictment of Supreme Court Justices Earl Welch and Nelson S. Corn for income tax evasion. In November of 1964 the Executive Council of the Oklahoma Bar Association resolved to establish a Clients' Security Fund to reimburse clients—as "a matter of grace, not right"—for dishonest acts of Oklahoma lawyers who were not covered by professional insurance, and who had since died, been adjudged mentally ill, or been suspended or disbarred. The Council appropriated $5000 to establish the fund as of January 1, 1965.[38]

The fund was raised to $50,000 and remained at that level for many years until the balance was depleted by payment of one substantial claim. The fund has since been increased under an arrangement requiring all disbursements to be made on a prorated basis. Lawyers are divided in opinion as to whether the fund should be publicized. To the chagrin of Bar officials, a few years ago their proud announcement that the fund balance had been expanded to $200,000 prompted the ill-phrased newspaper headline, "Bar Hikes Shyster Fund.'"[39]

Although the OBA had arranged to indemnify clients through the Client Security Fund for a lawyer's dishonest conduct, another problem arose out of the so-called "consumer movement" of the late 1960s and 1970s. While American consumers became more assertive in their demands for better products and improved service, some sophisticated clients insisted on error-free legal service. The dissatisfied clients could usually find a lawyer willing to initiate malpractice suits against his fellows. Such actions might allege errors of judgment, mistakes in pleadings, inexcusable mistakes during trials, and poor office management causing slip-ups in the form of missed dockets and failure to file suit within the statutory period.[40]

Thus the Oklahoma lawyer, like his peers on the national scene, was confronted with liability insurance rates that doubled each year and the prospect that insurance companies would discontinue legal liability insurance altogether.[41] The State Supreme Court directed the OBA in 1978 to conduct a study of lawyers' liabilities claims for the preceding six years in Oklahoma. The analysis showed some 200 comparatively small claims had been filed, a situation that convinced Bar Association officials that the Oklahoma practitioner was paying escalating premiums for losses sustained not in Oklahoma but in high claims areas such as New York and California.[42]

A quarter of a century earlier, after an extensive study begun in the administration of Bar President G. Ellis Gable and completed in Charles B. Duffy's administration, Oklahoma lawyers had cooperated in a group health and accident program that effected substantial savings to its participants.[43] Now Bar officials decided once again to enlist the cooperative effort of Association members, this time to organize a "captive" liability insurance company. The capital stock sales campaign that followed was one of the largest projects in the state Bar history, surpassed only by the building of the Bar Center. On November 20, 1980 the Oklahoma Bar Professional Liability Insurance Co. was launched with $1.3 million in capital provided from sale of stock to 900 lawyers and law firms. Generating $50,000 a month in premiums in 1981, the company seems well on its way to succeeding in its aim to provide protection for clients and furnish liability insurance coverage for Oklahoma lawyers at a reasonable cost.[44]

The cooperation exhibited by Oklahoma lawyers through participation in group health and professional liability insurance was not without precedent. Local Bar Associations of pre-Statehood days were well aware of the benefits of

standardized minimum fees and their *raison d'etre* could in large measure be attributed to a mutually agreed minimum fee schedule. When the Tulsa Bar Association was organized on October 3, 1903, appointment of a committee on fees was second on the agenda only to the appointment of a committee on constitution and by-laws. The fee schedule subsequently adopted included the following: Homicide and Rape, $200; Arson or Robbery, $150; Burglary, Larceny of horse or cow brute, $100; Misdemeanors, $10; Drafting a will, $5; Examination of an abstract, $2.50; Organization of a corporation, $15; Drawing a contract, $1; and a trip to the country, $7.50. A minimum fee of $10 for Attachment, Garnishment, and Replevin was later reduced to five dollars.[45]

The Texas County Bar Association, organized in Guymon in 1908, announced that its basic objective was to standardize legal fees.[46] The Committee on Commercial law of the original voluntary Oklahoma State Bar Association regularly included in its published annual report the following collection fees recommended by the Commercial Law League of America:[47] 10 percent on the first $300; 5 percent on the excess of $300, to $1,000; 2 1/2 percent on the excess of $1,000; Minimum fee of $3.00; and Minimum fee for suit $5.00.

The committee warned in its 1912 report that, "No attorney can handle business and give it the attention it deserves" for less than the recommended schedule, and anyone who did accept the business for less was guilty of "moral and business cowardice."[48]

State Bar officials had always refrained from taking a stand on adopting a minimum fee schedule until persuaded to do so by the Tulsa County Bar Association in 1937. The Tulsa Bar that year had undertaken a study of fees, resulting in a consensus among its members that compensation for legal services was too low. Lawyers in some instances charged so-called "starvation" fees in non-asset cases, principally bankruptcy and no-property divorce actions. The practice of "shopping" by mortgage and insurance companies also encouraged "starvation" fees. Officials of the state Bar acceded to a request of the Tulsa County Bar Association and on February 26, 1937, sanctioned adoption of an "Advisory Fee Schedule" by local associations on an optional basis. Tulsa immediately adopted a fee schedule.[49] Other Oklahoma communities had experienced problems similar to those in Tulsa. Clients bargained for the lowest fee, and lawyers found themselves involved in bidding contests. In one relatively prosperous county lawyers competed for divorce cases by bids of $15, $10, and even five dollars.[50]

Many lawyers feared that an established minimum fee would become the maximum fee. By the 1940s, however, most members of the profession believed a fee schedule could benefit not only the Bar itself but the public as well, primarily as a safeguard to discourage inferior service in return for unreasonable compensation. Proponents also reasoned that a fee schedule could help the younger, inexperienced attorney solve the often perplexing problem of arriving at a reasonable fee. Consequently the OBA's Central Committee in August of 1946 adopted a forthright stand in favor of recommended minimum fees and encouraged the use throughout the state of a fee guide prepared by the Committee on Minimum Fees.[51]

Bar associations all over the United States had about 500 different minimum fee schedules in use in 1975 when the United States Supreme Court in *Goldfarb v. Virginia State Bar* held that the practice of law is "commerce" subject to the antitrust laws. A minimum fee structure was deemed to be in restraint of trade and therefore illegal.[52] In Oklahoma the Board of Governors had already anticipated the court's decision. The Minimum Fee Schedule had been abolished in February of 1973 at the recommendation of the Professional Economics Committee and the Anti-Trust Law Committee.[53] Likewise, the Oklahoma legal profession needed no great foresight to realize that Bar rules against advertising were also in jeopardy.

After the Civil War a growing trend to advertise legal services in a manner misleading to the public caused the American Bar Association to adopt rules prohibiting advertising.[54] Lawyers in Oklahoma's territorial days usually confined advertising to "professional cards" describing the courts where the lawyers practiced and including a brief statement of the type of legal matters handled.[55] After Statehood Oklahoma attorneys complied with American Bar Association regulations except for occasional lapses. An obvious exception was Oklahoma City lawyer R.N. McConnell, whose full-page advertisement on the inside

cover of *Sturm's Magazine* in April and May of 1909 listed his four assistant attorneys and his "specialties," which included "Keeping Clients Out of Litigation." The advertisement said that McConnell practiced in all courts, offered opinions and advice by mail, and that depositions could be taken in his office by experienced notaries and stenographers.

The end of Bar rules against advertising began on February 22, 1976, when two young Arizona lawyers advertised a schedule of their fees in an Arizona newspaper. Fourteen months later by a five-to-four decision the United States Supreme Court struck down rules against advertising as being contrary to the free speech provision of the 1st Amendment.[56] The court left to the states the right to impose reasonable restrictions and prevent false, deceptive, or misleading advertising. An OBA committee quickly drafted rules which were approved by the State Supreme Court to prohibit radio and television advertising and to allow newspaper advertising limited in size, design, and content. However, court and Bar had a difficult time finding the elusive line between advertising that would provide pertinent information to the public and advertising that would accomplish little more that a lawyer's economic gain. Consequently, Oklahoma's revised advertising rules were subjected to attack as being among the most stringent in the nation.[57]

A Norman law firm placed advertisements in a local newspaper and in the yellow pages of the telephone directory.[58] An Oklahoma City lawyer followed with newspaper, radio, and television announcements. The Bar Association's disciplinary proceedings against him culminated in an Oklahoma Supreme Court ruling in July of 1982 that his advertisements constituted fairly presented "commercial speech" protected by the 1st Amendment.[59]

The court adopted more liberalized rules drafted by an OBA committee after two public hearings, which also took into consideration a January, 1982, United States Supreme Court case dealing with advertising in Missouri.[60] Under the court's new guidelines an Oklahoma attorney may state his fees in truthful informational advertising without self-adulation in any public media subject only to certain procedural requirements.[61]

As long ago as October of 1900 President Edgar Smith in his address to an Indian Territory Bar convention wondered whether the practice of law was developing into a mere trade rather than a profession.[62] Advertising rules have again raised the "trade vs. profession" issue, although advertising in the media to date indicates most Oklahoma practitioners still cherish the tradition that a lawyer should not commercialize his profession. Antlers attorney Joe Stamper, a 1935 University of Oklahoma law graduate, recalled that lawyers of his generation ranked "Thou shalt not advertise" and "Thou shalt not solicit" as 11th and 12th in the list of Great Commandments.[63] More experience with legalized advertising may determine whether it is indeed a service that the individual lawyer should provide and the general public will use.

The Oklahoma Bar Foundation, formed in 1946 to acquire a headquarters facility for the OBA, has evolved into an indispensable Public Relations arm for Oklahoma lawyers. Primarily from income derived from trust funds and contributions from lawyers, the Bar Foundation in recent years has made sizeable grants and awards to the University of Oklahoma, Oklahoma City University, and the University of Tulsa. It has financially assisted the Bar's Continuing Legal Education program and funded the purchase of updated Civil and Criminal Bench Books for Oklahoma trial judges.[64] Since 1983 the Foundation, with Edward H. Palmer as Executive Director, has administered the "Interest on Lawyers' Trust Accounts" program, now one of the Bar's most rewarding Public Relations projects.

The idea of IOLTA, an acronym for "Interest on Lawyers' Trust Accounts," originated during the 1982 OBA presidency of John L. Boyd, a 1950 law graduate of the University of Tulsa. Boyd had attended the Southern Conference of Bar Presidents where he learned of IOLTA, a project underway in Canada that made interest income available for worthwhile benevolent purposes. Following a revision of United States banking regulations permitting banks to pay interest on checking accounts, the Florida Bar Association adopted the IOLTA arrangements.[65]

President Boyd's Long Range Planning Committee, headed by Dale J. Briggs and a Board of Governors Special Committee chaired by Harry A. Woods, Jr., studied the IOLTA concept whereby clients' trust funds, typically too small

Justice Yvonne Kauger and Chief Justice John B. Doolin of Oklahoma's Supreme Court conducted this Indian Law Symposium funded by the Oklahoma Bar Foundtion. (Courtesy OBA.)

and deposited for too short a time to warrant the administrative costs typical of interest-bearing accounts, could in the aggregate earn substantial interest income when deposited in cooperating financial institutions. The income could then be transferred periodically to the Oklahoma Bar Foundation and devoted to worthwhile public projects.[66]

The OBA Board of Governors endorsed the IOLTA plan; however, Oklahoma disciplinary rules required lawyers to keep clients' funds in separate trust accounts, and any change of the rules required the Supreme Court's approval. The Court adopted an amendment to Disciplinary Rule DR 9-102 as recommended by the Board of Governors. The Internal Revenue Service and other governmental agencies have also approved the IOLTA provisions.[67] By 1989 approximately 1500 Oklahoma lawyers, along with 320 law firm-law office accounts and 140 financial institutions, were voluntarily participating in IOLTA, designating the Oklahoma Bar Foundation as sole beneficiary of interest earned from nominal, short-term funds deposited in interest-bearing accounts.

Oklahoma is now one of 48 states and the District of Columbia with an IOLTA program.[68] John L. Boyd, President of the Oklahoma Bar Foundation in 1987, has aptly termed IOLTA a "Painless Pro Bono" method by which a participating lawyer may to some extent fulfill the public interest legal service required by the Model Rules of Professional Conduct. For example, income from IOLTA deposits, averaging $26,000 monthly in

1989, has provided grants to Legal Aid of Western Oklahoma of $124,279 and Legal Services of Eastern Oklahoma of $115,318, along with sizeable sums to other organizations, such as Oklahoma Indian Legal Services and the Oklahoma Supreme Court Indian Law Symposium.[69]

The Oklahoma Bar Foundation advertises in metropolitan newspapers and the *Oklahoma Bar Journal*, requesting applications for grants and awards to support projects that (1) provide delivery of legal services to the poor; (2) promote quality legal education, and (3) improve the administration of justice and promote such other programs for the benefit of the public as are specifically approved by the Oklahoma Bar Association for exclusively public purposes.[70]

34

CONCLUSION

In the early days of the Twin Territories, the equipment in the average lawyer's office might consist of a roll-top desk, two or three straight-backed chairs, a pot-bellied stove, a cuspidor, and a minimum of law books. Joseph G. Ralls, while practicing in Atoka in the 1890s, made good use of his "Letter Press" book to produce copies of handwritten letters and legal documents by a rubbing process on chemically treated paper.[1] Two relatively new inventions, the telephone and the manual typewriter, earned their places in the lawyer's office of the early 20th century. In the years that followed, the lawyer's needs remained fairly constant, except for never-ending additions to his law library. Since the early 1950s, however, the legal profession has endured an explosion in overhead. More practitioners require expensive electric typewriters; dictating equipment is widely used; and the office copier is a near necessity. Sophisticated telephone systems are commonplace. Word processors and data processing equipment are acknowledged timesavers, while computers for research purposes threaten to replace law books.

The last three decades have also seen changes in the courtroom: robes worn by the judiciary, women on juries, more women lawyers, a minimum of Saturday court sessions, and in the realm of trial technique the widespread use of pre-trial discovery procedures to eliminate surprises in the course of the trial. An electronic marvel, television, came to Oklahoma in 1949 and started a debate about the propriety of televised courtroom proceedings.

Horace B. King, a former county judge who for 11 years worked as a legal assistant for the State Supreme Court, confronted the television question in a sensational case shortly after his election as county attorney in 1957. A 13-year-old youth killed two men and wounded another in the attempted robbery of a grocery store at Woodward. He claimed to have been influenced by criminal activities portrayed by movies and television. Newsmen as far away as London telephoned County Attorney King for information about the tragedy. The youth's grief-stricken parents and grandparents accompanied him at his arraignment before the county judge. When two television reporters appeared to film the proceedings, County Attorney King, in sympathy with the boy's relatives, objected to the intrusion of television cameras.

After the judge overruled his objections, King asked to be excused from the proceedings. He left the courtroom stating, "I will have no part in making a Roman circus of this unfortunate affair; I have too much respect for the feelings of the parents and grandparents of this unfortunate lad than to do so." Press reports widely publicized King's stand against the presence of cameras.[2]

The question of newspaper and television cameras in the courtroom received the attention of the Oklahoma Bar, and in February of 1958 the Committee on Judicial Administration of Justice asked the State Supreme Court to ban them from Oklahoma courts. The following year the court accepted the OBA's recommendation and adopted the American Bar Association's Canons of Judicial Ethics, including Canon 35 which banned radio and television from the courtroom as detracting from the dignity of the proceedings and distracting to the participants. Radio and television stations strongly objected, accusing the court of impairing freedom of the press.[3]

Supporters of television and photograhic equipment in the courtroom brought up the question again in 1978, insisting that technological improvements had eliminated the distraction of cameras, bright lights, flash bulbs, and busy technicians. Now, they contended, one person could operate a tiny, inconspicuous camera attached to a small cable leading to other equipment outside the nearest door; none of this would disturb the administration of justice.[4]

Chief Justice Ralph B. Hodges of the State Supreme Court announced that a committee of jurists and lawyers would study the matter and make recommendations.[5] By a six to three vote,

Oklahoma Bar Foundation Board of Trustees, 1988. Front row, L to R: Jayne N. Montgomery, Michael Burrage, Philip F. Horning, President V. Burns Hargis, President-Elect Richard L. McKnight, Past President John L. Boyd. Back row, L to R: Terry C. Kern, Judge Ed Parks, Robert J. Hays, Richard Hutton, Charles S. Chapel, Vice President Jon H. Trudgeon, William J. Baker, O.B. Johnston, III, Executive Director Edward H. Palmer. Not pictured: Mark A. Ashton, Burck Bailey, Marvin C. Emerson, Brian T. Hermanson, Anthony "Tony" M. Massad, David B. McKinney, Judge Mildred E. Otey, Jerry Otis, Judge Thomas C. Smith, Jr., Terry W. West. (Courtesy OBA.)

the court subsequently approved a trial period beginning on January 1, 1979, to allow camera coverage of court proceedings subject to prior approval of the judge, witnesses, and jurors. The defendant's consent was necessary in criminal cases.[6]

After a two-year experimental period, the findings of a special committee appointed to evaluate the results convinced a majority of the court that cameras in general did not adversely affect the proceedings. In May of 1981 Chief Justice Pat Irwin announced that cameras would continue to be allowed on a year-to-year basis subject to the judge's approval and the accused's consent in criminal cases. The court on February 22, 1982, adopted on a permanent basis the revised Canon 3A(7), Code of Judicial Conduct, permitting cameras and microphones into Oklahoma courtrooms. State journalists applauded the decision. The following April 2, Justice Hodges received the University of Oklahoma's H.H. Herbert School of Journalism and Mass Communication award for "significant contribution by a non-journalist to the practice of journalism in the public interest.[7]

Proponents of electronic equipment have suggested another innovation in the courtroom—the use of a videotape machine to produce a sound and visual record of trial proceedings. They argue that although video tape need not replace the court reporter's written account, it can furnish a more complete record for appellate purposes. They also believe that videotape can shorten the time required for appeal and thereby alleviate a frequent criticism of the judicial process.[8]

Lawyers have found the videotape machine helpful for other purposes. Not only can the expense of court appearances be reduced by the taping of expert and key witness testimony, but also the taped record can be used in damage suits to show a jury the nature of a plaintiff's injuries and the extent of property damage. The tape can also record accident scenes.[9] In Oklahoma City, history was made in legal circles when a Hollywood stunt man was employed to re-enact motor vehicles accidents on videotape.[10]

David K. Petty (right), 1987 OBA president, presents the prestigious President's Award to Marvin C. Emerson, Executive Director of the OBA, at the Bar Convention in November 1987. This award, a recognition of significant contribution to the legal profession, is always a well-kept secret and is awarded only occasionally, at the discretion of the current Bar president. In the background are Mrs. Petty, wife of the OBA president, and Chief Justice John B. Doolin of the State Supreme Court. (Courtesy OBA.)

The use of modern electronic equipment by the Oklahoma lawyer is the outgrowth of a complex society with constantly growing legal problems. From the beginning Oklahoma has been one of the most litigious states—a condition that has extended into 1981 when 208,088 civil suits ranked the state 14th among sister states in civil suits per thousand people.[11] The State Supreme Court reported that 550,000 cases of all kinds, including small claims and traffic violations, were filed in state district courts that year. The tremendous volume of detailed record keeping underscored the need for a state court data processing system; the Legislature responded with an appropriation of funds to initiate such a program.[12]

To reduce its case backlog the State Supreme Court in 1981 once again called on three-member panels of volunteer lawyers and judges to render opinions subject to the court's review, as had been done in the 1930s and 1960s.[13] The court also adopted a voluntary "fast track" procedure subject to mutual agreement of litigants whereby jus-

tices announced their decisions orally from the bench at the conclusion of oral argument.[14]

Federal courts in Oklahoma have participated in the rising tide of litigation which Oklahoma City's Circuit Court Justice William J. Holloway has attributed in part to the public's greater awareness that rights can be enforced through the courts.[15] The volume of legal business generated by the failure of Penn Square Bank in Oklahoma City has been compared to litigation that would result from the collision of two large passenger aircraft over the downtown section. In the criminal field, "kickback" cases burdened federal courts with the prosecution of numerous county commissioners and suppliers.[16]

While the case load in Oklahoma's federal courts grew at record rates, one federal judge called for more judges and criticized the "inexcusable waste" in overhead costs due to division of the state into three districts although all other states in the Tenth Circuit require only one district. His criticism recalled that Oklahoma was the

Anthony M. "Tony" Massad, Frederick, President of the Oklahoma Bar Association in 1989. (Courtesy OBA.)

Neil E. Bogan, Tulsa, elected President of the Oklahoma Bar Association for 1990, follows Thomas R. Brett (1970) and Deryl L. Gotcher (1974) as the third member of the firm of Jones, Givens, Gotcher, Bogan & Hilborne to become president of the OBA.

only state to enter the Union with two federal court districts—increased to three districts 18 years later largely because of the personal feud between Judges Robert L. Williams and F.E. Kennamer.[17]

An enlarged lawyer population corresponded with the greater volume of lawsuits in Oklahoma. Lawyers enrolled by the Supreme Court at Statehood numbered about 1800, but in the next few years court records showed a gain to about 3000—an increase no doubt attributable to late enrollment of local licensed attorneys as well as to immigration from other jurisdictions.[18] The lawyer-per-citizen ratio in 1910 stood at about one lawyer for every 550 citizens.[19] That ratio remained substantially the same for the next half-century as the active in-state rolls grew to a little more than 4200, with a proportionate rise in the state's population.[20]

At the Oklahoma Bar convention in December of 1959, President John D. Randall of the American Bar Association noted that the legal profes-

sion was endangered by the loss of top college graduates—a recent survey showed 50 percent had chosen to study science or engineering while only 3 percent preferred law.[21] But the era of the war in Vietnam followed by the Watergate scandal saw students flock to Oklahoma law schools in record numbers. In addition to more women finding the law attractive, some state educators attributed the rise in law school enrollment to a new breed of young idealists, both male and female, who believed the route to change in the social order was through the legal profession.[22] Veteran lawyer Hicks Epton observed in 1969, "When glamour sciences came along, we lost a lot of keen minds and brains from the legal profession, but now the pendulum in swinging back. The trouble is most want to stay away from the courthouse and that's the cradle of liberty—where your rights are tested. We must have men of courage who will walk into the courthouse as trial lawyers and put it on the line to preserve rights."[23] A dramatic increase of almost 52 percent occurred in the decade from 1970 to 1980, when active in-state lawyers grew from 4424 to 6717—one lawyer for every 450 Oklahoma citizens. By January of 1989 the active in-state lawyer population had expanded to 8637, a gain of almost 29 percent. The lawyer-ratio was about one to 378, based on an estimated Oklahoma population of 3,263,000. Total OBA membership of 11,988 included lawyers living outside the state and senior and associate members.[24]

The Bench and Bar of Oklahoma in 1989 could look back on a century of contribution to the development of the state. Lawyers had initiated the administration of justice through law in the Twin Territories, had led in the drive for Statehood, and had drafted the state Constitution. Always available to render public service, they have continued to provide leadership in state and federal government.

The Bar Association itself has grown from a voluntary organization of about 140 paid members in 1904 to a compulsory membership of 11,988 in 1989.[25] Mainly through the work of the organized Bar, Oklahoma has adopted a unified court system unsurpassed by sister states. The Bar Association's other notable accomplishments include improvement in the selection, tenure, and removal of judges, raising standards for admission to the practice of law, encouraging the observance of legal ethics and organizing a program of continued legal education.

The Bar has entered its second century of lawyer leadership in Oklahoma committed to the administration of justice for all, while inspiring high personal and professional standards for its members.[20]

LIST OF BAR PRESIDENTS

INDIAN TERRITORY BAR ASSOCIATION

1900	Edgar Smith*	Vinita
1901	Charles B. Stuart*	South McAlester
1902	C.L. Herbert*	Ardmore
1903	Clifford L. Jackson*	Muskogee
1904	Joseph G. Ralls*	Atoka

OKLAHOMA [TERRITORY] BAR ASSOCIATION

1890-97	Harper S. Cunningham*	Guthrie
1898-99	John W. Shartel*	Oklahoma City
1900-01	J.C. Strang*	Guthrie
1901	John H. Cotteral*	Guthrie
1902	Scott W. Denton*	Enid
1903	Jesse J. Dunn*	Alva
1904	Roy Hoffman*	Chandler

OKLAHOMA STATE BAR ASSOCIATION

1904	Charles B. Stuart* [Elected Dec. 1904]	Oklahoma City
1905	Charles B. Stuart*	Oklahoma City
1906	Samuel H. Harris*	Oklahoma City
1907	Clifford L. Jackson*	Muskogee
1908	Frank Wells*	Oklahoma City
1909	W.I. Gilbert*	Oklahoma City
1910	T.J. Womack*	Alva
1911	J.H. Burford*	Guthrie
1912	J.W. Hocker*	Purcell
1913	J.H. Gordon*	McAlester
1914	C.O. Blake*	El Reno
1915	George S. Ramsey*	Muskogee
1916	C.B. Ames*	Oklahoma City
1917	Frank M. Bailey*	Chickasha
1918	E.G. McAdams*	Oklahoma City
1919	H.H. Rogers*	Tulsa
1920	George L. Bowman*	Kingfisher
1921	Preston C. West*	Tulsa
1922	James A. Duff*	Tulsa
1923	N.A. Gibson*	Tulsa
1924	Walter A. Lybrand*	Oklahoma City
1925	Joseph C. Stone*	Muskogee
1926	C.B. Stuart*	Oklahoma City
1927	Edgar A. de Meules*	Tulsa
1928	Horace G. McKeever*	Enid
1929	John H. Kane*	Bartlesville
1930	J.R. Keaton*	Oklahoma City
1931	Alger Melton*	Chickasha
1932	W.E. Utterback*	Durant
1933	Thomas J. Horsley*	Wewoka
1934	Charles B. Cochran*	Oklahoma City
1935	Ben F. Williams*	Norman
1936	E.L. Richardson*	Lawton
1937	Felix Duvall*	Ponca City
1938	Frank M. Bailey*	Chickasha
1939	Logan Stephenson*	Tulsa

OKLAHOMA BAR ASSOCIATION

1940	John E. Luttrell*	Oklahoma City
1941	J.B. Moore*	Ardmore
1942	John H. Cantrell*	Oklahoma City
1943	Ray S. Fellows*	Tulsa
1944	A.W. Trice*	Ada
1945	Charles E. France*	Oklahoma City
1946	Gerald B. Klein*	Tulsa
1947	W.E. Crowe*	Enid
1948	Howard T. Tumilty*	Oklahoma City
1949	Wm. S. Hamilton*	Pawhuska
1950	T. Austin Gavin*	Tulsa
1951	C.D. Cund*	Duncan
1952	John H. Halley*	Oklahoma City
1953	Hicks Epton*	Wewoka
1954	G. Ellis Gable	Tulsa
1955	Charles B. Duffy*	Ponca City
1956	Eugene P. Ledbetter*	Oklahoma City
1957	Earl Q. Gray*	Ardmore
1958	Garrett Logan*	Tulsa
1959	John M. Holliman*	Bartlesville
1960	V.P. Crowe*	Oklahoma City
1961	Walter J. Arnote*	McAlester
1962	Jack N. Hays*	Tulsa
1963	Robert W. Blackstock	Bristow
1964	James D. Fellers	Oklahoma City
1965	T.D. Nicklas	Lawton
1966	LeRoy Blackstock	Tulsa
1967	Joseph M. Culp	Ardmore
1968	Paul C. Duncan*	Oklahoma City
1968	E.D. Hieronymus	Tulsa
1969	Winfrey D. Houston	Stillwater
1970	Thomas R. Brett	Tulsa
1971	Jim F. Gassaway	Ada
1972	Lee B. Thompson	Oklahoma City
1973	John R. Wallace	Miami
1974	Deryl L. Gotcher	Tulsa
1975	C.D. Northcutt	Ponca City
1976	William G. Paul	Oklahoma City
1977	Wilson Wallace	Ardmore
1978	William H. Bell*	Tulsa
1979	John M. Luttrell	Norman
1980	Leslie L. Conner, Jr.	Oklahoma City
1981	Ben T. Owens	Miami
1982	John L. Boyd	Tulsa
1983	Paul M. Vassar	Chandler
1984	Robert J. Turner	Oklahoma City
1985	John E. Shipp	Idabel
1986	James R. Eagleton	Tulsa
1987	David K. Petty	Guymon
1988	Burck Bailey	Oklahoma City
1989	Anthony M. Massad	Frederick
1990	Neil E. Bogan	Tulsa

*deceased

217

ENDNOTES

Special thanks to Burck Bailey, LeRoy Blackstock, Thomas R. Brett, Crowe & Dunlevy, Paul W. Dudman, G. Ellis Gable, T.D. Nicklas, Rogers & Bell, Lee B. Thompson, John R. Wallace, William H. Bell, Jap W. Blankenship, W.E. Crowe, James D. Fellers, Winfrey D. Houston, William G. Paul, John Joseph Snider, Terry W. Tippens, and the Chapman-McFarlin Barnard Interests for assisting in underwriting the research phase of the manuscript for this publication.

Chapter 1

[1] Luther B. Hill, *A History of the State of Oklahoma* (2 vols., Chicago: Lewis Publishing Co., 1910), I, 368-370; Irvin Hurst, *The 46th Star: A History of Oklahoma's Constitutional Convention and Early Statehood* (Oklahoma City: Semco Color Press, 1957), 32; Lerona Rosamond Morris, ed., *Oklahoma, Yesterday—Today—Tomorrow* (Guthrie: Co-Operative Publishing Co., 1930), 520-521.

[2] James A. Howard, II, "Charles Nathaniel Haskell, Governor of Oklahoma, 1907-1911," in LeRoy Fischer, ed., *Oklahoma's Governors, 1907-1929: Turbulent Politics,* (Oklahoma City: Oklahoma Historical Society, 1981), 29.

[3] Hurst, *The 46th Star,* 33-34; Howard, "Charles Nathaniel Haskell," 20-21.

[4] *Bartlesville Enterprise,* November 22, 1907, 1; *Dewey World,* November 20, 1907, 1; Hill, *History of the State of Oklahoma,* II, 384.

[5] "Address of Hon. Charles N. Haskell," *Chronicles of Oklahoma,* X (December, 1932), 464-466; Oklahoma, *Compiled Laws* (1909), c. 75, art. 1, secs. 4809-4819; *Kansas Natural Gas Co., v. Haskell et al,* 172 F. 545 (1909); Blue Clark, "The Beginning of Oil and Gas Conservation in Oklahoma, 1907-1931,"*Chronicles of Oklahoma,* LV, (Winter, 1977-1978), 375, 378.

[6] Joseph B. Thoburn and Muriel H. Wright, *Oklahoma: A History of the State and Its People* (4 vols.; New York: Lewis Historical Publishing Company, 1929), III, 271.

[7] Charles R. Goins and John W. Morris, *Oklahoma Homes Past and Present* (Norman: University of Oklahoma Press, 1980), 183.

[8] Evett Dumas Nix, as told to Gordon Hines, *Oklahombres* (St. Louis: Eden Publishing House, 1929), 113, 29.

[9] Blue Clark, "Delegates to the Constitutional Convention,"*Chronicles of Oklahoma,* XLVIII (Winter, 1970-1971), 400-415; W.B. Richards, comp., *Oklahoma Red Book* (2 vols.; Tulsa: Press of Tulsa Daily Democrat, 1912), II, 292-293.

[10] Act of March 26, 1804, U.S., *Statutes at Large,* Vol. II, 283, hereafter cited *Stat.,* preceded by Vol. number, followed by page number; George H. Shirk, "The Judicial System of Oklahoma," *The Oklahoma Almanac, 1961 edition,* ed. H.L. Fitzpatrick (Norman: Oklahoma Almanac, Inc., 1960), 77; Roy Gittinger, *The Formation of the State of Oklahoma* (Norman: University of Oklahoma Press, 1939), 3-4.

[11] Act of June 4, 1812, 2 *Stat.* 743; Act of March 2, 1819, 3 *Stat.* 493.

[12] Rex W. Strickland, "Establishment of 'Old' Miller County, Arkansas Territory," *Chronicles of Oklahoma,* XVIII (Summer, 1940), 154-161.

[13] Shirk, "The Judicial System of Oklahoma," 77; Arrell M. Gibson, *Oklahoma: A History of Five Centuries* (Norman: Harlow Publishing Corp., 1965), 68, 149.

[14] Andrew A. Lipscomb, ed., *The Writings of Thomas Jefferson* (Washington: Thomas Jefferson Memorial Association, 1905), X, 394-395.

[15] Shirk, "The Judicial System of Oklahoma," 77.

[16] *The Cherokee Nation v. The State of Georgia,* 5 Peters (U.S.), 1 (1831).

[17] *Samuel A. Worchester, Plaintiff in Errror v. The State of Georgia,* 6 Peters (U.S.), 515 (1832).

[18] Clement Eaton, *A History of the Old South* (New York: The Macmillan Company, 1965), 294.

Chapter 2

[1] John W. Morris and Edwin C. McReynolds, *Historical Atlas of Oklahoma* (Norman: University of Oklahoma Press, 1966), 21, 23.

[2] *Annual Report of the Commissioner of Indian Affairs, Transmitted with the Message of the President at the Opening of the Second Session of the Twenty-Eighth Congress, 1844-1845* (Washington: C Alexander, Printer, 1844), 19-20; Gittinger, *The Formation of Oklahoma,* 264.

[3] Indian Territory Bar Association, *Proceedings, Fourth Annual Meeting* (South McAlester, I. T.: June 9, 10, 1903), 47-51

[4] *Ibid.,* 41; Rennard Strickland, *Fire and the Spirits, Cherokee Law from Clan to Court* (Norman: University of Oklahoma Press, 1975), 168-169.

[5] *Ibid.,* 121-122, 124, 139, 141, 145; Kathleen Garrett, "Dartmouth Alumni in the Indian Territory," *Chronicles of Oklahoma,* XXXII (Summer, 1954), 123-141; J. Berry King, "Judge William Pressley Thompson," *Chronicles of Oklahoma,* XIX (March, 1941), 4-5.

[6] Strickland, *Fire and the Spirits,* 123.

[7] *Constitution and Laws of the Cherokee Nation* (Wilmington, Del.: Scholarly Resources, Inc., 1973), 313-316.

[8] *Ibid.,* 315-316; T.L. Ballenger, "The Life and Times of Jeff Thompson Parks: Pioneer, Educator and Jurist," *Chronicles of Oklahoma* XXX (Summer, 1952), 194.

[9] *Constitution and Laws of the Cherokee Nation,* 314-315.

[10] Strickland, *Fire and the Spirits,* 124, 141.

[11] *Constitution, Treaties and Laws of the Choctaw Nation* (Wilmington, Del.: Scholarly Resources, Inc., 1975), 142; for a review of Choctaw law, see Oliver Knight, "Fifty Years of Choctaw Law, 1834 to 1884," *Chronicles of Oklahoma,* XXXI (Spring, 1953), 76-95.

[12] L.C. Perryman, comp., *Constitution and Laws of the Muskogee Nation* (Wilmington, Del.: Scholarly Resources, Inc., 1975), 83-84.

[13] *Constitution, Treaties and Laws of the Chickasaw Nation* (Wilmington, Del.: Scholarly Resources, Inc., 1975), 107-108.

[14] Davis H. Homer, *Constitution and Laws of the Chickasaw Nation Together with the Treaties of 1832, 1833, 1834, 1837, 1852, 1855 and 1866,* Vol. II of *Constitution and Laws of the American Indian Tribes* (Wilmington, Del.: Scholarly Resources Inc., 1973), 294.

[15] *Ibid.,* 294-295.

[16] Indian Territory Bar Association, *Proceedings, Fourth Annual Meeting, pp. 42-43*; Czarina C. Conlan, "Chickasaw Courts, Reminiscences of Judge John H. Mashburn," *Chronicles of Oklahoma,* V. (September, 1927), 401.

[17] Indian Territory Bar Association, *Proceedings, Fourth Annual Meeting,* 41-43.

[18] Carolyn Thomas Foreman, "Joseph Absalom Scales," *Chronicles of Oklahoma,* XXVIII, (Winter, 1950-51), 429, citing Vinita *Indian Chieftain,* March 10, 1887.

[19] Indian Territory Bar Association, *Proceedings, Fourth Annual Meeting,* 59.

[20] *Ibid.,* 56.

[21] Conlan, "Chickasaw Courts," *Chronicles of Oklahoma,* V, 401; Indian Territory Bar Association, *Proceedings, Fourth Annual Meeting,* 62.

[22] *Ibid.,* 46; Perryman, *Constitution and Laws of Muskogee Nation,* 22-24; Angie Debo, *The Road to Disappearance* (Norman: University of Oklahoma Press, 1941), 185, 227.

[23] Perryman, *Constitution and Laws of Muskogee Nation,* 30.

[24] Kaye M. Teall, ed., *Black History in Oklahoma: A Resource Book* (Oklahoma City: Oklahoma City Public Schools, 1971), 92.

[25] *Ibid.,* 148-149.

[26] "Indian-Pioneer History," XL, 195; Teall, *Black History,* 149; L.W. Wilson, "Reminiscences of Jim Tomm," *Chronicles of Oklahoma,* XLIV, (Autumn, 1966), 300.

[27] Indian Territory Bar Association, *Proceedings, Fourth Annual Meeting,* 53-54.

[28] Garrett, "Dartmouth Alumni," *Chronicles of Oklahoma,* XXXII, 137.

[29] *Ibid.*

[30]Thoburn and Wright, *Oklahoma*, III, 225-226.

[31]A.D. Hefley, "Tobucksy County Courthouse," *Chronicles of Oklahoma*, XLVIII, (Spring, 1970), 31.

[32]*Ibid*, 32.

[33]*Ibid*,

[34]Indian Territory Bar Association, *Proceedings, Fourth Annual Meeting*, 53.

[35]Fanny Pate Hicks, "George A. Pate," *Chronicles of Oklahoma*, VIII, (March, 1930), 136-137.

[36]Indian Territory Bar Association, *Proceedings, Fourth Annual Meeting*, 47-51.

[37]*Annual Report of the Commissioner of Indian Affairs to the Secretary of the Interior for the Year 1877* (Washington: Government Printing Office, , 1877), 107-108; *Annual Report of the Commissioner of Indian Affairs to the Secretary of the Interior for the Year 1885* (Washington: Government Printing Office, 1885), 106; Clarence B. Douglas, *The History of Tulsa, Oklahoma*,(3 vols.; Chicago: S.J. Clarke Publishing Company, 1921), I, 59-60; Angie Debo, *The Rise and Fall of the Choctaw Republic* (Norman: University of Oklahoma Press, 1972), 184-185.

[38]"Indian-Pioneer History," XVII, 24-25.

[39]Grant Foreman, *The Five Civilized Tribes: Cherokee, Chickasaw, Choctaw, Creek, Seminole* (Norman: University of Oklahoma Press, 1974), 51-52.

[40]G.A. Crossett, "A Vanishing Race," *Chronicles of Oklahoma*, IV, (June, 1926), 110.

[41]Indian Territory Bar Association, *Proceedings, Fourth Annual Meeting*, 59-60.

[42]*Ibid.*, 60.

[43]William H. Murray, *Memoirs of Governor Murray and True History of Oklahoma*, (3 vols.; Boston: Meador Publishing Company, 1945), I, 229-230.

[44]Grant Foreman, "The Indian and the Law," Oklahoma Bar Association *Journal*, XVII, January 26, 1946, 88-91; hereafter the *Journal*, first published by the State Bar Association of Oklahoma and now published by the Oklahoma Bar Association, will be cited as Okla. B.J., Vol. No., and page no.

[45]Grant Foreman, ed., *Indian Justice, A Cherokee Murder Trial at Tahlequah in 1840, as Reported by John Howard Payne* (Muskogee: The Star Printery, Inc., 1962), 7.

[46]*Ibid.*, 8-9.

[47]Strickland, *Fire and the Spirits*, 124.

[48]*Ibid.*, 145, citing *Cherokee Phoenix*, October 22, 1828.

[49]Foreman, *Indian Justice*, 13-15, 26-27.

[50]*Ibid.*, 18.

[51]George E. Foster, "A Legal Episode in the Cherokee Nation," *The Green Bag: An Entertaining Magazine for Lawyers*, IV, (October, 1892), 489-490.

[52]*Ibid.*

[53]Foreman, *Five Civilized Tribes*, 33-34; Act of June 28, 1898, 30 Stat. 495.

Chapter 3

[1]Shirk, "The Judicial System of Oklahoma," 78; Gittinger: *Formation of Oklahoma*, 25-26; Act of June 30, 1834, 4 *Stat.* 729.

[2]Hill, *History of the State of Oklahoma*, I, 78; Gittenger, *Formation of Oklahoma*, 26-27; James D. Richardson, ed., *A Compilation of the Messages and Papers of the Presidents*, (Washington: Government Printing Office, 1896), III, 172.

[3]Edward Everett Dale and Morris L. Wardell, *History of Oklahoma* (Englewood Cliffs, N. J.,: Prentice Hall, Inc., 1963), 279-280.

[4]Foreman, *History of Oklahoma*, 282; LeRoy H. Fischer, "United States Indian Agents to the Five Civilized Tribes," *Chronicles of Oklahoma*, L, (Winter, 1972), 411.

[5]Foreman, *History of Oklahoma*, 199; Debo, *Rise and Fall of the Choctaw Republic*, 188.

[6]*Annual Report of the Commissioner of Indian Affairs to the Secretary of the Interior for the Year 1883* (Washington: Government Printing Office, 1883), 87.

[7]*The United States, Plaintiffs, v. William S. Rogers*, 4 Howard (U. S.), 567 (1846); Morris L. Wardell, *A Political History of the Cherokee Nation, 1838-1907* (Norman: University of Oklahoma Press, 1938), 100-101; *Report of the Commissioner of Indian Affairs Accompanying the Annual Report of the Secretary of the Interior for the Year 1857* (Washing-

ton: William A. Harris, Printer, 1958), 195-197; *Chickasaws and Choctaws: A Pamphlet of Information Concerning their History, Treaties, Government, Country, Laws, Politics and Affairs* (Wilmington, Del.: Scholarly Resources, Inc., 1975), 52; Louise Welsh, "The Development of Law and Order in the Cherokee Nation, 1838-1907" (unpublished Master of Arts thesis, Dept. of History, University of Oklahoma, 1932), 99.

[8]*Annual Report of the Commissioner of Indian Affairs, Transmitted with he Message of the President at the Opening of the Third Session of the Thirty-Fourth Congress, 1855* (Washington: A.O.P. Nicholson, Printer, 1856), 125-126; Foreman, *History of Oklahoma*, 52-53; Thomas Lee Ballenger, "The Development of Law and Legal Institutions among the Cherokees" (unpublished Ph.D. thesis, University of Oklahoma, 1938), 87-88; William T. Hagan, *Indian Police and Judges: Experiments in Acculturation and Control* (New Haven: Yale University Press, 1966), 22.

[9]Charles J. Kappler, comp., ed., *Indian Affairs: Laws and Treaties*, (5 vols.; Washington: Government Printing Office, 1904-1941), I, 2d ed., 18; Act of March 27, 1854, 10 *Stat.* 270; Foreman, *History of Oklahoma*, 52-53.

[10]*Report of the Commissioner of Indian Affairs, 1855*, 125-126; Foreman, *Five Civilized Tribes*, 413; Hagan, *Indian Police and Judges*, 22.

[11][S.W. Harman], *Hell on the Border* (Stockton, California: Frank L. Van Eaton, Publisher, 1953), 53-54.

[12]*Ibid.*, 62-65.

[13]Glenn Shirley, *Law West of Fort Smith: A History of Frontier Justice in the Indian Territory, 1836-1896* (New York: Henry Holt and Company,1957), 3-8.

[14]Act of March 21, 1866, 14 *Stat.* 755; Act of April 28, 1866, 14 *Stat.* 769; Act of June 14, 1866, 14 *Stat.* 785; Act of July 19, 1866, 14 *Stat.* 799; Kappler, *Indian Affairs*, II, 914, 922, 936, 946.

[15]Kappler, *Indian Affairs*, II, 946; Act of July 19, 1866, 14 *Stat.* 799.

[16]Daniel F. Littlefield, Jr., and Lonnie E. Underhill, "The Trial of Ezekiel Proctor and the Problem of Judicial Jurisdiction," *Chronicles of Oklahoma*, XLVIII, (Autumn, 1970), 307.

[17]*Ibid.*, 311-314.

[18]*Ibid.*, 318.

[19]*Ibid.*, 315.

[20]*Ibid.*, 319; Dr. Virgil Berry, "Uncle Sam's Treaty with One Man." *Chronicles of Oklahoma*, XXXII, (Summer, 1954), 228-229; Littlefield and Underhill, "The Trial of Exekiel Proctor," 319.

[21]Richardson, *Messages and Papers of the Presidents*, VII, 165-166; Ballenger, "The Development of Law and Legal Institutions among the Cherokees," 113; Grant Foreman, "The Tragedy of Going Snake Court House," *Daily Oklahoman*, October 7, 1934, 14-c.

[22]*Annual Report of the Commissioner of Indian Affairs to the Secretary of the Interior for the Year 1886* (Washington: Government Printing Office), 122.

Chapter 4

[1]Shirley, *Law West of Fort Smith*, 16-17; Harry P. Daily, "Judge Isaac C. Parker," *Chronicles of Oklahoma*, XI, (March, 1933), 675.

[2]J.H. Beadle, *The Undeveloped West* (Philadelphia: National Publishing Co., 1873), 393; V.V. Masterson, *The Katy Railroad and the Last Frontier* (Norman: University of Oklahoma Press, 1978), 145.

[3]Daily, "Judge Isaac C. Parker," *Chronicles of Oklahoma*, XI, 673-674.

[4]*Ibid.*, 673.

[5]*Ibid.*, 677-681.

[6]Indian-Pioneer History," CXII, 35.

[7]*Ibid.*, XII, 466-470.

[8]Foreman, *History of Oklahoma*, 280.

[9]*Fort Smith Elevator*, May 8, 1896, 3; Shirley, *Law West of Fort Smith*, 195.

[10]Shirley, *Law West of Fort Smith*, 35-40: Masterson, *The Katy Railroad*, 209.

[11]Shirley *Law West of Fort Smith*, 198.

[12]William F. Semple, "Isaac C. Parker, Judge of the United States Court," 12 Okla. B.J. 1263, August 25, 1951.

[13]Shirley, *Law West of Fort Smith*, passim; [Harman], *Hell on the Border*, passim; Daily, "Judge Isaac C. Parker," passim.

[14]Act of January 6, 1883, 22 *Stat.* 400.

[15]Thoburn and Wright, *History of Oklahoma*, II, 718-719.

[16]"Indian-Pioneer History," XCI, 280-282.

[17]Act of February 6, 1889, 25 *Stat.* 655.

[18]Act of March 3, 1891, 26 *Stat.* 826; Shirk, "Judicial System of Oklahoma," 79.

[19]Semple, 22 Okla. B.J. 1259-60, August 25, 1951; Daily, "Judge Isaac C. Parker," 686-689; Shirley, *Law West of Fort Smith*, 183-187.

[20]*Ibid.*, 187-190; Semple, 22 Okla B.J. 1264, August 25, 1951.

[21]Quoted in *National Law Journal*, October 19, 1981, 11; S.W. Harman, *Cherokee Bill: The Oklahoma Outlaw* (Houston: Frontier Press of Texas, 1954), 24-25.

[22]Daily, "Judge Isaac C. Parker," 686; *Goldsby, alias Cherokee Bill v. United States*, 160 U.S. 70; Harman, *Cherokee Bill*, 26 ff.; Shirley, *Law West of Fort Smith*, 134.

[23]*Ibid.*, 202.

[24]Act of March 1, 1889, 25 *Stat.* 783.

[25]Act of March 1, 1895, 28 *Stat.* 693.

[26][Harman], *Hell on the Border*, 38-39, 42.

Chapter 5

[1]Foreman, *History of Oklahoma*, 280-281; Act of March 1, 1889, 25 *Stat.* 783.

[2]Douglas, *History of Tulsa, Oklahoma*, I, 59-60; John D. Benedict, *Muskogee and Northeastern Oklahoma: Including the Counties of Muskogee, McIntosh, Wagoner, Cherokee, Sequoyah, Adair, Delaware, Mayes, Rogers, Washington, Nowata, Craig and Ottawa* (3 vols.; Chicage: S.J. Clarke Publishing Company, 1922), I, 381-382.

[3]Kappler, *Indian Affairs*, I, 2d ed., 39; Act of March 1, 1889, 25 *Stat.* 783.

[4]*Ibid.*, Foreman, *History of Oklahoma*, 280-281.

[5]Taped address by Joe C. Wallace, Living Legends Library, Oklahoma Christian University, Oklahoma City, Oklahoma.

[6]Carolyn Thomas Foreman, "Gen. James M. Shackelford," *Chronicles of Oklahoma*, XII, (March, 1934), 104-111.

[7]Thoburn and Wright, *Oklahoma*, II, 719; Grant Foreman, "Oklahoma's First Court," *Chronicles of Oklahoma*, XIII, (December, 1935), 462.

[8]Oklahoma State Bar Association, *Proceedings, Third Annual Meeting* (Oklahoma City, Oklahoma, February 14, 15, 1910), 228.

[9]Foreman, "Oklahoma's First Court," 458-459.

[10]Oklahoma State Bar Association *Proceedings, Eighteenth Annual Meeting* (Oklahoma City, Oklahoma, December 29, 30, 1924), 96-97.

[11]Thoburn and Wright, *Oklahoma*, II, 720.

[12]Foreman, "Oklahoma's First Court," 461.

[13]*Our brother in Red* (Muskogee), April 6, 1889, 1; May 25, 1889, 1, 3.

[14]Masterson, *The Katy Railroad*, 253; Marshall Houts, *From Gun to Gavel: The Courtroom Recollections of James Mathers of Oklahoma* (New York: William Morrow & Company, 1954), 13-14.

[15]*Our Brother in Red*, May 25, 1889, 5.

[16]*Ibid.*, Foreman, *History of Oklahoma*, 282.

[17]*Our Brother in Red*, June 8, 1889, 4; Foreman, "Oklahoma's First Court," 463.

[18]*Our Brother in Red*, June 8, 1889, 4.

[19]Foreman, "Oklahoma's First Court," 464.

[20]*Ibid.*, 462.

[21]*Wilson N. Jones, Plf. in Error v. Adolph Baer et., al.*, 37 L. Ed. 947, (1893), R.L. Williams, "The Judicial History of Oklahoma," Oklahoma State Bar Association, *Proceedings, Fifth Annual Meeting* (Oklahoma City, December 21, 22, 1911) 127; Benedict, *Muskgee and Northeastern Oklahoma*, I, 385; Foreman, *History of Oklahoma*, 282; Z.T. Walrond, "Early Annals of the Muskogee Bar Association," *Muskogee Phoenix*, September 23, 1905.

[22]Foreman, *History of Oklahoma*, 282.

[23]*Our Brother in Red*, June 8, 1889, 4; Foreman, *History of Oklahoma*, 463-465.

[24]*Our Brother in Red* June 22, 1889, 5.

[25]Benedict, *Muskogee and Northeastern Oklahoma*, I, 385-386; *Our Brother in Red*, October 12, 1889, 5, November 16, 1889, 1.

[26]*Ibid.*, September 28, 1889, 5, October 19, 1889, 1.

[27]Walrond, "Early Annals of the Muskogee Bar Association," *Muskogee Phoenix*, September 23, 1905.

[28]*Ibid.*

[29]Foreman, *History of Oklahoma*, 283.

[30]*Our Brother in Red*, September 28, 1889, 4-5; Thoburn and Wright, *Oklahoma*, II, 720; Walrond, "Early Annals of the Muskogee Bar Association," *Muskgoee Phoenix*, September 23, 1905.

[31]*Ibid.*, *Our Brother in Red*, September 28, 1889, 5.

[32]Thoburn and Wright, *Oklahoma*, II, 720.

[33]*Harlow's Weekly* (Oklahoma City), March 13, 1926, 3.

[34]*Daily Oklahoman*, January 28, 1934, 3-A; Thoburn and Wright, *Oklahoma*, II, 921-922, III, 387-389; *Harlow's Weekly*, March 13, 1926, 3; Joseph B. Thoburn, *A Standard History of Oklahoma*, (5 vols.; Chicago: The American Historical Society, 1916), III, 1015-1016.

[35]Act of May 2, 1890, 26 *Stat.* 81; Shirk, "Judicial System of Oklahoma," 79-80.

[36]Z.T. Walrond, "The Annals of the Muskogee Bar Association," Muskogee Bar Association, *Proceedings* (Muskogee, 1905-06), 16-17; Act of May 2, 1890, 26 *Stat.* 81.

[37]*Sixty-Second Annual Report of the Commissioner of Indian Affairs to the Secretary of the Interior*, 1893 (Washington: Government Printing Office, 1893), 149.

[38]Walrond, "The Annals of the Muskogee Bar Association," 17.

[39]Act of March 1, 1889, 25 *Stat.* 783.

[40]*Sixty-Second Annual Report of the Commissioner of Indian Affairs*, 149.

[41]Indian Territory Bar Association, *Proceedings, Fourth Annual Meeting*, 70.

[42]Hefley, "Tobucksy County Courthouse," 33.

[43]"Indian-Pioneer History," CI, 412.

[44]William P. Thompson, "Courts of the Cherokee Nation," *The Chronicles of Oklahoma*, II, (March, 1924), 72-73.

[45]Indian Territory Bar Association, *Proceedings, Fourth Annual Meeting*, 68.

[46]Walrond, "The Annals of the Muskogee Bar Association," 18.

[47]*Ibid.*, 17.

[48]*Ibid.*, 19.

[49]Indian Territory Bar Association, *Proceedings, Fourth Annual Meeting*, 69-70.

[50]"Indian-Pioneer History," XXVI, 456; [Howard Berry], *Moman Pruiett, Criminal Lawyer* (Oklahoma City: Harlow Publishing Co., 1945) 75.

[51]"Indian-Pioneer History," Vol. 31, 311-312.

Chapter 6

[1]S.J. Norton, *et al.*, "Resolution of Respect for and in Appreciation of Honorable Charles B. Stuart," *The Chronicles of Oklahoma*, XV, (June, 1937), 228-237.

[2]Indian Territory Bar Association, *Proceedings, Fourth Annual Meeting*, 53.

[3]Debo, *The Rise and Fall of the Choctaw Republic*, 173-174.

[4]Silian [sic.] Lewis Execution" envelope, Robert L. Williams Collection, Oklahoma State Historical Society, Oklahoma City, Oklahoma. Letter, March 20, 1989, T.F. Dukes to author, indicates the Choctaw attorney was Gilbert W. Dukes.

[5]*Life in Oklahoma*, (Oklahoma City), IX, May, 1940, 10-16; *Daily Oklahoman*, January 20, 1935, 11-C; "Indian-Pioneer History," XLI, 220-230.

[6]Indian Territory Bar Association, *Proceedings, Fourth Annual Meeting*, 53.

[7]Walrond, "The Annals of the Muskogee Bar Association," 17-18.

[8]*Ibid.*, 22-23.

[9]*Ibid.*

[10]D.C. Gideon, *Indian Territory* (New York: The Lewis Publishing Co., 1901), 511-512.

[11]"Napoleon Bonaparte Maxey," *Chronicles of Oklahoma*, X, (December, 1932), 611.

[12]*Sixty-Second Annual Report of the Commissioner of Indian Affairs*, 149.

[13]Foreman, *History of Oklahoma*, 285-286.

[14]*Sixty-Second Annual Report of the Commissioner of Indian Affairs*, 149.

[15]*Ibid.*, 149-150.

[16]Walrond, "The Annals of the Muskogee Bar Association," 18.

[17]Act of March 1, 1895, 28 *Stat.* 693.

[18]Foreman, *History of Oklahoma*, 285-287.

[19]Act to March 1, 1895, 28 *Stat.* 693.

[20]Thoburn and Wright, *Oklahoma*, II, 722.

[21]Act of March 1, 1895, 28 *Stat.* 693.

[22]Foreman, *History of Oklahoma*, 293-294.

[23]Walrond, "The Annals of the Muskogee Bar Association," 27, 28.

²⁴"In Memoriam, Hosea Townsend," 23 Okl. viii-ix.
²⁵Benedict, *Muskogee and Northeastern Oklahoma*, I, 389.
²⁶E. Benjamin Andrews, *The History of the Last Quarter Century in the United States, 1870-1895*, (2 vols.; New York: Charles Scribner's Sons, 1896), II, 172-173.
²⁷Houts, *From Gun to Gavel*, 28-30.
²⁸Act of June 7, 1897, 30 *Stat.* 84.
²⁹Act of April 28, 1904, 33 *Stat.* 573.
³⁰J. Stanley Clark, "The Career of John R. Thomas," *Chronicles of Oklahoma*, LII, (Summer, 1974), 152-179; J. Stanley Clark, "Carolyn Thomas Foreman," *Chronicles of Oklahoma* XLV, (Winter, 1967-68), 370, 371; *Harlow's Weekly*, January 24, 1914, 4.
³¹Clark, "The Career of John R. Thomas," 163-165.
³²*Annual Reports of the Department of the Interior for the Fiscal Year Ended June 30, 1898, Indian Affairs* (Washington: Government Printing Office, 1898), 96-100; Grant Foreman, "Horace Speed," *Chronicles of Oklahoma*, XXV, (Spring, 1947), 5-6; Clark, "The Career of John R. Thomas," 165-167; David R. Wrone and Russell S. Nelson, Jr., eds, *Who's the Savage? A Documentary History of the Mistreatment of the Native American Indians* (Greenwich, Conn.: Fawcett Publications, Inc., 1973), 443-451; Geraldine M. Smith, "Violence on the Oklahoma Territory-Seminole National Border: The Mont Ballard Case" (unpublished Master of Arts thesis, University of Oklahoma, 1957), 104.

Chapter 7
¹"Historical Oklahoma, Courts" vertical file, pamphlet, "Criminal Trial Docket," Western History Collection, University of Oklahoma.
²Houts, *From Gun to Gavel*, 35-36.
³"Indian-Pioneer History," XLIV, 459.
⁴Houts, *From Gun to Gavel*, 44-46; [Berry], *Moman Pruiett*, 156.
⁵"Indian-Pioneer History," XIX, 410-411; Thoburn and Wright, *Oklahoma*, III, 83-84.
⁶"Indian-Pioneer History," XIX, 409-410.
⁷Wellington Lee Merwine, "Old Fleetfoot, Okmulgee's Last Timber Wolf," *Harlow's Weekly*, September 16, 1922, 10.
⁸Walrond, "The Annals of the Muskogee Bar Association," 25-26.
⁹"Indian-Pioneer History," LXXIV, 433-434.
¹⁰*Ibid.*, 438.
¹¹*Ibid.*, XX, 403.
¹²*Ibid.*, XXI, 210-211.
¹³*Ibid.*, XV, 449.
¹⁴Julia K. Sparger, "Young Ardmore," *Chronicles of Oklahoma*, XLIII, (Winter, 1965-66), 405-406.
¹⁵May 23, 1895.
¹⁶"Indian-Pioneer History," CIX, 524.
¹⁷Walrond, "The Annals of the Muskogee Bar Association," 24-25.
¹⁸Hill, *A History of the State of Oklahoma*, II, (1909), 480-481; Douglas, *The History of Tulsa*, I, 166.
¹⁹Glenn Condon, "How Tulsa Became a Court Town," *Tulsa Daily World*, December 8, 1957, magazine section, 13.
²⁰Douglas, *The History of Tulsa*, I, 165-166; Charles Evans, "Harry Campbell," *Chronicles of Oklahoma*, XXVIII, (Winter, 1950-51), 380.
²¹"Indian-Pioneer History," LXXIX, 360-361.
²²Evans, "Harry Campbell," XXVIII, 377-378.
²³Lon R. Stansbery, *The Passing of 3-D Ranch* (New York: Buffalo-Head Press, 1966), 81.
²⁴Willams, "The Judicial History of Oklahoma," 134.
²⁵Joseph A. Gill, Jr., "Judge Joseph Albert Gill, 1854-1933," *Chronicles of Oklahoma*, XII, (September, 1934), 375-376.
²⁶La-vere Shoenfelt Anderson, "Judge Gill Recalls Days of 'Bad Men' and Tribal Justice," *Tulsa Daily World*, September 15, 1929, sec. 4, 12.
²⁷*Ibid.*

Chapter 8
¹"Life and Times of Robert L. Williams," Robert L. Williams Collection, Oklahoma Historical Society, Oklahoma City, Oklahoma, Manuscript No. 26, 14-16.
²James Ralph Scales, "Political History of Oklahoma, 1907-1949" (unpublished Ph.D. dissertation, University of Oklahoma, 1949), 176; *Daily Oklahoman*, April 10, 1948 25-A; Edward Everett Dale and James D. Morrison, *Pioneer Judge: The Life of Robert Lee Williams* (Cedar Rapids, Iowa: The Torch Press, 1958), 46-47: Charles Evans,

"Robert Lee Williams," *Chronicles of Oklahoma* , XXVI, (Summer, 1948), 128.
³*Ibid.*, Dale and Morrison, *Pioneer Judge*, 47.
⁴*Ibid.*, 48-61; Evans, "Robert Lee Williams," 129.
⁵*Ibid.*, 64-66; Mrs. Fanny Pate Hicks, "George L. Pate," *Chronicles of Oklahoma*, VIII, 137.
⁶"Life and Times of Robert L. Williams," Manuscript No. 16, 16-A.
⁷*Ibid.*, 1a-2a; Dale and Morrison, *Pioneer Judge*, 67-68.
⁸Judge R.L. Williams address, typescript, "Proceedings of the Annual Meeting of the State Bar of Oklahoma, 1933," Oklahoma Bar Association, Oklahoma City, Oklahoma, 147.
⁹Dale and Morrison, *Pioneer Judge*, 90-91.
¹⁰Keith L. Bryant, Jr., *Alfalfa Bill Murray* (Norman: University of Oklahoma Press, 1968), 3-19.
¹¹Murray, *Memoirs of Governor Murray*, I, 183-185.
¹²*Ibid.*, 184-185.
¹³Bryant, *Alfalfa Bill Murray*, 20.
¹⁴*Ibid.*; Murray, *Memoris of Governor Murray*, I, 199.
¹⁵*Ibid.*
¹⁶Bryant, *Alfalfa Bill Murray*, 22; Gordon Hines, *Alfalfa Bill: An Intimate Biography* (Oklahoma City, Oklahoma Press, 1932), 102-103; Murray, *Memoirs of Governor Murray*, I, 200.
¹⁷*Ibid.*
¹⁸*Ibid.*, 201.
¹⁹*Ibid.*, 201-202; Hines, *Alfalfa Bill*, 114.
²⁰Murray, *Memoirs of Governor Murray*, I, 210-211.
²¹*Ibid.*, 205.
²²*Ibid.*, 200; Hines, *Alfalfa Bill*, 118.
²³*Ibid.*, 139-140; Bryant, *Alfalfa Bill Murray*, 33.
²⁴Edwin C. McReynolds, *Oklahoma: A History of the Sooner State* (Norman: University of Oklahoma Press, 1960), 361.
²⁵Murray, *Memoirs of Governor Murray*, I, 246-247.
²⁶Bryant, *Alfalfa Bill Murray*, 28, 33; Murray, *Memoirs of Governor Murray*, I, 267-268.
²⁷*Ibid.*, 289, 295; Bryant, *Alfalfa Bill Murray* 33.

Chapter 9
¹"Indian-Pioneer History," XCVIII, 293-295.
²Kappler, *Indian Affairs*, I, 2d ed., 79; Act of March 3, 1893, 27 *Stat.* 645; U.S., Congress, House, Committee on Indian Affairs, *Laws Relating to the Five Civilized Tribes in Oklahoma, 1890 to 1914*, 63d Cong., 3d Sess., 1915 (Washington: Government Printing Office, 1915), 114-115.
³Muriel H. Wright, *Guide to the Indian Tribes of Oklahoma* (Norman: University of Oklahoma Press, 1979), 19.
⁴Kappler, *Indian Affairs*, I, 2d. ed., 81; Act of June 10, 896, 29 *Stat.* 339; *Laws Relating to the Five Civilized Tribes*, 193.
⁵*Ibid.*, 192; Kappler, *Indian Affairs*, I, 2d. ed., 81; Act of June 10, 1896, 29 *Stat.* 339.
⁶Loren N. Brown, "The Choctaw-Chickasaw Court Citizens," *Chronicles of Oklahoma*, XVI, (December, 1938), 428.
⁷*Ibid.*, 434-435.
⁸Edward Davis, "The Mississippi Choctaws," *Chronicles of Oklahoma*, X, (June, 1932), 263; *Wallace v. Adams*, 204 U.S. 415 (1907).
⁹Brown, "The Choctaw-Chickasaw Court Citizens," 437.
¹⁰Kappler, *Indian Affairs*, I, 2d. ed., 776-779; Act of July 1, 1902, 32 *Stat.* 641; *Laws Relating to the Five Civilized Tribes*, 397-401.
¹¹Angie Debo, *And Still The Waters Run* (Princeton: Princeton University Press, 1940), 39-40; Brown, "The Choctaw-Chickasaw Court Citizens," 441; Davis, "The Mississippi Choctaws," 264.
¹²Brown, "The Choctaw-Chickasaw Court Citizens," 442; Debo, *And Still the Waters Run*, 40; Davis, "The Mississippi Choctaws," 264.
¹³Debo, *And Still the Waters Run*, 40-41.
¹⁴Foreman, *History of Oklahoma*, 300-301; Gibson, *Oklahoma*, 325-326.
¹⁵Debo, *And Still The Waters Run*, 62-63.
¹⁶Walrond, "The Annals of the Muskogee Bar Association," 35.
¹⁷Stanley Clark, "Grant Foreman," *The Chronicles of Oklahoma*, XXXI, (Autumn, 1953), 226-242.
¹⁸George Elliott Sweet, *Gentleman in Oil* (Los Angeles: Science Press, 1966), 22-23.
¹⁹*Ibid.*, 35-37; Lyle H. Boren and Dale Boren, *Who Is Who In Oklahoma* (Guthrie: The Co-Operative Publishing Company, 1935), 169-170.

221

[20]Kappler, *Indian Affairs*, I, 2d ed., 100, 653-654, 726, 739, III, 24; Act of June 28, 1898, 30 *Stat.* 495; Act of July 1, 1898, 30 *Stat.*, 567; Act of March 1, 1901, 31 *Stat.* 848; Act of March 1, 1901, 31 *Stat.* 861; Act of March 3, 1903, 32 *Stat*, 1008; Gibson, *Oklahoma*, 324.

[21]Shirk, "The Judicial Systen of Oklahoma," 79.

Chapter 10

[1]Muriel H. Wright, "Notes on Colonel Elias C. Boudinot," *Chronicles of Oklahoma*, XLI (Winter, 1963-1964), 382-407.

[2]Kappler, *Indian Affairs*, II, 945; Act of July 19, 1866, 14 *Stat.* 801.

[3]Act of July 20, 1868, 15 *Stat.* 167; Wardell, *Political History of the Cherokee Nation*, 291.

[4]Robert K. Hiemann, "The Cherokee Tobacco Case," *Chronicles of Oklahoma*, XLI, (Autumn, 1963), 303-316; Foreman, *History of Oklahoma*, 187; "Indian-Pioneer History," XCVIII, 352-353.

[5]*The Cherokee Tobacco*, 11 Wallace (U.S.), 616 (1870); Foreman, *History of Oklahoma* 188.

[6]Edward Everett Dale and Gaston Litton, *Cherokee Cavaliers: Forty Years of Cherokee History as told in the Correspondence of the Ridge-Watie-Boudinot Family* (Norman: University of Oklahoma Press, 1969), 295.

[7]Hiemann, "The Cherokee Tobacco Case," 321.

[8]Hill, *History of Oklahoma*, I, 174.

[9]*Ibid.*, 170-183, 162-163; Dora Ann Stewart, *The Government and Development of Oklahoma Territory*, (Oklahoma City: Harlow Publishing Co., 1933), 331.

[10]Wright, "Notes on Colonel Elias C. Boudinot," 397.

[11]Gaston Litton, *History of Oklahoma at the Golden Anniversary of Statehood* (4 vols.; New York: Lewis Historical Publishing Co., 1957), I, 246.

[12]Edward Everett Dale and Jesse Lee Radar, *Readings in Oklahoma History* (Evanston, Illinois: Row, Peterson & Co., 1930), 442-444; Thoburn and Wright, *Oklahoma*, II, 887-888.

[13]Gibson, *Oklahoma*, 288-292; A recent biography of Payne is Stan Hoig, *David L. Payne: The Oklahoma Boomer* (Oklahoma City: Western Heritage Books, 1980).

[14]Gittinger, *Formation of Oklahoma*, 138-140.

[15]Carl Coke Rister, *Land Hunger: David L. Payne and the Oklahoma Boomers* (Norman: University of Oklahoma Press, 1942), 90-96; *United States v. David L. Payne*, 8 Fed.Rep. 883; *United States v. Payne et al*, 22 Fed. Rep. 426.

[16]Gittinger, *Formation of Oklahoma*, 140-141.

Chapter 11

[1]Act of March 3, 1885, 23 *Stat.* 362; Act of March 1, 1889, 25 *Stat.* 757; Act of March 2, 1889, 25 *Stat* 1003.

[2]Thoburn and Wright, *History of Oklahoma*, II, 533, 892.

[3]Act of March 2, 1889, 25 *Stat* 1003.

[4]Hill, *History of the State of Oklahoma*, I, 273; John Alley, *City Beginnings in Oklahoma Territory* (Norman: University of Oklahoma Press, 1939), 11.

[5]O.H. Richards, "Memories of an 89'er," *Chronicles of Oklahoma*, XXVI, 1 (Spring, 1948), 3.

[6]*Act of January 6, 1883*, 22 *Stat.* 400; Act of March 1, 1889, 25 *Stat.* 783; James L. Brown, "Early and Important Litigations," *Sturm's Oklahoma Magazine*, VIII, 2 (April, 1909), 26.

[7]Angelo C. Scott, *The Story of Oklahoma City* (Oklahoma City: Times-Journal Publishing Co., 1939), 21; Berlin B. Chapman, "Oklahoma City, from Public Land to Private Property," *Chronicles of Oklahoma*, XXXVII, 2 (Summer, 1959), 227-229.

[8]Hill, *History of the State of Oklahoma*, I, 272-274.

[9]Gittinger, *Formation of Oklahoma*, 192.

[10]Williams, "The Judicial History of Oklahoma," 136-137; *Guthrie Daily Leader*, April 18, 1976, Congressional section, 8.

[11]Hill, *History of the State of Oklahoma*, II (1908), 121-122.

[12]Richards, "Memories of an 89'er," 3.

[13]Rex Harlow, *Oklahoma Leaders* (Oklahoma City: Harlow Publishing Company 1928), 29-36, 397-406; Thoburn and Wright, *Oklahoma*, III, 271; *Guthrie Register News*, April 17, 1955.

[14]A.G.C. Bierer, "John Hazelton Cotteral," *Chronicles of Oklahoma*, XIV, 1 (March, 1936), 49-52; Harlow, *Oklahoma Leaders*, 29-36.

[15]Thoburn and Wright, *Oklahoma*, III, 271.

[16]Harlow, *Oklahoma Leaders*, 397-406.

[17]The 89ers, *Oklahoma: The Beautiful Land* (Oklahoma City: The Times-Journal Publishing Company, 1943), 60.

[18]*Ibid.*, 198; Harlow, *Oklahoma Leaders*, 177-178.

[19]89ers, *Oklahoma*, 199-201.

[20]*The Guthrie Daily Leader*, April 18, 1976, "Territorial Government Section," 7.

[21]89ers, *Oklahoma*, 202-203.

[22]*Ibid*, 203.

[23]Harlow, *Oklahoma Leaders*, 178-179.

[24]Thoburn and Wright, *Oklahoma*, II, 893.

[25]Dan Peery, "Introduction, "The First Two Years," *Chronicles of Oklahoma*, VII, 3 (September, 1929), 294-295.

[26]*Ibid.*, 298.

[27]Scott, *The Story of Oklahoma City*, 30, 121.

[28]*Ibid.*, 197.

[29]Alley, *City Beginnings*, 39.

[30]Peery, "Introduction, "The First Two Years," 298.

[31]*Ibid* 305-306.

[32]Thoburn and Wright, *Oklahoma*, IV, 524-525.; 89ers, *Oklahoma*, 323-324.

[33]*Ibid.*, 143-144.

[34]Carolyn Thomas Foreman, *Oklahoma Imprints, 1835-1907: A History of Printing in Oklahoma Before Statehood* (Norman: University of Oklahoma Press, 1936), 325-326; Nudie Williams, "The Black Press in Oklahoma: The Formative Years, 1889-1907," *Chronicles of Oklahoma*, LXI, 3 (Fall, 1983), 315; *Daily Oklahoman*, April 23, 1939, 45.

[35]Albert McRill, *And Satan Came Also: An Inside Story of a City's Social and Political History* (Oklahoma City: Britton Publishing Company, 1955), 16-17.

[36]Interview with Albert S. Gilles, Norman, Oklahoma, August 5, 1978.

[37]*Guthrie Daily Leader*, April 18, 1976, "Congressional Section," 8.

[38]Bunky [Irving Geffs], *The First Eight Months of Oklahoma City* (Oklahoma City: The McMaster Printing Co., 1890), 65-66; McRill, *And Satan Came Also*, 9-11.

[39]Alley, *City Beginnings*, 22-23.

[40]*Oklahoma Law Journal* (Oklahoma City), XIV, 3 (September, 1915), 19.

[41]Kingfisher Study Club, comp., *Echoes of Eighty-Nine* (Kingfisher: Kingfisher Times and Free Press, 1939), 192.

[42]Williams, "The Judicial History of Oklahoma," 140, 137-138; 89ers, *Oklahoma*, 168-169.

[43]Hill, *History of the State of Oklahoma*, I, 226.

[44]*Ibid.*, 239.

Chapter 12

[1]Act of May 2, 1890, 26 *Stat.* 81.

[2]Thomas Arthur Hazell, "George Washington Steele, Governor of Oklahoma Territory, 1890-1891," *Chronicles of Oklahoma*, LIII, 1 (Spring, 1975), 9-22.

[3]Berlin B. Chapman, *The Founding of Stillwater* (Oklahoma City: Times-Journal Publishing Co., 1948), 181.

[4]*Daily Oklahoman*, April 19, 1925, 26.

[5]June 7, 1890, 5.

[6]*Oklahoma State Capital*, May 31, 1890, 5; *Daily Oklahoman*, November 14, 1954, 32.

[7]*Oklahoma State Capital*, May 31, 1890, 2.

[8]*Ibid.*

[9]State Bar of Oklahoma, *Proceedings, First Special Meeting* (Oklahoma City, February 21, 22, 1930), 87-88.

[10]*Oklahoma State Capital*, June 14, 1890, 5; *Daily Oklahoman*, November 14, 1954, 32; Rock, *Illustrated History of Oklahoma*, 186-187.

[11]1-4 Okl. St. Anno. xi (1964).

[12]Act of May 2, 1890, 26 *Stat.* 87.

[13]A.G.C. Bierer, "Early Day Courts And Lawyers," *Chronicles of Oklahoma*, VIII, 1 (March, 1930), 9-10.

[14]*Guthrie Daily Leader*, April 18, 1976, 2B.

[15]*Ibid.*

[16]A.G.C. Bierer, "Early Day Courts and Lawyers," 2.

[17]*Ibid.*

[18]*William A. Allison v. Charles A. Berger et al.*, 1 Okl. 1, 25 P. 511 (1890).

[19]*Ex parte Halley*, 1 Okl. 12, 25 P. 514 (1890).

[20]26 *Stat.* 1546.

[21]Brown, "Early and Important Litigations," *Sturm's Oklahoma Magazine*, VIII, 28.

[22]Hill, *History of the State of Oklahoma*, I, 256-258.

[23]B.B. Chapman, "The Legal Sooners of 1889 in Oklahoma," *Chronicles of Oklahoma*, XXXV, 4 (Winter, 1957-1958), 388-389, 397-405; Hill, *History of the State of Oklahoma*, I, 258-259.

[24]Chapman, "The Legal Sooners of 1889 in Oklahoma,"405-408; *The Norman Transcript*, March 24, 1893, 1.

[25]*Alexander F. Smith, Appt., v. Eddy B. Townsend*, 1 Okl. 117, 148 U.S. 490 (1893).

[26]Hill, *History of the State of Oklahoma*, I, 259-263.

[27]*Ibid.*, 260-261.

[28]Peery, "Introduction, The First Two Years,"284-285.

[29]*The Autobiography of Charles Francis Colcord*, 1859-1934 (Tulsa: Privately printed, 1970), 158-160.

[30]*Ibid.*, 159-160.

[31]Hill, *History of the State of Oklahoma*, I, 261.

[32]*Ibid.*, II (1908), 36-37.

[33]*Ibid.*, 37; Foreman, "Horace Speed," 5.

[34]Hill, *History of the State of Oklahoma*, 1, 261.

[35]*Ibid.*, 261-262

[36]*Ibid.*

[37]*Ibid.*, 263.

Chapter 13

[1]Harry E. Henslick, "Abraham Jefferson Seay, Governor of Oklahoma Territory, 1892-1893,"in LeRoy H. Fischer, ed., *Territorial Governors of Oklahoma*, (Oklahoma City: Oklahoma Historical Society, 1975), 28-29; *Guthrie Daily Leader*, April 18, 1976, "Territorial Government Section," 5.

[2] Matthew J. Kane, "Recollections of the Judicial Career of Governor Seay, *Harlow's Weekly*, October 7, 1922, 7.

[3]Williams, "The Judicial History of Oklahoma," 143.

[4]Dan W. Peery, ed., "Autobiography of Governor A.J. Seay," *The Chronicles of Oklahoma*, XVII, (March, 1939), 44.

[5]Kane, "Recollections of the Judicial Career of Governor Seay," 6; Peery, "Autobiography of Governor A.J. Seay, 43.

[6]*Ibid.*, 45.

[7]89ers, *Oklahoma*, 65-66; Kingfisher Study Club, *Echoes of Eighty-nine*, 9.

[8]89ers, *Oklahoma*, 65-66.

[9]Homer Croy, *Trigger Marshal: The Story of Chris Madsen* (New York: Duell, Sloan & Pearce, 1958), 126.

[10]Peery, "Autobiography of Governor A.J. Seay," 44-45.

[11]Stewart, *The Government and Development of Oklahoma Territory*, 235-236.

[12]Kane, "Recollections of the Judicial Career of Governor Seay." 6.

[13]*Ibid.*

[14]Henslick, "Abraham Jefferson Seay," 44.

[15]Stewart, *The Government and Development of Oklahoma Territory*, 241.

[16]Berlin B. Chapman, "Oklahoma City, From Public Land to Private Property,"*Chronicles of Oklahoma*, XXXVII, 4 (Winter, 1959-60), 451, 452.

[17]Hill, History of the State of Oklahoma, II, 501-502.

[18]Berlin B. Chapman, "Oklahoma City, From Public Land to Private Property,"451.

[19]*Ibid.*, 451-452.

[20]*Ibid.*, 452.

[21]Williams, "The Judicial History of Oklahoma," 143.

[22] Thoburn and Wright, *Oklahoma*, II, 722.

[23]Carl Coke Rister, *No Man's Land* (Norman: University of Oklahoma Press, 1948), 160.

[24]Sanford Babcock, Taped Interview, Living Legends Library, Oklahoma Christian University, Oklahoma City, Oklahoma.

[25]*Harlow's Weekly*, June 18, 1932, p. 14; Scott, *The Story of Oklahoma City*, 135-136.

[26]C.A. Squire, "Old Grand, Ghost Town," *Chronicles of Oklahoma*, XXVIII, 4 (Winter, 1950-51), 400.

[27]"Indian-Pioneer History," XCV, 243-244.

[28]*Ibid.*

[29]*Ibid.*, 244.

[30]*Ibid.*

[31]*Ibid.*, 245.

[32]*Ibid.*, XC, 324.

[33]*Ibid.*, XCV, 246; Squire, "Old Grand, Ghost Town," 400.

[34]"Indian-Pioneer History," XCV, 246; *Harlow's Weekly*, March 20, 1937, 7.

[35]*Ibid.*

[36]O.H. Richards, "Early Days in Day County," *Chronicles of Oklahoma*, XXVI, 3, (Autumn, 1948), 315.

[37]*Harlow's Weekly*, June 24, 1939, 8.

[38]Erwin C. Surrency, "Federal District Court Judges and the History of Their Courts," *Federal Rule Decisions*, XL, 264, 268; Act of December 21, 1893, 28 *Stat.* 20; Thoburn and Wright, *Oklahoma*, II, 722.

[39]Squire, "Old Grand, Ghost Town," 401.

[40]"Indian-Pioneer History," XC, 325-326.

[41]Thoburn and Wright, *Oklahoma*, II, 722; *Oklahoma State Capital*, June 21, 1995, 1; Glenn Shirley, *West of Hell's Fringe* (Norman: University of Oklahoma Press, 1978), 285-286.

[42]*Daily Oklahoman*, April 19, 1925; *Edmond Sun-Democrat*, March 24, 1899, 4.

[43]*Daily Oklahoman*, April 19, 1925.

[44]Litton, *History of Oklahoma*, II, 471; Hill, *History of the State of Oklahoma*, II 501-502.

[45]Basil R. Wilson, comp., *Directory and Manual of the State of Oklahoma* (Oklahoma City: Oklahoma Election Board, 1967), 140.

[46]December 23, 1898, 6.

[47]89ers, *Oklahoma*, 99.

[48]*Ibid.*

[49]*Ibid.*

[50]Nat M. Taylor, *A Brief History of Roger Mills County*, n.p., n.d.

[51]Thoman A. Edwards, "Early Days in the C & A," *Chronicles of Oklahoma*, XXVII, (Summer, 1949), 148; Lawrence N. Morgan, "Judge Thomas A. Edwards,"*Chronicles of Oklahoma*, XXXIII, (Summer, 1955), 130.

[52] Edwards, "Early Days in the C & A," 154.

[53]*Ibid.*, 155.

[54]*Ibid.*, 155-156.

[55]*Ibid.*, 156.

[56]*Ibid.*

[57]*Ibid.*, 157.

[58]Morgan, "Judge Thomas A. Edwards," 130-131.

[59]Edwards, "Early days in the C & A," 148.

[60]*Harlow's Weekly*, April 2, 1938, 15.

[61]Williams, "The Judicial History of Oklahoma," 147; Surrency, "Federal District Judges," 268.

[62]Edwards, "Early Days in the C & A," 158-159.

[63]Thoman A. Higgins, "Stories Relating to Oklahoma Territorial Courts and Law,"*Chronicles of Oklahoma*, XXXVIII, (Spring, 1960), 106.

[64]Hill, *History of the State of Oklahoma*, II (1908), 529.

[65]"Indian-Pioneer History," XII, 424; Edwards, "Early Days in the C & A," 159-160.

[66]*Ibid.*, 160.

[67]*Ibid.*, 160-161.

[68]*Ibid.*, 161; Act of March 3, 1906, 34 *Stat.* 50.

Chapter 14

[1]Act of March 2, 1889, 25 *Stat.* 1003.

[2]Act of May 2, 1890, 26 *Stat.* 81.

[3]Foreman, *History of Oklahoma*, 244-245; Gibson, *Oklahoma*, 299-300.

[4]Litton, *History of Oklahoma*, IV, 616.

[5]"Indian-Pioneer History," Vol. LVIII, 325-326.

[6]*Ibid.*, 326-327.

[7]Interview with Albert S. Gilles, Norman, Oklahoma, September 17, 1978.

[8]Litton, *History of Oklahoma*, IV, 616.

[9]Stewart, *Government and Development of Oklahoma Territory*, 246.

[10]*Ibid.*, 246-247; Scott, *Story of Oklahoma City*, 110.

[11]Stewart, *Government and Development of Oklahoma Territory*, 254-255, citing *Weekly Oklahoma State Capital*, July 15, 1893.

[12]Williams, "Judicial History of Oklahoma," 144; Surrency, "Federal District Judges," 268.

[13]Scott, *Story of Oklahoma City* 151-152; Henry W. Scott, *Distinguished American Lawyers with Their Struggles and Triumphs in the Forum* (New York: Charles L. Webster & Co., 1891), *passim*.

[14]89ers, *Oklahoma*, 99-100.

[15]*Daily Oklahoman*, April 19, 1925.

[16]Thomas Wildcat Alford, *Civilization* (Norman: University of Oklahoma Press, 1979), 148-152.

[17]March 14, 1895, l.

[18]Scott, *Story of Oklahoma City*, 106.

[19]*Daily Oklahoman*, March 14, 1895, l.

[20]Nix, *Oklahombres*, 175-178.

[21]*Daily Oklahoman*, March 14, 1895, l.

[22]Scott, *Story of Oklahoma City*, 152

[23]*Ibid.*

[24]Hill, *History of the State of Oklahoma*, II 116-118; Foreman, *Oklahoma Imprints*, 371.

[25]*In the Matter of the Application of Frank McMaster for a writ of Habeas Corpus, 2 Okla. 435, 37 P. 598 (1894).*

[26]W.F. Kerr and Ina Gainer, *The Story of Oklahoma City*, (3 vols.; Chicago: S.J. Clarke Publishing Co., 1922), 152-153.

[27]Mrs. Tom B. Ferguson, *They Carried the Torch: The Story of Oklahoma's Pioneer Newspapers* (Kansas City: Burton Publsihing Co., 1937), 84.

[28]*In the Matter of the Application of Frank McMaster for a writ of Habeas Corpus, 2 Okla. 435, 37 P. 598 (1894).*

[29]Kerr and Gainer, *Story of Oklahoma City*, 152-153; 89ers, *Oklahoma*, 115.

[30]*In the Matter of Disbarment Proceedings Against J.L. Brown, 2 Okla. 590, 39 P. 469 (1895); J.L. Brown vs. J.H. Woods et al., 2 Okla. 601 (1895), 39 P. 473 (1895).*

[31]Oklahoma State Bar Association, *Proceedings, Fifth Annual Meeting*, 76-77; for another version of the Scott affair, see also Joseph B. Thoburn, *A Standard History of Oklahoma*, (5 vols.; Chicago: The American Historical Society, 1916), III, 1054.

[32]89ers, *Oklahoma*, 115-116.

Chapter 15

[1]*Daily Oklahoman*, April 19, 1925; Shirley, *West of Hell's Fringe*, 285.

[2]*Okl. Stat*, 1893, 875, ch. 66, sec. 665.

[3]89ers, *Oklahoma*, 258.

[4]Scott, *Story of Oklahoma City*, 141-142.

[5]*Daily Oklahoman*, April 19, 1925.

[6]*Ibid.*

[7]*The Central Law Journal* (St. Louis, Mo.), XXXVII, (July-December, 1893), 41.

[8]*Daily Oklahoman*, April 19, 1925.

[9]Scott, *Story of Oklahoma City*, 142.

[10]*Daily Oklahoman*, April 19, 1925.

[11]Scott, *Story of Oklahoma City*, 142-143.

[12]*Daily Oklahoman*, April 19, 1925.

[13]*Ibid.*

[14]Ferguson, *They Carried The Torch*, 52.

[15]*Lorenzo Irwin vs. Eliza Jane Irwin, 2 Okl. 180, 37 P. 548 (1894).* The framers of Oklahoma's Constitution made certain by Art. 7, Sec. 12, that county probate courts would not possess divorce jurisdiction.

[16]*Guthrie Daily Leader*, July 27, 1894, 2, September 9, 1894, 1; *The Central Law Journal*, XXXIX, (July-December, 1894), 415.

[17]*Okl. Laws*, 1895, 107, ch. XXII.

[18]*Anne M. Beach v. Charles F. Beach*, Jr., 4 Okl. 359, 46 P. 514 (1896).

[19]*Ibid.*, *Edmond Sun-Democrat*, September 11, 1896, 1.

[20]*Ibid.*

[21]*Ibid.*, March 20, 1896, 1.

[22]Act of May 25, 1896, 29 *Stat.* 136; Scott, *The Story of Oklahoma City*, 142.

Chapter 16

[1]Joe. B. Milam, "The Opening of the Cherokee Outlet,"*Chronicles of Oklahoma*, IX, (September, 1931), 269.

[2]*Ibid.*, 269-270; Dale and Rader, *Readings in Oklahoma History*, 431-434.

[3]Edward Everett Dale, "The Cherokee Strip Live Stock Association," *Chronicles of Oklahoma*, V, (March, 1927), 69-70; Dale and Rader, *Readings in Oklahoma History*, 434-440.

[4]Milam, "The Opening of the Cherokee Outlet," IX, 269.

[5]Dale and Rader, *Readings in Oklahoma History*, 431-434; Dale, "The Cherokee Strip Live Stock Assciation," V, 68-69.

[6]Kappler, *Indian Affairs*, I, 2d ed., 967; Proclamation of August 19, 1893, 28 *Stat.* 1222.

[7]*Daily Oklahoman*, April 26, 1914, 11-C; Thoburn, *Standard History of Oklahoma*, III, 1134-1135; August 19, 1893, 28 *Stat.* 1222; Act of June 6, 1900, 31 *Stat.* 680.

[8]George Rainey, *The Cherokee Strip* (Guthrie: Co-Operative Publishing Co., 1933), 282-283.

[9]Berlin B. Chapman, "Opening of the Cherokee Outlet, An Archival Study,"*Chronicles of Oklahoma*, XL, (Autumn, 1962), 265-266.

[10]Charles F. Barrett, *Oklahoma After Fifty Years* (4 vols.; Hopkinsville, Kentucky: The Historical Record Association, 1941), III, 770-771.

[11]Boren and Boren, *Who Is Who In Oklahoma*, 258; Kenneth L. Tracy, "Henry Simpson Johnston, Governor of Oklahoma, 1927-1929," in Fischer, *Oklahoma's Governors, 1927-1929*, 174-194.

[12]Robert E. Cunningham, *Perry: Pride of the Prairie*, (Stillwater: Frontier Printers, n.d.), 22.

[13]Chapman, "Opening of the Cherokee Outlet," 269-270.

[14]Rainey, *The Cherokee Strip*, 292-293.

[15]Litton, *History of Oklahoma*, III, 252-253; Boren and Boren, *Who Is Who In Oklahoma*, 175.

[16]T.P. Tripp, "Justice Cullison, Pioneer Jurist," *Harlow's Weekly*, November 4, 1933, 5; "Indian-Pioneer History," C, 465-466.

[17]Stephen Jones, "Percy Constance Simons," *Chronicles of Oklahoma*, XLIII, (Summer, 1965), 225-227.

[18]Robert L. Williams, "Judge Jesse James Dunn, 1867-1926," *Chronicles of Oklahoma*, XVIII, (March, 1940), 4-6; H.B. Kelly, "A Tragedy and Trial of No Man's Land,"*The Green Bag*, IX (1897), 494-498; *Cook et at., v. United States*, 138 U. S. 157 (1891).

[19]Williams, "Judge Jesse James Dunn," XVIII, 4.

[20]Manuscript, Justice Jesse J. Dunn Vertical File, Oklahoma Historical Society Library, Oklahoma City, Oklahoma.

[21]Williams, "Judge Jesse James Dunn," XVIII, 8; Walter M. Harrison, *Me and My Big Mouth* (Oklahoma City: Britton Printing Company, 1954), 221-223.

[22]Seigniora Russell Laune, *Sand in My Eyes* (Philadelphia: J.B. Lippincott Co., 1956), 58-59.

[23]Hill, *History of the State of Oklahoma*, II, 489-490; Laune, *Sand in My Eyes*, 59.

[24]*Ibid.*, 78-79.

[25]*Ibid.*, 36-53, *passim*.

Chapter 17

[1]Seigniora Russell Laune, "The Brilliant, Eccentric Temple Houston,"*Sturm's Oklahoma Magazine*, XII, (April, 1911), 20A. The definitive biography of Temple Houston is Glenn Shirley, *Temple Houston: Lawyer with a Gun* (Norman: University of Oklahoma Press, 1980).

[2]*The Sunday Oklahoman*, June 4, 1978, "Television News" section, 32

[3]Paul Laune, "Temple Houston,"*Oklahoma Today*, XIV, (Autumn, 1964), 16.

[4]Mrs. Lige Roberts, "True Son of the Raven Handled Gun at Tascosa Like Plainsman,"*Amarillo Sunday News and Globe*, Fred S. Barde Collection, Oklahoma Historical Society Library, Oklahoma City; R.C. Crane, "Temple Houston, Plains Statesman," *Amarillo Sunday News and Globe*, August 14, 1938; Laune, "Temple Houston," 16; Claude Weaver, "Personal Recollections of Temple Houston,"*Sturm's Oklahoma Magazine*, XII, No. 3 (May, 1911), 22.

[5]Laune, "Temple Houston," 16.

[6]Thoburn, *Standard History of Oklahoma*, IV, 1682-1683; Shirley, *West of Hell's Fringe*, 384-385; *Harlow's Weekly*, October 26, 1912, 9.

[7]Thoburn, *Standard History of Oklahoma*, IV, 1682-1683; Shirley, *West of Hell's Fringe*, 384-385; *Harlow's Weekly*, October 26, 1912, 9.

[8]Albert S. Gilles, Sr., "The Outlaw Who Ran for Governor," *True Frontier* (Fall, 1975), 4.

[9]"Indian-Pioneer History," LXXX, 431-432; CVIII, 481.

[10]*The South and West* (Beaver, Okla.), May 21, 1896, 1; *Daily Oklahoman*, May 16, 1896, 2; *Woodward News*, May 22, 1896, 1; "Indian-Pioneer History," CVIII, 478-486.

[11]Unidentified newspaper clipping, "Temple Houston in Constant Fear of Assassination," Fred S. Barde Collection, Oklahoma Historical Society Library, Oklahoma City; Duane Gage, "Al Jennings, the People's Choice,"*Chronicles of Oklahoma*, XLVI, 243.

[12]Shirley, *West of Hell's Fringe*, 393-411; Richard S. Graves, *Okla-*

homa Outlaws (Oklahoma City: State Printing and Publishing Co., 1915), 107-121; Zoe A. Tilghman, *Outlaw Days* (Oklahoma City: Harlow Publishing Co., 1926), 104-118; *Okmulgee Daily Times*, June 5, 1980, 4B.

[13]53 S.W. 456 (1899).

[14]In re Jennings, 118 F. 479 (1902).

[15]Shirley, *West of Hell's Fringe*, 413.

[16]Unidentified newspaper clipping, "Houston's Pride Wounded," Fred S. Barde Collection, Oklahoma Historical Society Library, Scrapbook, 124.

[17]Unidentified newspaper clipping, Temple Houston Vertical File, Oklahoma Historical Society Library.

[18]*Harlow's Weekly*, February 23, 1924, 13.

[19]Bernice Tune, "Temple Lea Houston," *Woodward County Pioneer Families Before 1915* (Woodward: Plains Indian and Pioneer Historical Foundation, 1975), 208; Frank X. Tolbert, "Sam's Youngest Boy," *True West*, X, (July-August, 1963), 52.

[20]*Daily Oklahoman*, August 20, 1905, 2.

[21]*Oklahoma State Capital*, September 12, 1905.

[22]"Indian-Pioneer History," LXXX, 439.

[23]*Oklahoma State Capital*, September 12, 1905.

[24]*Ibid.*

[25]Laune, "Temple Houston," 16.

[26]Claude Weaver, "Personal Recollections of Temple Houston," *Sturm's Oklahoma Magazine*, XII, 22.

[27]T.C. Richardson, *The Autobiography of the Rambling Longhorn* (Oklahoma City: Farmer-Stockman Magazine, 1959), 42-43.

[28]Higgins, "Stories Relating to Oklahoma Territorial Courts and Law," *Chronicles of Oklahoma*, XXXVIII, 105-106; Nix, *Oklahombres*, 242-243.

[29]*El Reno Democrat*, November 18, 1897, 8; *Alfred Son v. The Territory of Oklahoma*, 5 Okl. 526, 49 P. 923, (1897).

[30]*Ibid.*

[31]Unidentified Newspaper clipping, Fred S. Barde Collection, Oklahoma Historical Society Library, Oklahoma City.

[32]*El Reno Democrat*, November 18, 1897, 8.

[33]Typewritten manuscript, "Temple Houston's Plea in Defense of Alfred Son," Temple Houston Vertical File, Oklahoma Historical Society Library, Oklahoma City.

[34]*Ibid.*

[35]*Ibid.*

[36]*Daily Oklahoman*, August 20, 1905, 2.

[37]Typewritten Manuscript, "Temple Houston's Plea in Defense of Alfred Son," Temple Houston Vertical File, Oklahoma Historical Society Library, Oklahoma City.

[38]*Ibid.*

[39]*El Reno Democrat*, November 18, 1897, 8.

[40]*Woodward Democrat*, May 25, 1899; Harrison, *Me and My Big Mouth*, 263-266.

[41]*Ibid.*

[42]*Ibid.*, 266.

[43]Nix, *Oklahombres*, 243.

[44](New York: P.F. Collier & Son Corp., 1930), 268-273.

[45]Bernice Tune, "Temple Lea Houston," 208.

[46]"Indian-Pioneer History," XL, 379.

[47]Laune, "The Brilliant, Eccentric Temple Houston," *Sturm's Oklahoma Magazine*, XII, 22.

Chapter 18

[1]*United States v. Texas*, 162 U.S. 1 (1896).

[2]Act of May 4, 1896, 29 *Stat.* 113; Gittinger, *Formation of the State of Oklahoma*, 203-204.

[3]"Indian-Pioneer History," CXII, 265; Thomas F. Turner, "Prairie Dog Lawyers," *Panhandle Plains Historical Review*, XI, (1929), 104.

[4]*Ibid.*, 106.

[5]"Indian-Pioneer History," X, 297; LXXVII, 137.

[6]Turner, "Prairie Dog Lawyers," 106-107; Hill, *History of the State of Oklahoma*, II 348-349; "Indian-Pioneer History," CXII, 264.

[7]*Ibid.*, 265.

[8]Hill, History of the State of Oklahoma, II 360-361; *Oklahoma Law Journal*, XIV, (December, 1915), 110.

[9]J. Frank Dobie, *Cow People* (Boston: Little Brown & Co., 1964), 211; *Oklahoma Law Journal*, XIV, (October and November, 1915), 58; "Indian-Pioneer History," CXII, 265.

[10]"Indian-Pioneer History," LXXIII, 133.

[11]*Ibid.*

[12]*Ibid.*, X, 296-297; XL, 379.

[13]*Ibid.*, LXXXVIII, 320; XL, 380; Williams, "Judicial History of Oklahoma," 146.

[14]*Oklahoma Law Journal*, XIV, (October and November, 1915), 58.

[15]Oklahoma State Bar Association, *Proceedings, Seventh Annual Meeting* (Oklahoma City, December 29, 1913), 126-128.

[16]*Oklahoma Law Journal*, XIV, (October and November, 1915), 58.

[17]Berlin B. Chapman, "Dissolution of the Wichita Reservation," *Chronicles of Oklahoma*, XXII, (Summer, 1944), 194-198.

[18]*Ibid.*, 198-199.

[19]*Ibid.*, 194.

[20]*Ibid.*

[21]*Ibid.*, 196.

[22]*Ibid.*, 198

[23]*Ibid.*

[24]*Ibid.*, 202-203.

[25]Act of March 2, 1895, 28 *Stat.* 897.

[26]Act of June 6, 1900, 31 *Stat.* 676.

[27]*Annual Reports of the Department of the Interior for the Fiscal Year Ended June 30, 1903* (Washington: Government Printing Office, 1904), 261-266.

[28]*Lone Wolf, principal chief of the Kiowas, et al., appellants, v. Ethan A. Hitchcock, Secretary of the Interior, et al.*, 187 U.S. 553 (1903); Kappler, *Indian Affairs*, I, 2d ed., 1058-1065.

[29]*Ibid.*, 1010-1016.

[30]A. Emma Estill, "The Great Lottery," *Chronicles of Oklahoma*, IX, (December, 1931), 370, 372.

[31]Lawton Business and Professional Woman's Club, comp., '*Neath August Sun, 1901* (n.p., n.d.), 172-173.

[32]*Ibid.*, 176.

[33]Thoburn and Wright, *Oklahoma*, IV, 592.

[34]Lawton Business and Professional Woman's Club, '*Neath August Sun*, 62.

[35]*Harlow's Weekly*, June 27, 1925, 14.

[36]Lawton Business and Professional Woman's Club, '*Neath August Sun*, 62.

[37]*Ibid.*, 78.

[38]Hill, *History of the State of Oklahoma*, II (1908), 116; Monroe Lee Billington, *Thomas P. Gore, The Blind Senator from Oklahoma* (Lawrence, Kansas: University of Kansas Press, 1967), 10-11.

[39]John McClain Young, *The Life of John McLain Young During the Early Years of Oklahoma* (Miami: Engelhard Press, 1970), 8.

[40]Harlow, *Oklahoma Leaders*, 296-297.

[41]Lawton Business and Professional Woman's Club, '*Neath August Sun*, 74.

[42]*Ibid.*, 21.

[43]*Harlow's Weekly*, June 4, 1920, 5.

[44]Lawton Business and Professional Woman's Club, '*Neath August Sun*, 22

[45]Oklahoma and Indian Territory Bar Association, *Proceedings, First Annual Meeting* (Shawnee, O.T., December 29, 30, 1904), 212-215.

[46]*Ibid.*

[47]"Robert J. Ray, 1864-1931," *Chronicles of Oklahoma*, IX (December, 1931), 485; Wilson, *Directory and Manual of the State of Oklahoma, 1967*, 71.

[48]J.J. Methvin, *In the Limelight or History of Anadarko and Vicinity from the Earliest Days* (Oklahoma City: Walker-Wilson-Tayler Co., n.d.), 103-106.

[49]Berlin B. Chapman, "Settlers on the Neutral Strip," *Chronicles of Oklahoma*, XVIII, (March, 1940), 61-63.

[50]"Indian-Pioneer History," XC, 295.

[51]*Ibid.*, 296.

[52]*Ibid.*, 297-298; Kappler, *Indian Affairs*, I, 2d ed., 1014-1015.

[53]John S. Brooks, *First Administration of Oklahoma* (Oklahoma City: Oklahoma Eng. & Ptg. Co., 1908), 46: "Indian-Pioneer History," XC, 298.

Chapter 19

[1]*Congressional Record: Containing the Proceedings and Debates of the Fifty-First Congress, First Session, also Speical Session of the Senate* (Wash-

ington: Government Printing Office, 1889), XXI, 233; Stewart, *Government and Development of Oklahoma Territory,* 327.

²Victor E. Harlow, *Harlow's Oklahoma History* (Oklahoma City: Harlow Publishing Corporation, 1961), 382-383; Gibson, *Oklahoma,* 319-321.

³Douglas, *History of Tulsa,* I, 77-78.

⁴Charles Wayne Ellinger, "The Drive for Statehood in Oklahoma, 1889-1906," *Chronicles of Oklahoma,* XLI, (Spring, 1963), 15.

⁵Stewart, *Government and Development of Oklahoma Territory,* 327-328, 331; *Evening Gazette* (Oklahoma City), December 15, 1891, 3.

⁶*Ibid.,* December 16, 1891, 3; Thoburn, *Standard History of Oklahoma,* III, 1134.

⁷Thoburn and Wright, *Oklahoma,* III, 335-337; *Harlow's Weekly,* April 15, 1939, 9.

⁸*Congressional Record: Containing the Proceedings and Debates of the Fifty-Second Congress, First Session* (Washington: Government Printing Office, 1892), XXIII, Part 1, 522, H.B. 4629; Thoburn and Wright, *Oklahoma,* II, 589, 898-899; *Evening Gazette,* December 16, 1891, 3; Stewart, *Government and Development of Oklahoma Territory,* 329-331.

⁹*Ibid.*

¹⁰Thoburn and Wright, *Oklahoma,* II, 573.

¹¹Stewart, *Government and Development of Oklahoma Territory,* 334; *Evening Gazette, Fevruary 13, 1892,* 1.

¹²*Ibid.,* February 15, 1892, 2; Stewart, *Government and Development of Oklahoma Territory,* 335.

¹³Ellinger, "Drive for Statehood," 18; Thoburn and Wright, *Oklahoma,* II, 590.

¹⁴*Ibid.,* 899-900, citing Hearings of House Comm. on Terr., 52 Cong. 1st Sess. 46-49.

¹⁵*Ibid.,* 900.

¹⁶Stewart, *Government and Development of Oklahoma Territory,* 333, *Evening Gazette,* January 30, 1892, 2.

¹⁷Hill, *History of the State of Oklahoma,* I, 317-318, 340-341.

¹⁸*Ibid.,* 317.

¹⁹Thoburn and Wright, *Oklahoma,* II, 590.

²⁰Litton, *History of Oklahoma,* I, 491; Ellinger, "The Drive For Statehood in Oklahoma," 17-18.

²¹*El Reno News,* June 5, 1896, 1.

²²*Ibid.,* December 20, 1900, 2.

²³D.A. Richardson, "Judge Charles Bismark Ames," *Chronicles of Oklahoma,* XIII, (December, 1935), 391-398; Ben Ames Williams, "Charles Bismark Ames," (unpublished biography, Archives Room, St. Lukes United Methodist Church, Oklahoma City).

²⁴Thoburn and Wright, *Oklahoma,* III, 100, 101.

²⁵*Congressional Record: Containing the Proceedings and Debates of the Fifty-Seventh Congress, First Session, Also Special Session of the Senate;* (Washington: Government Printing Office, 1902), Vol. XXXV, Part 5, 5140-5141; Thoburn and Wright, *Oklahoma,* II, 595, 901-902.

²⁶Stewart, *Government and Development of Oklahoma Territory,* 350, 353; *Daily Oklahoman,* October 13, 1901, 9.

²⁷Thoburn and Wright, *Oklahoma,* III, 21.

²⁸Hill, *History of the State of Oklahoma,* I, 577-579.

²⁹Stewart, *Government and Development of Oklahoma Territory,* 358-359; *Daily Oklahoman,* October 17, 1901, 1.

³⁰*Ibid.*

³¹Hill, *History of the State of Oklahoma,* I, 578-579.

³²"Indian-Pioneer History," LXVII, 192.

³³Ellinger, "Drive for Statehood," 25.

³⁴Stewart, *Government and Development of Oklahoma Territory,* 365.

³⁵*Ibid.,* 365-375; *Daily Oklahoman,* November 14, 1901, 4, November 15, 1901, 1.

³⁶Thoburn, *Standard History of Oklahoma,* IV, 1492.

³⁷Stewart, *Government and Development of Oklahoma Territory,* 365; *Daily Oklahoman,* November 15, 1901, 1.

³⁸Thoburn, *Standard History of Oklahoma,* V, 2079-2081.

³⁹Stewart, *Government and Development of Oklahoma Territory,* 365-366; *Daily Oklahoman,* November 15, 1901, 1.

⁴⁰*Directory of Oklahoma, 1979* (Oklahoma City: State Election Board, 1979), 227.

⁴¹Thoburn and Wright, *Oklahoma,* II, 653.

⁴²Dale and Rader, *Readings in Oklahoma History,* 697-707, citing Hearings before the Committee on Territories of the House of Rep-

resentatives, January 20, 1904, Statement of Thomas H. Doyle, pp. 27-36; Morris, *Yesterday—Today—Tomorrow,* 498-508; Charles Evans, "Judge Thomas H. Doyle," *Chronicles of Oklahoma,* XXVII, (Summer, 1949), 138-144; see also Thomas H. Doyle, "Single versus Double Statehood." *Chronicles of Oklahoma,* V, (March, 1927), 18-41, (June, 1927), 117-148, (September, 1927), 266-286.

⁴³Morris, *Yesterday—Today—Tomorrow,* 504.

⁴⁴Stewart, *Government and Development of Oklahoma Territory,* 382.

⁴⁵Stewart, *Government and Development of Oklahoma Territory,* 380, *Daily Oklahoman,* July 12, 1905, 1.

⁴⁶Douglas, *History of Tulsa,* I, 64, 67.

⁴⁷Stewart, *Government and Development of Oklahoma Territory,* 383, *Daily Oklahoman,* July 13, 1905, 1.

⁴⁸William H. Murray, "The Constitutional Convention," *Chronicles of Oklahoma,* IX, (June, 1931), 126.

⁴⁹Harlow, *Harlow's Oklahoma History,* 386; Amos D. Maxwell, *The Sequoyah Constitutional Convention* (Boston: Meador Publishing Co., 1953), 48.

⁵⁰Oscar Priestly Fowler, *The Haskell Regime: The Intimate Life of Charles Nathaniel Haskell* (Oklahoma City: Boles Printing Co., 1933) 29.

⁵¹*Ibid.*

⁵²*Ibid.,* 31.

⁵³*Ibid.,* 32-33.

⁵⁴*Ibid.,* 33-44.

⁵⁵*Ibid.,* 41-42.

⁵⁶Benedict, *Muskogee and Northeastern Oklahoma,* I, 371; Hurst, *46th Star,* 38-39.

⁵⁷Fowler, *The Haskell Regime,* 49; U.S. Russell, "The Spark That Set Off Statehood Fire," *Harlow's Weekly,* May 22, 1937, 6-7.

⁵⁸Seth K. Corden and W.B. Richards, comps., *The Oklahoma Red Book* (2 vols.; Tulsa: Democrat Printing Company, 1912), I, 623-674.

⁵⁹*El Reno News,* September 27, 1900, 2; Debo, *And Still the Waters Run,* 100.

⁶⁰Maxwell, *The Sequoyah Constitutional Convention,* 73; *Muskogee :Phoenix,* August 30, 1905, 1; Corden and Richards, *The Oklahoma Red Book,* I, 624

⁶¹Bert Hodges, "Notes on the History of the Creek Nation and Some of Its Leaders," *Chronicles of Oklahoma,* XLIII, (Spring, 1965), 11, 13.

⁶²Maxwell, *The Sequoyah Constitutional Convention,* 73; *Muskogee Phoenix,* August 30, 1905, 1; Corden and Richards, *The Oklahoma Red Book,* I, 624, 633.

⁶³Louis M. Hacker and Benjamin B. Kendrick, *The United States Since 1865* (4th ed.; New York: Appleton-Century-Crofts, Inc., 1949), 225.

⁶⁴Film, Living Legends Library, Oklahoma Christian College, Oklahoma City.

⁶⁵Stewart, *Government and Development of Oklahoma Territory,* 309-310, citing *Daily Oklahoman,* December 10, 1901.

⁶⁶IX, (March, 1898), 447-452.

⁶⁷II, (August, 1899), 329.

⁶⁸Maxwell, *The Sequoyah Constitutional Convention,* 73; *Muskogee Phoenix,* August 30, 1905, 1; Corden and Richards, *The Oklahoma Red Book,* I, 650-651.

⁶⁹Dale and Morrison, *Pioneer Judge,* 146.

⁷⁰Murray, "The Constitutional Convention," 130.

⁷¹Litton, *History of Oklahoma,* I, 497.

⁷²Stewart, *Government and Development of Oklahoma Territory,* 383.

⁷³Hill, *History of the State of Oklahoma,* I, 352; Maxwell, *The Sequoyah Constitutional Convention,* 103, 105.

⁷⁴Act of June 16, 1906, 34 *Stat.* 267; Stewart, *Government and Development of Oklahoma Territory,* 383-384.

Chapter 20

¹Act of June 16, 1906, 34 *Stat.* 267.

²Hurst, *The 46th Star,* 2.

³Thoburn, *A Standard History of Oklahoma,* II, 842-843.

⁴*Ibid.,* 843.

⁵Scales, "Political History of Oklahoma, 1907-1908," 36-37.

⁶Hurst, *The 46th Star,* 4.

⁷Murray, *Memoirs of Governor Murray,* II, 88.

⁸Clark, "Delegates to the Constitutional Convention," 400-415.

⁹*Ibid.,* 412, 404; Murray, *Memoirs of Governor Murray,* II, 31.

[10]Clark, "Delegates to the Constitutional Convention," 414.

[11]*Ibid.*, 408.

[12]*Ibid.*, *Harlow's Weekly*, October 6, 1928, 8-9; Hill, *History of the State of Oklahoma*, II, 406.

[13]Robert L. Williams, "Relation Between the Three Branches of Government," Bar Association of Arkansas, *Proceedings, Nineteenth Annual Session* (Little Rock, Arkansas, May 30, 31, 1916), 152.

[14]H. Wayne Morgan and Anne Hodges Morgan, *Oklahoma: A Bicentennial History*, (New York: W.W. Norton & Company, 1977), 82.

[15]Williams, "Relation Between the Three Branches of Government," 152.

[16]Fowler, *The Haskell Regime*, 82; Benedict, *Muskogee and Northeastern Oklahoma*, 170-172.

[17]*Proceedings of the Constitutional Convention of the Proposed State of Oklahoma Held at Guthrie, Oklahoma, November 20, 1906 to November 16, 1907* (Muskogee: Muskogee Ptg. Co., 1908), 15-26; Dale and Morrison, *Pioneer Judge*, 166.

[18]*Proceedings of the Constitutional Convention of the Proposed State of Oklahoma*, 26; Dale and Morrison, *Pioneer Judge*, 166.

[19]Henry MacCreary, *A Story of Durant, Queen of Three Valleys* (Durant: Democrat Printing Co., 1946), 11; Hill, *History of the State of Oklahoma*, II, 284-285.

[20]Dale and Morrison, *Pioneer Judge*, 166-167.

[21]*Harlow's Weekly*, March 13, 1926, 3; William P. Thompson, "Courts of the Cherokee Nation," *Chronicles of Oklahoma*, II, 73.

[22]H.L. Stuart, "W.A. Ledbetter," *Chronicles of Oklahoma*, XII, (June, 1934) 236-239; Morris, Oklahoma, *Yesterday—Today—Tomorrow*, 517.

[23]John Rogers, "A History of the Constitution of Oklahoma," *Oklahoma Statutes Annotated* (St. Paul, Minn., West Publishing Co., 1952), Const. Arts. 1-4, xxvii.

[24]Murray, *Memoirs of Governor Murray*, II, 35.

[25]*Ibid.*, 23-27; Hurst, *The 46th Star*, 10-11; Albert H. Ellis, *A History of the Constitutional Convention of the State of Oklahoma* (Muskogee: Economy Printing Co., 1923), 97-102.

[26]Thoburn and Wright, *Oklahoma*, II, 346.

[27]Harrison, *Me and My Big Mouth*, 302.

[28]Hill, *History of the State of Oklahoma*, II, 31; Thoburn and Wright, *Oklahoma*, III, 346.

[29][Berry], *Moman Pruiett*, 46-47.

[30]*Ibid.*, 52.

[31]*Ibid.*, 53, 59-60.

[32]*Ibid.*, 57-59.

[33]*Ibid.*, 57-61.

[34]*Ibid.*, 62.

[35]*Ibid.*, 75.

[36]Harrison, *Me and My Big Mouth*, 301.

[37][Berry], *Moman Pruiett*, 196.

[38]*Ibid.*, 192-195.

[39]*Ibid.*, 198.

[40]*Ibid.*, 196.

[41]"Reproduction of the Original Constitution of the State of Oklahoma," *Oklahoma Statutes Annotated*, Const. (1981), 234-236, 262-263.

[42]Stephen Jones, "Captain Frank Frantz, The Rough Rider Governor of Oklahoma Territory," *Chronicles of Oklahoma*, XLIII, (Winter, 1965-1966), 386.

[43]Walrond, "The Annals of the Muskogee Bar Association," 26.

[44]Teall, *Black History in Oklahoma*, 181.

[45]*Ibid.*

[46]Foreman, *History of Oklahoma*, 315.

[47]*Proceedings of the Constitutional Convention for the Proposed State of Oklahoma*, 469; Hurst, *The 46th Star*, 24.

[48]Rex Harlow, *Oklahoma Leaders*, 122-133; D.A. Richardson, "Samuel W. Hayes," *Chronicles of Oklahoma*, XIX, (December, 1941), 309-313.

[49]Jones, "Captain Frank Frantz, The Rough Rider Governor of Oklahoma Territory," 387; Fowler, *The Haskell Regime*, 104-105; Murray, *Memoirs of Governor Murray*, II, 92-94.

[50]18 Okl. 561, 707, 710, 711, 712,; 91 P. 193, 239, 240, 238, (1907), Jones, "Captain Frank Frantz, the Rough Rider Governor of Oklahoma Territory," 386-387.

[51]Murray, *Memoirs of Governor Murray*, II, 54-55.

[52]*Proceedings of the Constitutional Convention for the Proposed State of Oklahoma*, 469.

[53]Surrency, "Federal District Court Judges and the History of Their Courts, 268; Williams, "Judicial History of Oklahoma," 148.

[54]Murray, *Memoirs of Governor Murray*, II, 54.

[55]*Ibid.*, 60.

[56]19 Okl. 561, 707, 710, 711, 712, 91 P. 193, 239, 240, 238, (1907).

[57]Hill, *History of the State of Oklahoma*, I, 399; *Daily Oklahoman*, October 14, 1909; Hurst, *The 46th Star*, 31; Fowler, *The Haskell Regime*, 124.

[58]Hurst, *The 46th Star*, 31; Hill, *History of the State of Oklahoma*, I, 398.

[59]Murray, *Memoirs of Governor Murray*, II, 12.

[60]*Tulsa Daily World*, June 9, 1912.

Chapter 21

[1]*Directory of Oklahoma*, 1979, 75-80. Trapp was admitted to the Bar in 1912; Thoburn and Wright, *Oklahoma*, II, 698.

[2]*Compiled Laws of Oklahoma*, 1909, Ch. 22, Art. VI, Sec. 1741.

[3]R.L. Williams, "John Bell Turner, 1860-1936," *Chronicles of Oklahoma*, XVII, (June, 1939), 253-254. For background of the other four justices see *supra*.

[4]Dale and Morrison, *Pioneer Judge*, 185-186.

[5]*Ibid.*, 192.

[6]*Ibid.*, 186; *Directory of Oklahoma*, 1979, 224.

[7]"Rules for the Supreme Court, State of Oklahoma, Adopted March 12, 1908, 20 Okl. vii-xiv.

[8]"Rules for admission to the Bar of the State of Oklahoma Adopted by the Supreme Court, (November, 19, 1907), 19 Okl. 598-605.

[9]Kane, "Recollections of the Judicial Career of Governor Seay," 7.

[10]*The Journal Record* (Oklahoma City), April 12, 1980, 1; Dave R. McKown, *The Dean: The Life of Julien C. Monnet* (Norman: University of Oklahoma Press, 1973), 239-245.

[11]Dale and Morrison, *Pioneer Judge*, 195.

[12]*Frank Guinn and J.J. Beal v. United States*, 238 U.S. 347, (1915).

[13]*The Oklahoma County Bar Association News*, II, (April, 1970), 3; *Oklahoma City Times*, December 9, 1974, 26.

[14]Richards, *Oklahoma Red Book*, II, 598, 589, 606.

[15]Hurst, *The 46th Star*, 129-137.

[16]*Coyle v. Smith, Secretary of State of the State of Oklahoma*, 28 Okl. 121, 113 P. 944, 221, U.S. 559, (1911).

[17]*Ibid.*; Thoburn and Wright, *Oklahoma*, III, 388.

[18]*Directory of Oklahoma*, 1979, 225.

[19]42 Okl. 478, 142 P. 305 (1914).

[20]Thoburn, *Standard History of Oklahoma*, IV, 1455-1456; Boren and Boren, *Who Is Who In Oklahoma*, 410.

[21]Thomas A. Edwards, "The Criminal Court of Appeals, Its History and Functions," State Bar of Oklahoma, *Proceedings, First Annual Meeting* (Oklahoma City, December 19, 20, 1930), 35, 37.

[22]Thoburn, *Standard History of Oklahoma*, V, 1804.

[23]Hill, *History of the State of Oklahoma*, II, 320.

[24]*Directory of Oklahoma*, 1979, 227.

[25]Dale and Morrison, *Pioneer Judge*, 193.

[26]*J.P. Crawford v. George W. Ferguson, County Judge*, 5 Okl. Cr. 377, 115 P. 278 (1911); Leslie A. McRill, "An Early Crusader for Law and Order in Oklahoma: Thompson Benton Ferguson," *Chronicles of Oklahoma*, XXXVI, (Spring, 1958), 85.

[27]Letter, C.C. West, Oklahoma State Penitentiary, to Governor Lee Cruce, October 27, 1926, Box 77, Cruce Collection, Western History Collection, University of Oklahoma, Norman.

[28]*Regular Biennial Message of Governor Lee Cruce to the Legislature of 1913, Oklahoma* (Vinita: Leader Printing Co., 1913), 42.

[29]*Henry v. State*, 10 Okl. Cr. 369, 136 P. 982 (1913); *Daily Oklahoman*, November 30, 1913.

[30]*Ex parte Crump*, 10 Okl. Cr. 133, 135 P. 428 (1913); *Harlow's Weekly*, August 30, 1913.

[31]*Ex parte Crump*, 10 Okl. Cr. 133, 135 P. 428 (1913); *Daily Oklahoman*, October 5, 1913; *Harlow's Weekly*, October 11, 1913.

[32]Frank Eagin, "Dean of American Judges of Criminal Courts," *Harlow's Weekly*, August 18, 1928, 6; *The Sunday Oklahoman*, March 30, 1969, 13A.

[33]Scales and Goble, *Oklahoma Politics; A History*, 29; Hurst, *The 46th Star*, 45.

[34]Richards, comp., *Oklahoma Red Book*, II, 121-122.

[35]*Enid Morning News*, April 7, 1976, 32.

[36]Goins and Morris, *Oklahoma Homes*, 135.

[37]Thoburn and Wright, *Oklahoma*, II, 643; Hurst, *The 46th Star*, 45.

[38]Litton, *History of Oklahoma*, I, 514.

[39]*Harlow's Weekly*, February 21, 1914, McRill, *And Satan Came Also*, 124.

[40]*Harlow's Weekly*, February 28, 1914, 11-12.

[41][Berry], *Moman Pruiett*, 319-320.

[42]Quoted in *Harlow's Weekly*, February 28, 1914, 11-12.

[43]Billington, "Honorable Thomas P. Gore: The Blind Senator," 121; [Berry], *Moman Pruiett*, 305, 308-311, 323-333.

[44]Billington, "Honorable Thomas P. Gore," 121.

[45]*Directory of Oklahoma*, 1979, 524.

[46]Boren and Boren, *Who Is Who In Oklahoma*, 171.

[47]Okla., *Laws* 1917, 350; Thomas Elton Brown, "Oklahoma's 'Bone-Dry Law' and the Roman Catholic Church," *Chronicles of Oklahoma*, LII, (Fall, 1974), 316.

[48]*Ibid.*, 321.

[49]*Harlow's Weekly*, October 17, 1917, 3; Richards, comp., *Oklahoma Red Book*, II, 524.

[50]*Harlow's Weekly*, October 17, 1917, 3.

[51]Brown, "Oklahoma's 'Bone-Dry Law' and the Roman Catholic Church," 324; Urban de Hasque, comp., "The Oklahoma Altar Wine Case," Vertical file, Oklahoma Historical Society Library, Oklahoma City, Oklahoma.

[52]Brown, "Oklahoma's 'Bone-Dry Law' and the Roman Catholic Church," 325-329; *Harlow's Weekly*, December 28, 1917, 3.

[53]*DeHasque v. Atchison, Topeka and Santa Fe Railway Company*, 68 Okla. 183, 173 P. 73 (1918); Brown, "Oklahoma's 'Bone-Dry Law' and the Roman Catholic Church," 328; *Harlow's Weekly*, May 22, 1918, 8-9.

[54]E.M. Kerr, "Thomas Horner Owen, 1873-1938," *Chronicles of Oklahoma*, XVII, (March, 1939), 119.

[55]*Harlow's Weekly*, February 24, 1922, 11.

[56]*State of Oklahoma v. State of Texas, United States*, Intervener 252 U.S. 372 (1920); 256 U.S. 70 (1921); 260 U.S. 606 (1923); 261 U.S. 340 (1923); Bunyan Hadley Andrew, "Oklahoma's Red River Boundary: Under U. S. Supreme Court Decision in 1927," *Chronicles of Oklahoma*, XLIV, (Autumn, 1966), 246-253.

[57]Foreman, *History of Oklahoma*, 334.

[58]Jim Feagin, *Fifty Years Under the Bench in Texas* (San Antonio: Naylor Co., 1950), 68-69.

[59]*State of Oklahoma v. State of Texas, United States*, Intervener, 256 U.S. 70 (1921); 260 U.S. 606 (1923); Andrew, "Oklahoma's Red River Boundary: Under U.S. Supreme Court Decision in 1927," *The Chronicles of Oklahoma*, XLIV, 246-253; see also C.A. Welborn, *The Red River Controversy: The Western Boundary of the Lousiana Purchase* (Austin: Nortex Offset Publications, Inc., 1973).

[60]*Harlow's Weekly*, February 24, 1922, 11.

[61]*Ibid.*

[62]*Ibid.*, May 31, 1924, 6.

[63]*Directory of Oklahoma*, 1979, 543.

[64]*Harlow's Weekly*, April 24, 1937, 6.

Chapter 22

[1]For an excellent study of the Oklahoma Federal Court, see William C. Kellough, "Power and Politics of the Oklahoma Federal Court," *Chronicles of Oklahoma*, LXV (1987), 182-213.

[2]Indian-Pioneer History," LXVII, 192.

[3]November 16, 1907, 1; *Supra*, 112.

[4]Harlow, *Oklahoma Leaders*, 31-32. See *Supra* for other references to Judge Cotteral.

[5]*Harlow's Weekly*, May 26, 1928, 10; *Sunday Oklahoman*, May 6, 1979, 23A.

[6]George H. Shirk, "Judge Edgar S. Vaught," *Chronicles of Oklahoma*, XXXVII, (Winter, 1959-60), 394-396.

[7]*Ibid.*, 397.

[8]*Harlow's Weekly*, May 9, 1925, 16.

[9]*Daily Oklahoman*, January 1, 1962, 23; Shirk, "Judge Edgar S. Vaught," 400.

[10]*Ibid.*, 400-401.

[11]Douglas, *History of Tulsa*, II, 14-18.

[12]Oklahoma State Bar Association, *Proceedings, Eleventh Annual Meeting* (Oklahoma City, December 27-29, 1917), 99-101.

[13]*Harlow's Weekly*, June 5, 1918, 5.

[14]Douglas, *History of Tulsa*, II, 18-19.

[15]Dale and Morrison, *Pioneer Judge*, 281.

[16]*Ibid.*, 282.

[17]*Ibid.*, 284.

[18]*Ibid.*, 288-289.

[19]*Ibid.*, 289; *Harlow's Weekly*, February 17, 1922, 13.

[20]Surrency, "Federal District Judges," 265, 269; *Harlow's Weekly*, October 6, 1923, 10, February 2, 1924, 3-6.

[21]Thoburn, *Standard History of Oklahoma*, IV, 1587; Thoburn and Wright, *Oklahoma*, III, 108-109.

[22]Barrett, *Oklahoma After Fifty Years*, IV, 1239.

[23]*Harlow's Weekly*, October 6, 1923, 10.

[24]*Ibid.*, February 2, 1924, 3-6, January 19, 1924, 8, 15.

[25]Thoburn and Wright, *Oklahoma*, III, 128-129.

[26]Oklahoma State Bar Association, *Proceedings, Twenty-first Annual Meeting* (Tulsa, December 2, 3, 1927), 15-16.

[27]*Ibid.*; *Daily Oklahoman*, March 10, 1929, 1-F.

[28]*Harlow's Weekly*, August 2, 1924, July 26, 1924.

[29]Condon, "How Tulsa Became a Court Town," *Tulsa Daily World*, December 8, 1957, magazine section, 13; Douglas, *History of Tulsa*, I, 165.

[30]Thoburn and Wright, *Oklahoma*, IV, 634-636.

[31]Kappler, *Indian Affairs*, III, 209-210; Act of June 21, 1906, 34 *Stat.* 342, 343; Douglas, *History of Tulsa*, I, 165.

[32]Benedict, *Muskogee and Northeastern Oklahoma*, I, 394; Douglas *History of Tulsa*, I, 72.

[33]Thoburn and Wright, *Oklahoma*, IV, 635.

[34]Interview with T. Austin Gavin, Tulsa, Oklahoma, June 25, 1979.

[35]Surrency, "Federal District Court Judges," p. 265; Act of February 16, 1925, 43 Stat. 945; *Harlow's Weekly*, September 9, 1921, February 9. 1924; February 21, 1925.

[36]Surrency, "Federal District Court Judges," 266.

[37]*Harlow's Weekly*, June 6, 1925, 13.

[38]Interview with T. Austin Gavin, June 25, 1979.

[39]Surrency "Federal District Court Judges," 266; Dale and Morrison, *Pioneer Judge*, 289.

[40]*Tulsa Daily World*, October 24, 1924, 1; Scales, "Political History of Oklahoma," 270.

[41]*Harlow's Weekly*, June 6, 1925, 13.

[42]*Harlow's Weekly*, September 5, 1925, 12-14.

[43]*Harlow's Weekly*, January 21, 1928, 9, March 10, 1928, 10-11, March 31, 1928, 4; 7 Okla. B.J. 164 (November, 1936).

[44]Harrison, *Me and My Big Mouth*, 208-210.

[45]*Tulsa Tribune*, February 14, 1935, 1, February 23, 1935, 1.

[46]*McAlester Democrat*, April 23, 1936.

[47]*Harlow's Weekly*, November 5, 1938, 6.

[48]Harrison, *Me and My Big Mouth*, 210-211.

[49]Interview with Royce H. Savage, Tulsa, Oklahoma, June 14, 1983; 11 Okla. B.J. 1183 (October 26, 1940).

[50]Interview with Royce H. Savage, June 14, 1983; *The Tulsa Bar News*, (October, 1961), 1.

[51]*Ibid.*

[52]*Ibid.*

[53]45 Okla. B.J. 1025 (April 27, 1974).

[54]*Saturday Oklahoman and Times*, February 10,1979, 3.

[55]50 Okla. B.J. 777 (April 14, 1979); *The Journal Record*, November 6, 1979, 1; *The Journal* (Oklahoma City), November 30, 1979, 3.

[56]Dale and Morrison, *Pioneer Judge*, 325-326.

[57]*Ibid.*, 328-332; *Harlow's Weekly*, January 30, 1937, April 24, 1937.

[58]Dale and Morrison, *Pioneer Judge*, 334-336.

[59]*Harlow's Weekly*, February 13, 1937, 9-10.

[60]*The Sunday Oklahoman*, May 6, 1979, 23-A; *Who's Who in the South and Southwest* (Chicago: Marquis—Who's Who, Inc., 1965), IX, 674.

[61]*Daily Oklahoman*, December 5, 1970.

[62]Litton, *History of Oklahoma*, III, 259; *Sunday Oklahoman*, May 6, 1979, 23-A.

[63]*Ibid.*, *The Journal Record*, November 20, 1979,

[64]Joseph C. Gouldon, *The Benchwarmers: The Private World of the Powerful Federal Judges* (New York: Weybright and Talley, 1974), 209.

[65]Interview with T. Austin Gavin, June 25, 1979; *Tulsa Tribune*, March 14, 1979, 1-B; *Daily Oklahoman*, February 13, 1979, 1.

[66]*Daily Oklahoman*, July 4, 1979, 41; *The Journal Record*, August 21, 1979, 1; Martin Haun, *He Buys Organs for Churches, Pianos for Bawdy Houses* (Oklahoma City: Midwest Political Publications, 1977), 170-171.

[67]Surrency, "Federal District Judges," 269; *Directory of Oklahoma, 1981* (Oklahoma City: State Election Board, 1981), 69-78; 45 Okla. B.J. 1025 (April 27, 1974); *Daily Oklahoman*, March 24, 1981, 21; 54 Okla. B.J. 2529 (October 8, 1983); 55 Okla. B.J. 1682 (September 8, 1984); 57 Okla. B.J. 502 (March 1, 1986); 58 Okla. B.J. 1806 (June 27, 1987).

Chapter 23

[1]Douglas, *History of Tulsa*, II, 103-105.

[2]Richards, comp., *Oklahoma Red Book*, II, 533.

[3]Gibson, *Oklahoma*, 325-326.

[4]Dale and Morrison, *Pioneer Judge*, 99-101.

[5]Debo, *And Still The Waters Run*, 98-99.

[6]Act of May 27, 1908, 35 Stat. 312; Kappler, *Indian Affairs*, III, 351-356; Debo, *And Still The Waters Run*, 179.

[7]*Ibid.*, 183; Foreman, *History of Oklahoma*, 355-356.

[8]*Daily Oklahoman*, January 1, 1911; Debo, *And Still The Waters Run*, 222; *Cobb v. Oklahoma Publishing Co.*, 42 Okl. 314, 140 P. 1079 (1914).

[9]Hill, *History of the State of Oklahoma*, II, 191.

[10]*Cobb v. Oklahoma Publishing Co.*, 42 Okl. 314, 140 P. 1079 (1914).

[11]*In re Horine*, 64 Okla. 315, 167 P. 1148 (1917); *In re Williams, et al.*, 64 Okla. 316, 167 P. 1149 (1917).

[12]Letter, Mott to Secretary of Interior, November 27, 1912, Lee Cruce administrative File, Division of Archives and Records, Oklahoma Department of Libraries, Oklahoma City; Debo, *And Still The Waters Run*, 232-234.

[13]*Ibid.*, 242.

[14]April 22, 1913, Lee Cruce Administrative File, Department of Archives and Records, Oklahoma Department of Libraries.

[15]Debo, *And Still The Waters Run*, 236-237.

[16]Oklahoma State Bar Association, *Proceedings, Seventh Annual Meeting* (Oklahoma City, December 29, 30, 1913), 67-70.

[17]Cato Sells, "Facts About the Indians in Oklahoma," Harlow's Weekly, August 13, 1920, 13-16; [Benjamin F.] Rice and [Thomas D.] Lyons, *The Oil Operator in Oklahoma* (New York: Dispatch Press, Inc., n.d.) 149-156; Debo, *And Still The Waters Run*, 243-245.

[18]Okla. *Laws* 1919, ch. 201, 288.

[19]Okla. *Laws* 1923-24, ch. 84, 100-102.

[20]Act of April 10, 1926, 44 *Stat.* 239; Kappler, *Indian Affairs*, IV, 518-520.

[21]Debo, *And Still The Waters Run*, 200.

[22]Jerry Rand, "Samuel Morton Rutherford, *Chronicles of Oklahoma*, XXX, (Summer, 1952), 149-159.

[23]Foreman, *History of Oklahoma*, 356; Debo, *And Still The Waters Run*, 208-210.

[24]56 L. Ed 820, 224 U.S. 413 (1912).

[25]*Muskogee Daily Phoenix*, May 8, 1914, 1; November 10, 14, 1915, 1, Douglas, *History of Tulsa*, II, 85-86.

[26]*Muskogee Daily Phoenix*, May 10, 1919, 1.

[27]Douglas, *History of Tulsa*, II, 85.

[28]*Harlow's Weekly*, December 5, 1917, 4.

[29]*State ex rel. Dale et al., v. Vernor et al*, 79 Okla. 124, 191 P. 729 (1920); *State ex rel. Dale et al., Com'rs. v. Sango* 80 Okla. 183, 194 P. 215 (1921), *State ex rel. Dale et al., Com'rs, v. Jefferson*, 79 Okla. 288, 193 P. 44 (1920); Debo, *And Still The Waters Run*, 313-314.

[30]*State ex rel. Dale et al., Com'rs. v. Johnson*, 78 Okla. 58, 188 P. 1053 (1920).

[31]*State ex rel. Dale et al., State Bar Com'rs. v. Curd*, 75 Okla. 15, 181 P. 484 (1919); *Muskogee Times-Democrat*, August 10, 1918, 1.

[32]*Harlow's Weekly*, January 21, 1919, 1.

[33]*United States v. Bessie Wildcat et al.*, 61 L. Ed. 1024, 244 U.S. III (1917); Debo, *And Still The Waters Run*, 274.

[34]*Daily Oklahoman*, March 10, 1929, 1-F.

[35]Thoburn and Wright, *Oklahoma*, III, 31.

[36]Debo, *And Still The Waters Run*, 274.

[37]Thoburn and Wright, *Oklahoma*, III, 31-32.

[38]Douglas, *History of Tulsa*, II, 98-105.

[39]*Ibid.*, 103-105; Boren and Boren, *Who Is Who In Oklahoma*, 316.

[40]*Harlow's Weekly*, December 23, 1939, 8; *Okemah Daily Leader*, April 17, 1941, 1; Dale and Morrison, *Pioneer Judge*, 306.

[41]*Harlow's Weekly*, February 18, 1920, 9; January 17, 1920, 8.

[42]Debo, *And Still The Waters Run*, 338-339.

[43]*Harlow's Weekly*, December 23, 1939, 8.

[44]Debo, *And Still The Waters Run*, 346.

[45]*Ibid.*, 349; Dale and Morrison, *Pioneer Judge*, 305; *Harlow's Weekly*, October 22, 1938, 7.

[46]Debo, *And Still The Waters Run*, 349; *Harlow's Weekly*, July 17, 1937, 3.

[47]Dale and Morrison, *Pioneer Judge*, 306.

[48]Dick Jones, *The Life of Judge Dick Jones* (Oklahoma City: Oklahoma Historical Society, 1983), 117-121.

[49]Debo, *And Still The Waters Run*, 349.

[50]*Okemah Daily Leader*, April 17, 1941, 1.

[51]Dale and Morrison, *Pioneer Judge*, 306.

[52]Dick Jones, *Life of Judge Dick Jones*, 121.

[53]Dale and Morrison, *Pioneer Judge*, 306.

[54]Acts of March 19, May 20, May 24, and June 7, 1924, 43 *Stats.* 27, 133, 139, 537, re Five Civilized Tribes.

[55]Debo, *And Still The Waters Run*, 386.

[56]W.F. Semple and Winnie Lewis Gravitt, "Grady Lewis, Choctaw Attorney," *Chronicles of Oklahoma*, XXXIII, (Autumn, 1955), 301, 303; Berlin Basil Chapman, *The Otoes and Missourias: A Study of Indian Removal and the Legal Aftermath* (Oklahoma City: Times Journal Publishing Co., 1965), 232; Wright, *Guide to the Indian Tribes of Oklahoma*, 25; Act of August 13, 1946, 60 *Stat.* 1049.

[57]Semple and Gravitt, "Grady Lewis, Choctaw Attorney," 303.

[58]Chapman, *The Otoes and Missourias*, 242.

[59]Odie B. Faulk, *A Full Service Banker: The Life of Louis W. Duncan* (Oklahoma City: Oklahoma Heritage Association, 1981), 106-107.

[60]Q.B. Boydstun, "Earl Boyd Pierce," *Chronicles of Oklahoma*, LXI, (Fall, 1983), 328-329.

[61]*The Oklahoma Journal*, April 18, 1975, 1.

[62]Chapman, *The Otoes and Missourias*, 237. Rennard Strickland discusses "Friends and Enemies of the American Indian: An Essay Review on Native American Law and Public Policy," in *American Indian Law Review*, III, 313-331.

Chapter 24

[1]Thoburn and Wright, *Oklahoma*, IV, 486; Oklahoma State Bar Association, *Proceedings, Second Annual Meeting*, 16-20.

[2]*Ibid.*, 20; Hiram Burris King, *Memoirs of an Oklahoma Jurist* (San Antonio: Naylor Co., 1973), 24-25.

[3]Oklahoma State Bar Association, *Proceedings, First Annual Meeting*, 67, 50-51.

[4]Maurice H. Merrill, "Random Thoughts on Legal Education in Oklahoma," *Tulsa Law Journal*, I, (January, 1964), 2; Dave R. McKown, *The Dean: The Life of Julien C. Monnet* (Norman: University of Oklahoma Press, 1973), 178-181.

[5]*Ibid.*, 150-151.

[6]The definitive biography of Dean Monnet is Dave R McKown, *The Dean: The Life of Julien C. Monnet*; see also 12 Oklahoma. B.J., 1052-1056 (July 26, 1941).

[7]McKown, *The Dean*, 182-186.

[8]Litton, *History of Oklahoma*, III, 343-344.

[9]*The Journal Record*, September 22, 1979, 1, March 22, 1979, 5; *Daily Oklahoman*, February 25, 1945.

[10]Thoburn and Wright, *Oklahoma*, III, 226.

[11]*Harlow's Weekly*, May 29, 1926, 4, 14-15; Guy William Logsdon, *The University of Tulsa: A History, 1882-1972*, ed. by Odie B. Faulk (Norman: University of Oklahoma Press, 1977), 161.

[12]*Ibid.*, 216-217; 21 Okla. B.J. 601-03 (April 29, 1950).

[13]50 Okla. B.J. 1613-15 (July 28, 1979).

[14]*Oklahoma City Times*, July 15, 1981, 10; *Daily Oklahoman*, January 26, 1982, 9; 57 Okla. B.J. 1676 (July 12, 1986).

[15]Teall, *Black History in Oklahoma*, 273-275; *The Black Dispatch* (Oklahoma City), January 19, 1946, 1.

[16]George Lynn Cross, *Blacks in White Colleges: Oklahoma's Landmark Cases* (Norman: University of Oklahoma Press, 1975), 35-46.

[17]*Sipuel v. Board of Regents of University of Oklahoma, et al.*, 199 Okl.

36, 180 P.2d 135, 332 U.S. 631 (1948); Cross, *Blacks in White Colleges*, 46-48.

[18]*Ibid.*, 52-54.

[19]*Ibid.*, 72-73, 114; Zella J. Black Patterson and Lynette L. Wert, *Langston University: A History* (Norman: University of Oklahoma Press, 1979), 234.

[20]Gene Aldrich, *Black Heritage of Oklahoma* (Edmond, Okla.: Thompson Book and Supply Co., 1973), 38, 40.

[21]Cross, *Blacks in White Colleges*, 80.

[22]*Ibid.*, 80-85.

[23]Oklahoma, *Laws* 1949, 608, Sec. 1.

[24]Cross, *Blacks in White Colleges*, 111-114.

[25]*McLaurin v. Oklahoma State Regents for Higher Education et al.*, 339 U.S. 637 (1950).

[26]Interview with Robert W. Blackstock, Bristow, Oklahoma, May 17, 1983; "Order,"S.C.B.D. No. 1256, "In RE: Application of Robert W. Blackstock to take the June, 1951 Bar Examination," June 18, 1951 [Supreme Court of State of Oklahoma]; *Regents of University of California, Petitioner, v. Allan Bakke*, 553 P. 2d 1152, 438 U.S. 265 (1978)

[27]Cross, *Blacks in White Colleges*, 134.

[28]*Sunday Oklahoman*, March 6, 1983, 18A.

[29]Letter, July 22, 1983, John Hope Franklin to author.

[30]Stephen Jones, *Oklahoma Politics in State and Nation*, 1907 to 1962 (Enid: The Haymaker Press, Inc., 1974), I, 10; *A.B. McDonald, Appellant, v. George. Key, Benjamin M. Cassity and J.Wm. Cordell, Appellees*, 224 F.2d 608 (1955).

[31]Wilson, comp., *State Directory*, 1967, 97, 121, 122

[32]Teall, *Black History in Oklahoma*, 227-228.

[33]Aldrich, *Black Heritage of Oklahoma*, 110-111; Teall, *Black History in Oklahoma*, 231

[34]Letter, July 22, 1983, John Hope Franklin to author.

[35]*Tulsa Lawyer*, XI, No. 4 (December, 1971), 10; Aldrich, *Black Heritage of Oklahoma*, 111.

Chapter 25

[1]*National Law Journal* (New York), August 24, 1981, 11.

[2]*Daily Oklahoman*, April 19, 1925; see also *Norman Transcript*, August 23, 1895, 1.

[3]Sara Thomason, "Necrology, Anabel Fleming Thomason, 1874-1949," *Chronicles of Oklahoma*, XXVIII, (Winter, 1950-51), 499-500, XXIX, (Autumn, 1951), 362; *Cleveland County Leader* (Lexington, Okla.,) December 2, 1899, 2, December 16, 1899, 5; *Krebs Eagle*, December 8, 1899, 1; *Oklahoma City Times*, December 14, 1978, 49.

[4]*Stillwater Advance*, December 11, 1902, 2.

[5]*Frederick Enterprise*, April 12, 1906, 6.

[6]State Bar of Oklahoma, *Proceedings, First Special Meeting*, 97-98, 99, 101-102; 9 Okla. B.J. 182, August, 1938.

[7]Oklahoma State Bar Association, *Proceedings, Fourteenth Annual Meeting* (Oklahoma City, December 29, 30, 1920), 70.

[8]*Ibid.*, *Fifteenth Annual Meeting*, 110.

[9]State Bar of Oklahoma, *Proceedings, First Special Meeting*, 98.

[10]9 Okla. B.J. 182, August 1938; Oklahoma State Bar Association, *Proceedings, Twentieth Annual Meeting* (Oklahoma City, December 27, 28, 1926), 52.

[11]Interview with Kittie C. Sturdevant, Oklahoma City, September 18, 1978; *Harlow's Weekly*, April 22, 1921, 6-7; Thoburn and Wright, *Oklahoma*, III, 37.

[12]Oklahoma State Bar Association, *Proceedings, Seventh Annual Meeting*, 17.

[13]*Ibid.*, 17-18.

[14]September 9, 1921, 7.

[15]*National Law Journal*, August 24, 1981, 11.

[16]Oklahoma State Bar Association, *Proceedings, Fifteenth Annual Meeting*, 6-7.

[17]*Harlow's Weekly*, September 9, 1921, 7.

[18]*Ibid.*, July 28, 1923, 15.

[19]53 Okla. B.J. 1741, July 24, 1982.

[20]*Harlow's Weekly*, August 13, 1920, 13; Boren and Boren, *Who's Who in Oklahoma*, 99-100; H.W. Carver, "Necrology, Forence E. Cobb, 1878-1946," *Chronicles of Oklahoma*, XXV, (Spring, 1947), 72-73.

[21]Harrison, *Me and My Big Mouth*, 65.

[22]*Harlow's Weekly*, August 27, 1920, 7-9.

[23]Thoburn and Wright, *Oklahoma*, III, 357; *Harlow's Weekly*, June 3, 1921, 2.

[24]*Ibid.*

[25]*Ibid.*, June 21, 1930, 7-8.

[26]Thoburn and Wright, *Oklahoma*, III, 357; *Harlow's Weekly*, June 21, 1930, 7-8.

[27]7 Okla. B.J. 243, March, 1937.

[28]Interview with Kathryn Goldman (Mrs. Van Leuven's niece), January 27, 1984.

[29]11 Okla. B.J. 182-83, April 23, 1940; 17 Okla. B.J. 230-31, February 23, 1946; Interview with G. Ellis Gable, Tulsa, Oklahoma, June 14, 1983.

[30]*Tulsa Tribune*, December 16, 1958, 55 Okla. B.J. 1113, June 2, 1984.

[31]*Tulsa Tribune*, December 16, 1958.

[32]*The Journal Record*, February 15, 1980, 1, August 20, 1981, 1A.

[33]*Ibid.*, February 15, 1980, 1.

[34]*Ibid.*, July 25, 1981, 4, February 15, 1980, 1; *Daily Oklahoman*, May 1, 1981, 16.

[35]*The Journal Record*, July 25, 1981, 4, February 15, 1980, 1; *Daily Oklahoman*, May 1, 1981, 16, *Sunday Oklahoman*, October 5, 1980, 20A; Letter, March 17, 1989, from Charlotte Nelson of Board of Bar Examiners.

[36]Interview with William G. Paul, of Crowe & Dunlevy, May 4, 1983; Letter, Crowe & Dunlevy to author, May 5, 1983; Interview with Thomas D. Gable of Hall, Estill, Hardwick, Gable, Collingsworth & Nelson, June 14, 1983, Tulsa, Oklahoma.

[37]*Daily Oklahoman*, November 15, 1979, 21; *The Journal Record*, November 20, 1979, 1.

[38]*Ibid*, April 21, 1983, 2, February 13, 1982, 4.

[39]*Sunday Oklahoman*, Sec. A, p. 15, October 23, 1988; 55 Okla. B.J. 650, March 24, 1984.

[40]*Sunday Oklahoman*, Sec. A., p. 15, October 23, 1988.

Chapter 26

[1]Indian Territory Bar Association, *Proceedings, Third Annual Meeting* (South McAlester, I. T., June 11, 1902), 17-18.

[2]*Ibid.*; Barrett, *Oklahoma After Fifty Years*, II, 393-395; George H. Shirk, "A Golden Anniversary for Lawyers," *Daily Oklahoman*, November 14, 1954, 32-33.

[3]Indian Territory Bar Association, *Proceedings, Third Annual Meeting*, 19.

[4]Barrett, *Oklahoma After Fifty Years*, II, 394-396.

[5]*Ibid.*, 397-398.

[6]Indian Territory Bar Association, *Proceedings, First Annual Meeting* (South McAlester, I. T., October 2, 3, 1900) 3, 4, 8-9.

[7]*Ibid.*, 12-13.

[8]*Oklahoma State Capital*, June 14, 1890, 5.

[9]*Ibid.*

[10]Marion Tuttle Rock, *Illustrated History of Oklahoma* (Topeka: O.B. Hamilton & Son, 1890), 186; Shirk, "A Golden Anniversary for Lawyers," 32.

[11]*Oklahoma State Capital*, June 14, 1890, 5.

[12]*State Bar of Oklahoma, Proceedings, First Special Meeting*, 87-88 and *supra* 65-66.

[13]*Portrait and Biographical Record of Oklahoma* (Chicago: Chapman Publishing Co., 1901), 51-53.

[14]Richards, *The Oklahoma Red Book*, II, 149, 159.

[15]Oklahoma and Indian Territory Bar Association, *Proceedings, First Annual Meeting*, 73-74.

[16]*Ibid.*

[17]The Oklahoma Bar Association, *Proceedings Annual Meeting* (Guthrie: January 9, 10, 1902), 3.

[18]Shirk, "A Golden Anniversary for Lawyers," 32.

[19]"Acts Concerning the Admission of Attorneys," 19 Okla. 605-607.

[20]Oklahoma Bar Association, *Proceedings, for the Year 1903-04* (Guthrie: January 7, 8, 1903 and January 6, 7, 1904), 99.

[21]Oklahoma State Bar Association, *Proceedings, Ninth Annual Meeting* (Oklahoma City: December 29, 30 1915), 184-185.

[22]Indian Territory Bar Association, *Proceedings, Fifth Annual Meeting* (South McAlester, I. T., June 14, 1904), 48.

[23]*Ibid.*, 52-53.

[24]*Ibid.*

[25]*Ibid.*, 54.

[26]*Ibid.*

[27]*Ibid.*, 56-57.

[28]*Ibid.*, 58-59.

[29]Norton, et al., "Resolution of Respect for and in Appreciation of Honorable Charles B. Stuart," 234; Ferguson, *They Carried the Torch*, 46-47.

[30]Oklahoma and Indian Territory Bar Association, *Proceedings, First Annual Meeting*, 7.

[31]*Ibid.*, 231-234.

[32]*Ibid.*, 77, 86, 109, 124, 128, 134.

[33]*Ibid.*, 106-107.

[34]Indian Territory Bar Association, *Proceedings, Annual Meeting*, (June 14, 1904), 49.

[35]Oklahoma State Bar Association, *Proceedings, First Annual Meeting* (Oklahoma City, December, 1907), 56.

[36]*Ibid.*, 328-331.

[37]*Ibid.*, 33.

[38]*Ibid.*

Chapter 27

[1]Oklahoma State Bar Association, *Proceedings, Seventh Annual Meeting*, 165.

[2]Oklahoma State Bar Association, *Proceedings, Seventeenth Annual Meeting* (Oklahoma City, December 27, 28, 1923), 129-130.

[3]*Ibid.*, 131.

[4]2 Okla. B.J. 3-4 (April, 1931).

[5]Oklahoma State Bar Association, *Proceedings, Seventeenth Annual Meeting*, 192-193; *Sixth Annual Meeting* (Oklahoma City, December 30, 31, 1912), 224.

[6]*Ibid.*, *Eighteenth Annual Meeting* (Oklahoma City, December 29, 30, 1924), 36-37.

[7]*Ibid.*, *Seventeenth Annual Meeting*, 130-131.

[8]*Ibid.*, *Thirteenth Annual Meeting* (Oklahoma City, December 18, 19, 1919), 1-2.

[9]*Ibid.*, *Tenth Annual Meeting* (Oklahoma City, December 29, 29, 1916), 6-9.

[10]*Ibid.*, *Second Annual Meeting* (Oklahoma City, January 4, 5, 1909), 14; Interview with Paul G. Darrough, November 29, 1978, Oklahoma City.

[11]Oklahoma State Bar Association, *Proceedings, Twenty-First Meeting*, 99.

[12]*Ibid.*, *Fourth Annual Meeting* (Oklahoma City, December 28, 29, 1910), 328.

[13]*Ibid.*, *Twenty-Second Annual Meeting* (Oklahoma City, December 28, 29, 1928), 232-233.

[14]*Ibid.*, *Seventeenth Annual Meeting*, 132-137; *Twenty-First Annual Meeting*, 102-104; State Bar of Oklahoma, *Proceedings, First Special Meeting* (Olkahoma City, February 21, 22, 1930), 126-127.

[15]Oklahoma State Bar Association, *Proceedings, Seventeenth Annual Meeting*, 109-110.

[16]*Ibid.*, 54-68.

[17]*Muskogee Times-Democrat*, April 14, 1924, 1.

[18]"Roll of Attorneys Admitted October 25, 1924 to June 22, 1925," 107 Okl. v.

[19]*Harlow's Weekly*, January 23, 1926, 5.

[20]"Roll of Attorneys Admitted from October 16, 1928 to March 5, 1929," 133 Okl. v; *Oklahoma City Times*, December 20, 1928.

[21]Oklahoma State Bar Association, Proceedings, *Ninth Annual Meeting*, 67.

[22]*Ibid.*, *Twenty-First Annual Meeting*, 14.

[23]*Ibid.*, *Ninth Annual Meeting*, 17-30.

[24]*Ibid.*, 21.

[25]*Ibid.*, 63.

[26]*Ibid.*, 74.

[27]*Ibid.*, 90-91.

[28]*Ibid.*, 92-92.

[29]*Ibid.*, 62-95.

[30]*Ibid.*, *Tenth Annual Meeting*, 171, e.g.

[31]*Harlow's Weekly*, February 21, 1931, 16; *Directory of Oklahoma*, 1979, 224.

[32]*Ibid.*, October 29, 1932, 13; *Daily Oklahoman*, January 8, 1933, 1, January 10, 1933, 8.

[33]*Bayless v. Kornegay*, 163 Okla. 184, 21. P. 2d 481 (1933); *Directory of Oklahoma*, 1979, 224.

[34]Oklahoma State Bar Association, *Proceedings, Twenty-First Annual Meeting*, 135-136.

[35]*Riverside Oil & Refining Co., a Corporation, et al...S.D. Lynch et al.*, 114 Okl. 198, 243 P. 967 (1925).

[36]*Harris, Receiver et al. v. Chambers*, 121 Okl. 75, 247 P. 695 (1926)

[37]October 24, 31, November 1, 2, 1926; Von Russell Creel, "Courts in Peril: The Legislative-Judicial Struggle of 1927-1929," *Chronicles of Oklahoma*, LII, (Summer, 1974), 225-227.

[38]*Directory of Oklahoma*, 1979, 175.

[39]*State ex rel. Attorney General v. Davenport et al.*, 125 Okl. 1, 256 P. 340 (1927); *State ex rel. Short, Atty. Gen., v. Owens*, 125 Okl. 66, 256 P. 704 (1927); *Harlow's Weekly*, May 14, 1927.

[40]*Dancy, Sheriff v. Owens*, 126 Okla. 37, 258 P. 879 (1927); *Ex parte Owens*, 37 Okl. Cr. 118, 258 P. 758 (1927); *Harlow's Weekly*, July 9, 1927, 13-14; Creel, "Court in Peril," 228-229.

[41]*Harlow's Weekly*, January 11, 1930, 4-5, 15, June 21, 1930, 2.

[42]*State ex rel. Short, Atty Gen., v. Martin*, 125 Okl. 51, 256 P. 667 (1927)

[43]Thoburn and Wright, *Oklahoma*, III, 140-141.

[44]*Ibid.*; *State ex rel. Attorney General v. Martin*, 125 Okl. 51, 256 P. 667 (1927); *Tulsa Tribune*, May 1, 1927, 18.

[45]Douglas, *History of Tulsa*, III, 553-554.

[46]*State ex rel. Attorney General v. Breckenridge*, 126 Okl. 86, 258 P. 744 (1927).

[47]*State ex rel. Dabney, Atty Gen., v. Ledbetter*, 127 Okl. 85, 260 P. 454 (1927), 162 Okl. 20, 18 P. 2d 1085 (1933); *Harlow's Weekly*, January 11, 1930, 4; 3 Okla. B.J. 297-299 (February, 1933).

[48]Creel, "Courts in Peril," 229-232; *Simpson v. Hill et al.*, 128 Okl. 269, 263 P. 635 (1927).

[49]*Harlow's Weekly*, May 26, 1928, 10-11, June 2, 1928, 10; Surrency, "Federal District Court Judges," 269.

[50]*Harlow's Weekly*, April 20, 1929, 16, May 11, 1929, 14.

[51]*Ibid.*, May 18, 1929, 8; Creel, "Courts in Peril," 235.

[52]*Harlow's Weekly*, May 18, 1929, 8. May 11, 1929, 14, April 27, 1929.

[53]*Harlow's Weekly*, June 6, 1929, 9.

[54]James R. Scales and Danney Goble, *Oklahoma Politics: A History* (Norman: University of Oklahoma Press, 1982), 149-150; Creel, "Courts in Peril," 235.

[55]*Harlow's Weekly*, November 12, 1927, 5.

[56]*Ibid.*, December 1, 1928, 12-13.

[57]*Owens et al. v. Clark*, 154 Okl. 108, 6 P.2d 755 (1931); *Harlow's Weekly*, May 23, 1931, 6.

[58]*Owens et al. v. Clark*, 177 Okl. 519, 61 P.2d 201 (1936).

[59]*Directory of Oklahoma*, 1979, 224-225.

[60]*Harlow's Weekly*, August 28, 1926, 10.

[61]*Tulsa Tribune*, December 16, 1942.

[62]Interview with Denver Davison, June 6, 1979.

[63]*Riley v. Cordell*, et al., 200 Okla. 390, 194 P.2d 857 (1948); *Directory of Oklahoma 1979*, 584.

Chapter 28

[1]Oklahoma State Bar Association, *Proceedings, Twenty-First Annual Meeting*, 102-104.

[2]State Bar of Oklahoma, *Proceedings, First Annual Meeting*, 23

[3]Oklahoma State Bar Association, *Proceedings, Fifteenth Annual Meeting* (Oklahoma City, December 29, 30, 1921), 95; *Eighteenth Annual Meeting* (Oklahoma City, December 29, 30, 1924), 110

[4]*Ibid.*, *Fifteenth Annual Meeting*, 95; *Sixteenth Annual Meeting* (Oklahoma City, December 27, 28, 1922), 10, 181

[5]*Ibid.*, *Twenty-First Annual Meeting*, 103

[6]*Ibid.*, *Twenty-Second Annual Meeting*, 22

[7]*Ibid.*, 262-263; State Bar of Oklahoma, *First Annual Meeting*, 22-23

[8]Oklahoma, *Laws* 1929, ch. 264, 376-385

[9]State Bar of Oklahoma, *Proceedings, First Special Meeting*, 116.

[10]"Address of Governor William J. Holloway," W.C. Austin Collection, Western History Collection, University of Oklahoma, Norman

[11]State Bar of Oklahoma, *Proceedings, Fifth Annual Meeting*, 182-191; The Brookings Institution, *Report on a Survey of Organization and Administration of Oklahoma Submitted to Governor E.W. Marland* (Oklahoma City: Harlow Publishing Corporation, 1935), 104; Okla-

homa *Laws*, 1929, ch. 264, 376-385; *Harlow's Weekly*, August 10, 1929, 4-5, 15.

[12]State Bar of Oklahoma, *Proceedings, First Special Meeting*, 130-131.

[13]Oklahoma State Bar Association, *Proceedings, Twenty-Third Annual Meeting* (Oklahoma City, February 21,22, 1930), 48.

[14]State Bar of Oklahoma, *Proceedings, First Special Meeting*, 187-188.

[15]*Ibid., First Annual Meeting*, 204-205; *Harlow's Weekly*, November 16, 1929, 12.

[16]State Bar of Oklahoma, *Proceedings, First Annual Meeting*, 87-89; *Third Annual Meeting* (Enid, Oklahoma, December 29, 30, 1932), 23.

[17]*Ibid., First Annual Meeting*, 166.

[18]*Ibid.*, 83, 90.

[19]*Ibid., First Special Meeting*, 117.

[20]*State Bar of Oklahoma v. McGhee*, 148 Okla. 219. 298 P. 580 (1931).

[21]19 Okla. 609-32; Oklahoma State Bar Association, *Proceedings, Fifth Annual Meeting*, 302-381; *Sixth Annual Meeting*, 264-265; *Seventh Annual Meeting*, (Oklahoma City, December 29, 30 1913), pp. 81, 311; *Eighth Annual Meeting* (Tulsa, December 28, 29, 1914), 258-260; *Ninth Annual Meeting*, 306-309; *Tenth Annual Meeting*, 209-211; *Twelfth Annual Meeting* (Oklahoma City, January 15, 16, 1919), 36-37; *Harlow's Weekly*, January 22, 1919, 14.

[22]Oklahoma State Bar Association, *Proceedings, Seventeenth Annual Meeting*, 210.

[23]6 Okla. B.J. 25, May, 1935; 7 Okla. B.J. 50, June, 1936.

[24]Brookings Institution, *Report on a Survey of Organization and Administration of Oklahoma*, 102-104.

[25]*Ibid.*, 104.

[26]*Ibid.*, 102-103.

Chapter 29
[1]Interview with John M. Holliman, Bartlesville, Oklahoma, June 27, 1979.

[2]*U. S. News and World Report*, March 7, 1983, 60.

[3]*Tulsa Daily World*, March 13, 1934, 1. March 23, 1934, 1; March 24, 1934, 1; Cheryl Haun Morris, *The Cutting Edge: The Life of John Rogers*, ed. by Odie B. Faulk (Norman: University of Oklahoma Press, 1976), 62-66.

[4]"Indian-Pioneer History," C, 333.

[5]The Oklahoma County Bar Association *BRIEFCASE*, XIII, (May, 1981), 1.

[6]Interview with E.D. Hieronymus, Tulsa, Oklahoma, June 25, 1979.

[7]Interview with Horace D. Ballaine, Tulsa, Oklahoma, June 14, 1983.

[8]Tape 485, Interview with Alfred Stevenson, Living Legends Collection, Oklahoma Christian College.

[9]Letter, Earl L. Stone to Williams, November 9, 1933, Miscellaneous "S" Folder, R.L. Williams Collection, Oklahoma Historical Society, Oklahoma City.

[10]Letter, Williams to Earl L. Stone, November 13, 1933, Miscellaneous "S" Folder, R.L. Williams Collection, Oklahoma Historical Society, Oklahoma City.

[11]*U. S. News and World Report*, March 7, 1983, 63.

[12]4 Okla. B.J. 243, March, 1934.

[13]*Harlow's Weekly*, October 29, 1932, 10.

[14]4 Okla. B.J. 30-31, May, 1933.

[15]*Harlow's Weekly*, September 17, 1932, 15.

[16]State Bar of Oklahoma, *Proceedings Second Annual Meeting* (Tulsa, December 29, 30, 1931), 22-26, 4 Okla. B.J. 191 January, 1934, p. 191; State Bar of Oklahoma, *Proceedings, Annual Meeting* (1933), "Report of the Board of Governors," Typescript, 32.

[17]3 Okla. B.J. 172, October, 1932.

[18]3 Okla. B.J. 6 (April, 1932).

[19]5 Okla. B.J. 165 (December, 1934), 236-238 (March, 1935); *State Bar of Oklahoma v. Retail Credit Association*, 170 Okla. 246, 37 P. 2d 954 (1934).

[20]State Bar of Oklahoma, *Proceedings, Second Annual Meeting*, 39.

[21]4 Okla. B.J. 84 (August, 1933).

[22]State Bar of Oklahoma, *Proceedings, Annual Meeting* (1933), "Report of the Board of Governors," Typescript, 32.

[23]*Ibid., Third Annual Meeting*, 33-34.

[24]8 Okla. B.J. 200 (January, 1938).

[25]*Daily Oklahoman*, May 7, 1937, 4.

[26]Interview with Winfrey Houston, Stillwater, Oklahoma, June 28, 1979; 8 Okla. B.J. 200 (January, 1938).

[27]Interview with John M. Holliman, June 27, 1979, LeRoy Blackstock, June 25, 1979.

[28]Interview with Denver Davison, June 6, 1979.

[29]Oklahoma Bar Association, House of Delegates, 1965 Mid-Year Meeting, Typescript, July 24, 1965.

[30]*Harlow's Weekly*, March 4, 1939, 5; *Daily Oklahoman*, May 28, 1939, June 9, 1939.

[31]*Harlow's Weekly*, May 13, 1939, 5-6, March 4, 1939, 5.

[32]*Ibid.*, May 13, 1939, 5-6, April 1, 1939, 6.

[33]*Ibid.*, April 22, 1939, 9-10.

[34]*Ibid.*

[35]*Ibid.*, Oklahoma, *Laws* (1939), ch. 22, 68-70.

[36]*Harlow's Weekly*, April 22, 1939, 10.

[37]Quoted in *Harlow's Weekly*, April 29, 1939, 16.

[38]*Harlow's Weekly*, May 13, 1939, 5, quoting *Mangum Star*.

[39]Interview with Denver Davison, June 6, 1979; *Daily Oklahoman*, June 9, 1939.

[40]*Harlow's Weekly*, October 14, 1939, 3. March 4, 1939, 5, December 30, 1939, 3.

[41]*Ibid.*, October 14, 1939, 3.

[42]*Ibid.*, December 9, 1939, 14; *In re Bledsoe*, 186 Okla. 264, 97 P. 2d 556 (1939).

[43]*Harlow's Weekly*, December 30, 1939, 3-4; *Daily Oklahoman*, December 29, 1939.

[44]Oklahoma Bar Association, *Proceedings, Annual Convention of the Oklahoma State Bar* (Oklahoma City, December 28, 29, 1939) Typescript, 10.

[45]*Ibid.*, 126.

[46]*Daily Oklahoman*, December 30, 1939; *Harlow's Weekly*, December 30, 1939, 3-4; 11 Okla. B.J. 729, August 24, 1940.

Chapter 30
[1]McRill, *And Satan Came Also*, 179-180.

[2]*Ibid.*, 180-181.

[3]Thoburn and Wright, *Oklahoma*, III, 148-149.

[4]*Daily Oklahoman*, February 1, 1940, 1, February 2, 1940, 1.

[5]McRill, *And Satan Came Also*, 181-183.

[6]Oklahoma, *Laws* (1919), ch. 70, 110-112.

[7]*The Daily Oklahoman*, May 25, 1941, 6D-7D; Harrison, *Me and My Big Mouth*, 270-273; *Harlow's Weekly*, March 4, 1939, 13, April 1, 1939, 11-12.

[8]2 Okla. B.J. 736 August 24, 1940.

[9]*Alan Shaw v. State*, 76 Okla. Cr. 271, 134 P. 2d 999 (1943); *Eli Jaffee v. State*, 76 Okla. Cr. 95, 134 P. 2d 1027 (1943); *Ina Wood v. State*, 76 Okla. Cr. 89, 134 P. 2d 1021 (1943); *Robert Wood v. State*, 77 Okla. Cr. 305, 141 P.2d 309 (1943); Jones, *The Life of Dick Jones*, 144. The cases are treated in detail in James Morton Smith, "Criminal Syndicalism in Oklahoma: A History of the Law and Its Application," (unpublished Master of Arts thesis, University of Oklahoma, 1946),, citing e.g., *Oklahoma City Times*, October 1, 1940, October 11, 1940, June 6, 1941.

[10]11 Okla. B.J. 1381 (December 14, 1940).

[11]12 Okla. B.J. 1693-95 (November 29, 1941).

[12]14 Okla. B.J. 1548-49 (October 23, 1943).

[13]Minnie Drowatzky, ed., *Who's Who In Greater Oklahoma City, 1965* (Oklahoma City: Oklahoma City Junior Chamber of Commerce, 1965), 375.

[14]13 Okla. B.J. 169 (June 27, 1942).

[15]14 Okla. B.J. 89 (January 30, 1943).

[16]40 Okla. B.J. 426, February 22, 1969.

[17]13 Okla. B.J. 1572, December 12, 1942; 14 Okla. B.J. 1549, October 23, 1943.

[18]13 Okla. B.J. 1572, December 12, 1942, 14 Okla. B.J. 1549, October 23, 1943.

[19]13 Okla. B.J. 168-71, June 27, 1942.

[20]15 Okla. B.J. 760, May 27, 1944.

[21]17 Okla. B.J. 247, February 23, 1946.

[22]Ibid., 247-50.

[23]30 Okla. B.J. 2102, December 26, 1959; 25 Okla. B.J. 2361, December 25, 1954; 43 Okla. B.J. 131-34, January 15, 1972.

[24]*Tulsa Lawyer*, March 1962, 2, April 13, 1962, 1, October 5, 1962,

1, November 6, 1962, 3; *Tulsa Tribune*, October 17, 1962, October 27, 1962.

²⁵17 Okla. B.J. 793, May 25, 1946, pp. 229-30, February 23, 1946.

²⁶40 Okla. B.J. 426, February 22, 1969.

²⁷Interview with Deryl L. Gotcher, Tulsa, Oklahoma, June 25, 1979; 18 Okla. B.J. 1718-19, November 29, 1947.

²⁸*Sunday Oklahoman*, January 10, 1971, 25.

²⁹Art. 5, sec. 43; 16 Okla. B.J. 1850, December 29, 1945.

³⁰*Harlow's Weekly*, March 12, 1938, 5-6.

³¹16 Okla. B.J. 1865, December 29, 1945.

³²17 Okla. B.J. 118-19, January 26, 1946; 18 Okla. B.J. 1960 December 27, 1947.

³³*Ibid.*; *Daily Oklahoman*, October 27, 1949, 1; 18 Okla. B.J. 248-50, February 22, 1947; Taped interview with Hicks Epton, November 17, 1969, Living Legends Library, Oklahoma Christian College, Oklahoma City.

³⁴24 Okla. B.J. 2115, December 26, 1953.

³⁵26 Okla. B.J. 2063, December 24, 1955; 34 Okla. B.J. 2375-76, December 28, 1963.

³⁶38 Okla. B.J. 2609, December 30, 1967; *Daily Oklahoman*, May 25, 1967, 1.

³⁷40 Okla. B.J. 407, February 22, 1969; Interview with E. H. Hieronymus, June 25, 1979.

³⁸*Ibid.*, 895, April 19, 1969; Daily Oklahoman, July 21, 1968, p. 4; 41 Okla. B.J. 1665, July 25, 1970.

³⁹Oklahoma City *Journal Record*, May 1, 1980, 12; 46 Okla. B.J. 103-04, June, 1975; *Oklahoma City Times*, December 3, 1979, N3.

⁴⁰Interview with C.E. Northcutt, Ponca City, Oklahoma June 27, 1979; 26 Okla. B.J. 2061, December 24, 1955.

⁴¹5 *Okla. Stat. Annotated*, ch. 1, app. 3, Canon 6; Interview with LeRoy Blackstock, June 25, 1979.

⁴²Oklahoma City *Journal Record*, December 29, 1979, 1.

⁴³56 Okla. B.J. 956, April 27, 1985.

⁴⁴56 Okla. 2732, November 23, 1985; 60 Okla. B.J. 430-36, February 25, 1989.

⁴⁵17 Okla. B.J. 1367-68, September 28, 1946; 20 Okla. B.J. 793-94, May 28, 1949; 49 Okla. B.J. 640, April 22, 1979; 40 Okla. B.J. 427, February 22, 1969.

⁴⁶Interview with John M. Holliman, June 27, 1979.

⁴⁷*Ibid.*, 33 Okla. B.J. 2470-71, December 29, 1962, p. 1639, September 1, 1962; letter, July 18, 1989, Neil E. Bogan to author.

⁴⁸56 Okla. B.J. 2664-65 (October 22, 1983).

⁴⁹60 Okla. B.J. 538 (March 4, 1989).

⁵⁰59 Okla. B.J. 2884-85 (November 5, 1988).

⁵¹59 Okla. 3506 (December 17, 1988).

⁵²Interview with Marvin C. Emerson, March 21, 1989; letter, July 18, 1989, Neil E. Bogan to author; 60 Okla. B.J. 1844 (July 29, 1989); interview with Edward H. Palmer, August 3, 1989.

Chapter 31
¹Oklahoma and Indian Territory Bar Association, *Proceedings, Third Annual Meeting* (Oklahoma City, December 20, 21, 1906), 44, 46-47.

²*Ibid.*, 49; Oklahoma, *Laws* (1965), ch. 256, 464-468; *Daily Oklahoman*, June 22, 1965, 14.

³Oklahoma State Bar Association, *Proceedings, Fifteenth Annual Meeting*, 196-207.

⁴*Directory of Oklahoma*, 1979, 226.

⁵Oklahoma State Bar Association, *Proceedings, Sixteenth Annual Meeting*, 63-64.

⁶August 20, 1927, 7.

⁷Oklahoma State Bar Association, *Proceedings, Nineteenth Annual Meeting* (Oklahoma City, December 28, 29, 1925), 72, 179-181; *Harlow's Weekly*, January 9, 1926, 4, 14.

⁸Oklahoma State Bar Association, *Proceedings, Fifteenth Annual Meeting*, 196-197.

⁹5 Okla. B.J. 47, June, 1934.

¹⁰State Bar of Oklahoma, *Proceedings, Second Annual Meeting*, 33-38.; *Harlow's Weekly*, January 9, 1932, 3.

¹¹4 Okla. B.J. 111, September 1933.

¹²4 Okla. B.J. 200, January, 1934.

¹³4 Okla. B.J. 111-113, September, 1933; 4 Okla. B.J. 201, January, 1934; *Harlow's Weekly*, March 4, 1939, 15.

¹⁴4 Okla. B.J. 196, January, 1934.

¹⁵*Ibid.*, 5 Okla. B.J. 4-5, April, 1934.

¹⁶4 Okla. B.J. 197, January 1934; *Directory of Oklahoma*, 1979, 230-231.

¹⁷5 Okla. B.J. 4-5, April, 1934; 5 Okla. B.J. 48-49, June 1934.

¹⁸*Harlow's Weekly*, June 2, 1934, 3.

¹⁹6 Okla. B.J. 54, June, 1935, quoting *Oklahoma City Times*, May 22, 1935; *Harlow's Weekly*, February 27, 1937, 7, March 4, 1939, 15; 7 Okla. B.J. 242, March, 1937.

²⁰Oklahoma, *Laws* (1937), 34, art. 2; *Harlow's Weekly*, March 4, 1939, 15.

²¹*Harlow's Weekly*, June 18, 1938, 4, March 19, 1938, 4.

²²15 Okla. B.J. 1306, November 25, 1944.

²³17 Okla. B.J. 1949-51, December 28, 1946.

²⁴*Ibid.*

²⁵25 Okla. B.J. 422, February 27, 1954, 1825-28, October 23, 1954; 20 Okla. B.J. 1630, November 26, 1949.

²⁶22 Okla. B.J. 2019, December 29, 1951.

²⁷22 Okla. B.J. 2020, December 29, 1951.

²⁸25 Okla. B.J. 2363, December 25, 1954.

²⁹25 Okla. B.J. 1825-28, October 23, 1954.

³⁰32 Okla. B.J. 2287, December 30, 1961.

³¹*Daily Oklahoman*, June 22, 1965, 14.

³²*Chambers v. Central Committee of the Oklahoma Bar Association et al.*, 203 Okla. 583, 224 P.2d 583 (1950).

³³32 Okla. B.J. 2288, December 30, 1961.

³⁴*Tulsa Daily World*, September 21, 1963, 19.

³⁵Interview with Winfrey Houston, June 28, 1979.

³⁶33 Okla. B.J. 2472, 2521-22, December 29, 1962; Oklahoma City Journal Record, May 1, 1981, 1.

³⁷*Tulsa World*, December 15, 1963; *Tulsa Tribune*, February 10, 1964, April 18, 1964.

³⁸35 Okla. B.J. 1870, October 31, 1964; *Directory of Oklahoma*, 1979, 671.

³⁹*Tulsa Tribune*, March 19, 1965, 1; Charles R. Ashman, *The Finest Judges Money Can Buy: And Other Forms of Judicial Pollution* (Los Angeles: Nash Publishing Corporation, 1973), 59-65.

⁴⁰36 Okla. B.J. 1507-09, August 28, 1965.

⁴¹*Daily Oklahoman* editorial, September 12, 1968, 1.

⁴²Interview with LeRoy Blackstock, June 15, 1979.

⁴³*Daily Oklahoman*, July 19, 1964, 1A; 36 Okla. B.J. 1509-10, August 28, 1965.

⁴⁴35 Okla. B.J. 1760, October 10, 1964.

⁴⁵*Tulsa Tribune*, March 19, 1965, 1; Ashman, *Finest Judges Money Can Buy*, 59-60.

⁴⁶Interview with Judge Luther Bohanon, Oklahoma City, May 10, 1983.

⁴⁷Interview with LeRoy Blackstock, June 25, 1979.

⁴⁸*Tulsa Tribune*, March 19, 1965, 1; 35 Okla. B.J. 1869, October 31, 1964; 35 Okla B.J. 2140, November 28, 1964; Ashman, *Finest Judges Money Can Buy*, 60-63.

⁴⁹36 Okla. B.J. Journal 1507-11, August 28, 1965.

⁵⁰State of Oklahoma, *Transcript of Proceedings of the Senate Sitting as a Court of Impeachment, Thirtieth Legislature, April 6, 1965*; 36 Okla. B.J. 1511-12, August 28, 1965.

⁵¹*Daily Oklahoman*, February 18, 1966; Ashman, *Finest Judges Money Can Buy*, 63-65.

⁵²*Daily Oklahoman*, July 28, 1965.

⁵³36 Okla. B.J. 1511, August 28, 1965.

⁵⁴36 Okla. B.J. 1513-14, August 28, 1965.

⁵⁵36 Okla. B.J. 1505, August 28, 1965; 36 Okla. B.J. 2341, December 18, 1965; *Oklahoma City Times*, August 10, 1965.

⁵⁶*Daily Oklahoman*, June 22, 1965, 14; Oklahoma, Laws (1965), ch. 256, pp. 464-468.

⁵⁷37 Okla. B.J. 804, April 23, 1966.

⁵⁸37 Okla. B.J. 2533, December 31, 1966.

⁵⁹Oklahoma, *Laws* (1974), ch. 251, 515-517; *Directory of Oklahoma*, 1979, 232; *The Journal Record*, May 1, 1980, 11.

⁶⁰37 Okla. B.J. 1198, June 25, 1966.

⁶¹*Ibid.*; *Daily Oklahoman*, July 17, 1980, 13.

⁶²58 Okla. B.J. 2041 (July 18, 1987); 60 Okla. B.J. 110 (January 21, 1989).

⁶³52 Okla. B.J. 2523, October 31, 1981; *Directory of Oklahoma, 1981*, 246-247; *Directory of Oklahoma, 1979*, 229-230.

[64]*Directory of Oklahoma, 1981*, 239-40.
[65]53 Okla. B.J. 340 (February 13, 1982).
[66]54 Okla. B.J. 3131 (December 17, 1983).
[67]55 Okla. B.J. 650 (March 24, 1984).
[68]55 Okla. B.J. 2088 (October 20, 1984).
[69]56 Okla. B.J. 119 (January 19, 1985).
[70]55 Okla. B.J. 2088 (October 20, 1984).
[71]56 Okla. B.J. 2915 (December 28, 1985).
[72]56 Okla. B.J. 1516 (July 6, 1985).
[73]58 Okla. B.J. 496 (February 28, 1987).
[74]58 Okla. B.J. 2124 (July 25, 1987).
[75]59 Okla. B.J. 2105 (August 6, 1988).

Chapter 32

[1]24 Okla. B.J. 2111-12, December 26, 1953.
[2]20 Okla. B.J. 1628-30, November 26, 1949; 20 Okla. B.J. 1522-24, October 29, 1949; 24 Okla. B.J. 2111-12, December 26, 1953.
[3]*Oklahoma City Times*, January 31, 1968.
[4]22 Okla. B.J. 2001, December 29, 1951; 25 Okla. B.J. 2361-62, December 25, 1954; 26 Okla. B.J. 2064, December 24, 1955.
[5]24 Okla. B.J. 2112, December 26, 1953.
[6]26 Okla. B.J. 2064, December 24, 1955.
[7]Newspaper Clipping form *Tulsa World* or *Tulsa Tribune* [ca. April 15, 1958], files of Newspaper Printing Corporation, Tulsa Oklahoma.
[8]*Daily Oklahoman*, June 9, 1959.
[9]31 Okla. B.J. 2260-61, December 31, 1960.
[10]49 Okla. B.J. 640, April 22, 1979.
[11]Interview with Robert W. Blackstock, Bristow, Oklahoma, May 17, 1983; Interview with LeRoy Blackstock, Tulsa, Oklahoma, June 25, 1979.
[12]*Tulsa Lawyer*, V, (November-December, 1965), 2-3; *Daily Oklahoman*, February 26, 1966, February 28, 1966 editorial, July 24, 1966; 37 Okla. B.J. 879-81, April 30, 1966; Interview with LeRoy Blackstock, June 25, 1979.
[13]37 Okla. B.J. 2533, 2585, December 31, 1966; Interview with LeRoy Blackstock, June 25, 1979.
[14]Oklahoma Bar Association, *Handbook*, 1978 edition, 4; 37 Okla. B.J. 2555, December 31, 1966; 37 Okla. B.J. 1239-41, June 25, 1966.
[15]Oklahoma Bar Association, *Handbook*, 1978 edition, 18; *Daily Oklahoman*, July 24, 1966, 1; 37 Okla. B.J. 1258, June 25, 1966.
[16]*Daily Oklahoman*, July 24, 1966; 37 Okla. B.J. 1244-52, 1242, June 25, 1966.
[17]49 Okla. B.J. 1687-90, September 23, 1978; *The Journal Record*, November 21, 1978, 1; 37 Okla. B.J. 1257, June 25, 1966; *Tulsa World*, December 3, 1977.
[18]*Tulsa Tribune*, October 19, 1978.
[19]49 Okla. B.J. 2339, December 9, 1978; *Tulsa World*, December 2, 1978; Interview with LeRoy Blackstock, June 25, 1979; 50 Okla. B.J. 225, February 3, 1979.
[20]*Oklahoma City Times*, August 22, 1969.
[21]42 Okla. B.J. 272, January 30, 1971; 47 Okla. B.J. 230, January 31, 1976.
[22]47 Okla. B.J. 8-9, January 3, 1976.
[23]Oklahoma Bar Association, *Handbook*, 1978 edition, 5; 48 Okla. B.J. 2126, October 1, 1977; 48 Okla. B.J. 2833-34, December 31, 1977.
[24]*Tulsa Tribune*, October 7, 1980; *The Sunday Oklahoman*, October 4, 1981, 13A.
[25]52 Okla. B.J. 1229, May 30, 1981; 52 Okla. B.J. 1519, June 27, 1981.
[26]*Daily Oklahoman*, March 4, 1981, p. 10, editorial, 8.
[27]60 Okla. B.J. 519, March 4, 1989.
[28]60 Okla. B.J. 745, March 25, 1989.
[29]58 Okla. B.J. 3531, December 26, 1987; interview with Marvin C. Emerson, March 21, 1989.
[30]60 Okla. B.J. 516-20, March 4, 1989.
[31]Statistics compiled from "Annual Report of Professional Responsibility Commission and Office of the General Counsel."
[32]59 Okla. B.J. 846, April 2, 1988.
[33]59 Okla. B.J. 706-08, March 19, 1988.
[34]56 Okla B.J. 959-61, April 27, 1985; 59 Okla. B.J. 3415-18, Dec. 10, 1988.

[35]58 Okla. B.J. 1477, May 30, 1987; 59 Okla. B.J. 636-38, March 12, 1988.

Chapter 33

[1]3 Okla. B.J. 60-61, June, 1932.
[2]5 Okla. B.J. 5, April, 1934.
[3]5 Okla. B.J. 27, May, 1934; 5 Okla. B.J. 50-51, June, 1934.
[4]Okla. B.J. 172-74, December, 1936.
[5]9 Okla. B.J. 287, December, 1938; 9 Okla. B.J. 342-43, January, 1939; *Daily Oklahoman*, December 10, 1938, 4, December 29, 1938, 3; *Harlow's Weekly*, December 17, 1938, 8, December 31, 1938, 1.
[6]33 Okla. B.J. 2470, December 29, 1962.
[7]58 Okla. B.J. 2143-44, July 25, 1987.
[8]60 Okla. B.J. 57, January 14, 1989.
[9]12 Okla. B.J. 1694, November 29, 1941.
[10]17 Okla. B.J. 1730, November 30, 1946.
[11]20 Okla. B.J. 1627, November 26, 1949.
[12]*The Sunday Oklahoman*, April 23, 1972, 26A.
[13]*Journal Record*, May 1, 1980, 1, May 1, 1981, 3.
[14]19 Okla. B.J. 583-84, April 24, 1948; 19 Okla. B.J. 1394, October 30, 1948.
[15]21 Okla. B.J. 529, April 15, 1950; 22 Okla. B.J. 439-40, March 31, 1951; 23 Okla. B.J. 532, March 29, 1952; 23 Okla. B.J. 781, April 26, 1952; 25 Okla. B.J. 575, March 29, 1954; Interview with Lee Thompson, June 13, 1979.
[16]25 Okla. B.J. 574, March 27, 1954.
[17]American Bar Association advertisement, "25 Years of Being Unreasonable," *U. S. News & World Report*, April 5, 1982; 42 Okla. B.J. 474, February 27, 1971.
[18]24 Okla. B.J. 2109, December 26, 1953; 25 Okla. B.J. 2359, December 25, 1954; 25 Okla. B.J. 1431-32, July 31, 1954.
[19]Interview with Winfrey Houston, June 28, 1979.
[20]35 Okla. B.J. 945-46, May 30, 1964; 35 Okla. B.J. 2324, December 26, 1964.
[21]20 Okla. B.J. 1251, September 24, 1949.
[22]47 Okla. B.J. 8, January 3, 1976.
[23]*Journal Record*, January 4, 1981, 4; 48 Okla. B.J. 16, January 1, 1977; 48 Okla. B.J. 1624, July 2, 1977.
[24]*Ibid.*, May 1, 1981, 1; Oklahoma County Bar Association *BRIEF-CASE*, May, 1981, 2.
[24]24 Okla. B.J. 2118-19, December 26, 1953; 25 Okla. B.J. 2360-61, December 25, 1954.
[26]7 Okla. B.J. 172-74, December, 1936.
[27]*Tulsa Tribune*, July 22, 1952, 16.
[28]*Tulsa Lawyer*, X, (April, May, June, 1970), 16; 25 Okla. B.J. 2360-61, December 25, 1954; 26 Okla. B.J. 2063, December 24, 1955.
[29]35 Okla. B.J. 2323, December 26, 1964.
[30]*Oklahoma City Times*, June 25, 1981, 11; *American Bar Association Journal*, LXII, (September, 1976), 1139-1142; *Journal Record*, March 28, 1981, 1, April 4, 1981, 4.
[31]*Daily Oklahoman*, June 5, 1981, 4N; 35 Okla. B.J. 1871-72, October 31, 1964; 629 P2d. 1269.
[32]24 Okla. B.J. 2118-19, December 26, 1953; 25 Okla. B.J. 2360, December 25, 1954.
[33]47 Okla. B.J. 9, January 3, 1976; see also *U. S. News & World Report*, December 1, 1980, 45.
[34]50 Okla. B.J. 1923, 2174, October 27, 1979; 50 Okla. B.J. 2076, October 13, 1979; *Sunday Oklahoman*, December 2, 1979, 37A; 52 Okla. B.J. 166, January 31, 1981; *Journal Record*, December 7, 1979, 1.
[35]*Daily Oklahoman*, July 9, 1981, 35; 50 Okla. B.J. 1085, May 26, 1979; 52 Okla. B.J. 1517, June 27, 1981.
[36]24 Okla. B.J. 2117-18, December 26, 1953.
[37]*Tulsa Tribune*, February 14, 1976.
[38]36 Okla. B.J. 1658-59, September 25, 1965; *Daily Oklahoman*, November 13, 1964, 24.
[39]*Oklahoma Journal*, (Oklahoma City), February 14, 1976; Interview with William G. Paul, Oklahoma City, Oklahoma, May 4, 1983; 50 Okla. B.J. 2709, December 29, 1979; *Tulsa Tribune*, February 14, 1976.
[40]*U. S. News & World Report*, May 11, 1981, 38-40; *Tulsa World*, May 14, 1977; *Journal Record*, December 22, 1978, 1.
[41]*Ibid.*, April 18, 1981, 4.

[42]*Ibid.*

[43]26 Okla. B.J. 2065, December 24, 1955; 26 Okla. B.J. 1023, June 18, 1955.

[44]*Journal Record*, April 18, 1981, 4. September 19, 1981, 4, December 29, 1979, 1.

[45]34 Okla. B.J. 1881, October 26, 1963.

[46]Roscoe Pound, *The Lawyer from Antiquity to Modern Times* (St. Paul: West Publishing Co., 1953), 329.

[47]Oklahoma State Bar Association, *Proceedings, Fourth Annual Meeting*, 333.

[48]Oklahoma State Bar Association, *Proceedings, Sixth Annual Meeting*, 213-14

[49]8 Okla. B.J. 75-79, July, 1937; 33 Okla. B.J. 1060, May 31, 1952.

[50]Interview with C.D. Northcutt, June 27, 1979.

[51]17 Okla. B.J. 1253-61, August 31, 1946; 33 Okla. B.J. 1060-61, May 31, 1952; Interviews with C.D. Northcutt, June 27, 1979, Lee B. Thompson, June 13, 1979, W.E. Crowe, June 28, 1979.

[52]421 U.S. 773 (1975); *American Bar Association Journal*, LXIV, (July, 1978), 1070; Interview with LeRoy Blackstock, June 25, 1979.

[53]44 Okla. B.J. 3316, November, 1973; *Oklahoma City Times*, June 16, 1975.

[54]*Oklahoma Journal* (Oklahoma City), July 10, 1976.

[55]E.g., *Blackwell Rock Record*, November 9, 1893, 1; *Oklahoma State Capital* (Guthrie), May 31, 1890, 2; *Chickasaw and Choctaw Herald*, February 11, 1859, 1, reprinted in Carolyn Thomas Foreman, *Oklahoma Imprints*, 118.

[56]*John R. Bates and Van O'Steen, Appellants, v. State Bar of Arizona*, 433 U.S. 350 (1977).

[57]49 Okla. B.J. 131-37, February 4, 1978; 49 Okla. B.J. 185-86, February 11, 1978; *Journal Record*, May 1, 1979, 3, October 27, 1979, 1.

[58]*Ibid.*

[59]*State of Oklahoma ex rel. Okla. Bar Association v. Peter K. Schaffer*, Okl. 648 P.2d 355 (1982); *Journal Record*, October 27, 1979, 1, October 30, 1979, 1.

[60]*Ibid.*, November 22, 1980, 4, November 20, 1982, 1; *Matter of R. M. J.*, 102 S.Ct. 929.

[61]54 Okla. B.J. 637, March 12, 1983; 54 Okla. B.J. 701-04, March 19, 1983.

[62]Indian Territory Bar Association, *Proceedings, First Annual Meeting* (South McAlester, I.T., October 2, 3, 1900), 14.

[63]49 Okla. B.J. 459, March 25, 1978.

[64]60 Okla. B.J. 527-30, March 4, 1989.

[65]59 Okla. B.J. 2049-51, July 30, 1988.

[66]53 Okla. B.J. 3041, December 31, 1982; 54 Okla. B.J. 1165, May 7, 1983.

[67]*Ibid.*

[68]60 Okla. B.J. 527-30, March 4, 1989.

[69]*Ibid.*

[70]*Ibid.*

Chapter 34

[1]J.G. Ralls Collection, Letter Press Book, Box No. 25, Western History Collection, University of Oklahoma, Norman.

[2]King, *Memoirs of an Oklahoma Jurist*, 63-67.

[3]30 Okla. B.J. 2096-97, December 26, 1959; *Daily Oklahoman*, November 10, 1959, 8, December 5, 1959, 7.

[4]49. Okla. B.J. 1241-44, July 8, 1978; *American Bar Association Journal*, LXIV, (April, 1978), 545-548; 49 Okla. B.J. 1488-90, September 2, 1978.

[5]49 Okla. B.J. 1241, July 8, 1978.

[6]49 Okla. B.J. 2150-51, November 11, 1978; *Sunday Oklahoman*, December 10, 1978, 50A; *Daily Oklahoman*, April 27, 1979, 16.

[7]*Saturday Oklahoman & Times*, May 2, 1981, 38; *Oklahoma City Times*, March 19, 1982, 9; 53 Okla. B.J. 827, April 3, 1982.

[8]40 Okla. B.J. 1213, May 31, 1969; 42 Okla. B.J. 3175-77, November 27, 1971; *American Bar Association Journal*, LIX, (February, 1973), 153-156.

[9]*Journal Record*, September 26, 1981. 4.

[10]*Ibid.*; *Time Magazine*, November 16, 1981, 97.

[11]*U. S. News and World Report*, March 7, 1983, 15.

[12]53 Okla. B.J. 51-52, January 16, 1982.

[13]52 Okla. B.J. 1465, June 20, 1981; *Sunday Oklahoman*, May 31, 1981, 18A; *National Law Journal*, June 1, 1981, 3.

[14]52 Okla. B.J. 748, April 4, 1981.

[15]*Journal Record*, June 8, 1979, 1.

[16]*Ibid.*, January 1, 1983, 4.

[17]*Sunday Oklahoman*, June 6, 1982, 10A; *Supra*, 135.

[18]"Roll of Attorneys," 19 Okl. 609; Oklahoma State Bar Association, *Proceedings, Sixth Annual Meeting*, 264-265, *Seventh Annual Meeting*, 311.

[19]*Directory of Oklahoma*, 1981, 638.

[20]Brookings Institution, *Report on a Survey of Organization and Administration of Oklahoma*, 58; 11 Okla. B.J. 743-74, August 24, 1940; 22 Okla. B.J. 2001, December 29, 1951; 32 Okla. B.J. 2282; *Directory of Oklahoma*, 1981, 638.

[21]*Daily Oklahoman*, December 5, 1979, 7.

[22]*Tulsa World*, April 16, 1972; *Journal Record*, November 29, 1980, 3.

[23]Taped Interview, November 17, 1969, Living Legends Library, Oklahoma Christian College.

[24]32 Okla. B.J. 2282, December 30, 1961; 42 Okla. B.J. 272, January 30, 1971; *Directory of Oklahoma*, 1981, 638; 52 Okla. B.J. 219, January 31, 1981; *Directory of Oklahoma*, 1981, 638; 60 Okla. B.J. 437, February 25, 1989.

[25]Oklahoma and Indian Territory Bar Association, *Proceedings, First Annual Meeting*, 231-234; 52 Okla. B.J. 219, January 31, 1981; 60 Okla. B.J. 437, February 25, 1989.

[26]52 Okla. B.J. 191, January 31, 1981; conference with Neil E. Bogan, February 10, 1989.

INDEX

110-113, 114, 115. See also Sequoyah
  Constitutional Convention
Oklahoma State Bar Journal, 155, 179
Oklahoma State Capital, 132, 158-59
Oklahoma State Election Board, 171-72
Oklahoma Station, 62
Oklahoma Supreme Court Indian Law
  Symposium, 210-11
Oklahoma Tax Commission, 194
Oklahoma Territory, 24, 26, 34, 37, 62, 65,
  69, 81, 84, 89, 114, 162; land openings,
  56-57, 73, 81, 90-91, 104-05;
  government created, 4, 27, 64; laws
  governing, 64, 66, 162; Legislature, 66,
  79, 84, 87, 88, 112, 160
Oklahoma Territory Bar, 89, 96, 152
Oklahoma [Territory] Bar Association, 76,
  93, 158-60
Oklahoma v. Texas, 130-31
Oklahoma Trust Companies
  Associations, 184
Oklahoma Turnpike Authority, 192
Okmulgee, OK, 39, 41, 138
O'Malley, Pat, 97
Opala, Marian P., 197-98
Oral Roberts University, O.W. Coburn
  School of Law, 147-48
"Organic Act for Oklahoma" (Act of May 2,
  1890), 27, 64, 66, 67, 70, 81, 121, 126
Orlando, OK, 43, 91
Osage Nation, 118
Oscar Rose Junior College, 187
Otey, Mildred E., 213
Otis, Jerry, 213
Ottawa County, OK, 6
Our Brother in Red, 24
Outlook Magazine, 128
Owen, Robert L., 17, 19, 23, 24, 86, 116,
  127, 129, 158
Owen, Thomas H., 130, 190
Owens, Ben T., 202
Owens, Charles L., 151
Owens, James G., 16
Owens, O.O., 168-71, 173
Pacific Reporter, 190
Page, Charles, 144
Paine, H.F., 48
Palmer, Edward H., 187-89, 210, 213
Palmer, Robert C., 70
Pancoast, J.L., 122
Panhandle, OK. See Oklahoma Panhandle
"Panic of 1893," 31, 87, 94, 111
Paralegals. See Legal assistants
Paris, T, 26, 29, 110, 120
Parker, Charles H., 5, 125
Parker, Isaac Charles, 18, 19, 20, 21,25-26,
  33, 36, 55, 110
Parker, Luman F., 165
Parker, Robert, 150
Parks, Ed, 213
Parmenter, Bert M., 105
Parris, Harry, 144
Paschal, Ridge, 23, 24
Pasco, G.W., 23
Pate, George A., 10, 43
Patterson, Orban C., 183-84
Patterson, W.N., 24
Paul, William G., 159
Pauls Valley, OK, 32, 44, 120, 121,
  136, 152
Pawhuska, OK, 38, 136
Pawnee County, OK, 91
Pawnee, OK, 38

Pawnee Indians, 90
Payne County, OK, 56, 64,65, 81
Payne, David L., 54, 55
Payne, John Howard, 12
Pearson, A.B., 8
Peck, Herbert M., 131
Peden, Preston E., 186
Peery, Dan, 61
Penn Square Bank, 214
Perjury, 36, 61, 67, 68, 69
Perkins, George N., 62
Perry Bar, 87
Perry, OK, 88, 91, 92, 113
Perry, Russell, 196
Petty, David K., 159, 187, 199, 203, 214
Petty, Mrs. David K., 214
Phelps, James I., 171
Philadelphia Record, 152
Phillips, Layn R., 139
Phillips, Leon C., 123, 137, 145, 171,
  179-81
Phillips, Orie, 186
Pierce, Earl Boyd, 145
Pike, Albert, 52, 102
Pike, Luther H., 102-03
"Pin" Indians, 17
Pine, W.B., 129, 135
Pinkerton, Amos M., 195
Pipe smoking, Cherokee courts, 12-13
Pittman, Charles H., 118
Pitzer, John, 98
"Plea for a Fallen Woman," Temple
  Houston case, 99
Pond Creek, OK, 92
Pontotoc County, OK, 40, 178
Populist Party, 68
Porta, A Francis, 180
Porter, E. Melvin, 150-51
Porter, Chief Pleasant, 22, 25, 26, 116
Posey, Alexander L., 51
Poteau, OK, 136
'Pott Line,' 68
Pottawatomie County, OK, 36, 81, 114
Pottawatomie Indian Reservation,
  68, 81, 103
Potter, B. Andrew, 194
Pound, Roscoe, 173
Powers, Bud, 76
"Prairie Dog Lawyers," 101
President's Award, 1987, 214
Price, Looney, 12
Probate attorneys, U.S. government,
  142, 154
"Pro bono" legal services, 204, 206, 210-11
Proctor, Zeke, 16, 17
Professional Responsibility Commission,
  Oklahoma Bar Association, 202
Professional Responsibility Tribunal,
  Oklahoma Bar Association, 202
"Professionalism," 203, 216
Proffett, Ethel. See Stephenson, Ethel M.
Prohibition of liquor, 68, 86, 107, 118, 122,
  128, 130, 134, 136, 162, 178
Provisional Government, Oklahoma
  Territory, 57, 59, 62, 63
Pruiett, Moman, 120-21, 129, 183
Purcell, OK, 16, 33, 38
Public relations, 204-07, 210-11
Pushmataha County, OK, 4
Quanah, T, 101, 131
Quapaw Indians, 6, 27, 33
Racial segregation, OK, 121, 125, 136, 138,
  148-49

Railroads, 16, 17, 28, 31, 47, 53, 54,55, 56,
  115, 116; free passes, 116; rate cases,
  128
Rainey, Robert M., 126, 134, 141
Ralls, Joseph G., 5, 9, 10, 23, 28, 158,
  174, 211
Ramsey, George S., 125, 136, 143, 168
Randall, John D., 215
Randlett, James F., 104
Ray, Robert, 96, 98, 106
Raymond, Charles R., 114
Rector, Sarah, estate, 143
Red River cases, 130-31
Red River, North Fork of, 6, 101
Reddick, Charles R., 83
Read, Jess G., 137
Reed, J. Warren, 21, 36
Reed, Thomas B., 34, 35
Regents for Higher Education, OK, 148
Rehnquist, William H., 150
Removal, Indian, 5, 14
Removal of capital from Guthrie,
  118, 125, 126
Renfrow, William C., 72, 84, 95
"Reverse discrimination," 150
Rice, Benjamin F., 144
Rice, Eugene, 138
Rice, John, 44
Richards, Alvin, 5, 186
Richardson, D.A., 43
Richardson, T.C., 98
Riley, Fletcher S., 171-72, 190-91
Ringo, Daniel, 15
Ristine, H.C., 49
Ritchey, W.H., 40
Riverside Oil and Refining Co., 168-69
Rizley, Ross, 139, 186
Roberts, T.M., 148
Roberts, Vernon, 196
Robertson, Alice M., 36
Robertson, J.B.A., 83, 123, 124, 143, 155
Roff, OK, 40, 41
Roger Mills County, OK, 73, 76
Rogers, Charles, 143
Rogers, Clement V., 119
Rogers County, OK, 180
Rogers, H.H., 142
Rogers, John, 147, 150
Rogers, Chief William C., 115
Roosevelt, Eleanor, 155
Roosevelt, Franklin D., 137
Roosevelt, Theodore, 3, 117, 121, 122,
  128, 132, 133
Root, Elihu, 173
Roper, Clay M., 173
Rose, David S., 118
Rose, John, 101
Ross, Chief John, 12
Rosser, Malcolm E., 143
Royal Hotel, Guthrie, 3, 84
Rummons, Nestor, 5, 125
"Run of '89," 56
Runkle, Lowe, 193
"Runners," 87, 164
Russell, David L., 139
Russell, Seigniora, 94
Russell, Stillwell, 120
Rutherford, Samuel Morton, 116, 142
Ryan, OK, 33, 121
Rydingsward, Carl (Baron von), 87
Sac and Fox tribes, 81
St. Lukes United Methodist Church, 202
Sallisaw Creek, 5

243

The author, Orben J. Casey, is a lifelong Oklahoman, born in Hanna and educated in Henryetta's public schools. He holds degrees of Bachelor of Science in business and Master of Arts in history from the University of Oklahoma. His Juris Doctor degree is from Oklahoma City University. A member of the Oklahoma Bar Association and the Oklahoma County Bar Association, Mr. Casey has been a businessman in Oklahoma most of his adult life and is now engaged in family business interests in Oklahoma City.